Black Scare / Red Scare

Black Scare / Red Scare

Theorizing Capitalist Racism in the United States

CHARISSE BURDEN-STELLY

The University of Chicago Press
Chicago and London

The University of Chicago Press, Chicago 60637
The University of Chicago Press, Ltd., London
© 2023 by The University of Chicago
Published 2023
Printed in the United States of America

32 31 30 29 28 27 26 25 24 23   1 2 3 4 5

ISBN-13: 978-0-226-83013-1 (cloth)
ISBN-13: 978-0-226-83015-5 (paper)
ISBN-13: 978-0-226-83014-8 (e-book)
DOI: https://doi.org/10.7208/chicago/9780226830148.001.0001

Library of Congress Cataloging-in-Publication Data

Names: Burden-Stelly, Charisse, author.
Title: Black scare / red scare : theorizing capitalist racism in the United States /
    Charisse Burden-Stelly.
Other titles: Theorizing capitalist racism in the United States
Description: Chicago : The University of Chicago Press, 2023. |
    Includes bibliographical references and index.
Identifiers: LCCN 2023019891 | ISBN 9780226830131 (cloth) |
    ISBN 9780226830155 (paperback) | ISBN 9780226830148 (ebook)
Subjects: LCSH: Anti-communist movements—United States—History—
    20th century. | Racism—Political aspects—United States—History—20th century. |
    African Americans—Politics and government—20th century. | United States—
    Politics and government—20th century. | Capitalism—United States—History—
    20th century. | United States—Race relations—History—20th century.
Classification: LCC E743.5 .B858 2023 | DDC 973.9—dc23/eng/20230425
LC record available at https://lccn.loc.gov/2023019891

♾ This paper meets the requirements of ANSI/NISO Z39.48-1992 (Permanence of Paper).

To Elizabeth, Layla, and the Black Alliance for Peace

Contents

INTRODUCTION

When William Edward Burghardt Du Bois testified before the US House Committee on Foreign Relations on August 8, 1949, in opposition to the Military Assistance Bill, the historian and vice chairman of the Council on African Affairs presented an invaluable assessment of the connections between capitalism, racism, imperialism, and war—and their legitimation through anticommunism. "Why in God's name do we want to control the earth?" Du Bois questioned. "Is it because of our success in ruling men? We want to rule Russia and we cannot rule Alabama. We tried to rule Porto [sic] Rico and gave it the highest suicide rate in the world."[1] He continued, "How have we equipped ourselves to teach the world? To teach the world democracy, we chose a Secretary trained in the democracy of South Carolina; when we wanted to unravel the worst economic snarl of the modern world, we chose a general trained in military tactics at West Point; when we want to study race relations in our own borders we summon a baseball player."[2] Here, he exposed that US global leadership was inseparable from violent imperialism, anti-Black racial oppression, and war-driven accumulation, a reality that undermined the government's claim that it needed to "rule Russia" for reasons of national security. "We who hate niggers and darkies," Du Bois chided, "propose to control a world full of colored people."[3]

The octogenarian went on to argue that, because the primary aim of the United States was to preserve economic exploitation rooted in racial hierarchy domestically and abroad, it "invented witchwords" to criminalize those who struggled for an alternative society. He explained: "If in 1850 an American disliked slavery, the word of exorcism was 'abolitionist.' He was a 'nigger lover.' He believed in free love and murder of kind slave masters. He ought to be lynched and mobbed. Today the word is 'communist.'" These witchwords were dangerous because they rationalized repression and reprisal: "If any-body questions the power of wealth, wants to build more [Tennessee Valley Authorities], or advocates civil rights for Negroes, he is a communist, a revo-lutionist, a scoundrel, and is liable to lose his job or land in jail."[4] The com-munist/revolutionist/scoundrel who believed in economic equality and Black liberation was a fundamental menace to profit, property, and racial propriety, and was therefore criminal, subversive, and un-American. These narrations not only normalized capitalism, imperialism, and racism over and against socialism, self-determination, and racial equality, but also dictated the distri-bution of rights, resources, life, and death.

Closing out his statement, Du Bois admonished: "Socialism, whether ac-complished by communism or reformed capitalism or both . . . is spreading to every civilized land today including the United States. To try stopping it by Red-baiting and hysterics is stupid. To turn back the clock by war is a crime."[5] The contradictions, critiques, and structures of domination Du Bois identi-fied are the subject of *Black Scare / Red Scare: Theorizing Capitalist Racism in the United States.*

Aims and Scope

Situated in the period spanning World War I and the early Cold War, *Black Scare / Red Scare* has four key objectives. The first is to define the relationship between and imbrication of racialism and capitalist exploitation, what I call "capitalist racism," and its inscription in the United States to produce what I call "US Capitalist Racist Society." The second is to theorize how capital-ist racism created the conditions for the Black Scare and the Red Scare and positioned Radical Blackness as a preeminent threat. The third is to explicate the codification of the Black Scare and the Red Scare in Wall Street Imperial-ism as the internal logic, anticommunism as the mode of governance, and True Americanism as the "legitimating architecture" of US Capitalist Racist Society. The final objective is to conceptualize the "Black Scare / Red Scare Longue Durée" as a problem space that illuminates *striking continuities* in the co-constitution of anti-Black and antiradical policy and practice.

Black Scare / Red Scare thus aims to intervene in and expand upon con-versations on racial capitalism that engage how racialism and capitalism ar-ticulate the relationship between racist governmentality and the maintenance of class division, the integral role of repressive discourse in maintaining ex-propriation and ongoing primitive accumulation in the capitalist mode of production, and how racial hierarchy structures economic exploitation.[6] It does so by recasting familiar and elucidating recondite events, concepts, and

issues to transform commonly held understandings about the interrelation-
ships of anti-Black racial oppression and anticommunism, or the Black Scare
and the Red Scare, to help readers to think anew about how the early twentieth century continues to inform the political challenges of the contemporary
moment.

To this end, *Black Scare / Red Scare* amplifies Black communist and anticapitalist ideas and praxis, which are too often marginalized—even in Black
studies. This radical knowledge production is used to read government documents and discourses against the grain to make plain their racist and antiradical logics; to correct archival distortions of Black realities; and to reevalu-
ate what counts as a legitimate source and whose knowledge is represented.
Attending not only to silences or omissions, but also to that which has been
overlooked or discounted, *Black Scare / Red Scare* is a work of Radical Black
resuscitation and reinterpretation that challenges racial and intellectual chauvinism to generate new ways of knowing and steward the counterhegemonic
scholarly traditions of African descendants.[7] This entails analyzing capitalism, imperialism, social oppression, and political repression through the scholarship, interpretations, experiences, and lives of Black people generally, and
Black political minorities particularly.

In addition, this work introduces and repurposes a constellation of vocabularies—US Capitalist Racist Society, Wall Street Imperialism, Structural
Location of Blackness, superexploitation, subproletarian, and legitimating
architecture, to name a few—to get at the complicated relationships between
anti-Black racial oppression and capitalism, imperialism and expropriation, discourse and material practice, and "Black" and "Red." This practice
of Africana Critical Theory is "inextricably linked to progressive political
practice(s), that highlights and accents Africana radicals' and revolutionaries'
answers to key questions posed by the major forms and forces of domination and discrimination." It is a method that requires a deep commitment to
human liberation and social transformation and an emphasis on the ideas,
analyses, and praxes of Black people like Benjamin Harrison Fletcher, Angelo
Herndon, Eslanda Goode Robeson, and Dorothy Hunton who have been
marginalized, erased, or distorted not only because of their race, but also because of their worldview and politics that defy US Capitalist Racist Society.[8]

Black Scare / Red Scare synthesizes the most emancipatory elements of
fields and disciplines including Black studies, political theory, and intellectual
history to offer a comprehensive criticism of a range of imperial impulses in
economic, political, social, and cultural phenomena to make ethical claims
for what should be.[9] In addition, the text aims to "constantly deconstruct and
reconstruct critical social theory to speak to the special needs of 'the new

times.'"[10] These "new times" include the age-old repression of radical and Black protest, coupled with new condemnations of "Critical Race Theory," "wokeism," and "cultural Marxism" in the context of increased racial and economic polarization that undergird creeping fascism in the United States and throughout the world. Offering a historical perspective on these current realities, *Black Scare / Red Scare* takes seriously the adage that "history doesn't repeat itself, but it rhymes." If the government and society invent witch-words, as Du Bois put it, to stymie progress, ossify the extant race and class order, criminalize radicalism, and condemn ideas and individuals committed to structural transformation, then the vocabularies, concepts, theories, and thinkers taken up in *Black Scare / Red Scare* aim not only to properly illuminate relations of domination and repression, but also to revive and reinvent how we speak and think about a Radical Black otherwise.

The Black Scare / Red Scare Longue Durée in US Capitalist Racist Society

US Capitalist Racist Society, defined as a racially hierarchical political economy and social order constituting labor superexploitation, expropriation by domination, and ongoing racial/colonial primitive accumulation, encompasses the "longue durée" of the Black Scare and the Red Scare. The Black Scare is the historically and contextually situated debasement, distortion, criminalization, and subjection of Blackness rooted in fearmongering about Black social equality, political domination, and economic parity, on the one hand, and the displacement, devalorization, and devaluation of whiteness, on the other hand. The "Red Scare" is operationalized as the criminalization and condemnation of anticapitalist ideas, politics, and/or practices through discourses of radical takeover, infiltration, and disruption of the American way of life to maintain a society dominated by a capitalist elite and organized along race and class lines.

The Black Scare derived from the "lateness in the abolition of the slavery in the United States"[11] and was a means of maintaining the "badge of slavery" that legitimated the economic, social, and ideological denigration of Blackness. It also followed from the US government's hostility to Black Nationalism, irrespective of its ideological orientation, not least because it is one of the most enduring and common political projects among African descendants. Classical Black Nationalism, spanning 1850 to 1925, was expressed through the efforts of Black people to "create a sovereign nation-state and formulate an ideological basis for a concept of a national culture." It was rooted in a desire for self-help, self-determination, independence, political autonomy, unity among the race, and the economic and military power to defend itself.[12] Modern Black Nationalism, which arose in the mid-twentieth century, shared the same desires of earlier forms but was more variable and experimental. Its primary aim was to confront powerlessness in US institutional life by closing ranks and cultivating a significant power bloc predicated on political, economic, cultural, and psychological unity.[13] Because Black Nationalism sought to empower the Black masses, challenge white authority, establish Black autonomy, and upend Black subordination, it was met with the Black Scare to both undermine and discredit these efforts. While Blackness and Black Nationalism are not reducible to each other, the potential of Black Nationalism to liberate Black people in the United States and connect them to Africans throughout the world animated the threat of Blackness articulated through the Black Scare.

The Black Scare reduced Blackness to a category of abjection and subjection through narrations of absolute biological or cultural difference; ruling-class monopolization of political power; negative and derogatory mass media propaganda; the use of discriminatory legislation to maintain and reinscribe inequality, not least various modes of segregation; and quotidian interactions in which distrust and antipathy toward Black people were normalized, as was the threat of mass violence.[14] Further, the Black Scare characterized Black agitation, protest, unrest, or dissent as dangerous, antithetical to the interests of the United States, and/or spurred by or susceptible to outside agitation. In doing so, it enunciated the US government's concern about national security, the ability to accumulate wealth, social organization along racialized lines of inequality, and the consolidation and maintenance of Wall Street Imperialism.

The Black Scare, moreover, was motivated by hysteria about how the linking up of the oppressed, the exploited, and the racialized could foment Black rebellion against global white domination. This perpetual panic legitimated overt anti-Black racial oppression and white supremacist terrorism through Jim Crow, lynching, and structural violence; economic exploitation through sharecropping, debt peonage, and unequal wages; high unemployment and exclusion from industry, or conversely, onerous and predatory inclusion into it; and the denial of full citizenship. Stated differently, the Black Scare was a means of preserving racial antagonism, hierarchy, and ordering instead of improving the social and material conditions that produced them.

Just as Black Nationalism was the specter of destabilization behind the Black Scare, the Red Scare was most prominently articulated through the threat of the communist/Bolshevist and the fellow traveler. In 1920, Attorney General A. Mitchell Palmer summed up this thinking in contending that the

"Red Movement" pretended to protest the supposed ills of US political and economic organization in the name of radical progress, but in actuality, it was a movement of those who despised liberty, aimed to destroy property ownership, and eschewed a belief in God. It was, therefore, both antidemocratic and a menace to US democracy insofar as it advocated the use of force to instill power by the few.

Moreover, for him, Bolshevists, syndicalists, Soviets, and industrial saboteurs were interchangeable "Reds" who were prone to criminality and violence, seeking to intimidate or confuse citizens into supporting their cause. As such, the US government was justified in waging "unflinching" war against these broadly conceived Reds not only for disturbing order, but also for leading people to radically question and/or distrust the government.[15] The Red Scare is thus the process by which "Red" became feared, hated, and obsessed about to the point that radicalism and militant challenges to the status quo became dangerous to the nation and portended the existence of traitors, conspirators, and agitators.[16] This anti-Red aggression facilitated the transmutation of social and economic reform into creeping socialism and ultimately communism; left-wing organization, discipline, and assembly into foreign-controlled conspiracy; left and progressive politics into authoritarianism; internationalist and industrial solidarity into potentially contagious insurrections; atheism into devilish "godlessness" and moral inferiority; communism into deceitfulness; and radical ideas, events, and protest into antidemocratic subversion and conspiracy.[17]

The Black Scare / Red Scare Longue Durée describes the joint and recursive unfolding of the Black Scare and the Red Scare starting in the midst of World War I and continuing through the early Cold War. Here, Blackness and radicalism were treated as vectors of subversion as the United States became the leading capitalist hegemon through methods of superexploitation, expropriation, and war—and their discursive legitimation.

Following Robbie Lieberman,[18] *Black Scare / Red Scare* takes seriously the *striking continuity* of antiradical repression and its inextricability from anti-Black racial oppression. The Black Scare / Red Scare Longue Durée roughly spans, on the front end, US entrance into World War I, the Bolshevik Revolution, and the deadly East Saint Louis Race riot in 1917, and on the back end, the formal end of "McCarthyism," the passage of the draconian Communist Control Act, and the *Brown v. Board of Education* ruling in 1954. These bookends, however, are guideposts and not hard edges. As such, *Black Scare / Red Scare* traces a longer trajectory that, while multidimensional in its ebbs and flows, was a persistent feature of US Capitalist Racist Society.

This longue durée makes plain the ways that the Red Scare was deeply informed by the Black Scare. The Black Scare, alongside antiforeignness,[19] shaped the racial anxiety of the Red Scare that is overlooked in much of the extant scholarship on the subject, even as it is acknowledged that the Black Scare was set to work by the Red Scare.[20] The co-constitution of these scares becomes evident in the analysis of the Black Scare / Red Scare Longue Durée as a "problem space," or a transtemporal network of repressive, racist, exploitative, and extractive dynamics that, while undergoing internal shifts, constitutes intractable continuities. These continuities are evidenced in several cases and documents that spanned the Black Scare / Red Scare Longue Durée.

In *Black Scare / Red Scare*, the entry into this Longue Durée is the passage of the Espionage Act of 1917 and the Sedition Act of 1918, which created the legal architecture for the punishment of Black agitation and manifold forms of radicalism as threatening to the wartime socioeconomic order, and thus to national security. As we will see, the disciplining of Benjamin Harrison Fletcher, leader in the Industrial Workers of the World (IWW) Local 8 of Philadelphia, illuminates this. The criminalization of Fletcher and the IWW represented the height of federal wartime Black Scare and Red Scare repression.[21]

The next important node in the network encompasses overlapping race riots, "Palmer Raids," and labor unrest during postwar demobilization that government authorities widely blamed on radicals, subversives, and agitators. In June 1919, Attorney General A. Mitchell Palmer had secured a $500,000 appropriation from Congress to build an investigative force to contend with the "criminal class"—not least Bolsheviks, anarchists, "huns," and those connected to and funded by them—and to "eradicate revolutionary agitation."[22] Out of this effort, the Radical Division of the Bureau of Investigation (BI), later renamed the General Intelligence Division (GID), was formed with J. Edgar Hoover at the helm.[23] It was Hoover who spearheaded the addition of Black people to the list of subversive elements and who worked doggedly to prove that Bolsheviks and other radicals were behind the race riots throughout the country. Indeed, Hoover is a central figure in the Black Scare / Red Scare Longue Durée. His hatred of working-class and labor dissidents, Black and white alike, fueled his collaboration with congressional committees in their anticommunist crusades and portended the use of hysteria to legitimate future repression.[24] In his roles in the GID, the Radical Division of the BI, and the Federal Bureau of Investigation (FBI), he was an architect of the Black Scare, the Red Scare, and their consocation. He combined criminal detection and political surveillance in one agency, sutured political counter-subversion and law enforcement, severed any real distinction between crime and radical dissent, and positioned struggles against racial hierarchy and agitation against capitalist exploitation as linked and mutually constitutive dangers.

This node also includes the rise of state-level antiradical actions and legislation that matched Palmer's federal initiative in the wake of the failure to pass a federal peacetime anti-sedition bill. In New York State, the Joint Legislative Committee to Investigate Seditious Activities, commonly known as the Lusk Committee, formed in 1919 to investigate "revolutionary radicalism." The broader goal of the committee was to compile evidence proving the interconnection of all left-wing political, industrial, and social organizations and their control by foreign powers. It further demonstrated that a key impetus of the Red Scare was fear of radical influence on Blacks and that a central aspect of the Black Scare was to forcefully repress efforts to fundamentally transform the racial and economic status quo.[25] In doing so, it set the standard for, and even influenced, later federal investigative reports and committees. The Lusk Committee did acknowledge that repressive measures against subversive and revolutionary organizations and movements must be accompanied by constructive action, which effectively meant compelling loyalty and uncritical acceptance of the status quo so as not to be rendered dangerous, subversive, or un-American.

The case of Marcus Garvey—his targeting, arrest, indictment, imprisonment, and ultimate deportation—is integral to the Black Scare / Red Scare Longue Durée topology. The attack on the "Black Moses," the infiltration of the Universal Negro Improvement Association by the BI, the demonization of the Black Star Line Corporation, and the criminalization of the UNIA's Liberia colonization plan were predicated on both the Black Scare *and* the Red Scare though Garvey was no Bolshevik and the UNIA was no "communist front." This was not least because, in the context of corporate monopolization and the spread of Wall Street Imperialism, Garvey's Black Nationalism was a powerful critique of US Capitalist Racist Society such that his encouragement of Black self-determination was, in its effect, rendered indistinct from communist propaganda by hostile government officials. Garvey's emphasis on race first, race pride, self-reliance, and the autonomous development of the Black race was considered radical agitation that encouraged and incited race hatred, and his back-to-Africa project was seen as a form of dangerous internationalism that challenged Western and Wall Street Imperialism. Likewise, his influence over ordinary Black people, whose purported ignorance made them particularly susceptible to subversive and foreign influences, was of great concern to the US government.[26] His persecution and ultimate deportation in 1927 created the conditions for the subsequent disciplining of manifold forms of Radical Blackness, framed as un-American, subversive, and dangerous.

The case of Angelo Herndon, the centerpiece of the Black Scare / Red Scare Longue Durée during the Great Depression, is perhaps the starkest example of virulent attacks on organizations, institutions, and individuals that demanded relief for workers generally, and Black workers particularly. Herndon was a nineteen-year-old Black communist who was arrested and convicted of insurrection in 1932 for his interracial labor organizing. He was targeted because, in situations of unrest and militancy, Blacks and those who crossed the color line were the most familiar and convenient scapegoats. As large swaths of the population shifted downward economically and either leftward or rightward politically based on skepticism about the durability of capitalism, radicals bore the brunt of government repression because their demands posed formidable challenges to US Capitalist Racist Society. Angelo Herndon's experience in the criminal legal/criminal punishment system will bring into sharp relief the convergence of the Black Scare, the Red Scare, and the conditions of capitalist racism that undergirded them during the Great Depression.

Like the Lusk Committee report, the *Survey of Racial Conditions in the United States* (*RACON*), a report commissioned by Hoover in 1942 and published in 1943, is invaluable to understanding the Black Scare / Red Scare Longue Durée. It elucidates the racial and economic tensions and contradictions at play in US Capitalist Racist Society during World War II. Throughout 1943, a nationwide wave of white terrorism rocked wartime industries in several cities, in response to increased Black presence in army camps and industrial centers.[27] This underscored that the Black Scare was set to work by the intersection of racial antagonism and economic subjection. At the same time, the Red Scare was employed to blame these conflicts on radical agitation and influence. The fourteen-month investigation—surveilling, documenting, and often mischaracterizing agitation by Black groups and individuals—and 743-page report constituting *RACON* condemned Black struggle for inclusion into wartime industry and unions as antithetical to the war effort, encouraged government disciplining of Black insurgency for political and economic equality by construing it as foreign inspired or subversive, and rationalized race riots aimed at undermining Black economic, political, and social gains. It also helped to deepen the Black Scare and the Red Scare by effectively defending and legitimizing the consolidation of Jim Crow power in national politics as World War II strengthened the "institutional grip" of forces supporting white supremacy. *RACON* laid the groundwork for the next eighteen years of surveillance and the all-out assault on Black and radical movements, making it a paradigmatic document of the Black Scare / Red Scare Longue Durée.[28]

At the tail end of the Black Scare / Red Scare Longue Durée, the meticulously documented 1951 United Nations petition *We Charge Genocide: The Historic Petition to the United Nations for Relief from a Crime of the United States Government against the Negro People* stands in contradistinction to the two government reports that codified and encouraged the Black Scare and the Red Scare. Prepared by the Civil Rights Congress under the guidance of its executive secretary, William L. Patterson, and collectively drafted and signed by notable Radical Black activists, organizers, journalists, and intellectuals, including Charlotta Bass, Louis E. Burnham, Benjamin J. Davis Jr., James Ford, Harry Haywood, Alphaeus and Dorothy Hunton, Claudia Jones, Maude White Katz, Amy Mallard, Rosalee McGee, Louise Thompson Patterson, Pettis Perry, Paul and Eslanda Goode Robeson, and Ferdinand Smith, the petition captured the war-driven intersections of capitalist exploitation, racial hierarchy, and social oppression. At the same time, it unearthed, critiqued, and offered a program to challenge the Black Scare and the Red Scare.

We Charge Genocide documented how economic crisis and a spike in racial violence immediately following the war converged with peacetime subversion legislation to wreak havoc on the lives of Blacks, radicals, and Radical Blacks. There had been a revival of lynchings and attacks on Black veterans in the South alongside a double-edged drive to roll back wartime gains made by Blacks in industry and to destroy the powerful alliance cultivated between labor and Blacks. To this was added the closing of Fair Employment Practices Committee (FEPC) offices, which tacitly sanctioned anti-Black economic, physical, and political assault.[29] Likewise, the Taft-Hartley Act was empowering employers to depress wages and eliminate the right to strike and collectively bargain.[30] The petition also described how Black women were hit worst of all, as their rights and living conditions were assaulted, the few gains they had made in industry during the war were eliminated, they were subjected to rising white chauvinism, and they were forced to battle "Jim Crow obstacles" that reduced millions of them to domestic labor.[31] As such, postwar economic realities particularly compounded women's "precarious economic position" emanating from low and unequal wages, work discrimination, and lack of opportunity.

We Charge Genocide documented and challenged on the world stage the Structural Location of Blackness that emanated from the interlocking realities of US Capitalist Racist Society and Wall Street Imperialism that animated the Black Scare / Red Scare Longue Durée.

Book Outline

Black Scare / Red Scare is organized into two thematic parts. Part 1, "Black Scare / Red Scare Foundation: Political Economy and the Threat of Radical Blackness," is divided into six chapters. Chapter 1 defines and establishes the relationship between US Capitalist Racist Society, Wall Street Imperialism, and the Structural Location of Blackness, and explicates how Wall Street Imperialism shaped different levels of development in the US North and South.

Chapter 2 theorizes the Black Scare, the Red Scare, and their entanglements and explicates Radical Blackness as the embodiment of these scares and thus the preeminent threat to US Capitalist Racist Society. Chapter 3 presents three genres of Radical Blackness targeted by the US state. The "West Indian" was integral to positioning Radical Blackness as foreign and as "alien anarchism" based on the convergence of immigrant status, undesirable ideas, and internationalism. The "Outside Agitator," who was educated, influential, and often disseminated ideas through the Black press, threatened to incite "unthinking" Blacks to violence, unrest, and defiance of the status quo. The "Red Black / Black Red" was perhaps the most odious of all genres as a card-carrying Red, an interracialist, and an advocate of social equality.

Chapter 4 builds on chapter 1 by explicating how the intersection of the Negro Question and Wall Street Imperialism gave the Structural Location of Blackness its national character and drove the demand for Black self-determination—a demand that was constructed as a preeminent threat to US Capitalist Racist Society. Chapter 5 focuses on the workings of Wall Street Imperialism in the Caribbean and in Africa. It hones in on how international expropriation was intimately linked to the Structural Location of Blackness in the United States, which, in turn was exported abroad through Wall Street Imperialism and its concomitant Black Scare and Red Scare methods. Finally, chapter 6 analyzes war, warmongering, and militarism as essential tools of capitalist racist accumulation and as means to employ the Black Scare and the Red Scare to expedite intervention, occupation, and economic domination.

Part 2, "Black Scare / Red Scare Codification: Governance and Legitimating Architecture," encompasses the remaining five chapters. Chapter 7 theorizes anticommunism as a mode of governance that, starting at the state and local levels, combined public authority and societal self-regulation to diffuse throughout society penalty for, and the marginalization, neutralization, and criminalization of, ideas and beliefs that challenged US Capitalist Racist Society. Chapter 8 begins the discussion of how all three branches of the US federal government participated in anticommunist governance by detailing the role of the executive and judicial branches, while chapter 9 focuses on the outsized role of the legislative branch through its production of a cacophony of legislation and its convening of antiradical congressional committees.

Chapter 10 examines the foundation of anticommunism in the "Counter-subversive Political Tradition," which describes the ongoing sanction of exclusion and repression predicated on the idea that foreigners and foreign ideologies were a threat to American ideals, values, and lifeways. Such fear of "others from without" was often linked to anxiety about "others from within," not least Black people and other racial, political, and religious minorities. The chapter ends with an examination of how the conjunction of the Countersubversive Political Tradition and anticommunist rule gave US Capitalist Racist Society a fascistic character.

The final chapter examines "True Americanism" as the paramount legitimating architecture of US Capitalist Racist Society during the Black Scare / Red Scare Longue Durée. True Americanism was the ideological enunciation of the Black Scare and the Red Scare that positioned capitalist racism as the preeminent system of political, economic, and social organization to which any challenge was dangerous, illicit, and illegitimate.

The epilogue reflects on the continuation of the Black Scare and the Red Scare in US Capitalist Racist Society today, especially through the convergence of neoliberalism and Black Lives Matter. One manifestation is the discourse of "Black Identity Extremism" that followed from a 2018 FBI memo.[32] More recently, the FBI's attack on the African People's Socialist Party,[33] Florida's 2021 bill "combatting public disorder"[34] and the 2021 Stop WOKE (Wrongs against Our Kids and Employees) Act[35] represent the reinvigoration of the Black Scare and the Red Scare as methods of criminalizing racial and radical militancy.

PART I

Black Scare / Red Scare Foundation:
Political Economy and the Threat of Radical Blackness

Theorizing US Capitalist Racist Society

Here was a paradise for the investor, which the state governments approved. Labor laws in the South were lax and carelessly enforced; company towns arose under complete corporate control; the police and militia were organized against labor. Race hate and fear and scab tactics were deliberately encouraged so as to make any complaint or effort at betterment liable to burst into riot, lynching, or race war.

W. E. B. DU BOIS, 1953

The Black Scare / Red Scare Longue Durée emanates from the coalescence of capitalist racism in the United States, Wall Street Imperialism, and the Structural Location of Blackness. US Capitalist Racist Society is defined as a racially hierarchical political economy and social order constituting labor superexploitation, expropriation by domination, and ongoing racial/colonial primitive accumulation.

Wall Street Imperialism, the highest stage of capitalist racism and the internal logic of US Capitalist Racist Society, had five key functions. The first was the consolidation of monopoly finance capital and its domination of all aspects of US domestic and foreign policy through the partnership between "big business" and the US government.[1] The second was to structure the unequal relationship between the US North and South with the "Negro Question" as its fulcrum. The third was to induce the national character of the Structural Location of Blackness. The fourth was to entangle expropriation and racial domination abroad, and the fifth, to employ war, warmongering, and militarism as principal tools of accumulation.

Finally, the Structural Location of Blackness describes an economic relationship that inscribes an inferiorized condition, a disempowered status, and a subordinated emplacement in the social order. Born out of capitalist racism and maintained through Wall Street Imperialism, the Structural Location of Blackness is an essential source of *superprofit* that engenders manifold discursive configurations to preserve and legitimate racial hierarchy and facilitate alliances across class between white capitalists and workers.[2] Given this structural location, "The entire history of the Negro people has been one of *radical* solution to a sorely oppressed status."[3] The Black Scare and the Red Scare have been instrumentalities to violently suppress that solution.

US Capitalist Racist Society

Labor superexploitation can be understood as a mode of surplus value extraction in which the intensity, form, and racial basis of exploitation emanates from, and often emulates, enforced servitude. Superexploitation results from the convergence of capitalism, racialism and white supremacy, imperialism, and brutality, which exceeds the conditions of exploitation to which white working classes are subjected. As Harry Haywood argued in 1948, "Beyond all doubt, the oppression of the Negro, which is the basis of the degradation of the 'poor whites,' is of separate character demanding a special approach."[4]

Labor superexploitation, coupled with structural exclusion from and discrimination in the labor market, reduces Black workers to a "subproletariat." The class composition of US Blacks was fundamentally altered between 1890 and 1940 as urban laborers became the decisive class, replacing "agrarian peons." In city-based factories and ghettos, they replaced European workers in the lowest-paying and most onerous jobs as the latter moved up.[5] As such, Black labor retained its subproletarian character insofar as such character is not a remnant of an earlier mode of production, but rather the "offspring" of US capitalist racism and imperialism that render Black labor cheap, unskilled, devalued, and superfluous when the productive forces are altered and tilted toward skilled, expert labor. This group is either set aside for capital's future need, not least to push labor costs down, or are warehoused in jails and prisons to remove them from the labor market permanently. The double move of the consolidation of monopoly capitalism and the shift of the Black masses from the Southern "Black Belt" to urban ghettos reified the Black subproletariat by holding their labor in reserve to keep it "dirt cheap," casual and precarious, and expendable when no longer required.

Labor superexploitation is especially manifest in the work of Black women, insofar as "capitalism and imperialism were [Black women's] main enemies" because they rendered it "economically profitable to exploit and oppress" this class of workers. Black women represented a cheap and surplus labor supply in the market and a free labor supply in their own homes—and often in the homes of white people. Likewise, the industries employing Black women were some of the most superexploitative across the country; this included "domestic workers, hospital workers, factory workers[,] farm laborers, [and garment workers]."[6]

A prime example of Black women's superexploitation during the Great Depression was the National Recovery Administration's (NRA) legal policy of differential wages, which were lowest of all for Black women workers in the

South.[7] Given Black women's subproletarian character, NRA codes worked especially against them because employers paying below the NRA minimum wage preferred to fire Black women workers instead of raising their wages. In other instances, the NRA cooperated with bosses to continue wage discrimination against Black women. At the Southland Manufacturing Company in Alabama, for example, employers were permitted to pay Black women nine dollars per week instead of the mandated twelve dollars because this despised group of workers was deemed incompetent.[8] Even though Black women were paid a pittance, their wages were considered to "compare favorably" to those of white women because in US Capitalist Racist Society, Black women's structural location meant that survival on less pay constituted their reality. According to employers, their standard of living was lower than that of whites, so they did not require as much remuneration.[9] Thus, "The super-exploitation of the Negro woman worker [was] revealed not only in that she receives, as a woman, less than equal pay for equal work with men, but in that the majority of Negro women get less than half the pay of white women."[10]

Expropriation by domination denotes the rapacious conscription of resources and labor for the purpose of *superprofits* through violent means that are generally reserved for populations racialized as inferior. It also designates the seizure and confiscation of land, assets, property, bodies, and other sources of material wealth that make the Structural Location of Blackness a function of imperialism domestically and abroad. This relationship exists both within and between nations and permeates the US South and North. The system of sharecropping and land tenancy that was widespread throughout the first half of the twentieth century was a cornerstone of US Capitalist Racist Society not least because of the relations of expropriation it engendered. Black croppers and tenants had their crops, wages, and livelihoods seized and were held in virtual bondage through crippling political and economic control by not only the landlords, but also by "banker-monopolists" who financed their operations.[11] Such control was rooted in relations of domination like disfranchisement, which not only stripped Blacks of the vote, but also subjected them to violence and terrorism if they attempted to exercise this right. Likewise, Black resistance was criminalized. White planters, employers, and merchants also maintained expropriation through "economic sanctions" like denying Black laborers land, housing, jobs, credit, and other tools necessary to forge an independent life. Northern capitalists and Southern landlords alike thereby accumulated immense wealth.

In the US North, one way expropriation by domination manifested was through housing policy. The well-documented New York mortgage conspiracy to limit Black housing to overcrowded ghettos and horrible slums for the purpose of superprofit was enforced through various forms of duress, not least violence, restrictive covenants, and court decisions. Black people never ceased resisting this violent imposition; throughout the 1920s, for example, under the leadership of the Black communist and African Blood Brotherhood members Grace Campbell and Hermina Huiswoud, the Harlem Tenants League organized the Black working class in Harlem against exorbitant rent, deplorable living conditions, rat infestation, neglectful and rapacious landlords, and disproportionate evictions and "dispossess notices."[12] This substandard living, which bred disease and subjected Blacks to premature death, was rooted in anti-Black domination. Such quotidian expropriation by domination was common knowledge; authorities agreed that Black ghettos were maintained in part because insurance companies, mortgage lenders, and real estate corporations wrested immense profit from this form of Black suffering that resulted from a "planned monopoly" that artificially restricted the housing supply.[13]

Relatedly, the prominent Black communist James Ford described expropriation by domination between nations. At the precipice of the Great Depression, the extant political economy, he explained, constituted the consolidation of Africa's partition and the "complete enslavement of its people"; the arresting of its industrialization, which hindered the development of the "toiling masses"; and the relegation of the continent to a source of raw material, a market for European goods, and a dumping ground for accumulated surplus capital. Further, the West Indies, subjected to US militarism and occupation on behalf of Wall Street, were largely transformed into a marketplace for US goods.

Finally, US Capitalist Racist Society constitutes ongoing racial/colonial primitive accumulation. Here, relations of settler colonialism intersect with anti-Black relations to configure the political economy of capitalist racism over time.[14] This primitive accumulation, emanating from the project of whiteness forged out of Pan-European "enslaving colonialism" and its violent suppression of "rebellious Africans and indigenes,"[15] links the Structural Location of Blackness to Indigenous dispossession through settler colonialism. Relatedly, "continental imperialism" describes the voracious appetite for land and labor that undergirds expansionist capitalism and links Blackness and Indigeneity through "dislocation and territorialization," discourses of absence, and "colonial and racial relations of control." These are rooted in the intimate relationship between slavery and colonialism, both of which are sutured to real estate property claims and the transformation of particular space into an invitation for aggressive exploitation and exploitative aggression.[16] Settler colonialism, the "primary social, economic, and political feature of the United

States" was the domestic iteration of Wall Street Imperialism abroad in its perpetuation of dispossession and plunder.[17] White and "free" wage labor are defined against the Structural Location of Blackness and Indigenous dispossession insofar as superexploitation and expropriation are constitutive of the latter but don't typically characterize the experience of the former. It is this *excess* that characterizes capitalist racism, reproduces US Capitalist Racist Society, and facilitates cross-class collaboration between capitalists and workers committed to white supremacy.[18]

Wall Steet Imperialism

Wall Street imperialism, the highest stage of capitalist racism in the United States, was more of a "lusty child of an already highly developed capitalism" than an exceptional capitalist power. The material conditions of the United States' rise to global hegemony included the intensive exploitation of its abundant natural resources, financial assistance from older capitalist powers, protective tariffs, and the development of a transportation and communication network that integrated mines, factories, and farms into "an effectively producing organism" with easy access to seaports.[19] It thrived off its large domestic market, and more importantly, its imbalance of Northern and Southern economies and its lack of investment in the political and economic welfare of the overwhelming masses of its population, least of all the descendants of the enslaved.[20]

As World War I wound down, the United States had shifted from a debtor to a creditor nation—extending $9.5 billion in loans to Allied powers during the war, for example[21]—and this elevated position allowed it to capture foreign markets, trade, and sites of investment. Additionally, the merger of banking and industrial capital matured in the United States in the second decade of the twentieth century, so that by the mid-1930s, eight groups of finance capital controlled 62 percent of large-scale industry, transportation, public utilities, and banking in the United States despite antitrust rhetoric and relatively ineffective legislation like the Sherman Antitrust Act.[22] These monopoly finance entities included Morgan electrical company and steel trusts, the Morgan Bank aluminum trust, the Kuhn-Loeb railroad mergers, and Rockefeller control of Chase National Bank. The internal expansion of the United States and the immense accumulation of capital at home required investments abroad and "an ever-widening foreign commerce," so "major entrepreneurs of the United States proceeded to step up their campaign for expansion abroad."[23] These forces merged with US militaristic foreign policy because "economic control require[d] political and military control" and spheres of influence.[24]

As such, though the owners of capital were a tiny fraction of the population, their aims were carried out and legitimated by politicians, the military, police, corporate managers, the media apparatus, labor union bureaucrats, and civil society organizations. In this way, imperialism became codified as "American policy," or stated differently, it became its internal logic.[25]

As the sociologist Oliver Cromwell Cox explained, imperialism was a "necessary component" of the capitalist system to "maximize and stabilize" the incomes of imperialist nations, and it was inseparable from the "propagation of, and dependence upon, racial prejudice when capitalist design [was] to keep a people exploitable" among and within nations.[26] Given this reality, racialism became "one of the main links of imperialism."[27] Likewise, Vladimir I. Lenin and W. E. B. Du Bois, "our American Lenin,"[28] analyze imperialism as the concentration of production and capital tending toward the creation of monopolies that take on a central role in economic life; the merging of bank and industrial capital to create finance capital and a financial elite, or oligarchy; the export of capital taking on increasing importance vis-à-vis the export of commodities; the formation of international capitalist monopolies that share in the exploitation and expropriation of the world; and the completion of the territorial division of the world among the capitalist powers. These dynamics became consolidated at the turn of the twentieth century.[29]

Furthermore, racialized exploitation and expropriation are the foundations of Euro-American imperialism. The deadly clash of imperialist powers, grounded in the white supremacist pact between the ruling and working classes to profit from the subjection of the darker nations, often led to war over spheres of plunder. In other words, the intersection of modern capitalism and Euro-American imperialism produced a class collaborationist project aimed at looting the labor and resources of those on the darker side of the color line. The shared vision of racialized labor exploitation and imperial expansion demanded the expropriation of wealth "from the darker nations of the world—Asia and Africa, South and Central America, the West Indies and the islands of the South Seas." At the same time, Black, Yellow, Brown, and Red men recognized that Europe's aggrandizement was predicated upon their dispossession, domination, and dehumanization.[30]

Black studies scholar Clarence J. Munford concurs that imperialist relations constituting the capitalist system were manifested in the United States in the superexploitation and racial oppression of African descendants, the "Lazarus-stratum" of workers. According to Munford, the capitalist mode of production wasn't inherently racist but US Capitalist Racist Society *was*, given that in "the U.S. system of political economy, racism and capitalism are inseparable aspects of the same reality," due not least to imperialism, which, "being inherently reactionary, [exhibits] a natural tendency to espouse racism."[31] The era of Reconstruction was important to the inscription of imperialism in the "color line," when whites asserted themselves against "the impudent ambition of blacks" in the US South at the same time that, worldwide, whites worked to restrict the "democratic development" and self-determination of the colonized through the promotion of race hatred. This program helped to "raise the scale of white labor," as it "in much greater proportion put wealth and power in the hands of great [Euro-American] captains of Industry and made modern industrial imperialism possible."[32]

At the same time, Wall Street Imperialism flourished by maintaining an extremely low standard of living in "dependent" countries. It did so through the extension of credit, aid, and loans to poor countries only if the conditions were favorable to US corporations; trade agreements and negotiations that allowed for US monopolies to destroy weaker local industries; employment of sanctions, embargos, and attacks on weaker countries' currencies to weaken or destroy their economies; preferences and favors for the most reactionary elements of societies in exchange for capitulation to Wall Street; treaty negotiations that encouraged unfettered pillaging of a countries' natural resources by US corporations; aggressive diplomacy to extract concessions for US companies; and the installation of US managers, advisers, and tax collectors to control the treasuries and finances of weaker countries.[33] Such policies were often couched in discourses of development, liberalization, democratization, and free trade—though most developing nations more accurately experienced these as violence—that conflated imperialism and Americanism.

The merging of bank and industrial capital, the formation of capitalist monopolies, and the territorial division of the world, coupled with racially hierarchical superexploitation and expropriation and its encouragement of white class collaboration, illuminates Wall Street Imperialism as a genre of imperialism inextricable from capitalist racism and the Structural Location of Blackness.

The Structural Location of Blackness

Wall Street Imperialism operated domestically and internationally, articulating racialized relations of inequality that spread outward and redounded back to the mainland.[34] One such relation was the Structural Location of Blackness. Born out of racial slavery, the Structural Location of Blackness exceeds the category of race, is not reducible to class, and does not fit the specifications of caste.[35] Whereas in the context of US capitalist political economy, race demarcates social status,[36] structural location describes a material relationship inextricable from imperialism and sustained through a combination of political, economic, and discursive processes to which any challenge is configured as destructive to US society. Likewise, while structural location has a class basis insofar as it exists within a capitalist system with an exploitative and antagonistic relationship between capital and labor, it is not reducible to a class relationship because it has generally served as a source of cross-class collaboration between whites—or as Du Bois described it, "democratic despotism"— not least through the ideology of white supremacy. The Structural Location of Blackness also facilities cross-class solidarity among Black people over and against interracial class solidarity at the same time that it encompasses intraracial class conflict that reifies and intensifies the superexploitation of Black workers. In other words, out of the Structural Location of Blackness, a dependent Black bourgeoisie was developed that excludes, marginalizes, discriminates against, and extracts from its subordinates even as this class experiences anti-Black racial oppression—albeit at a different intensity of violence.

The *political ontology* of Blackness as a structural location is the aporia of value minus worth, emanating from racial enslavement, whereby Blackness is a capacious category of surplus value extraction essential to an array of political economic functions, including accumulation, disaccumulation, exchange, use value, and the absorption of capital risk. At the same time, Blackness is also the quintessential condition of disposability, expendability, and reversibility. Techniques of obfuscation are essential to maintaining the irresolvable contradiction constituting the Structural Location of Blackness. The simultaneous reliance on the immense value extracted from Blacks and the denial of their indispensability engenders "a sense of worthlessness and unwantedness"[37] among Blacks and an unwarranted attitude of superiority among whites—an attitude whose material consequences emanate from a sense of white entitlement to Black production and productivity. As a result, oppression is mischaracterized as inferiority. For example, the Black masses' higher rates of sickness and death, worse quality of education, and higher rate of incarceration are markers of *oppression* that are construed as inferiority even though their "basic integrity . . . [is] untouched. Their aspirations for decency, humanity, justice—for them and of them—[is] present."[38] This obfuscation sets to work the Black Scare and the Red Scare by transforming such aspirations, and the struggle for them, into markers of backwardness, unbelonging, and subversion because they threaten the racial and economic order.

As a constant source of profit and extraction precisely through its devalorization, Blackness congeals oppression and exploitation. Because enslaved Africans were essential to the profits of the plantocracy, extreme violence and cruelty were essential to obfuscate their humanity. The aporia of value minus worth is especially legible in the fact that the immense value of enslaved Africans invited, instead of prevented, maximum cruelty.[39] Likewise, because every group that lives by exploiting another simultaneously despises that group, and that contempt is directly proportional to the degree of exploitation, the descendants of enslaved Africans are not only sources of extreme surplus value extraction, but also subjects of ongoing discourses and practices that render them constitutively lowly and worthless.[40]

Alongside political ontology is the *political economy* of the Structural Location of Blackness. This manifests most prominently in the reality that Blacks are "more essentially proletarian than any other American group"[41] given high proportion of workers and the comparative paucity, underdevelopment, and dependency of the Black bourgeoisie and petit bourgeoisie. More specifically, Blackness is *subproletarian* in character given that Black laborers have historically been "servants and serfs" and menial workers. Though Blacks theoretically belong to the world proletariat, the white proletariat subjected Black labor to physical assault, social degradation, economic exclusion, and interpersonal hatred. And, when Blacks attempted in self-defense to make a living, white workers denigrated them as scabs while ignoring the capitalists who were responsible for both groups' immiseration.[42] Black toilers were also excluded from the labor movement for much of their history because anti-Black racial oppression dictated that "*Negroes [were] servants; servants [were] Negroes.*"[43] The twin of routinized exclusion was burdened and onerous inclusion whereby Blacks got "less for their work" than any other workers, worked longer hours and under worse conditions, paid higher rents, and thereby experienced a form of exploitation—superexploitation—"keener than that of any group if white workers in America."[44] That Blacks felt the *dehumanizing* effects of the capitalist system most acutely is a testament of capitalist racism.[45]

The Negro Question and the Structural Location of Blackness

During the Black Scare / Red Scare Longue Durée, the Negro Question was the most direct engagement with the Structural Location of Blackness, given its preoccupation with how to incorporate Black people into society while maintaining racial hierarchy and managing Black subordination. The Negro Question was a direct result of the uncompensated expropriation of Southern slaveholders of their wealth in enslaved Africans after the Civil War. The South's anti-Black crusade could be traced to resentment arising from their loss of property in enslaved Africans, amounting to $3 billion, after they were routed in the Civil War. Their (temporary) subordination to the North and placement on equal footing with their former property during

Reconstruction; and their desire for "revenge and vindication" through extreme economic exploitation and cheap labor. The combination of greed and
vengeance was legitimated by the belief that inferior Blacks were ordained
by God to be the hewers of wood and drawers of water for superior whites.[46]
Upon the abolition of slavery in 1865, according to historian Gerald Horne,
the problem of massive expropriation without compensation led to a "fury"
among the descendants of those slave owners who were cast into poverty—
not unlike the despised Blacks—when their property was seized. To add insult to injury, the formerly enslaved sought parity with their former masters.[47]
This "uncompensated expropriation of private property in what had been the
slave holders republic—which left this 'property' and their progeny amidst
those made the poorer—was not a prescription of harmony" and resulted in
ongoing "acts of plunder, of incendiarism and of revenge."[48]

The convergence of economic imperative, white supremacist hostility, and
the drive to maintain racial hierarchy constituting the Negro Question was
not reducible to the US South. After the Civil War, "Northern Big Business as
well as humanitarianism secured the ratification of the Fourteenth Amendment, and Big Business soon decided that it could make more money out of a
stabilized racial situation in the South than it could out of agitation for Negro
rights."[49] Jim Crow policies were not only the product of white supremacy
and racial domination in the South, but were also a means by which "northern bankers and industrial monopolies tightened their grip on southern economic life to extract superprofits from the oppressed Negro people, and to a
lesser extent from white works and sharecroppers cut off from the Negroes by
economic favoritism and racist propaganda."[50] The Negro Question was central to the relationship between Northern capital and the Southern economy
because the high concentration and lowly status of Black people kept all labor
cheap.[51] Likewise, since Black labor, especially in the South, was the "chief
human factor" in wealth production, "the dominant economic class ha[d]
always been at the motivating center of the spreads of racial antagonism.
This [was] to be expected since the economic content of the antagonism,
especially at its proliferating source in the South, ha[d] been precisely that
of labor-capital relations."[52] Thus was the Structural Location of Blackness
codified in the Negro Question through Black codes, debt peonage, superexploitative sharecropping arrangements, racial lynching and routinized terror, and the generalized economic, political, and social subjection of the formerly enslaved. This domination and humiliation was sustained because the
federal government did very little to challenge this reality.[53]

By World War I, Wall Street was deeply invested in maintaining the conditions of the South. Black labor, resubjugated after Reconstruction, provided

the extra-exploited colonial-like labor within its own borders that lowered all workers' economic conditions. Superprofits were extracted from the lowest of the low: more than $4 billion of profit over and above that appropriated from white workers had been extracted especially from Black agricultural workers and from the "tens of thousands" of Black Southerners compelled into forced labor "on prison farms and roads for the profit of food companies and contractors who reap the fruits of their unpaid labor."[54]

Northern capitalists' investment in the oppression and exploitation of Southern Blacks meant that "the half-slave conditions in the Southern Black Belt continue[d] to set the pattern for the economic and social oppression of the Negroes in the North" and elsewhere.[55] During World War I, the labor crunch brought on by the European conflict and the concomitant halt to immigration was addressed by transforming the "black labor reserve in the Southern countryside" from a "potential" source of Northern industrial labor to an "active" source through mass migration.[56] This migratory process would be repeated during World War II in a more magnified and protracted way that signaled its irreversibility.[57] Around 1916, industrialists in the North, "impelled by visions of spectacular profits," opened up their factories to Black workers, and between 1916 and 1919, about a half-million Blacks relocated to Northern cities, with twice as many following throughout the 1920s.[58] By the end of World War I, there was an increase of 322,000 Black Southerners in the North.[59] There was also a simultaneous movement from rural to urban areas in the South. The meatpacking, steel, and automobile industries largely precipitated this move.[60] The convergence of Northern greed and the Structural Location of Blackness meant that the Negro Question was national in scope; market demands for cheap Black labor were not accompanied by a transformation in political and racial relations.[61] This was especially pronounced for Black women migrants. For them, the economic necessity of migration converged with the push factor of escaping sexual exploitation "within and outside their families," and sexual abuse at the hands of Southern white, and some Black, men. Nonetheless, they continued to be concentrated in the same types of domestic service jobs they had in the South—albeit at a slightly higher wage.[62]

As Blacks migrated out of the South, the North accepted Southern patterns of racial domination given their "longer experience with a vexatious problem"[63]—and the fact that Northern capital helped to maintain those patterns. Though there were comparatively more economic and industrial opportunities for Black men, advancement was virtually nonexistent, racial segregation and discrimination persisted, rents were exorbitant, and social ostracism was as ubiquitous in the North as it was in the South.[64] There was, for example, the employment of Black workers in "Negro jobs," a "classification openly avowed in the South" that reified the subproletarian character of Blackness but was rationalized as "merely the way things worked out through application of uniform standards."[65] In other words, because Black workers were forced into low-paid, onerous, dirty work in the South, in agriculture and in industry, this was considered to be the class of work for which they were ideally suited and against which white workers' standards would be set. Similarly, if a job started off as interracial but Blacks began to predominate, the wages would stagnate,[66] which meant that Blackness devalued labor, and devalued work was sutured to Blackness. In general, "in terms of day-to-day work, white labor was given a systematic advantage over black labor and a stake in the racist practices."[67]

Employers also fostered competition between Black and white workers, discouraged Blacks from unions and toward "open-shop" policies, and, more callously, employed Blacks as strikebreakers to undermine union militancy.[68] Northern capitalists' use of Blacks as strikebreakers increased racial tension and induced white trade unionists to excoriate Black workers as enemies of the labor movement.[69] On the one hand, strikebreaking was a function of the Structural Location of Blackness in several ways. It followed from the historical exclusion of Blacks from industrial labor until comparatively late except when it was used to discipline white militancy. It emanated from the long history of white labor's racist violence against their Black counterparts, which engendered Black workers' hostility. And it was used as a means to measure Black loyalty through obedience, obsequiousness, and docility.[70] On the other hand, Blacks did not break strikes with more frequency than whites, but the mere presence of Black workers was a "sore point" and the basis for "exceptional disorder."[71]

The dramatic increase in Black workers precipitated by the Great Migration, along with Northern capitalists' "stake in racist practices," stoked hostility in white workers who resented "the encroachment of Black newcomers," increased competition over housing, and heightened expectations among Blacks for economic and political parity. Whites were especially hostile to the "new racial militancy" expressed in Black periodicals and by Black militants.[72] Interracial tension, friction, antipathy, and antagonism developed among Black and white workers during the war and intensified thereafter. Postwar demobilization, surging inflation, stagnant wages, and widespread labor strikes converged with rampant unemployment among Black industrial workers, disrespect and destitution of Black veterans despite their valiant service, and an uptick in lynching.[73] This filled Blacks with "bitterness and disillusionment, with many swearing their conditions were worse than ever."[74] The result was more than twenty race riots throughout the nation immediately following World War I, where white violence and intimidation that accompanied perceived Black overreach was met with Black self-defense.[75] Even in the South, according to Major J. E. Cutler of the army Military Intelligence Division, there was "a New Negro to be reckoned with in [US] political and social life." He discovered during a tour of the region in August 1919 that a cross section of the Black press, trade unions, and political groups were challenging the existing power structure, linking up with activists and organizers outside of their community, cultivating Black Nationalist consciousness, and articulating a "leftist agenda focused on improving the economic status of laboring people."[76]

Wall Street Imperialism and the Relationship between the US North and South

The intersection of Wall Street Imperialism and the Negro Question structured the relationship between the industrialized North and the largely agrarian South in the United States during the Black Scare / Red Scare Longue Durée. Prior to World War I and the concomitant Great Migration, "Northern capital engaged Southern workers . . . by exporting capital to the South rather than by encouraging migration, thus enabling itself to exploit the low wage structure of the economically-backward South while avoiding any disturbances in its precarious political or economic balance."[77] The virtual enslavement of Black people was an "important prop" of Wall Street Imperialism insofar as "the preservation of the slave remnants in Southern agriculture" was a condition of extracting "superprofits."[78] Instrumental to this was the system of sharecropping and land tenancy that was widespread throughout the first half of the twentieth century and predominated in the South. Black and white croppers and tenants alike became key sources of accumulation for white planters, employers, and merchants. In terms of sheer numbers, more surplus was extracted from white croppers and tenants insofar as they made up two-thirds of that labor force. However, the political economy itself functioned through the Structural Location of Blackness, a remnant of the slave economy, which increased the vulnerability of all poor rural farmers and proletariats.

Wall Street Imperialism united Southern white capitalists and landlords and Northern monopolists in maintaining the direct and violent plunder of the Black masses.[79] Northern capitalists accepted a disempowered Black subproletariat concentrated in agriculture, rule of "Southern propertied interests," and racialized subjection as a means of stabilizing national politics, providing cheap raw materials for national mills and markets, and through this uneven development, facilitating rapid industrial expansion outside the South.[80] The ultimate aim of the "energetic" racist ideologies and policies in the United States was to conceal how Wall Street Imperialism decimated working conditions for all workers through the superexploitation of Black people. Here, the "fusion of finance capital with remnants of the pre-capitalist form in Southern agriculture, which [took] place in this period, [was] accompanied by a corresponding unity in the field of ideology,"[81] namely, anti-Black racialism.

The domination of monopolies was most pronounced in the South and resulted in a poorer standard of living and lower wages than any other section of the United States—phenomena that were largely predicated on the entrenchment of the Structural Location of Blackness originating from that region.[82] Here, the North was integral to the economic subordination of the South through Wall Street Imperialism. By 1900, investment there was more than double foreign investments. Southern farmers even referred to investments from Northern money lenders and bankers as "foreign capital." The imperialist relationship between Northern absentee corporate and financial entities and the South included the financing of Southern plantations by eastern banks' credit systems; the control of the majority of coalfields in the South by capitalist families like the Mellons, Fords, and Rockefellers; and the ownership of Southern natural gas and electric companies by Northern financial institutions.[83]

Particularly important given the South's agrarian makeup was the reality that the region's "industries most closely allied to agriculture, such as fertilizer plants and the tobacco plants, the cotton oil mills and the cotton compresses were dominated by giant corporations."[84] By 1949, US Steel Corporation, launched and dominated by Morgan, owned over 362,432 acres of coal mines and numerous plants throughout Alabama and Tennessee.[85] The E. I. du Pont de Nemours Corporation had numerous textile, plastic, explosives, and chemical plants spanning the South, including in Virginia, Tennessee, Alabama, and Texas. It also controlled General Motors plants in Memphis and Atlanta, sawmills in Louisiana and Tennessee, timber interests in Louisiana and Arkansas, and US Rubber Company plants in Georgia, South Carolina, Tennessee, and Virginia.[86] Large Northern corporations like Dow Chemical Company, Monsanto, du Pont, and Union Carbide and Carbon controlled nearly all of the chemical industry in the South. Corporations like American Bemberg and North American Rayon opened plants exclusively in the South to take advantage of low costs and higher profits.[87]

Petroleum, one of the South's most abundant natural resources, was largely in the hands of the Rockefellers—specifically Standard Oil Company—and its subsidiaries. Standard Oil Company of California controlled 2,018,866 acres of land in Texas, Mississippi, Louisiana, Georgia, and Alabama alone for oils wells and "further use," while the Rockefeller company Atlantic Refining Company owned oil rights on 3,665,000 acres across Alabama, Arkansas, Florida, Louisiana, Oklahoma, Texas, and Mississippi.[88] International Pulp & Paper, the world's largest paper company in the 1940s, had huge plants concentrated in the South, with three in Louisiana alone, and owned 1.5 million acres of timberland in the South. This allowed it to exercise expansive power over the press through ownership and sales.[89]

The meatpacking companies Swift & Company, Armour & Company, and the Cudahy Packing Company, along with the Buckeye Cotton Oil Company, Wesson Oil, and Snowdrift Company, worked together to control the price of cottonseed paid to Southern farmers and to dictate the extension of credit to cotton growers.[90] Additionally, while Southern textiles were one of the least concentrated US industries, they were nonetheless primarily owned or controlled by Northern corporations, especially after World War II, which "saw a veritable revolution in southern textiles, with whole chains of mills passing into northern ownership and merging with northern capital, as well as a general integration of industry."[91]

Moreover, Wall Street banks and insurance companies had taken over plantation land directly or indirectly through monopoly control of credit. The big insurance companies had a huge influence on the credit system of the South, which resulted in ownership of expansive tracts of land and, as such, the exercise of outsized influence on state governments, especially in times of economic crisis when they were trying to recoup loses or off-load land.[92] For example, in the 1940s, Metropolitan Life Insurance Company was the largest owner of agricultural loans in the South, and its profits were increased by the "special oppression" and exploitation of Black plantation workers—in other words, by the Structural Location of Blackness.[93] These patterns of ownership and control convey not only how Wall Street Imperialism structured economic relationships between the North and the South, but also how the North was deeply invested in Southern racial, social, and political relations that made immense profits possible.

The Structural Location of Blackness meant that Black labor was concentrated in stagnant or declining industries, including sawmills, coal mines, and cigar and tobacco factories, and its presence signaled devaluation insofar as these jobs generally meant low wages, terrible conditions, and drudgery. Of course, in times of labor market contraction, whites quickly ousted Blacks from the very jobs they otherwise avoided as "nigger jobs." This reality is manifested in the case of Angelo Herndon, a Southern Black communist who was a victim of the Black Scare and the Red Scare. His experience in the Great Depression conveyed the relationship between Wall Street Imperialism, the Negro Question, and the South as the preeminent site of superexploitation.

At the age of thirteen, Herndon worked in a coal mine in Lexington, Kentucky. After working ten- or eleven-hour days, the company often cheated him out of his pay, from which a substantial amount was deducted for "fantastic purposes." For example, he was charged schooling fees even though, being a child himself, he sent no children to school and did not attend himself. Segregation permeated the mines, with Blacks laborers confined to a separate area from white workers and denied the opportunity to rise to better-paying jobs. Blacks were relegated to the dirtiest, most arduous jobs like coal loading and serving as "mule boys," while whites worked in a variety of positions, including foremen, electricians, surveyors, engineers, and bank bosses. Likewise, Herndon and his brother lived in segregated, dilapidated company housing next to a garbage dump for which they were charged exorbitant rent. They ate horrible, often moldy, food that they were forced to purchase from the company shop at a premium. Not unlike sharecroppers, Herndon and the other (Black) workers went into debt to live in "subhuman" conditions and were "irretrievably mortgaged to these heartless ghouls who preyed upon them systematically."[94]

Insofar as the workers were banned from unionizing, they were "systematically robbed," and when they objected, the Black workers in particular were subjected to violence and racism. When Herndon protested that he had not been given full credit for the amount of coal he collected, the white foreman grabbed him by the throat and shouted, "You dirty little nigger shut your trap and don't let me hear a sound from you again. You take what you get and be grateful for it. If you don't like it, get the hell out of here and see if you are treated better elsewhere." Herndon knew that "wherever [he] would go, where Negro workers would go," they would be subjected to the same violence, indignity, and oppression. To add insult to injury, workers were subjected to surveillance by intimidating "hired gunmen" who patrolled the headquarters at all times.[95]

Herndon's condition did not improve when he went to work at the Tennessee Coal, Iron, and Railroad Company (TCI) in Birmingham, Alabama. He noted that TCI circumvented the union movement by forming sham company unions that excluded Black workers.[96] This approach was no doubt in response to the long history of labor unionizing in Alabama, which by 1940, was the most unionized state in the South. This labor movement was centered in Birmingham, a stronghold for unions like the United Mine Workers of America that had led a coalition in 1928 to abolish convict labor in the state. Coal miners were in the vanguard of labor organizing, helping to build unions across the state throughout the 1930s in industries including steel, woodworking, textile, and education. In addition, unionized areas in the state tended to be antiseg-regation and more supportive of liberal politics.[97] This reality no doubt shaped the TCI's vehement repression, where union busting also resulted in "hard work, maltreatment, ignorance and a bestial atmosphere [that] contrived to keep [the workers] blind as bats to their degradation."[98]

The "white exploiters" employed the Black Scare to create a "vicious atmosphere . . . about the Negro character as a further excuse to oppress" Black workers.[99] For example, when Herndon's Black work partner was electrocuted because the white foreman failed to properly shield a wire despite multiple complaints from workers, the foreman demanded that Herndon testify that the shielding had been there so the company would not have to pay out benefits to the family.[100] Herndon told the truth, much to the chagrin of the foreman, and his partner's family got some compensation. Though "it wasn't much. . . . Usually in similar cases, no redress or compensation is ever given to a worker's family."[101] Herndon's integrity, along with the threat of trade union organizing among disgruntled workers, allowed the family to wrest a paltry sum from the TCI.

The Black Scare and the Red Scare continued to coalesce around the threat of Black organizing and its challenge to Wall Street Imperialism. In 1930, Herndon was locked up by TCI company guards in the Big Rock Jail for associating with communists.[102] Presaging what was to befall him in Atlanta the next year, the judge found him guilty and stated, "I am only sorry that we haven't got an insurrection law here in Alabama as they have in Georgia so we could have your nec[k] broken in the court room without delay." He was sentenced to twelve months on the chain gang at hard labor and a $500 fine.[103] The case was subsequently overturned, but Herndon was black-listed in Birmingham. His experience conveyed the superexploitation, violence, and repression that accrued around poor Black workers generally, and Black "Reds" particularly, who labored in Northern-controlled or -dominated industries like mining. Wall Street Imperialism worked to entrench extremely low wages organized along racially hierarchical lines, horrible working conditions, backbreaking labor reserved for Blacks, and routinized violence against those who attempted to unionize to oppose these relations.

Wall Street Imperialism and the Structural Location of Black Women

The Wall Street Imperialist relationship between the US North and South meant that the Structural Location of Blackness was maintained to keep "semi-feudal" labor cheap, onerous, and easy to control. This was especially manifested in the gendered exploitation of Black women, namely, the hyper-extraction of their reproductive labor and accompanying social oppression through concentration in domestic service. Herndon confessed that he was "terribly distressed" by his mother's poverty, "wretchedness," and "helpless-ness" as a domestic servant. As a servant in the household of a rich white family, she was mistreated and overworked, leaving home before Herndon awoke and sometimes not returning until midnight. She received only ten dollars a week for her wages and was never paid overtime. Herndon under-stood that because his mother was a Black servant, she was at the bottom of the social scale, and was despised, poor, and oppressed. However, because this was the reality for the overwhelming majority of Black women, he did not see her condition as extraordinary, but rather as "the most natural thing in the world."[104] Herndon's description conveyed that "few occupations bet-ter symbolize Black women' work historically than domestic labor. . . . The cultural politics of household labor, in which white Americans cast African American women as content and loyal servants became a way to justify racial inequality."[105]

What Herndon recognized in his mother's plight was explained in 1928 by Grace Campbell, one of the first Black women to join the Communist Party. She explained, "Negro women workers are the most abused, exploited and dis-criminated against of all Americans workers, not only by the capitalist system and the employers, but by unenlightened race prejudice which is found even in the working class, and is used by the employers to drive a wedge between the black and white workers and thus destroy their unity and fighting power."[106] Black communists Eugene Gordon and Cyril Briggs noted in 1935, "the Negro woman worker is doubly victimized. She suffers both from general discrimina-tions against women works and from her identity as a member of a nationality singled out by the ruling class for special plundering, persecution, and oppres-sion . . . the dirty deal that falls to all working women in capitalist society falls heaviest upon the Negro woman worker."[107] Esther V. Cooper concurred that Black women, especially domestic workers, were discriminated and exploited "with double harshness."[108] According to Louise Thompson Patterson, though, women were *triply* exploited, "as workers, as women, and as Negroes."[109] This "special oppression," Claudia Jones argued, was maintained through "white chauvinist stereotype as to where her place should be" and was an imperialist device to ensure Black women would be understood as "'backward,' 'inferior,' and the 'natural slaves' of others."[110] Given their concentration in domestic ser-vice, the "owner-slave, lord-vassal, master-servant tradition remain[ed]" be-tween Black women and the white women and men they served.[111]

Up to 1910, Black women were relegated almost exclusively to work at the "drudgery and humiliation" of plantation labor or domestic or personal service. By 1930, though other labor avenues had opened up, Black women were still heavily concentrated in domestic and personal service—more than six hundred thousand out of the nearly two million who were working in the South.[112] While very young and very old white women were also represented in domestic work, it was the occupation of Black women of all ages.[113] The worst exploited were those, like Herndon's mother, who worked as cooks, chambermaids, household maids, and day workers.[114] Marvel Cooke and Ella Baker conveyed that this reality was not reducible to the South. They explained in the context of the Bronx, New York, how Black domestic workers attempted to sell their labor in virtual slave markets, the largest of which were located on 167th Street and Jerome Avenue and Simpson and Westchester Avenues. The work was highly irregular, and the entrance of Black women who had recently migrated from the South into the "slave market" who were willing to accept lower pay than more seasoned domestics meant that the newcomers would be threatened with violence or chased off the block in an effort to secure the highest wages possible for this class of beleaguered workers. This ad hoc organizing was necessary given the failure of the mainstream labor movement to spend any significant time organizing domestic workers.

In the "slave markets," "not only [was] human labor bartered and sold for slave wages, but human love also [was] a marketable commodity." Stated differently, these contingent workers were susceptible to sexual harassment and sexual exploitation by white men—the fathers, brothers, and husbands of the housewives who "rented" Black domestic day workers "at unbelievably low rates." Migration North did not save Black women from the onerous work and sexual violence that accrued around the Structural Location of Blackness.

The intensification of structural poverty during the Great Depression compelled Black domestic workers to auction their labor on these street corners for less than thirty cents an hour and to subject themselves to the indignity brought on by white housewives who often underpaid—or failed to pay altogether—these vulnerable laborers. While the Great Depression immiserated Black women's labor, it had brought a new employer class to the labor market, namely, lower middle-class white housewives who found the opportunity to secure the maid they had long dreamed about in the crushing poverty, starvation, and discrimination that pushed Black women onto street corners.[115] Moreover, it was the gross discrimination in the distribution of relief that forced Black women to seek this degrading employment.[116] As one woman explained, "The employment agencies are no good. All the white girls get the good jobs."[117]

Conditions were even worse in the South where Black women cooked, washed, cleaned, and nursed children for two to three dollars per week. This same group of women were also "field worker[s] by day, mother[s] and housewi[ves] by night."[118] Black domestics were reduced to "the feudal relationship and tie to the household" where they were "made to feel and acknowledge their social and racial lowliness."[119] Likewise, this class of workers generally suffered from lack of employment standards, long hours—averaging seventy-two hours a week in the late 1930s, for example—"starvation" wages, exclusion from social insurance benefits and other labor legislation, and social stigma that accompanied this type of labor.[120]

Other forms of service work Black women performed included stewards, waitresses, steam laundresses, untrained nurses and midwives, and charwomen.[121] Even as the US economy improved during World War II, in 1945 one million of 7.5 million Black women were in domestic and personal service, with 918,000 employed in private homes; 98,000 working as cooks, waitresses, and other services outside of private homes; and 60,000 Black women concentrated in personal service occupations. The next largest portion of Black women workers, 245,000, were in agricultural work.[122]

When Black women did begin to enter industry in significant numbers during World War II, their subordination continued in that they were paid some of the lowest wages for the heaviest and most hazardous jobs largely because they were inexperienced and largely unorganized. The only jobs available to them had been abandoned by workers who had moved to more highly compensated occupations.[123] This meant that Black women were making abysmal wages as others' wages and opportunities were increasing, exacerbating the divide between them and other groups of workers. In industries like textile, food, and tobacco, they were given the most menial, grueling, and poorly remunerated work. In the economic downturn after the war, Black women were the first to be cast out of most industries except for laundry, which was notorious for its terrible wages and working conditions and its "high speed-up."[124]

The Structural Location of Blackness and its gendered realities meant that even the tiny fraction of Black women working in the professions suffered discrimination and grossly unequal wages,[125] not least because the ruling class drew a sharp distinction between "Negro" and "white" white-collar jobs. Black professional women, for example, found it nearly impossible to be hired as anything other than porters and charwomen in department and chain stores and mercantile establishments given the deep racism of white customers and workers—and the need to maintain them as highly exploitable labor.[126] Likewise, as teachers—the largest Black professional group—Black women were forced into an economically and socially inferior status compared to white women, especially in the South, where white teachers made two-to-three times more money than their Black counterparts, who were also subjected to school closings for supposed lack of funding.[127] Neither were Black businesses able to provide significant employment, decent wages, or good working conditions for the majority of the Black community generally, and Black women particularly.[128]

Wall Street Imperialist investment in keeping the South cheap and unskilled meant that, throughout the Great Depression, Black Southern women's wages remained well below other groups. They also represented an outsized portion of unemployed workers throughout the nation; in New York in 1931, for example, 42 percent of Black women workers were unemployed compared with 18 percent of U.S.-born white women and 13 percent of foreign-born white women. Black women's unemployment was 75 percent in Detroit and over 40 percent in Chicago, Cleveland, Saint Louis, Houston, and Philadelphia.[129] Such unemployment had a detrimental impact on Black people as a whole as Black women were the largest percentage of women that headed households and were often the main breadwinners of their families.[130] Despite these extraordinary rates of unemployment, Black women were discriminated against in relief, were largely excluded from relief work, and were forced to pay high rents for the worst housing—all while being charged with raising and caring for their families.[131] In effect, Black women's structural location afforded them "the dirtiest deal at *all* times."[132]

While the superexploitation of Black domestic workers was checked somewhat at the start of World War II as they moved into other industries, after the war there was "wholesale firing" of Black women particularly from basic industry,[133] and as Black women were forced back into domestic work in droves, slave markets began to crop up again in places like New York City.[134] "Unemployment, which ha[d] always hit the Negro woman first and hardest, plus the high cost of living" coerced Black women back into domestic service. Likewise, the media perpetuated the idea that Black women preferred servile labor to industrial work.[135]

The superexploited position of Black women in the labor market was not only meant to keep them "at the bottom of capitalist society" to "subject them to greater exploitation," but also to "use them to depress the wages of all workers." In this way, the white ruling class forced Blacks into a lower position, created antagonism and prejudice between Black and white workers, and undermined their efforts to unite for better conditions.[136] As Gordon and Briggs argued, this reality was instrumental to the functioning of US Capitalist Racist Society: "To force Negro workers to exist on a lower standard of living and then use their impoverished conditions to justify lower wages and job-discrimination" was typical of capitalist racism, which was "based on the exploitation of the majority by a minority of capitalist and rich landlords, plus the special plundering and violent suppression of the Negro people."[137] This intersection of gender, the Negro Question, and Wall Street Imperialism transcended simple wage disparity or income inequality.[138]

The subordinated position of Black women, especially as domestic servants, also subjected them to the Black Scare and the Red Scare especially when they worked to improve their working conditions through organizing, unionization, and other forms of resistance. For example, J. Edgar Hoover's 1943 *Survey of Racial Conditions in the United States* (*RACON*) contained information about the purported formation of "Eleanor Clubs" that aimed to foment unrest in the South, primarily among Black women. The unrest would result from Black women demanding higher wages and better conditions for domestic work and from withholding their labor to force white employers to be in desperate need of their work. The slogan allegedly adopted was "a white woman in every kitchen by Christmas." In other words, a labor shortage of Black domestic workers during the war, the demand for better wages and conditions for Black women working in white peoples' homes, and the threat of Black women organizing was attributed to "Red" machinations and Black agitation.[139]

Relatedly, the threat of domestic workers' unionization was revealed when a confidential informant reported to the FBI that, in Richmond, Virginia, the Domestic Workers Union was attempting to organize "Negro domestics" and had distributed literature and pamphlets. Particularly threatening, the literature "show[ed] the advantages to be gained, including increase of salaries and better working conditions, by affiliating with the organization."[140] Here, the Black Scare and the Red Scare were operating on the assumption that Black women organizing for the wages and conditions they deserved was radical, dangerous, and threatening to the capitalist racist order. Indeed, the unionization of Black women domestics was easily subjected to the Red Scare because it was supported by organizations that had been labeled communist fronts, like the National Negro Congress (NNC) and the National Negro Labor Council (NNLC) and by Black women communists and fellow travelers like Esther V. Cooper, Claudia Jones, and Marvel Cooke. Two founders of the NNC who were members of the Domestic Workers Union, Rosa Raiside and Neva Ryan, were identified in *RACON* as "outstanding known or reported Communists."[141] At the inaugural NNC meeting, held February 14–16, 1936, it was resolved that "a national movement be instituted under the direction of the NNC to organize the domestic workers, who include 85 percent of all Negro women workers" to eradicate their low wages and long irregular hours, to improve their poor and unsanitary living quarters and conditions, to rectify employers' lack of respect for them, and to end their exploitation.[142]

Similarly, in 1951, the NNLC pushed for "full opportunities in industry for Negro women"[143] and recognized that Black women were denied the right to work in vast sections of US industry and had mostly been driven out of industries—even those with union contracts.[144] The result was that Black women were unable to get jobs any place but as domestic workers.[145] One of the biggest blind spots in the trade union movement, said Helen Lunelly, reporter for the panel on Negro women in industry, was its failure to fight against the abuse of Black women domestics and to organize them. Black women were sick and tired of working in other peoples' homes at the expense of their own kitchens and work. The NNLC, therefore, needed to open the doors of offices and factories to this weary group, and to organize Black women domestics for "livable" conditions and wages in the meantime.[146]

The NNLC also noted that often the unions refused to fight for the upgrading of Negro women, who were not considered for jobs other than as domestics or janitors.[147] Moreover, as Viola Brown explained, in 1946, as Black women were pushed out of factories, especially in the South, the Unemployment Compensation Commission would deny Black women their unemployment benefits and instead refer them to domestic jobs for as little as two dollars a week. If a woman refused to take the job, she would be denied her unemployment pay. It was only through Black women's refusal to accept a job that paid less than fifteen dollars a week, the union hiring an attorney, organizing pressure, and appeals that the denials were overturned. Black women were given their unemployment compensation, and the minimum wage for domestic workers was raised to ten dollars per week. Brown stressed that this success was due to the organization of these workers in the Black Belt— organization that needed to be extended to all Black women workers especially as employers were on the offensive, empowered by the Taft-Hartley Act, the McCarran Act, and the Smith Act.[148]

Illuminating the impact of the Wall Street Imperialism on the underdevelopment of the South and of the Black workers who lived there, Brown argued that almost nothing was being done to aid Southern workers in building unions, and even less was being to do win white workers to the necessity of unions for and unity with Blacks workers in the plants. It was the responsibility of organized workers in strong unions with sufficient finances to join with Southern workers and take on their "fair share" of the responsibility to confront and overcome violent reaction "on the unorganized Southern front."

She enjoined further that the South could not continue to be driven backward or to remain unorganized, because such conditions made the South a base for organized reaction and fascism. If a corner was to be turned, North and South had to come together.[149] Of particular importance in the South was the organization of domestic workers into unions because that was "where Negro women [were]."[150] Finally, the NNLC adopted a resolution titled "Economic Equality for the Negro Women" that called on the trade union movement to "accept the challenge" to win job opportunities for Black women in industry, offices, department stores, and public utilities, among other areas; to support the organization of domestic works in the North and the South; to give special attention to Black women and youth in job training and upgrading; and to afford Black women the right to lead in government, industry, and unions.[151]

Inside and in addition to these organizations, Black women communists excoriated "organized labor's limited concept of exploitation, which permits it to fight vigorously to secure itself against evil, yet passively or actively aids and abets the ruthless destruction of Negroes"—especially Black women.[152] Esther Cooper Jackson argued that because Black domestics were one of the most exploited groups in the labor force, their organization and unionization was essential to the labor struggle. The argument that they were "unorganizable"—because of, for example, isolation, the independence of each worker, lack of bargaining power, overcrowded labor market and resulting intense competition, worker mobility and employment change, and lack of class feeling and unity—was based on dubious assumptions that continued the social stigma and vulnerability of this class of workers. She noted that European countries had been successful in organizing domestic workers as early as 1910, and after the Russian Revolution, the Russian Domestic Worker Order ensured that domestics were afforded rest periods throughout the day and had equal social standing to any other worker, thereby eradicating the stigma attached to this class of work that was found in the US.[153]

To the extent that unionization had occurred among domestics workers in the US, it has been spearheaded by "those who suffered most from economic exploitation and racial discrimination . . . [those] who work[ed] by the day or night, who [were] hired and fired often, and who receive[d] far below a living wage."[154] However, by 1940, only two thousand of six hundred thousand Black women domestic workers were unionized, and they were concentrated in New York City; Newark, New Jersey; Washington, DC; and Chicago, Illinois. Attesting to intra-racial class contradictions, informed in part by the Red Scare and fear of Black Scare violence that often accompanied Black militancy, unionization was discouraged by certain women's clubs, employers, employment organizations, domestics who identified with their employers, and some newspapers and magazines. Nonetheless, Cooper insisted that "the problems faced by Negro domestic workers [were] responsive to amelioration through trade union organizations."[155] Claudia Jones contended that "one of the crassest manifestations of trade-union neglect of the problems of the Negro woman worker has been the failure, not only to fight against relegation of the Negro woman to domestic and similar menial work, but to the domestic worker." This was because domestic workers were unprotected by union standards and were excluded from all social and labor legislation, most importantly minimum wage legislation.

The drive to unionize Black domestic workers and to support the Domestic Workers Union was also dangerous to the capitalist racist order because it would fundamentally challenge the racial oppression, hyperexploitation, and indignity engendered by the Structural Location of Blackness. For one thing, it would help to eradicate white chauvinism, including the perpetuation of the "madam-maid" relationship, talking badly about or talking down to "maids," and paternalism.[156] Marvel Cooke noted that, without a union and bargaining power, much like during the Great Depression, after World War II the women of the "paper bag brigade" continued to do an "unspecified amount of work under unspecified conditions" without any guarantee that they would actually be paid by the end of the day. And, as they auctioned their labor on street corners, they continued to be humiliated and subjected to indignity by men who made "immoral advances."[157] When these women attempted to command the wage of one dollar an hour set by the Domestic Workers Union, they were chided by the white "local housewives" who insisted on paying them less.[158] As mentioned previously, without a union, "new" domestic workers, especially those who had recently migrated from the South, agreed to work for next to nothing, driving down the wages—and thus increasing the superexploitation—of workers who were more skilled at bargaining.[159]

The toiling masses in the US South and North, Black women workers, and Black domestic workers illuminated the relationship between US Capitalist Racist Society, its internal logic of Wall Street Imperialism, and the Structural Location of Blackness. Workers like Angelo Herndon conveyed how the South was maintained as a space of unskilled, poorly remunerated, oppressed workers given the high concentration of Black people. These conditions lowered the standards of Black workers throughout the nation—and for the working class writ large. As documented in *RACON*, among many other government instrumentalities, these material relationships were legitimated through the Black Scare, the Red Scare, and their embodiment in the threat of Radical Blackness.

The Black Scare, the Red Scare, and the Threat of Radical Blackness

To have been listed as "well behaved" in the eyes of Crackerdom would have forced us to cease publication and commit suicide since such a misfortune would have convinced us that there was something radically wrong with our radicalism and attitude on the race question. We thank God that we are among those who have been "flayed" by the crackerized Department of Justice.

CYRIL BRIGGS, 1920

The Black Scare and the Red Scare were extraordinarily effective instrumentalities of US Capitalist Racist Society that preserved and legitimated the racially hierarchical political economy. The Black Scare won the support of white exploited workers in making Black oppression a cornerstone of US social relations. The result was the elevation of "whiteness"[1] to a category of cultural and political leadership, irrespective of class; the granting of the white masses "the luxury of unbridled terror against Negro citizens with immunity from legal prosecution"; the offer of higher wages for the same work; and the reservation of the best jobs for whites. The cross-class collaboration engendered through these Black Scare tactics *seemed* to come with tangible benefits for white workers, who were presented with a higher standard of living when compared to Blacks. In reality, though, superexploitation lowered wages and living standards for everyone, with Blacks simply suffering worse of all. Though whiteness portended "an avenue of escape into a better life," this was a chimera made possible by the fact that Blacks were rendered the most destitute. The Structural Location of Blackness was the basis of accruing superprofits, and while a significant share did not ultimately accrue to white workers, the Black Scare benefited them by shifting "the grievous burdens of a domestic crisis" onto the backs of Blacks. In other words, though the economic gain was paltry, the comparative social and political advantage naturalized Blacks as the subproletariat of US Capitalist Racist Society.[2]

While the Black Scare could be used as the "carrot" for white workers, the Red Scare was the stick. The strength gained by Wall Street Imperialists following World War I allowed them to powerfully wield the Red Scare against the wave of labor unrest after the war as strikes and protests broke out in response to the soaring cost of living and decreased wages. Big business and their advocacy groups like the National Association of Manufacturers su-tured labor repression to the Red Scare to "convinc[e] millions of the middle class that every strike was the beginning of a revolution" so they could beat back workers' demands for higher wages, shorter hours, and better working conditions—in other words, for a fairer share of the massive war profits.[3] The steel strike launched on September 22, 1919, for example, was defeated in part because newspapers broadly supported the position of steel corporations, who construed the strike as a Bolshevist plot to seize their industry. Using the Red Scare to whip up fear helped to galvanize public sentiment against worker militancy, the closed shop, and general strikes.

These twin scares gained steam throughout the Black Scare / Red Scare Longue Durée based on a number of dynamics. International socialism was advancing, which illuminated the contrast between the rapid peacetime gains of the USSR starting in the 1920s and the relative decline and stagnation of capitalist production except in times of war. Militant Black consciousness and challenge to Euro-American domination took off. Capitalism entered a period of intense crisis during the Great Depression. Certain capitalist pow-ers turned to fascism while the Soviet Union played an instrumental role in destroying it. World War II brought on unparalleled devastation and destruc-tion. And, anti-imperialist and anticolonial movements ascended during the early Cold War.[4] Thus, the United States developed into "the strongest, most expansionist, *and most aggressive*, imperialist power in all history . . . [that] hasten[ed] to conquer and unite under its control the entire capital-ist world with the perspective of a new and more violent assault against the socialist [and decolonizing] world, which it fear[ed] to meet in peaceful competition."[5]

This anti-Black, anti-worker, aggressively imperialist posture made geno-cide a constitutive feature of US Capitalist Racist Society, which the Black Scare and the Red Scare encouraged, legitimated, and concealed. The *We Charge Genocide: The Historic Petition to the United Nations for Relief from a Crime of the United States Government against the Negro People* petition argued that the Black Scare was both a form of "direct and public incitement to commit genocide" and "complicity in genocide."[6] As incitement, the Black Scare "trained thousands of children in white supremacy" and encouraged the "numerous instances of Negroes killed or assaulted" when they attempted to exercise elementary rights such as voting, organizing, assembling, mi-grating, or protecting themselves from white violence.[7] As complicity, the Black Scare ensured that Black people would "not have the rights guaranteed [them] under the Constitution of the United States." In effect, the Black Scare, as a violent response to Black militancy, on the one hand, and a means of rationalizing Black subordination, on the other hand, transformed genocide "into civic virtue" constitutive of US Capitalist Racist Society.

The charge of genocide unearthed exposed, and analyzed what the Black Scare distorted, naturalized, and legitimized. Genocide, the petition stated, was "so embedded in law, so explained away by specious rationale, so hidden by talk of liberty, that even the conscience of the tender minded [was] sometimes dulled" because its commonplace nature and familiarity concealed its horror.[8] Similarly, the Black Scare narrated struggles against the wrongs meted out to Black people as detrimental to the US constitutional set up. The Structural Location of Blackness was hence maintained through a refusal to enforce foundational US constitutional law that had been written and passed to protect all US citizens.[9] The Black Scare also obfuscated "police brutality and murder, legal lynching, Ku Klux Klan and mob violence, racist laws enforced by city, state, and federal officials and courts, denial of the vote, jim-crow employment, the ghetto system . . . colonial-like relations in the Black Belt, [and] segregation in and denial of education"[10] as foundations of US Capitalist Racist Society through discourses of Black inferiority, disloyalty, and danger. In doing so, it facilitated the wrongful conviction and execution of thousands of innocent Blacks and stamped the Black skin with the brand of criminality. The Black Scare deployed dehumanizing, pseudoscientific, fascistic racism to reduce Blacks to second-class citizenship and subject them to a savage system of oppression, discrimination, and exclusion[11]—while presenting any challenge to this brutal reality as an attempt to undermine and destabilize US society as a whole. It thus accommodated anti-Black racial oppression while criminalizing mobilization against it. Just as "the object of this genocide, as of all genocide, [was] the perpetuation of economic and political power by the few," so too was the object of the Black Scare to maintain the racial order by eradicating the ability of the many to protest and dissent.[12]

We Charge Genocide also documented the genocidal logics of the Red Scare, which disciplined and criminalized radical dissent. It explained that the US government's indictment of W. E. B. Du Bois as a foreign agent in 1951 was just one example of how Red-baiting Black activism made "the Negro people in the United States the increasing target of genocidal fury."[13] The vitriol against Du Bois's peace activism was intimately linked to "the attempt to murder Paul Robeson at Peekskill, the failure of which immediately brought the State Department on the run to cancel the passport rights of that heroic black man in order . . . [to silence] the story of the crimes of the government against his peoples in his native land." These forms of Red Scare intimidation, repression, and persecution were inextricable from the numerous cases of

violence and lynching spelled out in the petition.[14] *We Charge Genocide* illuminated that "the frameup technique perfected by the government against
Negroes [was] now used against minority political parties and militant labor leaders," which made "the fight against genocide and against the Smith
Act . . . one fight."[15] In effect, the Red Scare served specific political and
economic aims, namely, splitting and neutering mass movements for peace
and democracy to continue reactionary control and the extraction of profits
higher than at any time in history. As an instrumentality of genocide, the Red
Scare "violate[d] every aspect of the United Nation's stated goal."[16]

The Black Scare and the Red Scare also gave the cases against Black victims of the Smith Act and the McCarran Act a genocidal character. The communist New York councilman Benjamin J. Davis Jr., the Communist Party
of the United States of America (CPUSA) leader Claudia Jones, the Council
on African Affairs and former NNC leader W. Alphaeus Hunton Jr., and the
radical sailor and labor organizer Ferdinand Smith were subjected to manifold forms of violent dehumanization, including harassment, confinement,
and expulsion because of their race and political orientation. As such, their
treatment fell under Article II (b) of the Genocide Convention, "Causing Serious Bodily and Mental Harm to Members of the Group."[17]

The Black Scare

An upsurge in Black agitation emerged during World War I out of a historically specific confluence of participation in the Great War, disillusionment
with continued racial terrorism despite (and because of) this participation,
the first successful socialist revolution, Radical Black internationalism, and
anti-imperialism that differed from earlier challenges to white supremacy.
The militancy of the "generation of 1917"[18] constituted a panoply of practice
and production that included linking US racism and Jim Crow to other forms
of colonial and imperial oppression, explorations of alternative modes of socioeconomic organization, expressions of the right to self-determination, and
assertions of Black modern subjectivity through cultural creativity.

The rise in political consciousness that challenged the racial and economic
order, and the population shifts resulting from migration from the US South
and the West Indies to Southern cities and industrial centers in the North,
produced an era of Black agitation and mobilization that was "substantively
distinct from previous historical epochs."[19] Though situated in a society and
world that continued to be defined in Eurocentric and white supremacist
terms and that persisted in the superexploitation and domination of Black labor, this agitation displayed a reticence to quietly accommodate second-class

citizenship, white violence, racial hierarchy as a transnational technology of expropriation, and imperial plunder. Black militancy emanating from shared international conditions of economic dispossession and assertive racial solidarity fundamentally challenged US Capitalist Racist Society, which marked Blackness as abject and reduced it to a reality of material dispossession.

Throughout the Black Scare / Red Scare Longue Durée, the Black Scare enunciated the US government's anxieties about its social organization along racialized lines of inequality, its ability to accumulate, and the proliferation and consolidation of its imperialist project. This was codified through concern about national security, foreignness, un-Americanism, subversion, and sedition, which significantly focused on the ability of radical propaganda to influence Black people to reject their position in US Capitalist Racist Society. Further, the Black Scare was motivated by hysteria about how the linking up of dispossessed groups on the darker side of the color line could foment Black rebellion against global white domination. Overt anti-Black racial oppression and terror through Jim Crow, lynching, and structural violence; economic superexploitation through sharecropping, debt peonage, and unequal wages; high unemployment and exclusion from industry; burdened, onerous, and predatory inclusion into unequal labor regimes; and the denial of full citizenship were certainly conditions that encouraged such rebellion.

The Black Scare was the dominant response to racial militancy, the spirit of defiance, racial consciousness, and international solidarity with African descendants who were subjected to colonial-imperial aggression and oppression. It construed discontent with racial and economic domination as antagonistic to the United States and in the direct or indirect service of enemies of the state, insofar as such critique could call into question US leadership of the capitalist world-system.[20] Black agitation was seen as a potential tool for anti-American propaganda because it put the savagery of capitalist racism on display for the world generally, and racialized and colonized peoples particularly. Critiquing official racial policies, upbraiding Jim Crow and disenfranchisement, condemning racial violence and hatred, advocating self-defense, or questioning Black participation in the war on behalf of a nation that reduced Blacks to "niggers" were all considered radicalism that effectively amounted to subversion because they purportedly caused or exacerbated internal racial strife, leaving the US vulnerable to external attack. From World War I onward, the Black Scare narrated Black protest as either foreign inspired and subversive or as disloyal and destabilizing.[21] Often these views reinforced each other, as "foreign inspiration" and "disloyal" racial agitation were seen as tandem forms of subverting the status quo.

During the First World War, the Black Scare was articulated through the fear of Black loyalty to the Germans and set the stage for the Red Scare from 1919 to 1920 that prompted the mass deportations of foreign radicals and dovetailed with mass violence against Blacks who were treated with consonant suspicion and fear. This hysteria continued throughout the Black Scare / Red Scare Longue Durée with, for example, the conflation of Garveyism and Bolshevism throughout the 1920s, the discourse of interracialism as a harbinger of Black and Red takeover throughout the Great Depression, the claim of foreign-inspired Black agitation and Black agitation facilitating Red infiltrating during World War II, and the Red-baiting and Black-baiting of peace activism in the early Cold War. Discourses of Black pro-Germanism presaged and laid the foundation for the convergence of the Black Scare and the Red Scare through accusations of Black loyalty to the Soviet Union.[22] Both underscored the threat and danger derived from the idea of "Black" as uniquely susceptible to foreign inspiration and thereby potentially seditious and un-American, and foreign Reds uniquely taking advantage of Black agitation to infiltrate and destabilize the United States.

Just as Black agitation for just treatment during the Great War was often traced to German influence based on the idea that Blacks were uniquely gullible, the government's investigation of Black unrest thereafter likewise attributed Black demands for "some of Woodrow Wilson's much-vaunted 'world-wide democracy'" to the influence of the new enemy of the state: Bolshevism.[23] Such alleged susceptibility to foreign-inspired subversion carried with it the threat of deportation and incarceration, "the twin ways that the United States has dealt with 'undesirables.'"[24] This "criminalizing and parallel conferring of statelessness on those with political positions deemed radical by the state"[25] produced a "socio-ontological structure" that "niggerized" Black and Red.[26]

Concomitantly, the reduction of Black protest to disloyalty meant, for example, that demands for lynching to be treated as a federal crime were, at best, dangerous Black agitation and at worst, a form of sedition. The possibility that Blacks were "taking advantage of the present existing conditions to force federal legislation to prevent lynchings, and also for recognition of themselves upon the same plane as the whites"[27] was deemed of the same caliber as collusion with enemies of the state. In other words, the call for a federal bill punishing the crime of lynching was anathema because inherent in such racial militancy was an attempt to subvert the racial order. This supported the argument that Black agitators should be prosecuted for sedition because they aimed to mobilize "colored" sentiment, or incite hatred, against whites. This Black Scare logic meant that racial unrest, even though it was the result of white violence and terrorism, was the fault of Black challenge that left the US vulnerable to outside enemies.

As one federal official put it during World War I, Black militants positioned "the attainment of their own objects, that is to say treatment which includes their being allowed to mix freely as they choose among white people, ahead of the stirring [*sic*] of the war." Even more than this, it was argued that agitation for basic rights and dignity put Blacks in harm's way, thereby intentionally creating unrest. The official continued, "they apparently put this object [racial equality] ahead even of the safety of their own race. Surely they must realize that by the constant stirring up of the fires of race prejudice they are doing what is in their power to make lynching more, rather than less, frequent. Surely the frequency of lynching interferes with the war and thus" Blacks engaging in this struggle were "obstructionist."[28] Here, Blacks were narrated as inciting violence against themselves and causing racial disorder, and thereby hampering the war effort, while the lynchers—understood as being provoked by Black assertion—were, in fact, the victims. So it was that Blackness, not white supremacy, posed the threat to national security.

Throughout the Black Scare / Red Scare Longue Durée, white racists freely employed the Black Scare to contest even the most liberal claims to civil rights and dignity. Blacks' refusal to submit to the racial status quo was considered the form of racial intolerance that menaced the social order. The equation of critiques of racial domination with opposition to the government naturalized white violence as a necessary condition of defending the sanctity of the state and was consistent with the demands of US society, organized around the idea of white supremacy and class hierarchy. "White citizenry" operated as a metonym for the state, and the Black Scare became fiat and dictum that commanded the subordination of Blackness as a prerequisite for national security. This reality was intimately linked to the Red Scare by, for instance, characterizing the demand for equality between the races as a communist plot. The interracial character of communist organizing not only concretized that suspicious, but also marked such radicalism as patently un-American.[29]

The Red Scare

The Red Scare was a durable feature of US Capitalist Racist Society, though it intensified at particular periods, like 1919–20, 1939–40, and 1947–54. While it has been argued that the Red Scare was most acute in times of "social unrest, domestic criticism or foreign crisis,"[30] Wall Street Imperialism functioned to ensure that social unrest and foreign crisis were ongoing such that virtually anything could be counted as domestic criticism. This was done by disciplining and criminalizing the most mundane challenges to capitalist racist authority. Through the Red Scare, a wide array of militant challenges were construed as foreign inspired, subversive, or un-American. As well, the Red

Scare shored up Wall Street Imperialism by defending corporate domination against labor, racism and white supremacy against Black self-determination, capitalist exploitation against transformative economic redistribution, and repression against radical opposition.

The specificities of Red Scare surveillance, discipline, and punishment were broad and far-reaching enough to incorporate all types of radicalism. Demands for equal protection under the law and civil rights became radical plots to rile up the otherwise complacent Negroes. Organizing unions—especially interracial unions—to empower workers became Bolshevik-influenced agitation. Strikes for better wages and working conditions became revolutionary plots to cripple industry so that enemies could overthrow the government. Organizations and individuals who espoused principles or tenets that challenged or criticized the pedagogy of the US capitalist racist state were subversives. Thus, the Red Scare was characterized by extensive injury, oppression, threat, and intimidation of all radicals, and "absolutely no attempt [was made] to distinguish among democratic liberalism, evolutionary socialism, and revolutionary communism." The Red Scare narrated "the Socialist, the [Wobbly], the pacifist, the anarchist, and the internationalist [as] Bolsheviki in everything but name,"[31] so anyone from militant labor organizers to race agitators were deemed political, social, moral, and economic threats to US Capitalist Racist Society.

The Red Scare subjected these "undesirables" to surveillance, infiltration, committee inquisitions, slander, reputation and character assassination, and other techniques of harassment with the result of undermining their right to free speech, press, assembly, association, and due process. It deprived the accused of the right to earn a living, destroyed or censored their works and works associated with them, subjected them to illegal inquiries about their personal beliefs and affiliations, and severely hampered their ability—and the ability of workers more broadly—to be involved with trade unions.[32] The totalizing construction of communism as menace legitimated the criminalization of ideas by construing them as subversive action; by claiming that these ideas aligned with or abetted the positions of "enemies" of the United States, from Germany to the Soviet Union; and by codifying radical opposition as constitutively violent, revolutionary, dangerous, illiberal, and destabilizing. Identifying such alignment, no matter how spurious or farfetched, allowed the US government, private corporations, and civil society to construe advocacy of even those ideals spelled out in the US Constitution as antithetical to the interests of the United States and therefore subject to surveillance and punishment. In this way, radicalism generally, and communism particularly, were positioned as "so uniquely threatening to America's survival that measures that might otherwise have been considered a serious violation of individual rights were justified on the grounds of national security."[33] The Red Scare shaped the "confidence of the American people in the honesty and integrity of national institutions and government"[34] by narrowing the boundaries of loyalty, belonging, and adherence to law and order.[35]

Black Scare / Red Scare

The Black Scare and the Red Scare were produced discursively as interaction metaphors[36] that undergirded the entire logic of Americanism and un-Americanism in US Capitalist Racist Society.[37] Interaction metaphors "interact" to proffer a network of meanings that result from the interaction of the two terms and cannot be reduced to literal comparison.[38] The Black Scare and the Red Scare interacted to produce a variety of linked discourses, including subversion, sedition, insurrection, un-Americanness, threat to internal/national security, foreign-inspired, deception, disloyalty, sowing division and confusion, and infiltration. The interaction between the two parts of the metaphor rendered legible the threat of "Black" through economic radicalism and the threat of "Red" through racial agitation given that both threatened racial hierarchy rooted in economic exploitation and capitalist accumulation ordered along the color line.

This "metaphorical system"[39] offered a way of seeing and experiencing the differences between belonging and unbelonging, True Americanism and un-American, citizen and foreigner, and democracy and authoritarianism. Hostility toward Blackness codified the dangers of radicalism, and vice versa, because, "in an interaction metaphor, a 'system of associated commonplaces' that strictly speaking belong only to one side of the metaphor are applied to the other . . . what makes the metaphor effective 'is not that the commonplaces shall be true, but that they should be readily and freely evoked.' "[40] Through metaphor, both Blackness and radicalism were "readily and freely evoked" as subversive whereby "Black" became constituted as radical/revolutionary/dangerous and "Red" as inferior/subordinate/disloyal. "Black," as an enunciation of unbelonging, lacked allegiance to the United States and was therefore primed for insurrection and sedition. "Red," inhered in a commitment to overthrow the US government, was understood as subversive and therefore unbelonging. Hence, "by their interactions and evoked associations both parts of [the] metaphor are changed. Each part is seen as more like the other in some characteristic way."[41] This is conveyed in the fact that "the activities of those who struggled for rights against racist domination were identified as subversive in every instance and were always linked to Communism, or called Communism outright, according to state ideologies and definition of Communism as identified in the *Congressional Record*, one of the sites of the nation's self-definition."[42]

The Black Scare and the Red Scare eviscerated the difference between challenges to white supremacy and challenges to capitalist exploitation because both opposed the organization of US Capitalist Racist Society. As such, "Black" and "Red" became essentially interchangeable as suspicious, outsider, and plausibly destabilizing. Both became represented as foreign, as aligned with enemies of the United States, and thereby undeserving of citizenship, rights, privileges, and entitlements. In effect, a "hegemonic, monologistic discourse"[43] was produced that helped to entangle the Black Scare and the Red Scare because it constructed "similarities that the metaphor itself helps constitute" by "'select[ing], emphasiz[ing], suppress[ing] and organiz[ing] features' of reality, thereby allowing us to see new connections between the two subjects of the metaphor, to pay attention to details hitherto unnoticed, to emphasize aspects of human experience otherwise treated as unimportant, to make new features into 'signs' signifying inferiority."[44]

The Red Scare targeted myriad forms of radicalism that, because of their purported subversive character, had the possibility of destabilizing the American economic and social order. Such subversion was heightened by proximity to Blackness. Here, the Red Scare provided the discursive opening for subversion and sedition to become the ideological purview of the Black Scare. The Red Scare helped to reconstitute Blackness as traitorous and universalize it as a fundamentally threatening to society, thus reifying and reinscribing the Black Scare in US Capitalist Racist Society. Concomitantly, the Black Scare, as a process of niggerization that reduced Blackness to a structural location, returned that distortion as the Black reality, and, through this "violent act of reduction and mutilation,"[45] positioned Blackness as economic, existential, and semantic surplus.[46] The Red Scare became legible in and through this "surplus" of meaning that entangled "Black" and "Red" as nigger. This helped to recapitulate radicalism as disloyal because, in rejecting the racialized economic order, it opened the way for "nigger" equality and takeover. Here, Blackness and Radicalism became interchangeable as the antithesis of US citizenship.[47] The simultaneous niggerization of Blackness and radicalism is "part of a larger historical imaginary, a social universe of white racist discourse that comes replete with long, enduring myths, perversions, distorted profiles, and imaginings of all sorts regarding"[48] subversion, unbelonging, and threat to the social and economic order of US society.

The True Un-American: Radical Blackness

Given the interaction of the Black Scare and the Red Scare in the US government's attempt to protect and preserve its racial hierarchy, class domination, and imperial expropriation, Radical Blackness became the preeminent threat to US Capitalist Racist Society. Radical Blackness encompassed a broad array of local, national, and global anticapitalist (e.g., communist, socialist, Marxist, revolutionary nationalist) analyses of, and forms of organizing against the nexus of capitalism, colonialism, war, racialism and white supremacy, and imperialism. It centered critical political economy, engaged Blackness as a special condition of surplus value extraction, promoted Black self-determination, attended to intra-racial class conflict and antagonism, and strove for the overthrow of capitalist racism by any means. Informed by and engaged with real world struggles, Radical Blackness enunciated African descendants' multivalent and persistent antisystemic and counterhegemonic challenges to political economies and legitimating architecture that sustained exploitation, exclusion, dispossession, and class-based domination rooted in racial hierarchy.[49] Radical Blackness was construed as dangerous because of its internationalist orientation, "foreignness," appeal to and influence on the masses of Black people, advocacy of self-defense, engagement in militant all-Black or interracial organizing, and unequivocal belief in social equality.

As the Radical Black poet Claude McKay explained: "The American government started to investigate and to suppress radical propaganda among Negroes, [and] the small radical Negro groups in America retaliated by publishing the fact that the Socialists stood for the emancipation of the Negroes. . . . Then I think for the first time in American history, the American Negroes found that Karl Marx had been interested in their emancipation, had fought valiantly for it."[50] This discovery—that socialism contained the promise of Black political, economic, and social equality and that Blacks embraced or were sympathetic to socialism because of this—not only helped to suture and secure "Black" and "Red" as forces that would destabilize US Capitalist Racist Society, but also helped to position Radical Blackness as the ultimate articulation of this subversion.

The specific targeting of Black struggles for basic rights in the context of the Korean War (1950–53), Gerald Horne contends, construed Black protest as more of a threat to national security than Southern racism and segregation.[51] Such targeting both preceded and exceeded the Korean War, permeating the Black Scare / Red Scare Longue Durée. During World War I, for example, the Military Intelligence Division sought to organize a subsection on Negro subversion as part of its Negative Branch that would be controlled by "some of the ablest leaders of the colored people" with the aim of countering unrest, especially civil rights protests; improving Black morale, with low morale understood as a harbinger of disloyalty; stopping disloyal propaganda by and among Black people; and compelling Black patriotism through a counterpropaganda campaign.[52] Likewise, the subsection would keep tabs on and assess Black opinion to contravene anything that approximated disloyalty.[53] Though this specific counterintelligence project did not ultimately come to fruition, the goal was also for the subsection on Negro subversion to shape public opinion and silence Black grievances that might hamper the war effort.[54] This attempt to silence Black dissent was considered a momentous, constructive, and positive "statesmanlike plan" that should not be questioned by the very people who would be subjected to its control.[55] It was claimed that the surveillance of Black people and efforts at whipping up their uncritical support for the war were critical to winning the war for democracy and civil rights for Blacks at home.[56]

Because political intelligence agents were generally hostile to Black striving, even more averse to agitation for advancement during times of "racial and national ferment," and committed to their role of maintaining the existing racial and economic "arrangements and proscriptions,"[57] expressing grievances about US Capitalist Racist Society and struggles to gain rights within it were seen as legitimate only if they were articulated as patriotism and aligned with the security state. This was so because federal officials had a narrow focus on preventing subversion and had no real understanding of Black lives, experiences, and issues.[58] Radical Blackness was therefore seen as not only anathema, but also dangerous and subversive, and struggle for material improvements in Black social, political, or economic rights was neutralized under the weight of the government's profound suspicion of challenges to the extant order or the war effort. The society writ large, inscribed in capitalist racism and its Black Scare and Red Scare repression—exacerbated by wartime patriotism—sanctioned intolerance, including lynching and other mob action, and willingly harnessed the idea of "national unity" to crushing Radical Blackness and doubling down on white supremacy.[59]

The punishment of militant struggle had a particularly deleterious impact on Radical Blackness, especially because articulations of freedom, including equitable distribution of property, better conditions for labor, eradication of poverty, improvement in living conditions, and an end to race-based job discrimination, were deemed subversive. Here, the Black Scare and the Red Scare reinforced each other insofar as Black demands for the redistribution of resources and the improvement of material conditions were cast as foreign inspired, whether German-backed, Soviet-backed, or supported by some other external or internal enemy. White supremacy was thus sutured to antiradicalism to defend capitalist property and privilege. In the process, Radical Black assertion came to be seen as a threat to national security. Indeed, during World War I and throughout the 1920s, there were six federal departments and numerous local agencies that specifically monitored Black people for radical activity. The assumption was always that "Blacks were potentially disloyal and especially receptive to the propaganda of enemy agents," an excuse that rationalized the opposition of white military officers and civilians alike to heightened demands for racial equality, the naturalization of Black inferiority, and the concomitant construal of efforts to combat capitalist racism as not only subversive of the "natural order," but also disloyal in times of war.[60] The "close identification between anti-Black and anti-red,"[61] that is, the imbrication of the Black Scare and the Red Scare, helped to preserve racial domination and to protect capitalism by suppressing Radical Blackness, which aimed to upend both racial oppression and economic exploitation.

J. Edgar Hoover, as the head of the Department of Justice's (DOJ) Radical Division,[62] and later the BI and the FBI, initiated a sweeping campaign of surveillance against Radical Blackness, which was presented as violent, terroristic, antidemocratic, and dangerous. As such, it required surveillance, punishment, and eradication. The Black Scare that took off alongside, and mutually constituted, the Red Scare against undesirable aliens—whether anarchists, Wobblies, or communists—during World War I was particularly concerned with the articulation of antiwhite hatred among Blacks, advocacy of self-defense during race riots, and migration that disrupted Southern superexploitation. Because Radical Blackness combined the dangers that propelled both the Black Scare and the Red Scare, it became an archetypal example of subversion, insurrection, sedition, and conspiracy. The dialectic between Radical Blackness and racial unrest led the US government, with the BI at the helm, to view "the newly awakened black militancy through the prism of the Red Scare . . . leading them to adopt against blacks many of the same repressive measures employed against so-called subversives."[63] Hoover fixated on forging links between racial militancy and communism/socialism even though relatively few Blacks subscribed to this ideology. Even though the BI found that the source of racial agitation during the 1919 race riots was "purely local"—that is, was a response to a combination of racial terror, economic exploitation, and systemic exclusion—the government continued to obsessively link Blackness with communism/socialism.[64] This was in part because communist/socialist advocacy of racial equality was considered to either sow the seeds of disorder or to fan the flames of dissent given its aim to redistribute wealth to those at the bottom, which fundamentally challenged racial hierarchy.[65] In effect, the fixation on subversion and disloyalty bound Black to Red to produce Radical Blackness as the ultimate enemy.

An early and representative case of disciplining Radical Blackness was the arrest, indictment, trial, and imprisonment of Benjamin Harrison Fletcher as part of the broader government repression of the IWW that followed from the passage of the Espionage Act of 1917 and the Sedition Act of 1918.[66] As the most prominent Black longshoreman in an interracial organization and a powerful interracial local with 3,500 members—Local 8 of Philadelphia—and an influential leader of workers of both races, Fletcher was a quintessential Black Scare and Red Scare target. As the socialist newspaper the *Messenger* explained, Fletcher was imprisoned "for trying to secure better working conditions for colored men and women in the United States. He has a vision far beyond that of almost any Negro leader whom we know. He threw in his lot with his fellow white workers, who work side by side with black men and black women to raise their standard of living."[67] Fletcher's Radical Blackness fit squarely within the IWW, which was a beacon of class and race radicalism with its organization of laborers irrespective of their race, color, or trade. This "abolition movement of the twentieth century" did not permit race prejudice in any aspect of their operations so as to model the new structure of society they were attempting to build.[68] This was, Fletcher argued, "the REASON WHY the IWW [was] damned, persecuted and lied about by the employing class and their minions. That [was] why [Big Bill] Haywood and ninety-three others including the writer . . . were sentenced to terms of years as high as twenty years."[69]

In 1912, Fletcher was the IWW's only Black speaker, but he "delivered the goods," captivating the "attentive" audience with his analysis of class struggle and cultivating interest among Black workers in the IWW.[70] He was also instrumental to the organization's agitational and educational work and took an active role in IWW conventions, underscoring its mission to "surmount[t] all barriers of race and color."[71] The combination of race and labor radicalism, coupled with Fletcher's reporting on, advocacy for, and organization of strikes and other forms of worker militancy, made him a prime target of the government. This was notwithstanding Local 8 closing ranks during the war by halting strikes. Striking, which was a key target of the wartime antiradical legislation, had subjected Fletcher's local to Red Scare repression virtually since its founding, and the interracial character of the strikes invited the Black Scare.

Fletcher explained in February 1914 that the Marine Transport Workers had successfully waged a battle against the shipping trust employers for "more control of industry." Despite the shipping trust's manifold attempts to

"use scabs, police, gunmen, bribery, race prejudice, etc." to undermine the
workers, "the solidarity of labor" ultimately won out.[72] It was both the interracial nature of the strike—that is, Black people asserting racial equality and
white people accepting it—and labor radicalism, he noted, at which violence
was directed. The response to this important labor victory was repression:
"Realizing the power wrought up in an organization of workers so trained
and fitted, they proceeded to make those of the Industrial Workers of the
World, who paved the way for this organization in Philadelphia, victims of
vengeance" in the form of police brutality and unjust prosecution and conviction.[73] Fletcher's call for IWW members to protest the "damnable conspiracy," organize for the release of their fellow workers, and "serve notice to
the master class that [they were] not going to permit [their] fellow workers
to be scarified"[74] were the actions of a radical agitator who was all the more
contemptible because he was Black. His continued call to protest repression,
alongside the interracial struggle for better wages and working conditions,[75]
helped to codify Fletcher as subversive and to ultimately put him in the cross-
hairs of the federal government.

By May 31, 1917, a few months before the passage of the Espionage Act
that kicked the persecution of the IWW into high gear, Fletcher was under
surveillance by federal agents and local police. He was targeted for his IWW
connections and for ostensibly passing out literature discouraging enlistment
in the war. Surveillance reports emphasized Fletcher's race, dark complex-
ion, and white wife and stepdaughter, and greatly exaggerated his height and
weight.[76] Here, the Black Scare was working alongside the Red Scare: it is
likely, for example, that his size was magnified to invoke the Black preda-
tor trope that usually accompanied trepidation over interracial coupling.[77]
In both his person and political actions, Fletcher was violating the capitalist
racist order, with his "interracial relationship and marriage only add[ing] further evidence of his willingness to tear down social norms."[78] Officials' contempt for Radical Blackness was conveyed by an investigator: "Fletcher is the
type of 'Southern Nigger agitator' with no education, poor grammar . . . [he]
is reputed by the police as a bad man or gun fighter. He did not display any
of that to agent." The agent also expressed Black Scare logic in another way,
stating that he did not think Fletcher was smart enough to write the subversive articles for which he was accused and thus was "not very harmful to the
federal government."[79] This did not deter the government, however, which
arrested and indicted him on September 28, 1917,[80] less than two months after
the Espionage Act came into effect, with more than 150 other IWW leaders.
This effort spanned federal agencies, including the Military Intelligence Division, the US Department of the Navy, and the US Department of War.[81]

Fletcher and his codefendants were accused of committing a litany of offenses that violated the Espionage Act, including:

> unlawfully and feloniously [conspiring] by force to prevent, hinder and delay the execution of the laws of the United States pertaining to the carrying on of the war with the Imperial German Government; to injure, oppress, threaten, and intimidate citizens in the free exercise and enjoyment of the right and privilege of supplying the United States with war munitions, supplies and transportation; to commit diverse offenses consisting of procuring persons to fail to comply with the registration and draft laws of the United States, and of causing disloyalty in the military and naval service; to obstruct the recruiting and enlistment service; and to commit divers offenses consisting of placing in the post office at Chicago of mail matter for the purpose of executing a scheme to defraud employers of labor.

As such, they were in violation of Sections 6, 19, and 37 of the Criminal Code of the United States and Section 4 of the Espionage Act.[82] Fletcher was the only Black Wobbly indicted[83] and was undoubtedly targeted because he was the IWW's most effective Black organizer and a member of its strongest interracial local. His incarceration was therefore a "tremendous blow"[84] to the organization. He was imprisoned despite the fact that his local was *aiding* the war effort: the local "loaded thousands of ships with but one short work stoppage. . . . Hundreds of members of the local were in the military, and others bought liberty bonds."[85] As such, Fletcher's persecution conveyed that, far from guarding the US against espionage and subversion, the government's goal was to crush the interracial Local 8 and the IWW more broadly.

No specific evidence was brought against Fletcher at the trial except for his IWW membership, but it was clear that this local, and its Black leader, were deemed dangerous precisely because it was powerful on the Philadelphia waterfront and its presence alone constituted a threat to the war effort.[86] Fletcher was ultimately sentenced to ten years in federal prison in Leavenworth, Kansas.[87] There, the federal government continued to target him for his Radical Blackness, with Hoover, for example, having his correspondence monitored for "Negro agitation."[88] The lone Black IWW victim of Black Scare and Red Scare repression was ultimately released on bail in 1920 and continued to recruit for and speak on behalf of the One Big Union despite the possibility of his bail being revoked.[89]

The repression of Radical Blackness redoubled in the next World War. *RACON*, prepared by the FBI under the guidance of J. Edgar Hoover, was instrumental in maligning Radical Blackness as either foreign inspired or against the interests of the United States, despite the reality that Black agitation

was a direct result of the structural and material conditions of capitalist racism. The report investigated and identified that outside influence emanating
from Axis propaganda and communism sowed the seeds of subversion by
fomenting struggles for racial equality where they did not previously exist or
by transforming extant protests into protracted unrest. Influential Northern
Black leaders and the Black press were also categorized as outside agitators.
Of these forces, *RACON* deemed communism the most pernicious influence
on Radical Blackness.

While the Northern Black press had the biggest influence on Black protest
in the South, it was reported that the activities of the CPUSA in larger Northern cities were most effective in stirring up racial unrest.[90] Likewise, agents
claimed that the significant "foreign influence" on Blacks in the West, who
worked primarily in agriculture, was from the CPUSA:[91] "By far the most active group or organization which attempts to influence the Negro population
in this area is the Communist Party, which, according to reports, is exceedingly active in attempting to obtain Negro recruits to allegedly advance the
cause of Negroes."[92] Communists were also accused of fanning the flames
of Radical Blackness by taking advantage of Black "discontent" with disenfranchisement by constantly raising the issue, with Jim Crow laws by espousing racial equality, with the poll tax by demanding the right to Black self-
determination in the Black Belt, with police brutality by urging protest, and
with discrimination broadly by drumming up cases to be brought before the
Fair Employment Practices Committee.[93] In other words, the CPUSA was accused of manufacturing Radical Black dissent by manipulating, exaggerating,
and bringing attention to these difficult issues with the aim of undermining
the US government. Radical Black demands for an end to inequality, discrimination, and racial violence were considered machinations of the CPUSA,
whether under the direction of Moscow or under the direct influence of local
Reds. As such, Radical Blackness was a subversive threat to national security.
"By linking the cause of civil rights with Communist subversion," Hoover
and *RACON* were able to effectively raise the specter of dangerous Radical
Blackness.[94]

In addition to the US State Department entities like the BI/FBI, federal and
state congressional investigative committees throughout the Black Scare / Red
Scare Longue Durée positioned Radical Blackness as extraordinarily disruptive to the status quo. Committees like the Overman Committee, the Lusk
Committee, the Fish Committee, the McCormick-Dickenstein Committee,
the Dies Committee, the House Committee on Un-American Activities, the
Senate Internal Security Subcommittee, and the Subversive Activities Control
Board employed the Black Scare and the Red Scare to suture Black agitation

to outside or foreign influence, thereby legitimating the repression of Radical Blackness. "The history of all congressional investigation committees from Martin Dies on down to the present McCarthy and Velde committees," argued Alphaeus Hunton, a favorite target of several of these witch hunts, "has been one of victimizing the fighters against jim crow." Finding "fault with the present system of discrimination against Negroes was subversive."[95] Hunton had experienced this reality firsthand while organizing in the NNC, which was formed in 1936 to agitate for the rights of Black workers. The Dies Committee targeted the NNC's campaign for Black jobs at Glenn Martin Aircraft Factory as subversive, claimed that it aimed to sabotage defense production, and branded Hunton, the leader of the campaign, a communist.[96] For the committee, Hunton's Radical Blackness made him interchangeably a communist, a subversive, a race agitator, and a threat to national security.

Relatedly, as the Black Scare and the Red Scare reached new heights at the intersection of the Cold War and the Korean War, legislation like the Internal Security Act of 1950 (the McCarran Act), which updated, revised, and made more draconian the Immigration Act of 1917, helped to recapitulate Radical Blackness as quintessentially foreign and un-American.[97] As the Black communist Pettis Perry explained in 1951, "in each situation like the present McCarran Bill, all these measures speak of Communists and Communist front organizations. And what organizations are considered Communist fronts? Every single organization that fights for the rights of Negro People."[98] In other words, the Radical Black struggle for rights that were supposed to be guaranteed by the US Constitution transformed Blackness into a vector of communism, brought the subversive intent of communism into sharp relief, and transformed the disciplining of Radical Blackness into a matter of national security. Three key genres elucidated the US government's trepidation about Radical Blackness: the West Indian, the Outside Agitator, and the Red Black / Black Red.

3

Genres of Radical Blackness

We invent witchwords. If in 1850 an American disliked slavery, the word of exorcism was "abolitionist." He was a "nigger lover." He believed in free love and murder of kind slave masters. He ought to be lynched and mobbed. Today the word is "communist." Never mind its meaning in a man's mind. If anybody questions the power of wealth, wants to build more TVA's, or advocates civil rights for Negroes, he is a communist, a revolutionist, a scoundrel, and is liable to lose his job or land in jail.

W. E. B. DU BOIS, 1949

Radical Blackness, as the embodiment of the overlapping perils that animated the Black Scare and the Red Scare, can be understood through three genres that were anathema to US Capitalist Racist Society. The "West Indian" was the archetype of foreignness, alien ideas, and subversive internationalism that menaced Wall Street Imperialism. The "Outside Agitator," encroaching upon spaces where they didn't belong, embodied subversive influence over the masses of Blacks, fomented white hatred, encouraged self-defense, and incited racial unrest that threatened the extant hierarchies of US Capitalist Racist Society. Finally, the "Red Black / Black Red," under the influence of CPUSA or Moscow, sought to overthrow the capitalist racist order through interracial organizing, advocacy of "social equality"—a shorthand for forms of equality that portended Black liberation—and instigating class antagonism. The West Indian, the Outside Agitator, and the Red Black / Black Red were not mutually exclusive, but rather mutually reinforcing, and shared characteristics that contravened the racial and economic status quo. This trifecta was fungible as a problem to be managed and a threat to be neutralized, and their dangerous attributes could be transferred and repurposed through the Black Scare and the Red Scare to codify and crush Radical Blackness.

The West Indian

The West Indian was the genre of Radical Blackness through which Blackness as type of foreignness was sutured to "alien anarchism." This was made possible through the convergence of immigrant status, undesirable ideas, and internationalism. The increased presence of West Indians in the United States starting in World War I aided in the explosion of Radical Blackness concentrated in Harlem, New York.[1] As the Jamaican-born radical Wilfred Adolphus Domingo asserted, "the genuinely radical movement among New York Negroes would be unworthy of attention" without the large presence of this group.[2] Whether or not this contention was a historical fact, the state and federal governments agreed and, in turn, subjected West Indians to intense repression and surveillance. By World War II, in New York City alone there were over one hundred thousand people of Caribbean origin, and this group played an active and decisive role in advancing the Black liberation struggle. They were also among the most active in trade unions. Additionally, "Caribbean intellectuals [came] to an understanding of class and race relations within more internationalist terms, in which colonial capitalism around the globe ha[d] constructed complex inegalitarian and hierarchical social structures, and in which class and racial differences both intertwine[d] and cut across each other through the region."[3] West Indians in the United States also tended to express concern about and support for the liberation struggles in the Caribbean, the eradication of coloniality and slavery, and self-determination and self-government.[4] This combination of race and class consciousness and internationalism helped to position the West Indian as an outsized threat to US Capitalist Racist Society by linking and challenging capitalism, colonialism, imperialism, and racialism. In other words, the analysis that combined race and class, domestic and international concerns, codified the perception of West Indians' "alien" subversion and undermined the authority of US domestic and foreign policy.

The West Indian inhabited manifold dangers of Radical Blackness. On the one hand, a number of the Black socialists and communists starting in the first two decades of the twentieth century were West Indian workers who analyzed the struggle of the Black working class in the United States as part of the larger fight of the international proletariat against captialism and imperialism.[5] If, as Domingo argued, West Indian intellectuals made up the majority of radicals in Harlem concerned with political economy because they understood race and class within an internationalist framework and in its relation to colonial capitalist relations and social hierarchy,[6] then it is fair to assume that their increased presence presented a formidable challenge to, and in, US Capitalist Racist Society. On the other hand, West Indians were heavily represented in Marcus Garvey's Universal Negro Improvement Association and African Communities League (UNIA), an organization that was seen as the preeminent site of "Negro agitation." The threat of the West Indian as communist/socialist and as Garveyite converged in the parallel militancy of the UNIA and the African Blood Brotherhood (ABB), a revolutionary Black National organization founded by Cyril V. Briggs in 1919 that combined Black liberation and socialism/communism. The struggle of these organizations on behalf of African descendants was inextricably linked to the world proletariat struggle since both served to "weaken the capitalist foe of both the subject peoples and the exploited white workers."[7]

The ABB, which included radicals like Richard B. Moore, Otto Huiswoud, Grace Campbell, and Harry Haywood, who would go on to be some of the earliest Black members of the CPUSA,[8] put forth a statement of aims including the liberation of the Black race, absolute racial equality, fostering racial self-respect, organized resistance to the Ku Klux Klan, "a united Negro front," Black industrial development, the eradication of Black superexploitation, fair education, and "cooperation with other darker races and with the class-conscious white workers."[9] Similarly, UNIA aims and objectives included universal "confraternity" among the Black race, Black pride and love, race solidarity and commitment, assistance to the most needy of the race, civilizing the "backward tribes of Africa," the development of independent Black communities and nations, commissions to protect African people wherever they were located, racial education, worldwide commerce among Blacks, and the betterment of conditions in Black communities.[10] Taken together, these West Indian–led and populated organizations sought to eradicate white supremacy and Euro-American domination, which meant the overthrow of the racial order in the US and abroad. They also sought to cultivate Black industrial development and economic independence, which would ultimately topple capitalist racism, Wall Street Imperialism, and European colonialism. It is no surprise, then, that BI undercover operations between 1917 and 1924 included a number of Black agents infiltrating Radical Black organizations like the ABB and the UNIA.[11] The West Indian, firmly outside the bounds of US citizenship, was perfect fodder for the Black Scare and the Red Scare.

The presence of the West Indian and other undesirable aliens spurred the BI/FBI, the DOJ, and other agencies to expunge radical organizations that heavily depended on both immigrants and racialized persons whose immigrant status *and* ideas rendered them foreign and whose citizenship could be easily denied or revoked through criminalization. West Indians were especially targeted as disloyal and dangerous, and confronted with exclusion, defamation, deportation, and incarceration. Such treatment inspired the American Committee for the Protection of the Foreign Born (ACPFB), organized in 1933, to call an emergency conference on April 4, 1948, to contest the deportation of scores of noncitizen activists on the grounds of "political opinion," including the West Indians Claudia Jones and Ferdinand Smith. The ACPFB argued that these deportations were meant to deny constitutional rights to "aliens" *and* to undermine the civil liberties of Americans.[12] The punishment imposed on the foreign for "thinking, saying, writing, or belonging to anything which the Government might disapprove or from reading any newspaper or book or associating with any person whom the Government might claim to be subversive"[13] harnessed the Black Scare and the Red Scare to destabilize the citizenship of all radicals irrespective of national origin.

Hostility toward the West Indian was evident in the ultimatum delivered by Special Assistant Attorney General Robert L. Van in 1934: "If you West Indians don't like how we do things in this country, you should go back home where you come from; we Americans will not tolerate your butting into our affairs. We are good and tired of you. . . . There should be a law deporting the whole gang of you."[14] Van's suggestion ultimately became policy. Jones noted, for example, that she was deported under the "reactionary" Walter-McCarran law, which was notorious for its particular racism against West Indians and Asians. The West Indian was a target of the reactionary repression of progressive ideas, she reasoned, for repudiating the counterrevolutionary foundations of US Capitalist Racist Society. She noted further that the law restricted West Indian immigration to one hundred persons per year from the entire Caribbean.[15]

*

The disciplining of Marcus Garvey conveys how the West Indian's race consciousness, mass appeal, internationalism, and demand for Black economic self-determination sutured the Black Scare and the Red Scare and positioned them as a vector of communism, *irrespective of ideology*. Garvey's Black Nationalism became a threat akin to communism despite his expressed anticommunism. The US government viewed Garvey, the UNIA, and the espousal of Black Nationalism as Black conduits of Bolshevism and the CPUSA. Government surveillance reports made ample mention of advocacy of socialism and Bolshevism at UNIA meetings,[16] and Hoover claimed that "in his paper the 'Negro World' the Soviet Russian Rule is upheld and there is open advocation of Bolshevism."[17] Another report mentioned the "Red speeches and the anti-White talks" that abounded at UNIA meetings and asserted, "Liberty Hall is today the greatest hot-bed for the teaching of race antagonism, race hatred, and class hatred, and Garvey is the head of the stress."[18] Garvey would go on to oppose support from the IWW, socialists, or Bolsheviks and claim that in the struggle between capital and labor he would side with whoever gave Blacks their just due.[19] Nonetheless, the Black Scare and the Red Scare came together to criminalize the West Indian by coupling "antiwhite" with "Red," race "hatred" with class "hatred."

As the literal embodiment of the West Indian, Garvey became the quint-essential "undesirable alien"[20] who drew the ire of Hoover and the BI as early as 1918. The UNIA and its Black Nationalism combined the threat of Black-ness, foreignness, and subversive and un-American influence over poor Black folks. One of the earliest Black BI informants, William Wormley, helped to establish the link between the UNIA's Radical Blackness and the West Indian as dangerous foreigner. He wrote, "at the meetings I have attended at Liberty Hall I have seen not more than one or two American negroes. . . . I can report definitely that those expressing radical sympathies are, with the few excep-tions mentioned, all foreign negroes, mostly of West Indian Birth."[21] The Red Scare drive to eradicate the political threat of radical "aliens" was harnessed to the Black Scare to place Garveyites alongside anarchists, Wobblies, and communists as offenders to be neutralized and punished.[22] Though peace-time following World War I forced authorities to "pay more attention to legal forms" and indict Garvey for a commercial crime, his prosecution was deeply political in its aim to expel a West Indian.[23]

The US government charged that Garvey

> would by means of false and fraudulent representations, pretenses and prom-ises induce, solicit and procure divers persons . . . referred to as the victims, to pay and transmit to him, the said defendant, money and property for the purchase of stock in the Black Star Line, Inc., and for the purpose of inducing said victims to part with their money and property in the purchase of said stock and said memberships so intended to be sold and offered for sale.

This indictment for fraud was simultaneously an indictment of Radical Black-ness. Garvey's alleged crime—illegally selling stocks of the Black Star Line—contained the threat of Black working-class and mass appeal, international-ism, and advocacy of an economic program apart from Euro-American-led capitalism. His widespread influence among Black workers allowed him to successfully market shares to purchase ships as a step toward to connecting African peoples throughout the diaspora. This would challenge Wall Street Imperialism and European colonialism through the establishment of trade and commerce in the Black World that would build up Black economic power and promote Black self-determination and self-sufficiency. That the threat of Radical Blackness, not concern about fraud, ultimately drove Garvey's re-pression was underscored by the fact that if the mail fraud charge had been unsuccessful, the BI was prepared to make a case against him based on "radi-cal statements." Such a case would fall under the alien anarchist provision of the Immigration Act of 1917.[24] Concern for Black shareholders, the purported reason for Garvey's mail fraud conviction, was a patently superficial excuse

used to conceal the blatant attack on Radical Blackness that drove his prosecution.[25] Garvey's actual crime was articulating a counterhegemonic racial
and economic program that could empower the Black masses against Wall
Street Imperialism and capitalist racism.

The ability of the West Indian to galvanize the Black masses with foreign
ideas was a key threat to US Capitalist Racist Society. On the mass, working-
class appeal of Garvey and the UNIA's Black Nationalism, Cyril Briggs wrote:
"The leadership of the Garvey movement consisted of the poorest stratum
of the Negro intellectuals—declassed elements, struggling businessmen and
preachers, lawyers without a brief, etc.—who stood more or less close to the
Negro masses and felt sharply the effects of" capitalist racism. Significantly,
Garvey's movement was a sharp break from the Black bourgeois leadership
of the NAACP, which was effectively a mouthpiece of imperialism.[26] Garvey's
archnemesis, W. E. B. Du Bois, claimed that the UNIA leader had made the
most inroads among the "West Indian peasantry" given their "great and long
suffering grievances," "leaderless" reality, "rudiments of education," and lack
of "economic chances" that left them "groveling at the bottom."[27] Negative
connotation notwithstanding, Garvey's Black Nationalism posed a formidable challenge to US Capitalist Racist Society by inspiring those from whom
superprofits were extracted and by offering an alternative to control and
management by the white elite and the Black bourgeoisie. The West Indian's
appeal to the masses domestically and abroad menaced profit, property, and
law and order by encouraging race "arrogance" and inciting racial "hatred"
in the US and the colonized world among the "hard working poor men and
women who absolutely refuse[d] to think and reason for themselves."[28] Like
Du Bois, the US and colonial governments assumed that poor and working-
class Blacks were ignorant and therefore the most susceptible to Garvey's dangerous propaganda, while intelligent upper-class Blacks rejected his program.[29]
Indeed the claim that Garvey's followers had "crude minds and undeveloped
faculties"[30] fit the Black Scare and Red Scare discourse that the combination of
ignorance and foreignness resulted in susceptibility to subversive influence and
fraud. This discourse provided the basis for Garvey's indictment.

The West Indian's mass appeal was made all the more dangerous by the
Radical Black internationalist challenge to Wall Street Imperialism and European colonialism. Garvey's anti-imperialism was, ironically, predicated on his
conception of an African empire that would lead to Black empowerment and
self-determination. In arguing that "the fullest opportunity should be given
to both races to develop independently a civilization of their own," Garvey
rejected white domination in all its forms and encouraged social, cultural,
and political development through Black autonomy and self-determination.

These could be achieved only through the displacement of Euro-American capitalists, imperialists, and colonizers and through the development of a powerful African empire. Garvey's counterhegemonic vision of empire did not advocate conquest, but rather transterritorial linkages to the end of political, economic, and social development and collective defense. The totality of the race, scattered throughout the world, would have to unite, as empire building would inevitably require the violent overthrow of arrogant and technologically advanced whites because "the imperial powers would never willingly surrender control of their African colonies."[31]

Though Garvey accepted the dominant claim that Africa and its descendants had slipped into a state of degeneration, he believed the UNIA would reverse this historical trend. The rise of European superiority meant that Africa needed its descendants to redeem it from the decay and backwardness that had resulted from colonization and white domination.[32] Yet Garvey also highlighted the role of *Euro-American barbarism* in arresting the development of the darker race. Garvey's declaration that "Pilgrim Fathers we must have if Africa is to rise from her slumber and darkness"[33] revealed his conviction that Garveyites and the UNIA had the responsibility to expel Euro-Americans from Africa as a step in rehabilitating the continent from the savagery wrought by capitalist racism, colonialism, and Wall Street Imperialism. This Black offensive was possible as European powers continued to tear each other asunder through world war, and Africans continued to organize for power and control. As Garvey saw it: "The Seat of Empire Northward Moves was true to history and poetry during the period of Negro decline. But its Northern limit has been reached and with the revival of Negro activity its path has again turned South. For Empire has not only a Seat but a Home and that Home is in Africa."[34]

The program promoted by Garvey and the UNIA portended the end of white dominance, wealth, control over the labor supply, and ability to accumulate. It also threatened the Structural Location of Blackness in its advocacy of Black emigration and sovereignty beyond the white man's land—in Africa, the original site of civilization, where the darker race could have complete self-determination. Inclusion into, as much as exclusion from, US Capitalist Racist Society reproduced racial domination. The realization of global African self-determination through the unification of the race to the end of a united, disciplined, strong Black empire-state on the African continent was the most viable alternative. For Garvey, the focus on integration into the United States, the West Indies, and Europe ultimately distracted Blacks from developing their own territory and wasted energy on something that would never be realized. It made more sense for Black people to work and fight for their own land than to expect white people to concede equality to a group they deemed inferior. "Even in basing his program upon fantastic claims of empire," it was noted, "Garvey always impressed in his followers that his promise was more realistic than that of those who were constantly arguing for the theoretical rights of the Negro."[35] In his view, demand for these "theoretical rights" ultimately meant negotiating the terms of Black immiseration. This assessment invalidated the linear progressive narrative of the United States in which Black people would attain full rights and equality at some point in the future—a narration that allowed the US to both position itself as democratic and to maintain racial hierarchy.

Garvey's two-pronged claim that Blacks had the capacity to develop a strong sovereign state in Africa and that that Euro-Americans' world-historical dominance was coming to an end brought together Black Scare and Red Scare fears of Black self-determination, antiwhite sentiment, expropriation of their property and wealth, and displacement of whites at the top of the racial hierarchy.

For the US government, moreover, the West Indian's advocacy of independent Black economic organization was as dangerous, subversive, and foreign inspired as socialism/communism. Garvey wrote, "One important factor in the marketability of the UNIA's latest economic venture was the mounting concerns of black workers over the consolidation of corporate capital, the accelerated rate of mechanization, and the ubiquitous problem of labor redundancy in many parts of the urban South."[36] His program, in other words, was popular among the superexploited because it sought to upend the Structural Location of Blackness. The Black Star Line Corporation, organized in 1919, and later the Black Cross Navigation and Trading Company in 1927, would help to bring this vision into fruition by connecting Blacks dispersed throughout the world through business and trade. Initially, even Du Bois conceded that, "shorn of its bombast," Garvey's political economic vision was wholly feasible insofar as it encouraged US Blacks to accumulate and control their own capital, organize independent industry, and unite with other centers of the African diaspora through commercial enterprise. In doing so, Africa would be redeemed and fitted for Black autonomy. This was not only "true" and "feasible," Du Bois reasoned, but was a longstanding idea among Blacks even as Garvey popularized it.[37] The possibility and popularity of this plan is precisely what made it subversive. According to Garvey in the article "Why the Black Star Line Failed,"

> There was no doubt that several governments of Europe were feeling the effects of the new spirit of racial consciousness that had come over the Negro people of the world. Big commercial houses in America were afraid of the

result of my encouraging Negroes to develop their own business enterprises
and trading among themselves. . . . The big shipping companies were also
determined to keep the Negro off the high seas.[38]

Garvey's plan, though neither communist nor socialist, incited the Red
Scare because Black economic autonomy and Pan-African economic coordination directly challenged Wall Street Imperialism and its rootedness in the
racial ordering of peoples and nations. His anti-Western internationalism and
Radical Black encouragement of racial self-possession, which was construed
by the white power structure as encouraging white hatred, racial hostility,
and Black insubordination, underscored the West Indian's foreignness and
fanned the flames of the Black Scare. Even as Garvey's vision was construed
as naive, irresponsible, incompetent, and even criminal, it was nonetheless a
dangerous form of Radical Blackness. The West Indian, who appealed to the
masses, organized internationally, and rejected white imperial domination
through Black counterimperial autonomy, was an inexorable menace to US
Capitalist Racist Society.

The Outside Agitator

During the Black Scare / Red Scare Longue Durée, the Outside Agitator, generally hailing from the US North, was the genre of Radical Blackness that
illuminated a deep contradiction in US Capitalist Racist Society. On the one
hand, a Black leadership class was needed to control and manage the ignorant
masses, but, on the other hand, this "uppity" class possessed a penchant for
subversion. The Outside Agitator also embodied the paradox of Black education: education was necessary to stave off foreign influence among the ignorant, but as Black people became more educated they tended to become more
dissatisfied with the Structural Location of Blackness and more likely to agitate against it. Likewise, the more educated Blacks became, the more *amenable*—as opposed to susceptible—they ostensibly were to "foreign" propaganda.
Whereas ignorant Blacks might fall prey to radicalism, Outside Agitators
welcomed subversive ideas. Even worse, on the logic of the US government,
the Outside Agitator, taking direction from, or in collaboration with, radicals
including Wobblies, socialists, and "Bolsheviki," spread incendiary information among the "uneducated classes in the Southern States,"[39] thus imperiling
white supremacy and superprofits. This genre of Radical Blackness revealed
that, whether poor and ignorant or affluent and educated, Blackness was always already a potential vector of radicalism, and Radical Blackness required
vigilant repression.

The Outside Agitator was not only literate and educated but also articulate and influential, and therefore had the maximum potential to incite ignorant Blacks to violence, unrest, and defiance of the status quo. Stated differently, Outside Agitators were incendiary because their leadership, erudition, persuasiveness, and free circulation of ideas throughout the Black community could easily sway the gullible Black masses toward subversion. Importantly, the Outside Agitator often wielded influence through the Black press—especially with its rapid increase during the 1920s—where they not only held up a mirror to the contradictions of US Capitalist Racist Society, but also expressed criticism and cynicism about continued oppression and inequality. Even worse, they viewed Black fightback against white violence and terrorism favorably.[40] As such, the Outside Agitator was considered insolent, ill-governed, intemperate, inflammatory, insubordinate, and belligerent—all of which portended disloyalty and subversion.

Relatedly, this genre of Radical Blackness undermined national unity in wartime and peacetime by defying tenets of race, class, and religious "tolerance" that were a shorthand for accommodating and naturalizing inequality. Such defiance included disloyal protests of the racial status quo, "sensationalizing" acts of discrimination and white violence to encourage dissent, promoting "white hatred" by advocating self-defense, and threatening to upend the social order by demanding equality irrespective of "class, race, caste, or religious distinctions."[41] The Outside Agitator was the enemy of national unity and a source of unrest by constantly incensing the Black population, whose loyalty was already suspect. As one federal agent claimed, Radical Blackness should be concerning to "all right thinking people, white and black" because it sought to "openly create a feeling of resentment among certain negro elements" and was readily received by the "ignorant." If the words and ideas of Outside Agitators turned into action, it would "lead to results that all good citizens [would] deplore."[42]

In 1919, Attorney General A. Mitchell Palmer delivered a report to the Senate Committee on the Judiciary, *The Attorney General Report on the Activities of the Bureau of Investigation of the Department of Justice against Persons Advising Anarchy, Sedition, and the Forcible Overthrow of the Government*, that aimed to persuade the Senate to pass a peacetime sedition act.[43] With such an act, Palmer, in collaboration with J. Edgar Hoover, would pursue criminal charges against Outside Agitators who used the Black press to sow seeds of discontent.[44] To strengthen his effort, Palmer included an appendix titled "Radicalism and Sedition among the Negro as Reflected in Their Publications," a report prepared by either J. Edgar Hoover or Robert Bowen of the US post office. It constructed the danger of the Outside Agitator by appending

Black influence, education, and dissatisfaction with US Capitalist Racist Society to "radicalism" and "sedition." As the report claimed, "There can no
longer be any question of a well-concerted movement among a certain class
of Negro leaders of thought and action to constitute themselves a determined
and persistent source of a radical opposition to the Government, and to the
established rule of law and order."[45] Alarmingly, the editors of these newspapers were "men of education" who were "seeing red" and sought to inculcate
this politics in its readership.[46]

   A similar claim would be made in a parallel state-level report, *Revolutionary Radicalism: Its History, Purpose and Tactics with an Exposition and Discussion of the Steps Being Taken and Required to Curb It*, in 1920. Also known
as the Lusk Committee Report, it came about because, after the federal government failed to pass the peacetime sedition act, individual states rushed
to pass legislation that would muzzle all manner of radicalism. Of particular
concern was Bolshevism and those it might influence, not least the Outside
Agitator. Through extensive documentation of New York–based Black publications that circulated throughout the country, the Lusk Committee Report
emphasized "the mental calibre of the leaders of radical movements among
negroes"—that is, Outside Agitators—who were ostensibly moving in lockstep with the Socialist Party and the subversive Rand School of Social Science
to convince ordinary Blacks to abolish the extant form of government. Here,
their appeal to "class consciousness" was said to be a rejection of remedying
Jim Crow, disenfranchisement, and lynching "in a lawful manner." On this
logic, the Outside Agitator's critique, not to mention action, was unlawful
and thus criminal.[47]

   "Radicalism and Sedition" likewise claimed that newspapers including
Negro World, the *Veteran*, *Crusader*, the *Challenge*, the *Messenger*, the *New
Negro*, and the *Crisis* articulated "the dangerous spirit of defiance and vengeance at work among the Negro leaders, and, to an ever-increasing extent,
among their followers."[48] Of these, the *Messenger* was considered to be the
most "able" and "dangerous" in that it offered "the most educated thought
among Negroes" and "threw all discretion to the winds, and became the exponent of open defiance and sedition."[49] Here, the potential subversion of
educated Blacks was again emphasized. The Lusk Committee Report also
homed in on the *Messenger*, which was especially concerning given the influence it sought to "exert upon the colored men in this country looking toward
their conversion to revolutionary radicalism," and its broad circulation in
major cities where Blacks had recently moved during the Great Migration,
including New York City, Chicago, Philadelphia, and Los Angeles, and in key
Southern cities like Atlanta; Washington, DC; Charleston; and Columbia.[50]

A November 23, 1919, *New York Times* article titled "Radicalism and Sedition," which brought the report to the public's attention, zoomed in on the *Messenger,* in particular an October 1919 article that promoted "sex equality." The first of its kind in a Black publication, the article emphasized the social equality with which Black soldiers were treated in France, including between one thousand and two thousand marriages between French white women and US Black men. The outsized attention given to "sex equality" implied that Outside Agitators sought to impose a subversive order that would upend the social underpinnings of US Capitalist Racist Society. The *New York Times* article also focused on the UNIA's *Negro World.* Here, the particular concern was its advocacy of armed self-defense, construed as "bitter expression" emanating from a "sense of oppression" that was both cultivated and encouraged by Outside Agitators through "insolently race-centered condemnation of the white race."[51] In both instances, the Black press, and the Outside Agitators who used it as a catalyst for unrest, were presented as dangerously defiant of the extant racial and political order, which legitimated the US government's suppressive efforts.

In "Radicalism and Sedition," articles, editors, and entire publications fell under scrutiny for a wide range of assertions "antagonistic to the white race," including purported incitement or encouragement of antiwhite violence, promotion of armed self-defense, hostility to white rule, dissatisfaction with Black economic subordination, and advocacy of migration out of the South. The Black Scare was appended to the Red Scare by linking up the Outside Agitator's encouragement of "antiwhite" aggression, support for Blacks joining radical labor unions, antiwar positions, and sympathy for communism as identical forms of subversion.[52] As well, the Outside Agitator was scrutinized for rejecting "Old Negro" leadership, often supported or selected by the white elite, and for excoriating "Old Negroes" for being complacent, backward, and too accommodating of the status quo.

Moreover, "Radicalism and Sedition" illuminated the need to control and silence the Outside Agitator by meticulously documenting subversive, incendiary, disloyal, and offensive content in the Radical Black press. *Negro World,* edited by Marcus Garvey and W. A. Domingo,[53] was dangerous because of its "race first" ideology that demanded an end to lynching and white terrorism by any means necessary; advocated matching racist "fire with hell-fire"[54]; and condemned the idea that Blacks and Africans must capitulate to white superiority and serve white civilization.[55] The short-lived periodical the *Veteran,* which represented the views of Blacks who had returned from World War I, was inflammatory because it celebrated that Blacks had fought back during race riots. It also connected the violence "at Chicago, at Washington, and at

Longview, Texas" to that of war because both had produced a New Negro who valued liberty and was willing to fight for it.[56] The *Crusader*, the publication of the ABB, was "full of significant material"—that is, seditious material— that excoriated the US government for not protecting its Black citizens from lynching and mob violence, denounced "conservative" Black leadership, asserted the superiority of Blackness to whiteness, encouraged Blacks to vote for the socialist ticket, incited Black agitation, insisted that Blacks and Africans were fit for self-government, and rejected US imperialism and intervention in Mexico. In short, the *Crusader* circulated a wide range of the positions that conveyed Radical Blackness as anathema to US Capitalist Racist Society and the Outside Agitator as subversive.

An editorial titled "Six Demands" in the *Challenge*, edited by William Bridges, also appeared in "Radicalism and Sedition" and encapsulated the incendiary nature of that publication. It eschewed "re-Americanization" and loyalty to a government that did not protect it; pointed out the contradiction that the "detested" Germans had more social, political, and industrial opportunities than Blacks; argued that the US government bore the responsibility for lynching because it allowed its "component parts," that is, state and local governments, to operate above its laws; demanded that lynchers and white terrorists be hunted down by federal forces with the same vigor as whiskey makers; insisted that "it [was] more honorable to die defending [Black] lives than to die pleading with some illiterate white dog to spare them"; and warned that until Negro life became as valuable as that of any senator, peace was impossible. Because of positions like this, the paper was considered "offensive" and "inflammatory."[57] Similarly, the *New Negro*, edited by Hubert H. Harrison and August Valentine Bernier, was a dangerous radical publication in its assertion that "if white men are to kill unoffending negroes, negroes must kill white men in defense of their lives and property."[58] "Radicalism and Sedition" presented two papers, the *Crisis* and the *New York Amsterdam News*, in contradistinction to these reckless Radical Black publications, though even these were "not always above reproach" because any critique of, lamentation about, or challenge to capitalist racism was offensive to whites, could potentially incite the impressionable Black masses, and should therefore be punished.

The "Radicalism and Sedition" appendix to Palmer's Senate report and the Lusk Committee Report hysterically documented the "dangerous spirit of defiance and vengeance at work" among Black people, fomented by Outside Agitators. It drew no distinction between economic radicalism, demands for social equality, the right to self-defense, or the promotion of militant race consciousness. All of these were equally seditious articulations of Radical Blackness. As such, suppression and repression were legitimate means of muzzling

the Outside Agitator and the Black press used to spread insolent and dangerous ideas.

The Red Black / Black Red

The Red Black / Black Red, or the "Nigger Communist," as Mississippi congressman John Rankin called Paul Robeson in 1949,[59] was perhaps the most
odious of all genres of Radical Blackness. They were identified in a number of
ways. First, the Red Black / Black Red belonged to the CPUSA, a "communist
front," or an organization that abetted communists by accepting them among
its ranks. Second, they introduced conspiracy into every idea, organization,
institution, movement, and/or network in which they were involved. Third,
their militant agitation for a federal antilynching bill, the enforcement of the
Fair Employment Practices Committee, the right to strike for higher wages
and better working conditions, equal access to the nation's resources, self-
defense against anti-Black violence, and the enforcement of the Thirteenth,
Fourteenth, and Fifteenth Amendments were veiled support for the overthrow of the US government by force or violence.[60]

Fourth, the Red Black / Black Red took advantage of discrimination to
sow seeds of dissent among Blacks; focused on exploitation, antagonism, and
inequality instead of unity to encourage discontent; introduced tension and
hostility in the labor movement; and rejected gradualism in favor of transformative change. This was because they did not actually care about the plight
of, and sought to manipulate and take advantage of, Black people for their
own nefarious ends—not least promoting the communist line and imposing socialism. Fifth, the Red Black / Black Red understood anti-Black racial
oppression not as a flaw or shortcoming of otherwise perfect US democracy,
but rather as a constitutive feature and function of US Capitalist Racist Society. Such an interpretation was rooted in the anti-American rejection of the
United States and a penchant for disloyalty.

Finally, the Red Blacks / Black Reds could be identified by their very subjection to political repression. In other words, they were subversive because
they were disciplined; they were disciplined because they were subversive. Indeed, state-sanctioned "terror was aimed at blacks generally, at breaking the
black-Left tie, and at breaking black Reds."[61] They were denigrated in the mainstream press; barred from speaking; arrested and brutalized by police on largely
trumped-up charges; arrested, indicted, and prosecuted; investigated as "un-
American"; surveilled and harassed by the FBI; forced to leave the country or
barred from traveling abroad; and beaten or murdered. The right to free speech,
assembly, press, or association did not extend to them. Becoming a "political

refugee" by going underground or into exile to avoid this repression underscored their criminality and disregard for law and order.[62] Taken together, the Red Black / Black Red was a fecund and fungible problem: they were an existential threat to US Capitalist Racist Society, which rationalized their rightlessness. At the same time, the specifications of their rightlessness legitimated the narrowing of rights for the entire society. The Red Black / Black Red, then, was both the cause and the effect of the Black Scare and the Red Scare.

Moreover, the Red Black / Black Red brought these scares together through their consummate interracialism, namely, their practice of economic, political, and racial equality. Interracial class struggle tended to be seen as foreign inspired and un-American because interracial protest against segregation and white supremacy contravened the American way of life.[63] According to the arch-racist South Carolina senator J. Strom Thurmond, for example, integration would be "the most un-American law ever proposed. It would undermine our government, our constitution, and our way of life. It was borrowed from the Communists who know well that they can never gain control of America so long as our fundamental rights are preserved to the States."[64] Through interracialism, the Red Black / Black Red sought to upend the very foundations of the United States by abrogating white power and concomitant ruling class domination.

Ironically, despite being Black, the Red Black / Black Red was also constructed as the quintessential enemy of Black people because their association with "nigger lovers" invited anti-Black violence and repression.[65] "If Southern 'gentleman' hate 'niggers,'" it was reasoned, "they hate even more what they call 'nigger lovers,'"[66] and the gathering together of the Red Black / Black Red and "nigger lover" inevitably incited white terrorism. Thus, it was those who contested racial inequality and defied segregation—not white vigilantes, police, or other agents of the state—who were the real enemies of, and dangers to, Black people. "Nigger lovers" included white communists, militant union leaders, and other radicals who, because they believed in immediate civil rights and racial equality, were disloyal race traitors. Likewise, by uniting with Blacks, they caused confusion and division among whites and thereby undermined law and order.

The entanglements of the Black Scare and the Red Scare, positioned the "nigger lover" and "fellow traveler"—someone who held similar ideas to, a common cause with, and was willing to work alongside, Reds even though they did not belong to the CPUSA—were two sides of the same coin. By sympathizing with and legitimizing communism, the fellow traveler, like the "nigger lover," caused confusion and division among the American population and goaded them into disloyalty. The House Committee on Un-American

Activities claimed that the fellow traveler "sympathize[d] with the Party's aims and serve[d] the Party's purpose in one or more respects without actually holding a Party card" and was "the HOOK with which the Party reache[d] out for funds and respectability and the WEDGE [driven] between people who [tried] to move against it."[67] Just as the nigger lover was a traitor to white supremacy, the fellow traveler was a traitor to capitalist individualism and liberal democracy. Likewise, the "nigger lover" and fellow traveler were brought together through their critique of the surveillance, disciplining, and punishment of Red Blacks / Black Reds on moral or constitutional grounds.

In many ways, the "nigger lover" / fellow traveler was even more pernicious than the Red Black / Black Red because they did not carry the signs and significations of the maligned Black/Red identity and could thus more easily dupe or manipulate those who would never of their own accord be "agents" of subversion.[68] The "nigger lover" / fellow traveler was "a deadly weapon" that "deceive[d] others and often himself";[69] a turncoat that bestowed respectability upon the Red Black / Black Red; and an impediment to legitimizing the use of state-sanctioned violence to extirpate threats to the status quo. Hence, the Red Black / Black Red, the "nigger lover," and the fellow traveler were a contemptable cabal of conduits of Radical Black subversion.

✳

The case of Angelo Herndon illuminates the Red Black / Black Red as the most hated genre of Radical Blackness. The child of a coal miner and a domestic servant, he was galvanized by his position at the absolute bottom of US Capitalist Racist Society. His Radical Blackness sprang from his experiences as a Southern Black worker who endured superexploitation, expropriation, dispossession, violence, and surveillance starting at the age of thirteen. Though the 1920s were the "prosperity era" when "wages were high," Herndon and his brother Leo could only find "piece-work" jobs that came with countless deductions for amenities Herndon and other Black workers were barred from accessing. About this predicament Herndon wrote, "They robbed us with an undisguised brazenness . . . the company rob[bed] us of the fruits of our labor which we earned by the sweat of our brows and the ache of our limbs."[70] He also noted how company housing became a means of expropriation by domination: the rent for his shack was fifty dollars a month—almost three-fourths of his paycheck—even though it had no electricity or private toilet and was in the segregated section next to a putrid garbage dump. He paid more rent than the white workers despite exponentially worse conditions.

To add insult to injury—or domination to expropriation—the shacks were patrolled by armed gunmen to make sure the workers did not steal the company's property. Such surveillance and repression were perpetual features of subproletarian Black toil. During Herndon's work on a dam in Birmingham, Alabama, for example, he was watched over by a "whole army" of "floor walkers" who lorded over the laborers day and night, ensuring that they did not escape.[71] Workers were bound to this abysmal situation through indebtedness, which meant that "miners . . . were irretrievably mortgaged to these heartless ghouls [disreputable loan sharks and credit stores]" who preyed upon them systematically. All in all, the standards Herndon endured were nothing short of dehumanizing.[72]

The ongoing subjection Herndon endured primed the development of his Radical Black political consciousness—and prepared him for the violence that accrued to the Red Black / Black Red. One day during a trolley ride, he could endure no more and railed against capitalist racism. When a white man attempted to force him to vacate his seat, Herndon shouted, "You white people are so civilized that you seem to think that you can afford to behave worse than savages towards us defenseless Negroes. I know you hate us, but it strikes me awfully funny that you are ready to accept money from a black hand as well as from a white. Now understand me clearly, I've paid my fare to ride this car and I won't give up my seat to any white man until hell freezes over!"[73] Here, Herndon rejected the contradictions of US Capitalist Racist Society: white savagery amid claims of civilization, white violence legitimated as law and order, and Black defenselessness obfuscated as danger. Likewise, Herndon conveyed that if dollar equality was possible, so too was racial equality. The latter, after all, was perversely conveyed when workers rose up, insofar as Black cops beat white women and white cops attacked Black women; race prejudice was not a factor when it came to brutalizing workers.[74] Herndon's analyses of and challenges to US Capitalist Racist Society emanated from the violence and indignity he experienced as a Black toiler and later as a Red Black / Black Red.

The Black Scare and the Red Scare meant that, especially in the South, the only thing worse than Blackness was Radical Blackness, and worst of all was to be a Red Black / Black Red. As one historian put it, "Reds were persecuted and black Reds were virtually flagellated."[75] In 1930, Herndon joined the Unemployed Council, and that same year he was locked up by Tennessee Coal, Iron, and Railroad guards in the Big Rock Jail for associating with communists. When he went to court after his arrest, townspeople gathered to gawk at the "*Negro Red*" freak with "cruel and depraved" curiosity.[76] The prosecutor did not hide his hatred of the Red Black / Black Red, and the Black Scare and the Red Scare stood in for any semblance of fact in the case. According to Herndon, this officer of the court

talked vaguely and bitterly about bewhiskered devils that carried bombs in
their pockets and threatened the virtue of every white woman. He referred to
Communists and Bolsheviks as if they were two separate kinds of radicals and
talked about Russians as if they were all Jews. . . . [He] demanded that society
protect itself against such horrible creatures by giving us the fullest punishment under the law.[77]

Here, the Red Black / Black Red was interchangeable as terrorist, potential
rapist, interracialist, foreign and foreign inspired, communist/Bolshevik/radi-
cal, and creature to be put down for the sake of society.

A police chief in Birmingham, Alabama, made a similar statement when
Herndon was later arrested alongside two white communists:

Too bad I can't make a public example of you Reds, Russians, Jews, and niggers. . . . That God-damn Legislature of ours—it won't enact the criminal-
anarchy law I recommended against you bastards! If it were up to me alone
I wouldn't be treating you as leniently as the courts do. Trials should be only
for Americans and not for such Red trash as you. You've been agitating far too
much and stirring up trouble among our steel workers and miners. If I had
my own way about it I'd line you all up against the wall and shoot you down
like dogs.[78]

The Red Black / Black Red, appended to the Russian and the Jew, was a for-
eign/foreign-inspired subversive, a criminal-anarchist, an agitator, and a piece
of trash to be disposed of. No law or punishment was too harsh for this bastard,
troublemaker, dog. Herndon's Radical Blackness, coupled with his interracial
organizing activities, made him an abomination to US Capitalist Racist Society
generally, and in the Southern Black Belt particularly, because he challenged
the trifecta of class domination, racist oppression, and dehumanizing poverty as the capitalist system was being called into question during the Great
Depression.

Herndon's repression as a Red Black / Black Red began when he became
involved with the CPUSA-led Unemployed Councils. While working in a
coal mine in Birmingham, Alabama, he saw a handbill advertising a meeting
at which the dire situation of the city's workers would be discussed.[79] He was
drawn as much to the CPUSA's staunch reproach of Jim Crow and emphasis
on interracial cooperation as he was to the class analysis the Party offered.
The very first meeting he attended was raided by police because of these very
factors, and from then on Herndon became a persistent target of police harassment. As a Red Black / Black Red, he was persona non grata throughout
the South and was subjected to "an orgy of repression and brutality"[80] that
included arrest, interrogation, surveillance, harassment, and torture. "Time

and again I was now picked up on the street and arrested," he wrote. "I became reconciled to the idea of being arrested. . . . Inevitably I would walk straight into the dragnet the police set for me. It got to be such a habit that every time I looked at a policeman I knew 'it' was coming."[81]

Herndon's experience of repression combined public and private deployment of the Black Scare and the Red Scare. When he was arrested for "vagrancy" in Birmingham on the way to a Labor Day rally coordinated by the CPUSA and other organizations, he was held in jail for eleven days and put in the "dog house" for mentally insane prisoners. This was because any "nigger" who chose to be a communist must be crazy—and dangerous. Then, after hearing the case, the judge attempted to have him murdered by the Ku Klux Klan.[82] In New Orleans, Louisiana, he was arrested for participating in a longshoreman's strike and charged with "violation of the Federal Injunction, inciting to riot, dangerous and suspicious, distributing circulars without a permit, and having no visible means of support."[83] The latter charge, not unlike his vagrancy charge in Birmingham, was a means of imposing forced labor through the criminalization of Blackness. The "inciting to riot" charge no doubt had to do with the fact that he was a Red Black / Black Red supporting workers' militancy.

Herndon was policed and harassed further when he attended the All-Southern Conference for the Scottsboro Defense in Chattanooga, Tennessee, on May 31, 1931. The police had gathered in a show of extraordinary force against interracialism and against the Northern communists who would be speaking.[84] Moreover, authorities had no problem creating trumped-up charges to frame the Red Black / Black Red—a process organizations like the International Labor Defense called "legal lynching." Then, on August 3, 1931, Herndon was accused of murdering three white girls in an all-white suburb of Birmingham. After beating him in an interrogation room, several officers took him out to the woods and brutalized him with a rubber hose. When he wouldn't confess to the crime, they returned him to the Birmingham County Jail and threw him in solitary confinement with no medical attention.[85] When the murder charge did not stick, Herndon was convicted of vagrancy along with two other comrades.[86] This dragnet of unmitigated torment conveyed that no punishment was too harsh, no violence was too brutal, no rationalization was too outlandish, and no crime was beyond the realm of possibility for the Red Black / Black Red.

Finally, because of the incessant threat of arrest, lynching, and police assassination, in 1932 the party reassigned Herndon to Atlanta, Georgia, where he would continue his organizing work. Unfortunately, he would face ultimate repression there—and the fight of, and for, his life. Herndon's arrest and conviction under Georgia's anti-insurrection law was the archetypal punishment for being a Red Black / Black Red. The law was a manifestation of an earlier confluence of the Black and Red Scares, namely, fear surrounding the Nat Turner rebellion of 1831 and hostility to increased abolitionist militancy. These laws sanctioned the full use of the state to suppress actual and suspected slave revolts and conspiracies and aimed to criminalize any public opposition to the slave system.[87] After the Civil War, references to slaves were removed, but the definition and harsh penalization of insurrection remained. The Georgia Penal Code was updated to read: "Attempt, by persuasion or otherwise, to induce others to join in any combined resistance to the lawful authority of the State, shall constitute an attempt to incite insurrection." Unless the jury recommended mercy, insurrection was a capital crime.[88] Indictment of the Red Black / Black Red under a law enacted in response to white fear of slave rebellions and the collapse of the slave system gave credence to the connection Du Bois drew between the abolitionist and the communist as the victim of "witchwords."[89] As Herndon understood it, "The fact that I am a Communist infuriated the rulers of Georgia. They would rather see their Negro servants come crawling on their knees asking for their hypocritical mercy."[90]

Leading up to his arrest, Herndon, now a leader in the Atlanta Unemployed Council, called for an interracial demonstration at the Fulton County Courthouse after the city of Atlanta, in the throes of the Great Depression, closed all relief stations and attempted to drop twenty-three thousand families from the relief rolls and send them back to the farms, where there was no work— effectively a death sentence for the impoverished masses. Herndon and his comrades drafted a list of demands and organized a protest of this decision. More than one thousand Black and white, male and female, workers participated in the action, striking fear into the hearts of politicians and authorities because a gathering of that size of Black and white workers had never taken place in the South. Despite the efforts of authorities to foment racial animosity among protesters by only negotiating with whites and excluding Blacks, the protest was a success: the twenty-three thousand families remained on the relief rolls and $6,000 of additional funds were appropriated for relief.[91] As a direct result of this interracial, militant protest, Herndon was arrested on July 11, 1932, and incarcerated for eleven days under "suspicion" without being formally charged. He was eventually indicted for three counts under Section 56 of the Georgia Penal Code, which criminalized "any attempt by persuasion or otherwise, to induce others to join in any combined resistance to the lawful authority of the State." Such action constituted "an attempt to incite insurrection."

As a Red Black / Black Red, Herndon's contravention of racial hierarchy through interracialism, challenge to the ruling elite by organizing workers, and rejection of capitalist racism by demanding economic relief for Black and white families were not expressions of freedom of speech and assembly, but rather dangerous rioting aimed at overthrowing the government. Likewise, Herndon's membership in and organizing on behalf of the CPUSA amounted to foreign-inspired subversion and an attempt to undermine democracy with dictatorship, upend property relations, and foment revolution. Further, for circulating radical *ideas*, the Red Black / Black Red was guilty of insurrection because his analysis threatened the Jim Crow regime that obfuscated Georgia's capitalist exploitation of Black and white workers alike—albeit at different levels of intensity.[92] Not unlike enslaved Africans gaining literacy, the circulation of revolutionary ideas was considered dangerous and unlawful such that one Radical Black possessing "subversive" literature, like an enslaved African possessing a book, menaced the whole system.[93]

The Black Scare and Red Scare were activated throughout Herndon's trial to underscore the danger of the Red Black / Black Red, with the racial position of the CPUSA targeted as much as its economic program.[94] The prosecutor argued: "The defendant claims to be interested in the unemployed, but that is just a disguise. He is only trying to stir up the races, to foment and create trouble that will bring about an industrial revolution so he and his Communist friends can set up a godless dictatorship in this country based on the style of the Bolsheviki dictatorship in Soviet Russia." Here, the Red Black / Black Red was accused of taking of Depression conditions to manipulate the unemployed, to stir up race hatred—thus agitating whites and leaving Blacks open to their wrath—to overthrow the economic order, and to subject the United States to foreign domination. The prosecutor also asserted that because Herndon was an admitted member of the CPUSA, he should legally be sent to the electric chair, along with "other Reds who might plan to invade" the state of Georgia. "As fast as the Communists come here," the prosecutor warned, "we shall indict them and I shall demand the death penalty in every case." In less than two hours, Herndon was found guilty, but, in act of Southern "mercy," the jury recommended twenty years on the chain gang instead of the electric chair.

Through the logic and discourse of the Black Scare and the Red Scare, the West Indian, the Outside Agitator, and the Red Black / Black Red posed acute threats to the life and limb of superior whites, the racial order, the capitalist system of private property, Wall Street Imperialism, and European colonialism. In addition to their attempt to subvert the extant order, all three genres of Radical Blackness were linked through their promotion a dire threat to US Capitalist Racist Society: Black self-determination.

The Negro Question as a National Question, the Structural Location of Blackness, and the Problem of Black Self-Determination

The fact can be stressed again that the Negro is such an integral part of American life that almost every struggle of the workers has its Negro side.
WILLIANA BURROUGHS, 1928

During the Black Scare / Red Scare Longue Durée, the demand and struggle for Black self-determination arose from the interrelation of Wall Street Imperialism, the Negro Question, and the Structural Location of Blackness. Self-determination was understood expansively by both its proponents and opponents as encompassing a wide array of political, economic, and social demands rooted in economic and racial justice and, importantly, self-defense against arbitrary violence and routinized mob terror. As the Southern Black communist Hosea Hudson explained, the goal of self-determination encompassed practical, day-to-day concerns like the right to vote and other democratic rights, eradicating lynching and police brutality, and the right of poor rural Blacks to control their economic destiny.[1] Thus, Black self-determination portended the end of white domination, challenged superexploitation and superprofits, and threatened collaboration between Blacks and enemies of the US state—worst of all the communists. Federal and state governments instrumentalized the Black Scare and the Red Scare to construe Black self-determination as a perpetual danger to US Capitalist Racist Society. Within the borders of the United States, the most subversive forms of Black self-determination were the advocacy of self-defense against racial violence, the encouragement of Black workers' political economic autonomy, and the understanding of the Negro Question as a national question, especially as it was articulated through the Black Belt Nation Thesis.

Black self-determination posed formidable threats to capitalist political economy rooted in racial hierarchy and was a persistent target of Black Scare and Red Scare hysteria, violence, and repression. For example, during the first Great Migration, Southern landowners Red-baited and Black-baited

Black exodus because it depleted their superexploited agricultural labor supply, which threatened to drive wages up.[2] Politicians employed the Red Scare in their efforts to criminalize labor agents and migrants by painting them as subversives, often accusing them of pro-German attitudes. Those encouraging migration were also subjected to the Black Scare. They were accused of inciting race hatred among Blacks and of being agents of a Northern conspiracy to cajole Blacks into leaving,[3] and were subjected to Civil War–era anti-incitement laws. After the US declared war on Germany on April 6, 1917, white Southerners began to inform the BI about the *Chicago Defender*'s efforts to incite Blacks against whites and to influence mass meetings "to encourage northward migration."[4]

Support for Black migration was considered disloyal because it ostensibly disrupted agriculture in the South, which had the potential to undermine the war effort.[5] Whites used the Black Scare to blame this mass departure on the "outside influence" of Northern white agitators, simultaneously attempting to criminalize and deny Black self-determination in the form of migration.[6] By insisting that Blacks wanted to stay and were too docile or lazy to leave of their own accord, whites conveyed their investment in the Southern racial system while helping to construct Black self-determination as a means of threatening and subverting capitalist prosperity.[7] The Black Scare and the Red Scare used discourses of Black docility, dependency, and shiftlessness to conflate Black outmigration and subversion because it threatened the very foundation of the Southern socioeconomic order.[8]

Similarly, Black self-determination in the form of self-defense during race riots in the North and South was met with the Black Scare and the Red Scare by all factions of US Capitalist Racist Society. As "the country appeared headed toward a racial civil war[,] white America, trying to make sense of it all, blamed it on the Reds." Indeed, "the taint of Communism added yet another dose of poison to the image of blacks in the white mind. The public was now being encouraged to view Negroes, particularly those clamoring for change, as traitors."[9] The German scapegoat for Black migration during World War I soon transformed into the specter of the Bolshevik encouraging Black resistance to racial violence. The "militant resistance of the Negroes to the white rioters and their readiness to use retaliatory violence" during race riots, kicked off by a violent clash in Charleston, South Carolina, in 1919, was "attributed to a 'Bolshevik plot.'"[10] The entanglement of the communist menace and Black self-determination as subversion was exacerbated by two developments: theorizing the Negro Question as a national question, thereby clarifying Wall Street imperialism as the source of Black superexploitation and transforming Black liberation into an international struggle;

and positioning the Black Belt—the citadel of white supremacist semifeudal power—as Black man's land.

Race Riots, Racial Conflict, and the Threat
of Black Self-Determination

A more militant enunciation of Black self-determination during the Black Scare / Red Scare Longue Durée extended back to World War I and its immediate aftermath. An article in the Black newspaper the *Pittsburgh Courier* explained the rationale behind, and US government response to, this militancy:

> When the Negro returned home [from WWI] . . . and at once began to fight back. . . . Then went up the cry from all over the country: The Negro is joining the Bolshevists. As long as the Negro submits to lynchings, burnings, and oppressions—and says nothing, he is a loyal American citizen. But when he decides that lynchings and burnings shall cease even at the cost of some human bloodshed in America, then he is a Bolshevist.[11]

Here, it was effectively argued that any articulation of Black self-determination was subjected to the Black Scare and the Red Scare. As early as 1919, for example, the US government and the capitalist class in the United States set its sights on the ABB precisely because it was a "radical black organization whose programme [was] based on the destruction of capitalism" and because it was the only organization to wage a "brilliant and brave struggle" during the Tulsa race riots.[12] Those who defended the status quo were adept at combining the twin scares with violence, especially in the form of race riots and mob violence, to undermine Black self-determination. They did so by construing Black assertion as foreign inspired, un-American, and criminal.

During World War I, and in the subsequent context of the "first" Red Scare, white supremacists, the US government, local officials, and citizens socialized into maintaining the capitalist racist order had a powerful technique of repression in branding any action for Black self-determination as communist or subversive, and therefore "illegitimate and unpatriotic."[13] Those who advocated self-determination by "opposing World War I or the selective service . . . advocat[ing] self-defense during the race riots of the 'Red Summer' of 1919, or [getting] involved in radical labor unions fared no better at the hands of federal agencies than black Communists and Socialists."[14] Such advocacy made ideologically distinct factions, like the UNIA and the CPUSA, identically subversive in the eyes of the government. At the same time, the communists' positioning of the Negro Question as a national question, and later, their support of self-determination in the Southern Black Belt, rendered them uniquely dangerous because they incorporated, expanded, attempted to build organizations around, and internationalized articulations of Black self-determination.

The confluence of labor radicalism, New Negro militancy, race riots, economic demobilization following World War I, and the global impact of the Bolshevik Revolution helped to suture struggles for Black self-determination and the communist "menace." As Black and white worker competition exploded into race riots in the North and collided with government demands for loyalty, "labor strife and racial tension could now be blamed on 'Bolshevism.'"[15] As argued in the *Crusader*, a publication targeted by the US government as seditious, "Bolshevik" was being applied to "bad agitators" who challenged the idea that Black people should "forever be enslaved in the clutches of the cut-throat, child-exploiting, capitalist-imperialist crew" and who were willing to ally with groups that supported Black liberation.[16] More moderate voices insisted that the charge of Bolshevism by "Southernized officials and Negro haters" allowed whites to "shut their eyes to the real fundamental cause for the 'unrest and intense feeling'" among Blacks, namely, segregation, disenfranchisement, discrimination, and lynching.[17] Ironically, even as conservative voices warned Blacks to steer clear of communism and argued for government protection of Black life and property as the "surest antidote for Bolshevism,"[18] the government rebuffed that suggestion, instead insisting that Blacks were inexorably susceptible to Bolshevik machinations.

Authorities found fodder for their hysteria in the decidedly militant tone taken by some editorials, like the one that stated that because "Uncle Sam [had] prevaricated" and Republicans and Democrats had "lied themselves out of the good graces of the thinking colored folks," Blacks were "angry and [were] paying more attention to the propaganda that [was] being spread and listening to the soothing words of the Soviets, Bolsheviks, Reds, and Radicals."[19] In effect, because the conditions undergirding the "national chaotic crisis which loom[ed] behind strikes, discontent, mobs and burners of human flesh"[20] were inscribed in US Capitalist Racist Society and maintained through Wall Street Imperialism, the government had no intention of changing them and instead relied on the Black Scare and the Red Scare as tools to both deny and criminalize Black self-determination.

Especially during the explosion of race riots following World War I, the federal government employed the Black Scare and the Red Scare to link racial conflict with the peril of Black self-determination. One example was the race riot in Elaine, Arkansas, which spanned September 30 and October 1, 1919. It brought into sharp relief the threat Black attempts to unionize posed to white supremacy, the assumption that communists catalyzed these attempts, and the willingness of whites to violently maintain the Structural Location of Blackness.

The organization of Black agricultural workers and tenant farmers was seen as a form of subversive Black self-determination not least because it "played on long-held fears of a black insurrection" by fundamentally challenging racial and economic subjection. This Black self-assertion, on the one hand, and white fear, on the other hand, helped "to create a potent blend that led to horrific violence."[21] In typical Black Scare fashion, the Elaine massacre was construed in the white press as "a negro conspiracy . . . to massacre the whites."[22] That the Progressive Farmers and Household Union of America, a "semi-secret fraternal order" of Black farmers aiming to wrest some economic power from the landlords, was "virtually revolutionary in nature" in rural Phillips County, Arkansas, attests to the superexploitative nature of US Capitalist Racist Society generally, and the US South particularly. After a special agent for the Missouri Pacific Railroad was killed and a deputy sheriff was wounded in a shootout with Black laborers at one of their meetings, a reign of terror was unleashed, and at least twenty-five Blacks and five whites were killed over the span of two days.[23] This massacre elucidates the violent repression used to maintain race and class hierarchy.

This race riot was wholly interpreted through the Black Scare. Federal troops arrested several hundred Blacks, corralling them into a criminal legal system in which their structural location denied them any hope for fairness or justice. While the majority were led to believe that if they pleaded guilty to murder they would be "let off" with light prison sentences, in reality seventy-five Blacks were railroaded into "penitentiary terms ranging from five to twenty-one years; [and] twelve were sentenced to the electric chair." The Arkansas Supreme Court eventually issued stays for the death penalty convictions.[24]

The hysteria demonstrated in the Elaine massacre was ubiquitous throughout 1919 thanks in large part to the Black Scare and Red Scare tactics of the Justice Department, the Military Intelligence Division of the army, the BI, and other federal and state entities. They attributed the race riots not to white supremacy and racist backlash, but rather to radical influence on, and outside agitation for, Black self-determination.[25] In fact, one newspaper reported that the cause of the racial clash in Elaine was propaganda spread among the Black farmers that convinced them to demand higher prices for their labor and cotton. "Certain well-known Negroes"—the ever-present Outside Agitator—were said to be organizing this dispossessed group to refuse to work for landlords unless they were paid higher wages. It was also claimed that they were organizing this group for self-defense, and that a white lawyer had "influenced" the group to adopt a "defiant and independent attitude."[26] This interpretation put the blame on Black farmers generally, and radical organizing for self-determination particularly. By contrast, another newspaper article stated plainly that "the cause of the disturbances in Arkansas was systematic robbery of negro tenant farmers and sharecroppers," which resulted in the organization of the Progressive Farmers and Household Union of America.[27] The story that the massacre had been planned by the Black farmers was concocted to "cloak the robbery of Negroes by white landlords and agents."[28] In other words, blaming Black farmers and radicals was a means of sustaining white supremacy and superexploitation and of subjecting Black self-determination to the Black Scare and the Red Scare.

Following the Elaine massacre, major race riots had broken out throughout 1919 in Charleston, South Carolina; Atlanta, Georgia; Norfolk, Virginia; Longview, Texas; Chicago, Illinois; Knoxville, Tennessee; and Omaha, Nebraska. The flashpoints varied, but Black self-determination, whether in the form of self-defense, defiance of the racial and/or economic order, or refusal to bow to white terrorism, was often construed as the culprit. In the Lusk Committee's *Revolutionary Radicalism*, one of the most influential antiradical reports of the post–World War I period, the Black Scare and the Red Scare abounded. The report asserted that problems affecting "peace and public safety" had been created by radical propaganda encouraging social unrest and was "in large measure the product of subversive doctrines."[29] Likewise, social and racial unrest, "with its revolutionary implications" were not the result of "spontaneous" economic factors, but rather the effect of radicals spreading "false ideas respecting government and the present social order."[30] This meant the source of race riots was not the contradictions and antagonisms of US Capitalist Racist Society, but rather attempts to resolve them.

Attesting to the international correlation of forces that produced the dialectic between Wall Street Imperialism and European colonialism and the rise in practices of Black self-determination, the findings of the Lusk Committee dovetailed with those of other Western imperialists disturbed by widespread Black militancy in their colonies. In October 1919, the British government sent a report, "Unrest among the Negroes," to the US State Department that expressed concern about Radical Blackness in the United States spreading to the Caribbean and Africa. The report contended that US race riots were not a response to "race prejudice," but were rather "the fruits of the doctrine of socialistic equality preached by agitators to negro audiences."[31] In Black Scare and Red Scare fashion, "socialistic equality" implied the collapse of both racial and class hierarchy—and colonial domination. In the appendix "Radical and Nationalistic Groups—Negro Riots," it was further asserted that "smoldering antagonism of race" was behind the riots in the United States. This was evidence of "vicious and well financed propaganda, which [was] directed against the white people" by organizations like the IWW, the radical Socialists, and the Bolshevists who, through incendiary utterings, aimed to incite "the uneducated class in the Southern States" to violent action. Here, it was Blacks—under the influence of subversives—who were the antagonists, not the individuals, institutions, and conditions that made self-defense and the struggle for self-determination necessary. Of equal concern, based on Black Scare logic, was Black discontent with economic subjection in the context of postwar deindustrialization and the desire of the "negro race for race equality."[32] The British government's assessment was identical to that of the Lusk Committee.

Revolutionary Radicalism spotlighted articles that were deemed abjectly revolutionary or seditious or that were apologetic or sympathetic to subversive movements. One criterion was support for Black self-determination, whether in the form of self-defense or agitation for equal rights. The first item selected from *Russky Golos*, "a Russian daily with a circulation of 20,000," was a July 29, 1919, editorial titled "Race Pogroms (Riots)." It argued that whites, mostly soldiers and sailors, were brutalizing Black people throughout the nation, and that "the conservative American press . . . [attempted] only to blame not the white rioters, but those same blacks [by] spreading the rumor that 'Reds' and 'Bolsheviks' [were] carrying out an intensive propaganda among the negros [and] that this red propaganda [was] inciting the negroes, [who were] beginning to revolt." On this logic the soldiers and police were simply pacifying the dangerous Blacks. The article concluded that "pogroms will continue until negroes will be given equal rights with whites."[33] This piece was undoubtedly considered "revolutionary and seditious" because it offered a radical critique of race riots, revealed how the Black Scare and Red Scare legitimated white violence and concealed the roots of race antagonism, and demanded Black rights.

Among the numerous articles selected from *Liberator*, a monthly magazine edited by the socialists Max and Crystal Eastman with a circulation of fifty thousand, was a September 1919 editorial titled "Race and Class" that praised Black "resistance to white" persecution. It argued that the more Blacks defended themselves, the less white mobs would assault them, and called for Blacks to "join revolutionary organizations of the general proletariat rather than special organizations of their own race." This praise and encouragement helped to propel the idea that (white) Reds were behind Black militancy—and that interracial organizing was subversive.[34]

Throughout *Revolutionary Radicalism,* the *Messenger* and its editors A. Philip Randolph and Chandler Owen were given outsized attention. The paper

was considered especially dangerous because it was published by Radical
Blacks, had a large portion of white stockholders, and was circulated among
Blacks with the aim of converting them to "revolutionary radicalism."[35] Likewise, it was "revolutionary in tone" and "committed to the principles of the
Soviet government of Russia and the proposition of organizing the negroes
for the class struggle."[36] The *Messenger* embodied the dangers of Black self-
determination in its excoriation of race riots and advocacy of defense against
them. In the editorial "The Cause and Remedy for Race Riots," *Revolutionary
Radicalism* quoted the sections that called for the socialization of industry,
the nationalization of land, the organization of the masses, an independent
Black press, control over how Blacks were portrayed on the screen and stage,
"physical force and self-defense," and revolution.[37] Revolution meant "the
complete change in the organization of society" because "just as the absence
of industrial democracy is productive of riots and race clashes, so the introduction of industrial democracy will be the longest step toward removing
that cause."[38] Likewise, the editorial contended that "capitalism must go."

These writings helped authorities to construe race riots as attempts by
radicals, Blacks, and Radical Blacks—whether West Indians, Outside Agitators, Red Blacks / Black Reds, "nigger lovers," or fellow travelers—to upend
the capitalist order and, by extension, to expropriate and dominate (propertied) whites. Such interpretation was buoyed by "Thanksgiving," a November 1919 *Messenger* editorial that asserted, "On the field of physical force, the
negro has been right on the job for the protection of his home, his life and
his loved ones. The Washington, Chicago, Longview, Knoxville, Elaine and
Omaha riots are bright spots in New Negroes' attitude toward American
lawlessness and anarchy. They present the New Negro upholding the dignity
of the law against both white hoodlums and the government—the latter of
whom should have seen that law was upheld." Here, Black self-defense could
readily be construed not only as self-determination, but also as aggression
against US Capitalist Racist Society writ large.

The position taken up in the *Messenger* regarding race riots was repeated
in the "extremely inflammatory" and "extremely radical magazine" *Challenge*,
which editorialized in October 1919, "When we shoot down the mobist who
will burn our properties and destroy our lives, they shout 'Bolshevist.' "[39] The
issue, for the US government and white civil society, was not that Blacks were
"abandoned, cast off, maligned, shackled, shoved down the hill towards Gol-
gotha in 'The Land of the Free and the Home of the Brave,'" but rather that
they attempted to mitigate that reality—ostensibly under the influence of enemies of the United States.[40] *Revolutionary Radicalism* confirmed this analysis by claiming Black self-determination—which, on their logic, linked the

"Socialist elements," the UNIA, and the NAACP[41]—was "being cleverly fostered by the Socialist Party and the Rand School of Social Science"; was a refusal to challenge lynching, race riots, Jim Crow, and disenfranchisement "in a lawful matter"; was an attempt to raise class consciousness among Blacks; and was a means to abolish the US form of government.[42]

Vehement rebuke of Black self-determination manifested at the federal level in A. Mitchell Palmer's 1919 *Attorney General Report*, especially in the appendix "Radicalism and Sedition among the Negroes as Reflected in Their Publications." Articulating a position in lockstep with to the Lusk Committee Report, it identified the *Messenger* as the voice of the "Negro radical movement" because of its denunciation of US imperialism and racial barbarism, and its support for Black "physical force" and "economic force."[43] This "insolently offensive" publication, moreover, took extreme pride in Blacks fighting back, warning that "the old order is passing. It is passing in race relations. It is passing in class relations."[44] In its support for Black self-determination, the *Messenger* "threw all discretion to the winds, and became an exponent of open defiance and sedition."[45]

Tellingly, "Radicalism and Sedition" opened with an examination of the role of Blacks in recent race riots.[46] Black reporting on and self-defense in these race riots was construed as "a well-concerted movement among a certain class of Negro leaders"—Outside Agitators—who espoused "radical opposition to the Government, and to established rule of law and order."[47] The effectiveness of their treacherous propaganda was demonstrated in increased race consciousness, antagonism to "the white race," and defiant assertions of equality "and even superiority."[48] The Black press, which not only reported on the ubiquity of racial terror but also made recommendations on how Blacks might protect themselves, was thus a key factor in the rise of unsavory Black self-determination by facilitating the spread of Radical Black ideas. Palmer lamented that, while these types of publications had been kept in check during World War I by the Espionage and Subversion Acts, there was now no way to curb publications ostensibly aimed at fomenting industrial and social revolution, the forcible overthrow of the US government, and the installation of a proletarian dictatorship.[49] As a result, the whole of US Capitalist Racist Society was imperiled.

Even the most mundane details gave Palmer ammunition for the Black Scare. He noted that many of these Black periodicals were "expensive in manufacture," "well-printed," and gave "evidence of the possession of ample funds,"[50] which demonstrated alternative—presumably nefarious and/or foreign—funding sources. Radical Black and foreign-language publications were notable, Palmer argued, in that "a great many [were] . . . devoid of advertising matter which indicat[ed] that they [were] receiving money from outside sources to further their propaganda."[51] Such funding was likely the primary reasons why those newspapers and publications espoused the "Bolshevik, revolutionary, and extreme radical doctrines" spreading throughout the country. The link Palmer made between lack of advertising and radical machinations implied the threat of Black self-determination insofar as the ability of these papers to sustain themselves without utilizing a capitalist instrument like advertising meant that the editors rejected US Capitalist Racist Society and instead chose to align with foreign enemies. Palmer's analysis made liberal use of the Black Scare and the Red Scare in its coupling of (Radical Black) financial independence and the spread of foreign ideology; its interpretation of the rejection of a capitalist convention like advertising as hostility to the American way of life; and its positioning of "discontent, race prejudice, and class hatred" as the purview of foreign and Black radicalism that "urge[d] the overthrow of the government."[52] Likewise, in noting that radical organizations had been relatively successful in attracting Blacks to their side, Palmer appended Black self-determination to external influence.[53]

The Black Belt Nation Thesis, Wall Street Imperialism, and the Structural Location of Blackness

The "Bolshevik plot" that came to be of particular concern to the US government was the communists' Black Belt Nation Thesis (BBNT). This thesis drew on Lenin's analysis of imperialism, the national question, and the colonial question and offered one theorization of, and site for articulating, the demand for self-determination during the Black Scare / Red Scare Longue Durée. In the midst of World War I, Lenin published *The Socialist Revolution and the Right to Self-Determination (Theses)* in which he meticulously theorized self-determination as an essential aspect of the struggle against capitalism and the realization of international socialism. In the first thesis, he wrote:

> Victorious socialism must achieve complete democracy and, consequently not only bring about the complete equality of nations, but also give effect to the right of oppressed nations to self-determination, *i.e.*, the right to free political secession. . . . Socialist Parties [must] prove . . . that they will free the enslaved nations and establish relations with them on the basis of a free union—and a free union is a lying phrase without right to secession.[54]

The BBNT was an imperfect application of Lenin's position to the realities of Black people in the Southern United States, and as such, it was hotly contested within the CPUSA and the Communist International. It was also largely ineffective at attracting and galvanizing Black people when compared to the UNIA's Black Nationalism. Nonetheless, the BBNT was a revolutionary means of understanding the relationship between Wall Street Imperialism and the Structural Location of Blackness and of making the demand for Black self-determination. Its promotion of Black self-determination to organize the Black (and white) masses in the South, its critique of Wall Street Imperialism, and its *potential* ability to incite a segment of the Black population to revolutionary action was characterized by the defenders of US Capitalist Racist Society as the communists' efforts to sow the seeds of subversion among Blacks and to overthrow the US government by force or violence.

The BBNT situated the origins of the Structural Location of Blackness in the US South and in Wall Street Imperialism, analyzed the Negro Question as a national question, and argued that Black self-determination was foundational to Black liberation as one aspect of the global proletarian struggle. It posited that the "Black Belt" of the United States—the "old slave South" encompassing "the old cotton country" that traversed twelve Southern states from the south of Maryland to the Mississippi delta and that contained roughly five million Blacks, over 60 percent of the Black population[55]—was a nation with the right to secede from the United States if it so desired. The Black Belt was where the national oppression of Blacks, or their structural location, took on its most acute form. There, "the plantation system and all its accompanying evils (peonage, share cropping, debt slavery, etc.) persist[ed] . . . in all their most brutal forms."[56]

In 1922, the Negro Question was taken up for the first time by the Communist International at the Fourth Congress.[57] In "Report on the Black Question," Otto Huiswoud, a US Black delegate, argued that the Negro Question was of "great interest and supreme importance."[58] Though it was primarily an economic question, he explained, it also emanated from Blacks' "mark of bondage," which resulted in antagonism between Black and white workers in addition to overall class conflict.[59] Another remnant of slavery was that, in the South, nearly 80 percent of Blacks lived in the countryside. Hence, the Black Belt was "almost a separate country" where the class struggle was waged in its most brutal form. Given the dire economic conditions there, when strikes broke out among white workers in the North, the ruling class was easily able to introduce Southern Blacks as strike breakers, which exacerbated racial violence and pushed down the wages and working conditions of the entire working class. The latter was also possible because Blacks were largely barred from trade unions. Given this oppression and the fact that Wall Street Imperialism had turned its attention to "the peaceful penetration of Africa," Huiswoud argued that the Black struggle must be understood as an international one against capitalism and imperialism.

Given this reality, Lenin's *Theses on the National and Colonial Question* must be applied to the Negro Question.[60] Lenin had written that, though he lacked "concrete information" about the situation of "Negroes in America," they undoubtedly fell under the purview of the national question.[61] In 1925, the Communist International's American Commission went on to affirm that the Negro Question in the United States represented the "most characteristic form of national oppression in a capitalist state whose historic roots are connected with the birth of class society" and exposed "the class substance of racial antagonism."[62]

Drawing on *The Socialist Revolution and the Right to Self-Determination (Theses)* and other of Lenin's writings, Harry Haywood, the key proponent of the BBNT, argued that the special suffering of African Americans emanating from the history of transatlantic enslavement, the failure of the Civil War to completely overthrow the feudal order in the US South, and the continuation of Wall Street Imperialism gave the Structural Location of Blackness its national character. Its "real economic and social essence" was not in racial difference but rather in the difference in economic and cultural development between Black and white workers under conditions of US Capitalist Racist Society. Skin color, as a proxy for racial superiority and inferiority, was both the means by which the ruling class concealed the national character of the Structural Location of Blackness and the physical characteristic through which the latter was expressed.[63] Such efforts aided in the perpetuation of Black superexploitation in Southern agriculture and in unskilled industry through a sociopolitical "superstructure"—i.e., the Black Scare—that consisted of "Jim Crowism" and segregation as technologies to deny Black people democratic rights, full equality, and the right to self-determination.[64] The Black communist leader James Ford added that Blacks suffered from capitalist exploitation as members of the working class and from imperialist oppression through anti-Black racial antagonism, the deprivation of rights, subjection to lynch-law and mob rule, and foreclosure from justice. Black striving for liberation therefore amounted to a national struggle for self-government and self-determination. For Haywood, a revolutionary movement led by a Black peasant-proletariat alliance was the most effective approach to fighting Wall Street Imperialism.[65]

The understanding of the Negro Question as a national question and the Structural Location of Blackness as a form of national oppression was concretized in the Communist International's 1928 BBNT.[66] Its specific authorship is unclear. According to historian Minkah Makalani, "It remains a point of some debate as to whether these Black Communists [James Ford, Williana Burroughs, Otto Hall, Harry Haywood, William Patterson, and Maude White] or one of Stalin's functionaries played the key role" in drafting it.[67] Historian Keith Griffler more firmly asserted, "It is clear that no American had a hand in drafting it," which was reflected in "its extremely clumsy presentation" and "theoretical ineptitude."[68] Another historian, Mark Solomon, contended that the BBNT followed from a collaboration between the Siberian communist Charles Nasanov and Harry Haywood, whose position attacked white chauvinism and emphasized social equality and self-determination.[69] Whatever its origins, the subcommittee offered a "diasporic frame" for the BBNT and conceptualized race as nation, "which in Marxist thought . . . established a more 'objective' grounds on which to discuss what would otherwise remain a mere bourgeois chimera obscuring class."[70]

A parallel formulation was happening with regard to South Africa, when in 1928 James La Guma and Harry Haywood coauthored a resolution with Soviet theorists in the Anglo-American Secretariat calling for an independent republic of South African natives with equal rights for all races. This was a particularly important resolution given that the Communist Party of South Africa (CPSA) had the largest number of Black members, and because it emanated from a protracted struggle between the Comintern and white South African communists in 1920 and 1922 over the failure of the CPSA to recognize the need to organize among the African masses and to understand their revolutionary potential. Though the party had passed an "Africanization" policy in 1924, it wasn't until La Guma was invited to Moscow in 1927 and the passage of the Black Republic Thesis in 1928 that this work began in earnest.[71]

Interestingly, many Black communists, including James Ford, Otto Hall, Lovett Fort-Whiteman, Otto Huiswoud, and later, Doxey Wilkerson, opposed the BBNT, instead arguing that Blackness was a question of *racial discrimination* and that US Blacks demanded full equality *within the United States*. Like the Black and white South African communists who argued against the Black Republic Thesis,[72] their US counterparts "cautioned against pursuing [the BBNT] too aggressively, feeling that it was . . . 'more Garveyism than Garvey himself.'"[73] Ford argued that because of class differentiation among Blacks, there could not be a common national ideology of an oppressed proletariat and any emphasis on nationalism would play into the hands of the bourgeoisie. Otto Hall argued that no Black nationality existed as such, and that Blacks wanted to be considered part of the US nation.[74]

By contrast, Haywood contended that the national oppression of Black people—or the Structural Location of Blackness as a form of national oppression—could be traced to the "remnants of slavery" in the South, which

ensured a cheap supply of labor and lower wages for them throughout US
Capitalist Racist Society. Haywood argued further that the "peasant question" formed the basis of Blacks' national oppression insofar as their persecution emanated from the fact that they lived in "large masses" in the agrarian South—a phenomenon that was reproduced through the development
of separate living areas in Northern cities—and this was the precondition
for a revolutionary movement among the Black nation.[75] In other words, the
conditions of the South, at the intersection of Wall Street Imperialism and the
Negro Question, gave the Structural Location of Blackness both a national
and a potentially revolutionary character. Thus, spearheaded by Haywood,
the 1928 BBNT articulated three central points: that Blacks were an oppressed
nation in the South of the United States; that the Black masses possessed the
capacity to organize and liberate themselves; and that as a national question,
the Black struggle in the United States was one iteration of international socialist revolution. The "Black Bolshevik" counseled the CPUSA to take up its
duty to not only fight for full social and political rights, but also to unreserv-
edly support the right of national self-determination "up to the erection of an
independent Negro state."[76]

The BBNT and Self-Determination

Haywood's position won the day, and the emphasis on Black self-determination
underscored that, as a national question, the Negro Question had a special
character and was of international importance similar to the Irish and Jewish questions. As well, as Claudia Jones explained, the Negro Question posed
linked but distinct problems for the North and the South. For Blacks in the
North, whose "problems [were] akin to those of an oppressed national minority," the fight was for *equal rights* and was primarily being waged by the
presence of a large and growing Black proletariat that provided the critical
link between the broader working class and the toilers in the Black Belt. In
the South, by contrast, the struggle was for *emancipation*—to wipe out the
economic, political, and social survival of slavery emanating from the Wall
Street Imperialism, and to enforce equal rights through the exercise of the
right to self-determination.

Self-determination, though, did not exclude "the struggle for partial demands" that aided "the class struggle against exploitation."[77] Furthermore, the
objective reality of workers in the Black Belt demonstrated that they desired
self-determination as a means of overcoming superexploitation, that they ab-
horred their oppressed status under Jim Crow, and that the ideology of white
supremacy denied them full freedom and equality. Failure to acknowledge

this reality was to deny the obligation of the working class to struggle for conditions in which Blacks could make their own choice regarding national liberation.[78] Given this objective reality, the Black struggle was fundamentally a revolutionary struggle against *national oppression* and for the right to self-determination in the Black Belt.[79]

Jones's position was predicated on a revision of the BBNT between 1928 and 1930 that resulted from heated debate concerning the lived realities of Black people in the South. The 1930 resolution argued that Northern Black folks were involved in a struggle for integration and assimilation, while the demand for self-determination was to be applied to the South. But the quest for racial equality, irrespective of region, was a revolutionary demand. The updated resolution, passed at the Seventh National Convention of the CPUSA, stated in part:

> The Party must openly and unreservedly fight for the right of Negroes for national self-determination in the South, where Negroes comprise a majority of the population. Self-determination for the negro masses in the logical continuation and highest expression of the struggle for equal rights (social equality). As the Negro liberation movement develops, it will, in the territories and states with the majority of Negro population, take more and more the form of a struggle against the rule of the white bourgeoisie, for self-determination.[80]

In other words, the realities of Wall Street Imperialism elicited the urgent need for self-determination in the South as one expression of the struggle for complete social equality everywhere.

The Black communist B. D. Amis concurred that the only solution to break "the iron clutch of imperialism which [held] in subjection the Negro masses" was "self-determination for the majority of the Negro population in the Black Belt . . . thru [sic] revolutionary struggles."[81] The mischaracterization of the Structural Location of Blackness as a function of racial discrimination as opposed to national oppression betrayed a lack of faith in the Black masses, expressed politically in the underestimation of Black liberation struggles. It treated the Black movement as detracting from and contradictory to "pure" class struggle instead of as an ally to and a means of strengthening proletarian struggle.[82] Likewise, the misrecognition of the Negro Question as merely racial antagonism underestimated the revolutionary content of the Black struggle for national liberation and, objectively, "reduce[d] the movement to a feeble opposition against American imperialism."[83] For Amis, Haywood, and other supporters of the BBNT, the struggle for Black self-determination meant the overthrow of class rule in the Black Belt, and by extension, the yoke of Wall Street Imperialism. This was because the "right to self-determination

raise[d] the question of power for the Negro population in the Black Belt. It
mean[t] wrestling the power from the white minority of exploiters. . . . It
[was] a *basic, fundamental* demand of the liberation struggle of the Negroes
in the Black Belt . . . [and] a slogan of national rebellion."[84]

Perhaps most important, the emphasis on Black self-determination pushed
the party to redouble its work among Blacks especially by establishing roots
in the South.[85] Practically, it led to the establishment of the CPUSA's District 17
in Birmingham, Alabama in 1929, which encompassed Alabama, Georgia,
Louisiana, Florida, Tennessee, and Mississippi. It also inaugurated the earnest work of organizing Black and white workers and farmers, establishing
a weekly periodical, and starting a workers' school.[86] Self-determination as a
slogan didn't always translate into material gains for Black workers, but it was
a powerful way to encourage Black-white unity while focusing on the specific
plight of Black workers, to support the armed self-defense of sharecroppers,
and to support autonomous Black organizations like the Share Cropper's
Union, organized in 1931.[87] This work also opened up political space for Black
workers to articulate their "rich culture of opposition" amid the CPUSA
"framework for understanding the roots of poverty and racism," to link local
struggles to world politics," and to "challenge not only hegemonic ideology
of white supremacy but the petit bourgeois racial politics of the Black middle
class" so that "ordinary people could analyze, discuss, and criticize the society in which they lived."[88] In addition, the emphasis on self-determination
"propelled African Americans to national and international party offices. For
example, the Red International of Labor Unions World Conference in the
summer of 1930 required that one-third of the American delegates be 'black
proletarians.'"[89]

This emphasis on Black self-determination was undermined by the rise
of Earl Browder to power in the CPUSA during the Popular Front era. "Brow-
derism," as his "opportunist" and "revisionist" policies were called, included
advocacy of peaceful coexistence between socialism and capitalism, the replacement of the CPUSA with the Communist Party Association, and the
suspension of the Black self-determination slogan.[90] In 1944, Browder's position, which, according to Jones, distorted the teachings of Lenin who, in
1913, made "a *direct* reference to the Negro people as an *oppressed nation*,"[91]
obfuscated the liberatory content of Black self-determination by contending
that US Blacks desired full integration into US society, not separation.[92] His
main fallacy, according to Jones, was the conflation of separation with self-
determination; a rigorous understanding of the historical and material conditions of US Blacks showed that "integration [could not] be considered a
substitute for the right to self-determination," that "National liberation [was]

not synonymous with integration," and that "the two concepts [were not] mutually exclusive."[93] Jones advocated for a return to pre-Browder analysis not least because the communist position on the Negro Question had put the CPUSA at the forefront of the struggle against Wall Street Imperialism and US Capitalist Racist Society more broadly.[94]

Ultimately, the BBNT helped to illuminate that Wall Street imperialism transformed the Negro question into a national question—and that the Structural Location of Blackness was a form of national oppression that required special consideration, systematic struggle against white supremacy and white chauvinism, and an emphasis on Black self-determination.[95]

The Black Scare and the Red Scare against the BBNT and Black Self-Determination

From its inception, the BBNT and its emphasis on Black self-determination was of particular concern to federal and state governments alike. In 1931 the New York congressman Hamilton Fish Jr., chair of the notorious Special Committee to Investigate Communist Activities in the United States, argued that one of the most dangerous aspects of the communists was their work among Blacks, particularly the Communist International's emphasis on Black self-determination starting in 1928. According to Fish, the communists were working to "rouse the racial hatred of the Negroes and develop a revolutionary spirit against government" by promoting self-determination, social and racial equality, and intermarriage. He reasoned that while loyal Blacks rejected such propaganda—that is, accepted their subordinated status—subversive "colored men and women [were] going to Moscow all the time to be trained in the revolutionary schools."[96] Similarly, the prosecutor in Angelo Herndon's trial for insurrection in Atlanta 1932 argued that it was simultaneously a trial of every white person who united with Blacks and who believed in a "nigger Soviet Republic in the Black Belt."[97] This argument was reiterated before the Supreme Court in 1935. When pressed by the justices on what crime Herndon had committed, J. Walter LeCraw, representing the State of Georgia, replied, "He tried to set up a Nigger Republic in the Black Belt."[98]

These preoccupations were evident in the early Cold War: in a 1953 FBI report, "The Communist Party and the Negro," it was argued that "equal rights" and "self-determination" were the primary means by which the Communist Party had attempted to gain Black support, and that the theory of self-determination was "originally formulated in Moscow." Even as self-determination in the Black Belt was said to be deeply unpopular among US Blacks who wanted total equality "within American society," it remined an

area of focus for the communists, according to the FBI, as a means of upend-
ing the current form of government.[99]

"The Communist Party and the Negro" recapitulated the position articulated in *RACON*, which considered the BBNT and the call for Black
self-determination to be one of the communists' most pernicious forms of
subversion. In an October 1942 bulletin, the FBI specifically instructed that
a report titled "Communist Party—Negro Question" should be prepared
"when matter of evidentiary value [were] obtained indicating the activity
of the Communist Party among the negro race which [was] in furtherance
of its program of self-determination for the Negro . . . that [was] in violation of a Federal law under jurisdiction of this Bureau." The memo further
noted that "the Communist Party ha[d] re-emphasized its Marxist-Leninist
theory of self-determination for the negro race which [was] one of its more
revolutionary tactics."[100] A confidential informant who was purportedly a
former high-ranking member of the CPUSA claimed that the communists
"exploited" Black grievances about lynching, the poll tax, and Jim Crow to
"stir up the Negroes" and to promote the formation of an independent Black
government in the Black Belt—a claim that gave credence to the idea that
Black self-determination was subversive and subversives promoted Black
self-determination.[101]

The *RACON* appendix "The Communist Party and Negroes" documented
CPUSA and Comintern resolutions and directives "allegedly" directed at US
Blacks since 1920, with a particular focus on the constitution of the Negro
Question as a national question and the slogan of self-determination in the
Black Belt.[102] The appendix noted that the Third International regarded US
Blacks as connected to the revolutionary work they were doing in various colonies.[103] Likewise, the CPUSA's intention to overthrow the US government by
force or violence was claimed to manifest in 1930 in its work among Blacks, not
least its self-determination slogan. The revision of the 1928 BBNT was considered by the FBI to be a precursor to "perhaps the most important directive to
the [CPUSA] issued by the Communist International . . . adopted by the Executive Committee of the Third (Communist) International in October 1930" on
the handling of the Negro Question. The FBI erroneously claimed that it was
"still" in effect during World War II and "evidence of it being followed [was]
constantly being reported."[104] In reality, as mentioned above, the BBNT and the
self-determination slogan had been suspended with the rise of Earl Browder
and the Popular Front strategy in 1935. It returned only after Browder's ouster
and the installation of William Z. Foster at the helm of the CPUSA. These details mattered little to the FBI insofar as they were committed to tracing a long
pattern of communist subversion rooted in their work among Blacks.

The 1930 resolution was extensively excerpted in *RACON* from the February 1931 volume of the *Communist*. Passages of concern included that Blacks were considered an oppressed nation, that the main slogan in the South was Negroes' right to self-determination in the Black Belt, that the past and ongoing slavery of Blacks was the basis of their special demand for equality, that Blacks were subjected to both the arbitrary will of white exploiters and to social ostracism, and that "the origins of all this [was] not difficult to find: This Yankee arrogance towards the negroes stinks of the disgusting atmosphere of the old slave market."[105] *RACON* also documented the communist position that the struggle for equal rights was linked to Black national demands put forth by the masses and was one of the most important proletarian class struggles in the US, and that even though the "Negro zone" of the South was not a colony of the US, the "peculiar situation in the Black Belt" meant that the right to self-determination was the correct slogan. Especially concerning to the FBI was the contention that self-determination occupied "the central place in the liberation of the negro population in the Black Belt against the yoke of imperialism," necessitated the "confiscation of the land and property of the white landowners and capitalists for the benefit of Negro farmers," and required the "establishment of the state unity of the Black Belt." Further, self-determination meant that Blacks had the complete and unlimited right to exercise governmental control throughout the Black Belt, to decide how they would relate to the United States and other nations, and to overthrow class rule in the Black Belt. It was the decision of the Black masses, the communists resolved, whether to separate from or federate with the United States, and separation would be rejected only in the event that there was a proletarian takeover within the United States.[106]

Providing fodder for the FBI's entanglement of the Black Scare and the Red Scare, the communists analyzed that it was essential for the CPUSA to organize the masses of Black and white workers against Black oppression to promote rebellion, whether the latter would be the catalyst for or would follow from proletarian struggle or dictatorship.[107] On this logic, the Black masses were an invaluable revolutionary force, especially in conjunction with the Communist Party. *RACON* fallaciously asserted that these positions "continued" to characterize the approach of the Communist Party during World War II because the Black communist Pettis Perry of the Los Angeles Workers School taught a course on the Negro Question as a national question that emphasized the characteristics of the Black Belt and self-determination. The course also included recommended reading by Harry Haywood, who, *RACON* stated, "ha[d] been a Communist Party member [and made] reference to the program of the Communist International on 'the Negro Question.'"[108] Again, the self-determination line was not, in fact, in operation at the time *RACON* was compiled, but facts and accuracy were not necessary to construe Black self-determination, and its links to the CPUSA, as subversive.

In another appendix, "Communist Party Front Organizations and Negroes," *RACON* outlined how the League of Struggle for Negro Rights (LSNR) was subversive in its promotion of the BBNT. Born out of the American Negro Labor Congress (ANLC), the LSNR was organized in 1930 with the mission to destroy the plantation system in the South, confiscate without compensation the land of big landlords, and declare Black self-determination in the Black Belt. Drawing on information from a confidential informant who had been in the CPUSA, *RACON* claimed that the LSNR was "based on the program of the Communist International relative to the Negro question in the United States" and was the entity through which landowners in the Black Belt would be overthrown and an autonomous Black government would be established.[109] The LSNR was understood as the vessel through which communist subversion and potential Black revolution would be actualized precisely because it emphasized Black self-determination and organizing the Black and white masses and segments of the Black petit bourgeoisie to this end.[110]

According to a confidential informant, the aim of self-determination was to be achieved through "organizing white and negro farmers and workers to fight against lynching, the poll tax, right to sell their crops, Jim Crowism, and the right to ownership of land."[111] Likewise, the LSNR set forth a program against segregation and the social system in which "Negroes are set apart from the rest of the population as a despised and outlawed people"; the denial of ordinary human and civil rights to Black people throughout the country; forced labor, chain gangs, and "the hangover from chattel slavery"; and ideas of white supremacy and superiority that justified the enslavement of Blacks by white rulers.[112] Such actions and advocacy were easily construed as both communist plots and Black subversion.

RACON also noted that the September 1, 1932, issue of *Liberator*, the LSNR's official organ, included a map of eleven Southern states with shaded regions referred to as the "Black Belt." It was stated that the Black Belt included the 195 counties with over 50 percent Blacks and 220 counties with 35–50 percent Blacks, and these counties constituted a continuous area in which Blacks amounted to over 50 percent of the total population. Underneath the map was written "The Communist Party and the League of Struggle for Negro Rights demand the right of the Negros of the 'Black Belt' to rule over this territory, including any white minority residing there, and even to separate this territory from the United States if they so desire."[113] The FBI seemed unaware or unconcerned that the LSNR was little more than a paper organization that, like the ANLC, was more of a propaganda machine that put forth forceful rhetoric and analysis but was relatively ineffective at organizing Black workers. The CPUSA was compelled to form these organizations when it failed to capture the Garvey movement and the Negro Sanhedrin. The latter was an organization established by the moderate intellectual and political activist Kelley Miller that held an influential, ideologically diverse "All-Race Conference" from February 11 to 15, 1924.[114] But, for the US government, ideas, rhetoric, and possibilities were in and of themselves subversive *acts* when articulated by organizations it despised.

RACON focused on the Comintern because the FBI believed that the CPUSA's emphasis on Black self-determination and the BBNT was directed by Moscow. On the one hand, during the 1920s, US Black communists did turn to the Comintern to offer up policies and resolutions on the Negro Question, given its relative neglect by US communists up until that point. On the other hand, Black communists and fellow travelers, like Otto Huiswoud and Claude McKay, along with those from other parts of the colonized world, offered analysis of the Black conditions in the United States to influence the Comintern to understand the Black struggle in international and revolutionary terms.[115] In particular, the ABB did much to shape "Negro work," the Negro Question, and the constitution of all-Black organizations as potentially revolutionary and as essential to developing the consciousness of Black workers.[116] Historian Hakim Adi contended, "Certainly the views of the ABB on the significance of the worldwide Negro movement, its recognition of the influence of Garveyism and the particular vanguard role that African Americans should play seem to have become more significant in the approaches of American Communists and the [Comintern] to the Negro Question in this period."[117] In other words, commitment to Black self-determination was a combination of Moscow directives and day-to-day organizing, analysis, and struggle of Black and other communists in the United States. Even the establishment of the ANLC in 1924 at the behest of the Executive Committee of the Communist International was a product of Radical Black influencing the party: "they had tirelessly pressed the party to make it the 'duty of all party members under all conditions' to demand 'social equality' for Negroes" and to place "segregated housing, Jim Crow, lynching, race riots, and imperialism at the center of" communist work under the control of Blacks.[118]

Relatedly, at the International Congress against Colonial Oppression and Imperialism convened in Brussels in 1927, which was a multi-tendency gathering with significant communist influence, a five-member Negro Commission was established and created "The Common Resolution on the Negro Question." It linked the histories of Blacks in Africa, the Caribbean, and

100

CHAPTER FOUR

the United States; offered the most comprehensive statement on the Negro Question and self-determination up until that point; and created the political foundation for the BBNT in 1928. It argued for Black self-determination globally through complete freedom of African descendants; complete equality of the races; control of the African land by Africans; abolition of forced labor and expropriative taxation; eradication of social, political, and economic racial restrictions; the end of military conscription; Black freedom of movement; freedom of speech, press, and assembly; the right to education; and the right to unionize.[119] This meeting and resolution demonstrated not the domination of Moscow, but rather collaboration between Moscow and Radical Blacks throughout the African diaspora. Though Moscow certainly provided ongoing financial, material, and organizational support, claims by the US government that US communists generally, and Black communists particularly, were under totalizing foreign influence and uncritically followed the dictates of the Soviet Union were more of a reflection of the Black Scare and Red Scare than of political reality.

✶

Government reports spanning the Black Scare / Red Scare Longue Durée demonstrate that Black self-determination, in the form of defense against white violence; analysis of the national character of the Structural Location of Blackness in the South; and the linked demand for the right to self-determination in the Black Belt were subjected to the Black Scare and the Red Scare at the state, national, and international levels. Irrespective of the viability or popularity of an articulation of Black self-determination, its very existence added fodder to the claim that Black assertion was inseparable from foreign influence and outside agitation. These reports also demonstrated that counterhegemonic words, ideas, and rhetoric concerning any militant resolution to the Negro Question counted as subversive *acts* because these positions offered up the possibility of galvanizing the Black masses against the internal logic of US Capitalist Racist Society—that is, Wall Street Imperialism. The latter not only engendered hostility to Black self-determination in the United States, but also to any struggle against expropriation and for autonomy abroad, especially in the African diaspora.

5

Wall Street Imperialism and Expropriation Abroad

> Africa is imperialism's greatest and most characteristic expression.
> RALPH BUNCHE, 1936

During the Black Scare / Red Scare Longue Durée, Wall Street Imperialism wreaked havoc abroad, especially in the Black World. From 1920 to 1948, US capitalists made $18 billion in income on foreign investments—"only a *fraction* of the actual booty of imperialism."[1] Such pillaging was aided by the rapid development of "militarism and navalism," the use of force against foreign competitors for markets, the transformation of markets into fields for the investment of surplus superprofit, the takeover of governments of selected areas to guarantee profit, and the establishment of spheres of influence.[2] Investment and trade treaties were unequivocally backed by military force—"the only force sufficient to compel a foreign government to sign away its resources" and the only force that could create a temporary law and order climate demanded by Wall Street Imperialists to conduct business. This had particularly devastating consequences for the Caribbean and Africa insofar as "having subjected its workers and exploited its natural resources at home," Wall Street Imperialism "turn[ed] with grim determination to undeveloped races and new areas to renew the same process there"—and those on the darkest side of the color line were considered particularly suited for expropriation.[3]

Expropriation abroad began at home, with the subjection of racialized workers elsewhere following from the successful superexploitation of racialized workers domestically.[4] Relatedly, earlier capital accumulation from westward land dispossession and subsequent industrialization, corporate consolidation, and economic expansion created the conditions for the internationalization of Wall Street—of the appending of Wall Street to imperialism.[5] The First World War accelerated that process and strengthened the relationship between banking, finance capital, and US imperialism.[6] New York was newly able to compete with London, Paris, and Berlin largely because the Great War "drastically reordered global credit flows," with the United States transforming from a debtor into a creditor nation.[7] Latin American and Caribbean nations and businesses turned to the United States for financing, and credit and domestic saving and investment patterns were altered to the benefit of Wall Street Imperialist institutions like the City Bank.[8] Likewise, fomenting war in Latin American and the Caribbean was an invaluable tool used by Wall Street to run the economic affairs of these countries and to develop partnerships with the US State Department to establish the repressive political conditions—through militarism or dollar diplomacy—necessary for this contravention of sovereignty.

These processes were entwined with the Black Scare and Red Scare that transformed racial and cultural difference into the basis for white rule over "inferior" Blacks and "Others" deemed unfit for self-government.[9] Wall Street Imperialism and its agents exported domestic practices of Black subjection "to the Caribbean [and] instrumentalized white racism in imperial banking policy and practice through their everyday encounters and transactions with Caribbean peoples."[10] As banks looked overseas for outlets for unproductive capital, Wall Street Imperialism clashed with "the peoples, nations, and colonies of the Caribbean and Latin America, [and] participated in the creation, replication, and reordering of Caribbean economies on racial lines while helping to reproduce the racist imaginaries and cultures in which finance capital was embedded and through which banking functioned."[11]

In 1927, the West Indian–born communist Richard B. Moore analyzed the relationship between Wall Street Imperialism and the denigration of the African continent, the Caribbean, and the African diaspora more broadly. He argued that this convergence of finance and industrial capitalism had facilitated the colonization of Africa in the late nineteenth century and had robbed Liberia, through a "great concession made to a Wall Street corporation," of its nominal freedom. The imbrication of US imperialism and finance had facilitated the decimation of Haiti by US military occupation, expropriated the republic of its land and resources, and subjected Haitians—and Caribbean labor in general—to virtual enslavement and the denial of basic liberties. To end this region-wide economic and political brutality, Moore demanded economic autonomy and the immediate withdrawal of imperialist troops and institutions.[12]

Two years later, James Ford expanded Moore's analysis, insisting that the looming crisis of capitalism was especially significant to the international working class, to oppressed people generally, and to African descendants particularly. He explained that the extant stage of capitalist development, characterized by Wall Street Imperialism, constituted the consolidation of Africa's partition and the "complete enslavement of its people"; the arresting of industrialization, which hindered the development of the "toiling masses"; and the relegation of the continent to a source of raw material, a market for European goods, and a dumping ground for accumulated surplus capital.[13] In the United States, poor Blacks suffered dehumanizing exploitation by Wall Street, "white big business," and the "rising Negro bourgeoisie," whose condition of possibility was the subjection of the Black working class.[14] The exacerbation of these conditions by rigid racial barriers, disenfranchisement, and lynching gave Black exploitation its special character: superexploitation. The West Indies, subjected to US militarism and occupation on behalf of Wall Street, was largely transformed into a marketplace for American goods. Moreover, throughout Africa, the US South, and the Caribbean, Black workers were impressed into forced labor, laying railroads, building roads and bridges, and working in mines; were entrapped on plantations through peonage; and were subjected to convict leasing. In addition, they suffered intolerable working conditions and routinized violence. Liberation from the imperialist oppression of Black people throughout the world, Ford argued, was wholly contingent on "how they estimate[d] the present period of imperialism, the concrete task of organization they set themselves to achieve these things[,] and the unity they establish[ed] with the international working class in the struggle against imperialism."[15] Both Moore and Ford revealed the connections between Wall Street Imperialism, capitalist racism, and the denial of self-determination to peoples and nations at the bottom of the racial hierarchy.

Wall Street Imperialism in Haiti

The archetypal example of Wall Street Imperialism and racist domination in the Black World generally, and the Caribbean particularly, during the Black Scare / Red Scare Longue Durée was the US occupation of Haiti from 1915 to 1934. This independent nation of African descendants had their government overtaken and their liberty revoked by the US Navy even though war had not been formally declared by Congress.[16] The occupation was a collaborative effort between the US government and finance capital, a hallmark of Wall Street Imperialism. The public-private partnership was manifested in the fact that Secretary of State William Jennings Bryan solicited the advice of City Bank's vice president Roger Leslie Farnham about "a long-term solution to the unsettled political and economic conditions in Haiti." It was Farnham who offered military intervention as a solution based on "ideas of Haitian racial backwardness and civilizational underdevelopment."[17] City Bank was able to wield this power because the marines and the civil servants who helped to maintain the occupation were at the service of US financial interests, though the federal government paid their salary.[18]

Haiti was particularly appealing as a location for a strategic naval base in the Caribbean and for the investment of finance capital in the development of exports like coffee, cotton, tobacco, cocoa, and sugar.[19] The motivations of this joint enterprise were purely expropriative in its aim to establish a coaling station, to impose a protocol to settle outstanding financial claims of US citizens against the Haitian government, and to revise Article 6 of the Haitian constitution that prevented non-Haitians from owning property in Haiti.[20] This change, implemented under conditions of economic coercion and political duress, helped to facilitate the expropriation of Haitian land and resources. During the occupation, the majority of fertile land was taken over by Wall Street Imperialists and turned into foreign-controlled plantations.[21] Expropriation was further facilitated through mandates that only US financial interests could develop mining, commercial, and agricultural resources in Haiti; the United States would be the sole financial adviser and exercise complete control over revenue; Haitians could not float new loans or raise tariffs without US consent; Haiti could not lease or cede its sovereign territory to any foreign power; and the United States would be the sole provider of officers for the Haitian police force.[22] To assure these interests, President Woodrow Wilson promoted an aggressive posture toward Haiti to assume control of the country's finances.[23] In turn, as the NAACP field secretary James Weldon Johnson explained in 1920, Haitians had been murdered with "American rifles and machine guns" because "the National City Bank of New York [was] very much interested in Haiti."[24] To ensure—and insure—its expropriation schemes, Wall Street Imperialists insisted that the State Department maintain war vessels at Port-au-Prince "as a warning sign to potential insurrectionists."[25]

Haiti's total population—elites, politicians, peasants, and laborers alike—were subjected to a brutal administration that reproduced the realities of the Structural Location of Blackness on the island. In this way, the US occupation of Haiti under Wall Street Imperialism mirrored European imperialist political partition of Africa, in which the Indigenous elite was deliberately destroyed, historian Walter Rodney explained, due to "the racism spawned in the earlier phase of capitalist expansion when genocide in Latin America and the enslavement of Africans had to be given pseudo-scientific and obscurantist philosophical justification."[26] The constitutive indignity of the Structural Location of Blackness in US Capitalist Racist Society was on full display in Haiti. Haiti's political and elite classes were muzzled, humiliated, and "unceremoniously dethroned from their positions of political power [by] the codes and cultures of US racism [that] demoted them to the status of the black peasant."[27] They were also subjected to arbitrary brutality; a marine captain, for example, found great humor in kicking a well-dressed ex-member of the Haitian Assembly into the street with a pair of heavy boots for walking on the sidewalk.[28] This routine disrespect was meant to remind Haitians, irrespective of class, of their subordination. As Johnson explained, "Americans have carried American hatred to Haiti. They have planted the feeling of caste and color prejudice where it never before existed."[29] Here, "caste" could be understood as the lowly status imposed by the Structural Location of Blackness.

A particularly violent method of expropriating Haitian labor, resources, and sovereignty was the implementation of a road project that the US government used to maintain law and order, entrench military control, and surveil and contain the insurgent Cacos. The US Marines established martial law, enforced by a brutal militia, and activated the 1864 Haitian corvée law to conscript free labor for the road project. Corvée required peasants to work on local roads instead of paying road taxes, and this system, under exogenous administration, approximated a return to racial slavery. In the control of the US Marines, it was an extension of the chain gangs of the US South into Haiti.[30] Occupation forces "seized" workers from all corners of the island, and these raids "closely resembled the African slave raids of past centuries. And slavery it was—though temporary." Workers were brutalized, intimidated, and killed if they tried to resist, and their families were left to fend for themselves as the male members were impressed into unfree labor.[31] Corvée illuminated how the Wall Street Imperialist relationship between the US North and South that ensured cheap Black labor, land dispossession, and brutal oppression in the Black Belt was transferable to other populations that shared a similar structural location. Not unlike the race riots that peppered US Capitalist Racist Society, as the laborers revolted, "some 3,000 Haitians were killed in the first five years of occupation" as hunting Cacos and torturing peasants became a "sport" for the marines.[32] Cacos were also subjected to bombing campaigns— the first recorded occurrence of coordinated air-ground combat.[33] When labor was compensated, it was at the rate of between twenty and thirty cents per day, and workers were forced to endure long hours and brutalization by cruel US managers. For women and children, the wages were even more abysmal— fifteen cents and ten cents, respectively. These wages were comparable to what Black women made in the Bronx Slave Market and demonstrated how Wall Street imperialism subproletarianized and denigrated Black labor in general, and Black women's labor in particular, wherever it was located. Likewise, similar to the way Angelo Herndon's wages were garnished to pay for goods and services he did not enjoy, a portion of many Haitian workers' wages were deducted to pay the interest on foreign loans—a quotidian form of expropriation.[34]

As in the US South, debt became a tool to immiserate the Haitian people. The ruthless expropriation by Wall Street Imperialists resulted in the Haitian government defaulting on its internal and external debt—something that had never occurred before the occupation. Failure to pay on state and municipal bonds resulted in the complete destitution of numerous families who were formerly wealthy or middle class.[35] As the "father of Harlem Radicalism," Hubert Harrison, explained, the same agents terrorizing Blacks in the US were expropriating Haitians: "In their own land, their civil liberties have been taken way, their governments have been blackjacked and their property stolen. And all this by the 'cracker' statesmanship of 'the South,' without one word of protest from that defunct department, the Congress of the United States!" The "cracker" policy of keeping the "nigger" in its place based on the establishment of the "cracker democracy" of the US South in Haiti linked Wall Street Imperialism at home and abroad; indeed, if the "crackers" of the South were able to expropriate Blacks overseas, then "God help [the] Negroes in America in the years to come!"[36]

This violence, domination, occupation, and total control of Haiti's finances and politics were accompanied by the Black Scare, enunciated through "a paternalistic view of Haitians," "a naturalized sense of Haitian inferiority," the rejection of Haitian "capacity for self-government," and belief in "the necessity of white intervention to guide and guarantee Haitian development."[37] Here too, the Black Scare was inextricably linked to the Red Scare through Wall Street Imperialists' anxieties about radicalism, in the form of revolution, insurgency, protest, rebellion, subversion, nationalization, and rejection of US domination. For example, as was the case for radicals and militants during and after World War I in the United States, there was strict censorship of the Haitian press, with newspapers being prohibited from publishing anything critical of the occupation or the Haitian government.[38]

More generally, the repeated attack on Haiti's sovereignty by imperial powers aiming to reestablish white supremacy there[39] was a manifestation of the disdain for the radical uprising that led to Haitian independence in 1804. The indemnity Haiti was coerced into paying to France on pain of invasion was meant to punish the revolutionary expropriation of private property and the audacity of enslaved Africans to be self-determining and to assert their Black selves as equal to whites. The reversal of San Domingue from the most prosperous colony in the world to an independent Black nation demanded the unrelenting and systematic punishment of its incessant revolutionary movements, threats of revolution, uprisings in the service of revolution, and overall position as a "chronically revolutionary country."[40] This revolutionary spirit was linked to Haiti's purported racial backwardness and civilizational lack.[41] In other words, the entanglements of the Black Scare and the Red Scare were manifested in the belief that not only had "Haiti's development [been] marred by black sovereignty," but "chronic revolution, anarchy, barbarism, and ruin" would reign in Haiti if US Marines withdrew.[42] All modes of radicalism, even (or especially) in the struggle for sovereignty and self-determination, and particularly when accompanied by an uncompensated loss of property or profit by foreign interests, were codified as savagery and backwardness that necessitated white intervention, tutelage, and/or occupation. In effect, the Black Scare and Red Scare undergirding the US occupation of Haiti ensured that US "supervision" amounted to military domination to the end of superexploitation and expropriation.[43]

Wall Street Imperialism in Africa

The Marxist Pan-Africanist George Padmore and the Council on African Affairs leader W. Alphaeus Hunton Jr. linked Wall Street Imperialism in Haiti to that of the nominally free nations in Africa, Ethiopia and Liberia, during the Black Scare / Red Scare Longue Durée. Each of these nations had "intolerable" condition for laborers given internal economic and political organization exacerbated by incessant colonial and imperial encroachments upon their sovereignty. Likewise, these two politically independent nations were linked through powerful racism that made Euro-Americans deeply hostile to them, even as both were enmeshed in the capitalist world-system.[44] The same racist disdain for Black self-government held true for Haiti.

Though Ethiopia was a constitutional monarchy, in 1930 it began to be "drawn into the orbit" of Wall Street Imperialism. Over British objections, a US engineering company secured a contract to build a dam for $25 million largely because the Emperor Haile Selassie I (Ras Tafari) was sympathetic to US capitalists and their desire to industrialize the country. Workers in Ethiopia were "exploited in the worst way" given the feudal order and the reality of domestic slavery. With the cooperation of Selassie, Wall Street Imperialism threatened to facilitate brutal exploitation and expropriation by procuring decades-long leases on large tracts of land, foreign concessions, and slave labor leased by the "Rasses" that would allow the enslaved to eventually purchase their freedom.[45] In 1945, Sinclair Oil Company, a US outfit, secured a fifty-year concession that gave it exclusive and advantageous prospecting rights for fifteen years; at the end of the latter it would maintain a monopoly even as prospecting was opened up to competitors. Relatedly, during and after World War II,

US technical experts began to predominate in government-owned entities, and US advisers worked closely with the emperor on foreign affairs, finance, and commerce.[46] As well, the US military replaced the British in training the Ethiopian army and advising the emperor on military matters. The US also received ninety-nine-year rights to establish a military base.[47] Though some aspects of these agreements appeared to be mutually beneficial, their foundation in Wall Street Imperialism ensured that terms were most favorable to the US government and US corporations and were to the extreme detriment of the Ethiopian masses.

Liberia was the most important site of Wall Street Imperialism in Africa prior to the Second World War since US finance capital had been largely excluded from the rest of the continent by European monopolies.[48] Similar to Haiti, though nominally free, Liberia was a "typical colonial country" that became the site of a "Firestone dictatorship" when, after World War I, the United States needed to compete against the British rubber monopoly. In July 1925, Firestone secured one million acres of land from the Liberian government at the expropriative sum of six cents per acre. The Liberian government was also coerced into taking on a $7 million loan to fund the building of a railway and roads to facilitate Firestone's extraction. To run its large-scale plantations, Firestone, with the aid of the Liberian government, expropriated native land, thereby forcing many to work on the rubber plantations. The government also formed a Labor Bureau that conscripted able-bodied workers for the plantations. Exceeding the terrible superexploitation of workers in Haiti, the US Black Belt, and the Bronx Slave Market, Liberian workers who were actually paid made about three cents a day and worked for fourteen to fifteen hours a day under violent and dehumanizing conditions, while others were forced into literal slavery.[49]

Moreover, not unlike the shipping of Haitian workers to Cuba and Colombia to work under unimaginable conditions during the US occupation, "large contingents of laborers were recruited from indigenous populations and shipped to Fernando Po and French Gabon on conditions scarcely distinguishable from the old methods of slave trading and slave raids." Wall Street Imperialism in Liberia was also manifested in the partnership between Firestone and the US government to ensure that the corporation's support and use of unfree labor was concealed so as not to embarrass either party.[50] By 1941, Wall Street Imperialism in Liberia had become even more entrenched, with 90 percent or more of Liberian exports going to, and more than two-thirds of its important coming from, the United States. Likewise, Liberia's national bank became a subsidiary of the First National City Bank of New York—the same bank at the helm of Haiti's occupation.[51]

Further expropriation was facilitated through the December 13, 1943, Port Construction Agreement: the US agreed to build a port—a project abandoned early on by Firestone given the cost—in exchange for the right to use, maintain, and control naval, air, and military facilities and installations at the port "for the protection of the strategic interests of the United States of America and the South Atlantic." No time limit was specified. The Liberian government would not gain control of the port until the $22 million it cost was repaid; control rested in the hands of Monrovia Port Management Company, which was organized by the US State Department and consisted of seven US corporations: Firestone, Liberia Company, two oil companies, two shipping lines, and a mining company.[52] Wall Street Imperialism's imbrication of the US government and capitalist interests was demonstrated through the port agreement:

> The late Edward R. Stettinius, Jr. a director of U.S. Steel, General Motors, General Electric, Metropolitan Life and other corporations, was Land-Lease Administrator and then Under-Secretary of State during 1943 when the agreement for construction of a port and port works at Monrovia, Liberia, was negotiated and signed. Soon after leaving the post of Secretary of State in 1945, Mr. Stettinius organized the Liberia Co.[53]

Moreover, wide-ranging concessions agreements with US rubber, timber, mineral, and other corporations had enriched the ruling aristocracy of Liberia while impoverishing workers, who were still earning an average of twenty-eight cents a day. When strikes did occur, they were met with machine guns.[54]

Wall Street Imperialism in the Black World and the Disciplining of Marcus Garvey

Wall Street Imperialism in Liberia, Central America, and the Caribbean—underwritten by the Black Scare and the Red Scare—was central to the disciplining, indictment, imprisonment, and ultimate deportation of Marcus Garvey throughout the 1920s. Garvey was central to the "New Negro" spirit of the post–World War I era, taking the lead in igniting worldwide defiance against the lack of Black autonomy due to colonialism and imperialism. As such, the US government targeted him "because they considered all black radicals subversive," and Wall Street Imperialists and European colonialists were hell-bent on stamping out his influence because he threatened the stability of colonial-imperial expropriation.[55] In the context of violent race riots spreading throughout the United States, on the one hand, and the extension of Wall Street Imperialism throughout the Black World, on the other hand, Garvey was branded an agitator and an alien radical. An archetype of the West In-dian genre of Radical Blackness who migrated to the United States during World War I, Garvey was a menace to capitalist racism. His commitment to African liberation and Black self-determination; his organization, UNIA; his Black Nationalist ideology; and his Black Star Line Steamship Corporation—though underfunded and poorly run—posed a quintessential threat to white supremacy, Wall Street Imperialism, and European colonialism. This was enough to subject him and members of his organization to intense Black Scare and Red Scare surveillance and repression.

In 1919, after the governor of the Panama Canal warned about Garvey's attempt to sell stocks in the Black Star Line to "Negroes" in the Canal Zone and the West Indies, J. Edgar Hoover, then the head of the Justice Depart-ment's Alien Radical Division, suggested that deportation proceedings might be pursued against Garvey for "fraud in connection with his Black Star line propaganda."[56] This was after the government had failed to secure enough evidence to deport Garvey as a subversive alien.[57] In keeping with their at-tempt to discipline any assertion of Black self-determination and any chal-lenge to Wall Street Imperialism, in May 1920 the DOJ attempted to block two UNIA members, Hubert Harrison and J. W. H. Eason—who according to a BI letter were "being sent to Africa by Marcus Garvey"—from obtain-ing passports to travel to Liberia to negotiate a settlement plan. Likewise, in 1921, when Garvey toured Central America and the Caribbean to sell Black Star Line stock, Hoover attempted to have Garvey barred from reentering the United States based on "utterances either by word of mouth, or in writing, advocating the overthrow of the Government by force or violence, or urg-ing the unlawful destruction of property." US consulate officials in Kingston, Jamaica, and throughout Central America were ordered by the secretary of state to deny Garvey a reentry visa because of his activities in "political and race agitation."[58] Through the Black and Red Scares, both Garvey's effective-ness in raising race consciousness and promoting Black self-determination and his efforts to build up the Black Star Line Corporation as a means of connecting the Black World outside of Euro-American influence were con-sidered subversive acts against the interests of the US government.

When the claim of subversion alone was not effective, the charge of "fraud" provided cover for the Euro-American officials' disquietude about the disrup-tion Garvey, the UNIA, and *Negro World*, the organization's weekly newspa-per, were inspiring in areas being expropriated by these imperial powers. The British expressed their concern in a February 1924 Colonial Office Report that documented Garvey's endeavor to start a "great Negro State in Africa" and to oust "the white man." These efforts were accompanied by propaganda among Blacks in the United States, the West Indies, and to a lesser extent West Africa, with the intent of developing a sense a nationality among the peoples, which, for the British, amounted to "sowing the seeds of discontent and revolt." Even more subversive was the attempt to organize the masses against "their existing conditions of life." It was further asserted that through *Negro World*, the UNIA deliberately attempted to incite racial antagonism, which was "seditious and revolutionary," and all the more dangerous because it was widely circulated in the West Indies and had to be banned in Nigeria, the Gold Coast, and Gambia. The Colonial Office Report also mentioned the UNIA's efforts to raise money for the Black Star Line to "provide means for transporting negroes from other parts of the world to Africa and for laying the foundation of the commerce of the Negro State." Likewise, despite the UNIA having made "little headway" in the British West African colonies, Garvey had defrauded some "natives" by convincing them to purchase stock in the Black Star Line.[59] The accusation of Garvey "sowing seeds of discontent," encouraging "revolt," and circulating "seditious and revolutionary" materials was quintessential Red Scare language, and, coupled with Black Scare claims of "fomenting racial antagonism," conveyed how Black self-determination menaced imperial expropriation.

Interestingly, in a 1919 report, the British used Liberia as an example of the unlikelihood that "race solidarity" would develop in the Black World because when the "coloured" president of Liberia was asked his opinion about US Black "agitation," he remarked that such matters pertained only to that group and as a Liberian, he was concerned about Liberian politics.[60] Assuming that this was a true representation of his position, and that his position represented that of all Liberians, it was no wonder that once the UNIA showed up on the West African shores to center Black self-determination in Liberian politics, the threat of "race solidarity"—and its potential disruption of Euro-American expropriation—became much more real, threatening, and "revolutionary." In other words, for imperialists, if Liberia had been a potential bulwark against anti-imperial Black solidarity prior to Garvey's arrival, it was a potential hub of it thereafter.

As the 1920s unfolded, the charge of fraud became another tool to criminalize Garvey's attempt to contravene expropriation throughout the African diaspora. As Garvey explained, "They found that ridicule alone would not drive Negroes away from me, nor from the ideal. They added 'villain' to my denunciations in a more spirited and scientifically arranged propaganda against me." Further, "They used the power of Government to intimidate me in my business efforts, started with the purpose of raising the necessary funds with which to execute the plans of real race emancipation."[61] Garvey's

contention is confirmed in the 1919 report, in which the British government
had made no mention of fraud, instead focusing on the danger Garvey's "agitation" might have on increasing race consciousness, connection, and discontent among Blacks in the British colonies.[62]

Representatives of the UNIA approached the Liberian government in
1920 to obtain permission to move its headquarters there; to procure land for
business, agricultural, and industrial projects; and to provide the government
with "financial and moral assistance" in building institutions of higher education and raising the international prestige of the nation "by organizing outside of the country development corporations backed by the entire membership of the UNIA."[63] The association also promised to aid the government in
alleviating its economic plight and servicing its external debts; establish trade
routes between Liberia, the Americas, and the West Indies through the Black
Star Line Corporation; encourage immigration from throughout the Black
World to help develop the country; and provide skilled personnel to build
hospitals and other facilities for the betterment of the local population.[64]
These efforts were initially received favorably by the Liberian government,[65]
which ignited the disfavor of French, British, and Wall Street Imperialists.
As early as 1921, the French and British governments had expressed concern
about UNIA involvement in Liberia[66] not least because both countries had
effectively promised to invade or occupy the country unless the Liberian government quelled "anarchical conditions."[67] The threat was all too real given
that the claim of "chaotic conditions" served as the basis for Wall Street Imperialist occupation of Haiti in 1915. And, like in Haiti, such occupation would
have surely included expropriation and (further) economic domination.
Likewise, prior to the arrival of Firestone, usurious debt-payment arrangements had been established between Liberia and the US government, which
effectively meant "the election of a white [American] king over Liberia" given
the "insulting and humiliating" terms of the loan. Such terms would "be a
great inconvenience to the UNIA" in its establishment of a settlement,[68] while
the UNIA commitment to help Liberia become debt free would hinder US
financial extraction.

In April 1921, the United States gained detailed accounts of the UNIA's
plans in Liberia after a dispute erupted between Cyril A. Crichlow, the secretary to the UNIA commission to Liberia, and Gabriel M. Johnson, who
was the mayor of Liberia's capital city, Monrovia, the president of the UNIA
Monrovia division, and the UNIA potentate. To resolve the issue, Crichlow
had appealed to the US minister in Liberia and turned over numerous documents, including "confidential reports to Garvey, confidential correspondence, Garvey's instructions to him, and the transcript between the Liberian

cabinet and the UNIA." All of these documents were promptly forwarded to the US Department of State,[69] which undoubtedly gave more urgency—and ammunition—to the US government's claims that Garvey was an alien subversive and agitator and to their efforts to criminalize, incarcerate, and ultimately deport him. Indeed, the US government's investigation hit paydirt less than six months after the Liberia documents had been received and only two months after Garvey's return from the West Indies. After a memorandum from a confidential informant to J. Edgar Hoover stipulated that Garvey planned to publish a false advertisement in *Negro World* to secure more Black Star Line stock purchases, the BI began their effort to prosecute Garvey for violating postal regulations.[70]

As is the case with imperialism anywhere, Wall Street Imperialism in Liberia would not have been possible without the consent and collaboration of the country's petit bourgeois class, which controlled the government. Thus, over time, the US government's hostility to Garvey influenced, and was matched by, the Liberian political oligarchy, which increasingly began to see the UNIA settlement scheme as a challenge to its authority—and the ability to accumulate wealth that came with its support of Wall Street Imperialism. Elie Garcia, who had been sent to Liberia in April 1920 to appraise the government's response to the UNIA's colonization plans, levied a vehement critique of the America-Liberian political class in private correspondence with Garvey. For starters, he found the political leadership to be "*the most despicable element in Liberia.*"[71] He wrote:

> Dishonesty is prevalent. To any man that can read and write, there is but one goal: a government office, *where he can graft*. . . . The Liberian politicians understand clearly that they are degenerated and weak morally and they know that if any of number of honest Negroes with brains, energy, and experience come to Liberia and are permitted to take part in the ruling of the nation they will be absorbed and ousted in a [very] short time.[72]

He went on to warn, "the Liberians are opposed to any element which may be instrumental in bringing to [*an*] end *their political tyranny, their habits of graft and their polygamic freedom.*"[73] While the UNIA threatened to end such rule, Wall Street Imperialism was keen to preserve it insofar as it was precisely this class that facilitated their expropriation. Liberia's secretary of state was already showing his government's imperialist allegiance, telling the British consul that Garvey's schemes would not be endorsed and that President Charles Dunbar Burgess King was already taking steps to put an end to the UNIA's "unauthorized and unwarranted exploitation of Liberia."[74] It was the ruling elite, especially the king—"the favorite of the U.S. State Department"—that had entered into predatory loan agreements with the US government and facilitated Firestone's and other corporations' domination of Liberia, so this class balked at the "revolutionary purposes of the UNIA in Liberia."[75] While Garvey sought to "standardize the wages of the black race and dignify the social life of the people," *Negro World* claimed, the Liberian political elite sought to exploit and subject the people to enrich themselves and the "unreasonable" machinations of capitalist racism in Africa.[76]

Despite a downturn in Liberian colonization efforts due to Garvey's arrest, trial, and brief incarceration between 1922 and 1923, by 1924 plans were made to build four "colonies" in Liberia, the first on the Cavalla River, where a group of civil and mechanical engineers had already started preparing for the first "batch of colonists" from New York.[77] On August 5, Garvey was rearrested on perjury charges regarding his income tax from 1921. On the very same day, the Liberian secretary of state ordered the consul in the United States to withhold visas from Garveyites, claiming that Garvey's proposed settlement would "supplant the constitutional regime of President King of Liberia."[78] Such language was strikingly similar to that levied at communists and other radicals—that their very presence and beliefs portended the overthrow of the government. The Liberian government instructed its consuls to "make public declarations that would prevent the immigration of black Americans to Liberia under the auspices of the UNIA."[79] On August 25, Liberia's secretary of state Edwin Barclay stated the government was "irrevocably opposed both in principle and in fact" to the UNIA settlement plan given that it could adversely affect the country's foreign relations. Barclay also encouraged US government efforts to prohibit UNIA-influenced Black emigration to Liberia.[80]

Though Garvey and the UNIA blamed the Liberian government's seeming about-face on W. E. B. Du Bois and the NAACP,[81] they also aptly noted that the "hypocrisy and double-crossing" of the Liberian political elite began shortly after they had conceded one million acres of land to Firestone.[82] In December 1923, with the support of the US government, Donald A. Ross had arrived in Liberia on behalf of Firestone to investigate the possibility of establishing a rubber plantation, since its plans in the Philippines had failed. After Ross discovered that the "growth, yield, and latex quality" of trees on an abandoned British plantation would be ideal, Firestone began negotiations with the Liberian government.[83] In August 1925, Secretary Barclay welcomed Firestone and celebrated the corporation's million-acre concession and access to cheap laborers. He also stated plainly that Garvey, his followers, and anyone associated with them would be turned away from Liberia. Unfortunately for Garvey and the UNIA, the Liberian government had not only enriched itself on, but had also encouraged, Wall Street Imperialism "by putting [it] in the rubber-producing field,"[84] which not only stymied Garvey's colonization efforts, but also aided in his persecution by the US government.

It is important to note that, despite Garvey's hostility to communism, and communists' distaste for him because he supposedly "successfully kept the Black workers from them,"[85] the Black Scare and the Red Scare construed his rejection of Wall Street Imperialism and European colonialism and commitment to Black self-determination as open advocacy of Bolshevism. The mutual disdain between the UNIA and the communists/socialists did not protect Garvey because his anti-imperialism and popularity among the workers were seen as either inspired by, in league with, or of the same type as that of the communists/socialists. Similarly, the cooperation of Black communists/socialists like Cyril Briggs, A. Philip Randolph, Chandler Owen, and Hubert Harrison (a former UNIA leader) with the US government in its efforts to deport Garvey did not save them from government repression because their belief in the empowerment of Black workers to upend capitalist racism and promotion of Black self-determination made them subversives.

Such resonance between the UNIA and the communists was manifested in a signed press release titled "Importance of Organization of Negroes" issued by the Workers (Communist) Party of America protesting the attack on Garvey and the UNIA by the US government. Despite their misgivings about Garvey, they castigated this repression because of the effect it "was having on the morale of the negro workers."[86] After pointing out the Structural Location of Blackness, the letter argued that the Black movement would play an instrumental part in the "world-struggle against capitalist-imperialism." Black liberation in the US, the statement held, was linked to the anti-imperialist struggles of West Indians and Africans as well as "the awakening" of the masses of China and India.[87] Likewise, the increasing attunement of US Black people to internationalism was manifested in the efforts to strengthen Liberia and to win independence for the whole of Africa—efforts in which the UNIA had played a "confused" but major role.

This internationalism and rejection of Wall Street Imperialism and European colonialism, the Workers (Communist) Party of America asserted, was the source of the government's vehement attack on the UNIA and the efforts of US, British, and French authorities to outlaw it on African soil. In fact, the Liberian president had openly admitted "obligation to the great powers" was central to the UNIA's banishment, and land concessions initially promised to the UNIA were "given to a big American corporation (the Firestone Tire Co.), thru the machinations of an American diplomatic minister at the same moment the United States government made its final assault to break up the [UNIA]." This two-pronged attack represented Wall Street Imperialism's determination to penetrate and plunder the African continent just as it had done to Haiti, Puerto Rico, and the Virgin Islands, among other localities.[88] Insofar as the party was committed to working-class solidarity, it could not support the efforts of the "capitalist dictatorship" to eviscerate "a mass organization of the exploited Negro people" or to deny the Black masses the right to organize.[89]

The statement called on all workers to protest the persecution of the UNIA, to demand the immediate and unconditional release of Marcus Garvey, to cease efforts to deport Garvey, and to end the financial terrorism against the association by the courts and the law. These demands were linked to the struggle to keep the "bloody hand" of Wall Street Imperialism from "strangl[ing] the African people" and to cultivate the full, free, and unimpeded "intercourse of American Negroes with their brothers of the African continent."[90] Such convergence of purpose was central to the government's Black Scare and Red Scare construal of these antagonistic factions as two sides of the same coin that menaced Wall Street Imperialism in and beyond the United States.

In the final analysis, Garvey's promotion of Black self-determination, challenge to Wall Street Imperialism in Liberia, and excoriation of Euro-American expropriation of the African continent, made all-the-more dangerous by his ability to garner financial support for the Black Star Line from Black workers everywhere, propelled the US government's Black Scare and Red Scare construction of him as a radical agitator, an alien subversive, and an undercover Bolshevik, and aided in its rabid attack on him under the auspices of fraud.

Wall Street Imperialism against African Liberation

The expropriation of Africa through Wall Street Imperialism reached new heights during and after World War II. The United States used the Second World War to establish military bases throughout the continent and to develop unequal trade relationships. Between 1938 and 1948 its trade with the continent rose from $150 million to $1.2 billion.[91] After the war, "Africa offered the best outlet for billions of dollars in surplus capital [and] the best new source for a rich variety of strategic war materials," and Marshall Plan money was used to facilitate Wall Street Imperialist penetration there.[92] The US invested in mines and other colonial enterprises with the ultimate aim of wresting control of them from their European partners: "the prospecting for new mineral deposits, the railroad expansion, and the new harbor facilities financed by the United States were designed to pave the way primarily for

American private investment."[93] These projects sought to intensify the exploitation of Africans and to accelerate the expropriation of resources.[94] American "big business" planned to move into Africa to invest surplus capital and gain massive profit "with the help of guns from the United States, arsenal of world imperialism" by engaging in a campaign of violent repression against Africans to postpone their independence.[95] In effect, the pervasive penetration of US capital into Africa was a gross negation of the state's purported anticolonialism because the presence of US corporations was accompanied by abysmal wages from twenty cents to one dollar per day and by strong support for the most brutal colonial regimes whose oppression facilitated expropriation.[96]

Agitation for African liberation and self-determination was rooted in anti-imperialist demands including "democracy, political power and independence; for the return of land robbed from the Africans; for an end to the profiteering and strangle-hold of the monopolies; for a decent living wage and better living standards; for the right to manage and develop their country for their own benefit."[97] As the Radical Black Pan-Africanist Eslanda Goode Robeson explained, this was because "the people of Africa, like those of Asia, [did] not want their land staked out for foreign military bases, drained by foreign investment projects or dug up for raw materials for foreigners to take away and use for themselves in other lands. They want[ed] to plan and build and run things for themselves [and would] ask for outside help if and when and how they need[ed] and want[ed] it."[98] The Black Scare and the Red Scare used this clamor for self-determination, especially as it became more organized and intense over time, to legitimate the use of force as "even the native capitalists compromised as they [were] by imperialism, utilize[d] every weakening of the foreign grip, every distraction which temporarily remove[d] the master's military force, to push their own enterprises and limit the loot of the imperialists."

In turn, US militarism backing Wall Street Imperialism "me[t] with serious resistance, and some setbacks even in the Western hemisphere."[99] During the early Cold War, the Black Scare and Red Scare in Africa heightened in direct proportion to the amplification of the call for independence and rejection of Wall Street Imperialism, on the one hand, and as the battle between capitalism and socialism heated up, on the other hand. Hunton elucidated,

> We and the Africans were told that a Soviet military invasion threatened the continent, and that an insidious campaign of Communist subversion and propaganda was under way to stir up riot and insurrection. . . . But it seems we were misinformed. The "enemy" came . . . offering trade deals and technical

know-how. . . . This offer of economic assistance was also a threat to Africa and the "free world," we were informed . . . the price of such Communist aid was a "rope around the neck." . . . It seem[ed] more likely that what worrie[d] Washington [was] not so much the interests of the prospective recipients of Soviet aid as its *own* interests. What it fear[ed] [was] the weakening or loss of its *exclusive* controlling influence in the countries concerned; it fear[ed] giving these countries the chance to make choices and decisions on their own. . . . [Such position] reflect[ed] the attitude . . . of one talking about inferior people who *can't know* which way to go but must be pulled this way or that.[100]

Here, it was believed that Africans' inferiority rendered their independence a liability because they were either uniquely susceptible to communist influence or they could not be trusted to make the "correct" decision to align with anticommunism of their own volition. Indeed, as Goode Robeson analyzed, a general pattern accompanied all struggles against expropriation and for liberation.

There is always the beating of drums and the calling to arms, the name-calling, the flood of pious declarations of peaceful intentions, the "benefits" of civilization by the oppressors, who scream about the evil intentions, the savagery and backwardness, the troublemaking, disloyalty, subversiveness and sedition of the people who insist upon equal rights, self-government, human rights, an end to oppression, and payment for services rendered.

In this general pattern there is always the jailing and exile and persecution of the freedom leaders, the confiscation of their lands and resources, the use of real force and violence—the army, navy, air force. There is always the attack upon the freedom organizations, the banning of the publications, the forbidding of public meetings, the threats and the terror.[101]

Thus, the Black Scare and Red Scare were simply harnessed to colonial discourse aimed at illegitimating African demands for self-determination over and against Wall Street Imperialism.

A report prepared by US vice president Richard M. Nixon entitled "The Emergence of Africa" encapsulated how the Black Scare and the Red Scare were used to legitimate Wall Street Imperialism in Africa. Nixon acknowledged that Africa was growing increasingly important to the future of the United States and the Free World, so developing relations there needed to be assigned a higher priority.[102] He noted that one of the impediments to that was "the skillful propaganda . . . [of] enemies of freedom" about the treatment of minority races in the United States. African leaders had a "false impression" of racial prejudice in the belly of the beast that resulted in "irreparable damage to the cause of freedom which [was] at stake."[103] Nixon recommended that the administration get at the root of the problem by ensuring "orderly progress" toward the eradication of discrimination in the US, and doing a more effective job of "telling the true story" of the progress that was being made toward that end.[104]

"Orderly progress" was rooted in the Black Scare because it ensured the continued superexploitation of Black people based on the logic that too much freedom would be dangerous to the capitalist racist status quo. While such gradualism "may [have been] attractive to academicians, politicians, statisticians, it [was] a good deal less so" for African descendants suffering under the yoke of Wall Street Imperialism and capitalist racism given their genocidal reality.[105] William Patterson underscored that the "bankrupt and immoral theory of gradualism" could only lead to "infamy and death,"[106] while Paul Robeson added that it was simply "another form of race discrimination" that afforded "lawbreakers" infinite time "to comply with the provision of law."[107] Nixon's statement was also rooted in the Red Scare because he raised the issue of racial prejudice and discrimination not because Black people deserved equality and dignity, but because the communists could use these issues as "skillful propaganda" to hinder the expansion of Wall Street Imperialism in Africa. The primary concern was the transnational reach of communism, and US racism was a liability for US efforts to gain a foothold in the parts of the world that were agitating for independence.

Nixon asserted that Africa was a prime target of the international communist movement, which was presenting itself as the true champion of independence, equality, and economic development. The United States was obligated, then, to assist these countries in maintaining their independence—from the Soviet Union, that is, not the West—and to eradicate conditions of "want and instability" specifically because they bred communism or sympathy to it. For Nixon, African independence wasn't important on its own terms, but rather to ensure the strength and stability of the "Free World," which needed to take every step to mitigate the (communist) "danger" Africa faced.[108] Nixon used the Red Scare to link African alliance with communist countries with the circumscription of their sovereignty and the destabilization of the "Free World"—that is, the United States and its allies. This was the same logic that sutured Black struggles for self-determination in US Capitalist Racist Society to outside agitation, foreign inspiration, and communist conspiracy. The implication was that, for the US government, African/Black self-determination was an invitation for communist intrigue that contravened US interests. As such, international cooperation between communists and Africans came to be viewed as dangerous precisely because it threatened to upend Wall Street Imperialism on the continent, the ability of the West to accumulate, and thus the latter's safety and stability. This rationalized a policy aimed at the containment of communism, on the one hand, and intervention into African politics and economics, on the other.

On this Black Scare and Red Scare logic, the entrance of African countries into the international community of nations required extensive surveillance and control because if they went in the wrong direction, US national security could be in jeopardy. Nixon reasoned that one way to ensure that Africans wouldn't be seduced by radicalism was to "familiarize" them with the culture, technology, ideals, aspirations, traditions, and institutions of the "American character." Africans could be brought to the United States for study and travel so that these potential enemies could be scrutinized, on the one hand, and "educated" into being reliable allies, on the other hand.[109] His promotion of cultural imperialism underscored the Black Scare and Red Scare assumption that Africans could only resist communism and other forms of radicalism by taking up American methods of organizing their state and society.

*

Expropriation of the Black World, from Haiti to Liberia, strengthened Wall Street imperialism throughout the Black Scare / Red Scare Longue Durée. As such, Black self-determination and African liberation had to be undermined, and Radical Blacks like Marcus Garvey who promoted it, punished. During the early Cold War, Africa in particular was of geostrategic importance to Wall Street Imperialism, so the United States had to ensure that the only foreign influence on the continent was its own. Black Scare and Red Scare logic dictated that African independence could be supported only when appended to concerns about US security and stability, which provided cover for ongoing expropriation and exogenous control. The latter was inextricable from US war, warmongering, and militarism, cornerstones of US Capitalist Racist Society that sustained, supported, and generated revenue for Wall Street Imperialism and helped to compel consent for Black Scare and Red Scare repression.

6

War, Wall Street Imperialism, and (Inter-)National Accumulation

> The War in Europe is a war of the white race wherein the stakes of the conflict are the titles to possessions of the lands and destines of his colored majority in Asia, Africa, and the islands of the sea.
>
> HUBERT HARRISON, 1917

War, warmongering, and militarism were the backbone of Wall Street Imperialism nationally and internationally and helped to externalize the Black Scare and the Red Scare. The Spanish-American War of 1898 allowed the United States to redivide the world to gain a larger portion of its markets and profit. The nascent global hegemon wrested direct control of the Philippines and Puerto Rico, indirect control of Cuba, and Central and South America as its sphere of influence. It also gained strategic domination of the Caribbean and naval power in the Pacific through the expansion of its military base apparatus. As these racialized peoples resisted Wall Street Imperialism, the United States launched armed intervention and wars of conquest and pacification in countries including Mexico, Haiti, Panama, Colombia, the Dominican Republic, Honduras, and China. In these acts of aggression, the US military effectively functioned as an armed force "for Big Business, for Wall Street, and for the bankers."[1] Wall Street Imperialism connected the subjugation of the Philippines, Puerto Rico, and Cuba and the reduction of Latin America to an appendage of US economic exploitation to the Structural Location of Blackness through the consolidation of segregation laws and disenfranchisement in the South. The very same people who brutalized the darker nations abroad to extract land, labor, and resources terrorized Black people in the belly of the beast for the same purpose. White supremacy, for example, was codified in the *Plessy vs. Ferguson* Supreme Court decision just two years before Wall Street Imperialism took off in the Pacific, with the court proclaiming that "if one race be inferior to the other socially, the Constitution of the United States cannot put them upon the same plane."[2] This idea of white superiority was the justification for the military conquest that accompanied capitalist racist accumulation.

Wall Street Imperialism continually expanded through hot and cold war, including the two world wars, the Korean War, and the Cold War. The United States entered both world wars in an advantageous position—after other combatants were exhausted from fighting and as the primary supplier of their armaments. In effect, the diametric reality of war—US enrichment and the devastation of other imperialist countries—was the central factor in the economic, financial, and military power of Wall Street Imperialism.[3] As the Great War raged, for example, "the Caribbean Sea region transformed into an American lake," and by the end of the war, the US dominated this region, the Canal Zone, and the Virgin Islands, with Haiti, the Dominican Republic, Cuba, and Nicaragua operating as protectorates.[4] Wall Street became the financial center after World War I, and the United States was consolidated as "the decisive holder of the purse strings, with the London bankers not only subordinate, but themselves dependent on New York." Similarly, World War II reversed trends in foreign investment in favor of the United States, and by the end of the war the imperialist positions of Germany, Japan, and Italy had been completely eliminated.[5] By 1949, US private foreign investments exceeded the combined investments of all other imperialists powers.[6] Moreover, the United States had developed overwhelmingly superior military power among capitalist countries.[7]

War, Warmongering, and Wall Street Imperialism

War, warmongering, and militarism went hand in hand with Wall Street Imperialism inasmuch as economic power provided the basis for military domination, while political and economic diplomacy were successful when backed by the threat or reality of military invasion.[8] In turn, both were in lockstep with the Black and Red Scares. The Espionage Act of 1917 and the Sedition Act of 1918 helped to codify this link by widely construing interference with "foreign commerce" as promotion of the success of its enemies and making this a punishable offense—hence, the conflation of sabotage and treason.[9] In particular, the 1918 Sedition Act made synonymous the obstruction of the sale of bonds or securities or the ability of the US to make loans during wartime; "urg[ing], incit[ing], or advocat[ing]" the curtailment of production of goods necessary to the prosecution of war to cripple or hinder the waging of war; willfully "uterr[ing], print[ing], writ[ing], or publish[ing] any disloyal, profane, scurrilous, or abusive language about the form of government of the United States" or the Constitution, flag, military or naval forces or their uniforms and inciting, provoking, or encouraging resistance to the United States; and promoting the cause or displaying the flag of its enemies.

The interchangeability of interfering with the government's financial and production aims, critiquing the government, and showing support for a hostile government aided in the punishment, under the rubric of sedition, of challenges to economic exploitation in its manifold forms, racial discrimination and oppression as it related to wartime industry, or war itself as a tool of capitalism and imperialism. The provision that the Sedition Act should operate for the "better enforce[ment of] the criminal laws of the United States" and, vaguely, "for other purposes," supported this broad application.[10]

During World War I, the IWW suffered the Red Scare vitriol of the US federal government given the connections it drew between war and imperialism. The organization understood that imperialist wars enriched powerful businesses and the ruling class while working people sacrificed their lives.[11] The position of the IWW was that wars by nation-states violated the internationalism upon which socialism was predicated and that the only sanctioned war was class war.[12] The government targeted the IWW despite the fact that during WWI "as a precautionary measure, the IWW ceased calling for anti-militarist actions . . . [though] it did not endorse the government's war efforts."[13] As would be the case during the anticommunist Smith Act trials starting in 1948, the indictment of IWW leaders was based solely on writings and ideas. One such idea was sabotage.

According to the lifelong radical Elizabeth Gurley Flynn's 1915 pamphlet *Sabotage*, "Sabotage means either to slacken up and interfere with the quantity, or to botch in your skill and interfere with the quality of capitalist production so as to give poor service. It is something that is fought out within the walls of the shop. Sabotage is not physical violence; sabotage is an internal industrial process. It is simply another form of coercion."[14] The IWW had supported sabotage as a tactic of asserting workers' power, and its writings "were used [by the US government] to affirm that the Wobblies had advocated violence and clandestine action for years. Moreover, the anti-militarist stances of the organization, albeit prior to April 6, 1917, allowed the enemies of the IWW to accuse it of obstructing the war effort."[15] The targeting of the IWW under the Espionage Act based on antiwar, anti-imperialist, and anticapitalist ideas expressed *before* US entrance into WWI conveyed how, in US Capitalist Racist Society, radicalism transformed individuals and organizations into perpetual enemies. The IWW was accused of abetting German sabotage prior to the United States' entrance into the war, not unlike the accusation that Black outmigration from the South sat at the intersection of German influence and Black disloyalty. Both the IWW and Blacks were construed as potential saboteurs, and thus traitors[16]—and IWW support of interracial unionizing and the improvement of Black labor conditions confirmed this connection. This signifying chain allowed "sabotage" to apply both to impeding capitalist production and to contravening the racial order. During World War I, both forms of "sabotage" became "synonymous with subversive and clandestine acts in the service of a foreign power."[17]

Ironically, Wobblies did the opposite of obstructing and sabotaging US war efforts. In fact, the IWW's predominately Black Local 8, under the leadership of Ben Fletcher, encouraged support for the Allied war effort and voted not to strike for its duration. Nonetheless, government repression engulfed the IWW shortly after the passage of the Espionage Act. Fletcher was targeted for his prominence in the organization and was deemed a "tremendous" threat.[18] Likewise, according to the *Messenger*, Fletcher's "unremitting fight in the class war" was inextricably linked to his willingness to "sin against the sacred creed and dogma of imperialism."[19] "Fletcher's unwavering class-consciousness, commitment to industrial organization and opposition to imperialism made him" not only "an ideal leader of the New Negroes,"[20] but also a prime target of the US government. Fletcher and his IWW codefendants were indicted for conspiring to prevent, hinder, and delay the execution of the war against "Imperial" Germany; hindering citizens from supplying the US with war munitions, supplies, and transportation; encouraging persons to defy the draft and causing disloyalty in the military and naval services; and using the mails in an attempt to defraud employers of labor.

The charge of defrauding employers of labor can be interpreted to have Black Scare implications in Fletcher's case. His success in recruiting and organizing Black dockworkers, getting them pay equal to whites, and leading successful strikes meant that he was hampering the ability of owners to extract superprofits from Black workers, an effectively criminal act in US Capitalist Racist Society. It didn't matter that Fletcher had ceased such activity during the war; his interracial labor militancy—or sabotage of the racial order—was enough to render him subversive and guilty. As Fletcher saw it, "No genuine attempt by Organized Labor to wrest any worthwhile and lasting concessions from the Employing class can succeed as long as organized Labor for the most part is indifferent and in opposition to the fate of Negro Labor."[21] If organizing Black labor and improving their material conditions, both domestically and abroad, was a means of "wresting concessions"—or defrauding employers in the parlance of the US government—then this action fell under the purview of the 1917 and 1918 acts. So too did the simultaneous fight against Black disenfranchisement in the South.[22] Relatedly, if Black loyalty meant loyalty to the "employer class," that is, the Wall Street Imperialists, then Black labor militancy was inherently disloyal and an impediment to the wartime effort.

To stem the tide of Black labor radicalism encouraged by the IWW, "an alliance of big business, government, and conservative labor officials set out to take advantage of the wartime hysteria to overwhelm and destroy the IWW." Its "crime" was actively organizing the exploited and superexploited, especially Black workers who had been ignored and excluded by other labor organizations like the American Federation of Labor. Cutting into the profit of employers by rendering ineffective their battle-tested tactic of sowing antagonism between Black and white workers could be construed as disloyal and traitorous given the broad scope of the 1917 and 1918 acts.[23] Likewise, the Black Scare and the Red Scare meant that Fletcher, an influential Radical Black leader of the Outside Agitator variety who organized some of the most important workers during the war, was the literal embodiment of conspiracy.[24]

We Charge Genocide deftly made the connection between warmongering and Wall Street Imperialism and explicated how, historically, war and the threat of war intensified Black Scare violence and Red Scare silencing of the American people generally, and proponents of peace particularly. The petition gathered evidence of anti-Black genocide from 1945 onward that "gain[ed] in deadliness and in number of cases almost in direct ratio to the surge towards [the Korean] war."[25] The drafters noted that in times of war or threat of war—which were virtually ongoing given its active role in facilitating accumulation in US Capitalist Racist Society—violence against Black people intensified, especially when they agitated for rights and equality. This was because their struggle undermined the idea that "all iniquity" rested with the enemies of the United States, so "the very presence of the Negro people in the United States" was "an indictment and exposure that evoked hatred against them."[26]

One example of such hatred was the murder of Black war veterans by civilians and police. Denice Harris in Atlanta, Georgia, in 1945; St. Clair Pressley in Johnsonville, South Carolina, in 1945; Roland T. Price in Rochester, New York, in 1947; Isaiah Nixon in Montgomery County, Georgia, in 1948; Otis Newsom in Wilson, North Carolina, in 1948; Herman Burns in Los Angeles, California, in 1948; James Perry in Saint Louis, Missouri, in 1949; and Eugene Jones in West Bank, Louisiana, in 1949 were all slain on the basis of race despite—and because of—their service.[27] Such violence against Black servicemen who "exposed the fictions cutting through the narrative of white supremacy"[28] was a repeat of what transpired after World War I; Black veterans faced physical and economic lynching, anti-Black racial oppression, and a flurry of race riots that peaked in the Red Summer of 1919.[29]

The intersection of the Red Scare and war "increased oppression throughout America" and eased the ability of the ruling class to superexploit, expropriate, and dispossess.[30] In the Korean War context of *We Charge Geno-cide*, its drafters analyzed that the increased terror against African Americans could be accounted for by the Cold War and the drive to another world war, and that this, in turn, was the basis for aggression in Korea. "The jelly bombs dropped in Korea," the petition argued, "prove[d] that racism is an export commodity to be forced upon colored peoples."[31] The fate of the superexploited in the United States was thus the fate of mankind because "the continuance of this American crime against the Negro people of the United States [would] strengthen those reactionary American forces driving towards World War III." Further, "White supremacy at home [made] for colored massacres aboard" since both were predicated on utter disdain for racialized life. As well, "The lyncher and the atom bomber [were] related. The first cannot murder unpunished and unrebuked without so encouraging the latter," with the intimate link between the two being "economic profit and political control."[32] In "Genocide Stalks the USA," Paul Robeson wrote that, as the petition was being finalized, a delegation of the Women's International Democratic Federation witnessed in Korea "how the American government was practicing genocide against a colored people struggling for their independence." The women's report and *We Charge Genocide* needed to be understood together, he argued, because the subjection of Black Americans and the massacre of Koreans were twin functions of Wall Street Imperialism and its will to war.[33]

W. E. B. Du Bois made a similar connection that brought together US domestic and foreign policy. He reasoned that the use of fear by "powerful interests in the United States" to rationalize armament and aggression had particularly detrimental consequences on the racialized, the colonized, and the working class. Through perpetual war, the ruling class extracted cheap land and labor from Africa, Asia, Russia, and the Balkans; weakened organized labor power in the US and Europe to increase private profit; and continued corporate control in Latin America and the Caribbean.[34] Additionally, Wall Street Imperialism meant increasing war expenditures, training young men "for murder," and overshadowing any possibility for peace with the threat of nuclear war. It also linked seemingly disparate forms of US aggression, including the oppression and hyperincarceration of US Black folks, denial of human rights to the oppressed throughout the world, intervention in the Korean Civil War, exclusion of China from the United Nations, occupation of the Philippines, and violent slander of the Soviet Union and communism as the source of all international problems.[35] In Du Bois's estimation, the only remedy to Wall Street Imperialism was to "cease fire now. Bring back our troops . . . dismantle our costly forts that encircle the world. Stop our aid to

empires trying to conquer colonial peoples struggle desperately to be free. . . .
Cut our impossible tax burden, house our people, educate our children and
declare a world policy of peace on earth, goodwill toward men."[36] The Korean
delegation to the 1953 World Congress of Women concurred that only an end
to the Korean War could stave off the senseless death and condemnation of
American sons, and "only peace can insure the freedom of nations and the
security of homes."[37]

Wall Street Imperialism and the Threat of Peace

War and Wall Street Imperialism were also intimately linked through the
disciplining of peace activism and objection to war. Protesting the war, like
Black militancy, was thought to be antithetical to US interests and therefore
seditious. Many promoters of peace were surveilled, jailed, or exiled. Radical Black peace activists were considered particularly prone to subversion
because historically, the injustice, racism, and oppression inherent in war
tended to inspire Black opposition. Additionally, when Black people did support the United States in international conflicts, their stance was contingent
upon an assessment of whether it had the potential to improve their lived
conditions.[38] Dating back to World War I, such calculations were considered
rank opportunism that amounted to disloyalty.[39]

Radical Blacks who promoted peace and freedom were also considered
disloyal because they critiqued how US foreign policy used the discourse of
democracy to dominate racialized folks the world over. The early Cold War
was characterized by vehement repression of peace activism for two reasons:
first, because peace was an essential component of USSR propaganda, and,
second, because international peace activism linked US militarism and warmongering to capitalist racism and Wall Street Imperialism. As such, it challenged the hegemony of the United States as the arbiter of freedom, democracy, and equality. Official US discourse construed mobilization for peace and
progress as support for a communist plot to undermine the United States.
Officials also contended that communists were using the language of peace
to hoodwink, exploit, and confuse Americans. Peace activism, according to
this logic, was not only dangerous and subversive, but was also another example of Black peoples' susceptibility to exogenous forms of manipulation and
trickery that illuminated their inferiority and legitimated their subjection.

We Charge Genocide linked the persecution of W. E. B. Du Bois for his peace
activism to the inscription of war in Wall Street Imperialism. "The majority of
Negroes are for peace," the petition explained, "and peace endangers profits."

As such, the "venerable" Du Bois, "elder statesman of the Negro people," had been indicted for his peace advocacy because his position "endanger[ed] the profits from war."[40] The petition noted that Du Bois was targeted because he understood that Wall Street Imperialism not only imposed its economic agenda through war, but also used it to disenfranchise Blacks, abet illegal mob violence against Black people when they did attempt to vote, and control the government to draft and sustain racist laws and policies aimed at subjugating Black people.[41] Peace promoted "the growing awareness that the fight against anti-Negro genocide and anti-democratic drives against the entire people [was] one struggle" particularly because "frame-up" techniques perfected through the Black Scare were extended through the Red Scare to repress political minorities and militant labor leaders. This made the struggle against genocide, war, and repression a common struggle.[42] This dragnet of repression fell under Article II (b) of the Genocide Convention, "Causing Serious Bodily and Mental Harm to Members of the Group."[43]

According to Du Bois, since World War I, the United States had become a land "approaching universal military service" with armed forces on every continent and sea. Uncle Sam had demonstrated its commitment to control the masses domestically and abroad, to control the beliefs of nations throughout the world, and to spend on these aims "more money than it ever spent for religion, education or social uplift altogether." And, by the end of the World War II, the United States stood out as the supreme warmonger, increasingly preparing for war, forcing other nations to fight, and compelling Americans to choose impoverishment and to sacrifice for and sanction a "Jim-Crow army." All of this devastation was on behalf of a suicidal drive for another world war "that nobody want[ed] but the rich Americans who profit[ed] by it."[44] To this Du Bois added that the Korean War was a product of a unilateral executive decision to start "a little police action" so that big business could interfere with the governments of Asia.[45]

The US had caught the imperial fever at the end of the nineteenth century, Du Bois continued, and its small but significant territorial gains through military conquest inexorably entangled Wall Street Imperialism and the will to war. During World War I, it rushed to grab the spoils of European imperialism with so little concern for the effects that the whole industrial system was brought down temporarily less than two decades later.[46] But not even the Great Depression deterred the United States and its big business rulers from war despite the fact that Wall Street Imperialism and its inscription in monopoly capitalism "had [met] a terrible and costly reverse."[47] Those who owned the earth, industry, and the press, continued the drive for profit by waging a Red Scare fight on "ideas" through "organizing war, murder and destruction on people who dare[d] to try to plan plenty for all mankind." The US did so by becoming the hegemonic imperialist nation and bribing workers and thinkers in rich countries with comparatively high wages and privileges to "build a false and dishonest prosperity on the slavery and degradation, the low wage and disease, of Africa and Asia and the islands of the sea."[48]

As the undisputed leader of the capitalist world-system after World War II, the United States was reproducing "the African roots of war" that undergirded imperialist rivalry in the Great War. In 1915, Du Bois argued that the German-British imperialist rivalry for the booty on offer in Africa drove the conflict. "With the waning possibility of Big Fortune . . . at home, arose more magnificently the dream of exploitation abroad," and white labor also sought to share in the "golden stream" of racialized expropriation. This "democratic despotism" allowed for the white working class to "share the spoil of exploiting 'chinks and niggers,'" which implicated not simply the ruling class but "the nation; a new democratic nation composed of united capital and labor"[49] that perpetuated war and imperialism through cross-class collaboration. Du Bois noted that the disrespect and dehumanization of the racialized toilers and peasants in the plundered colonies mitigated the exploitation and impoverishment of the white working class in imperial countries. This superexploitation allowed white workers to get a share, however pitiful, of "wealth, power, and luxury . . . on a scale the world never saw before"[50] and to benefit from the "new wealth" accumulated from the "darker nations of the world" through cross-class consent "for governance by white folk and economic subjection to them"—a consensus solidified through the doctrine of "the natural inferiority of most men to the few."[51]

Consistent with his argument against Wall Street Imperialism, Du Bois argued, "The domination of one people by another without the other's consent, be they subject people black or white, must stop. The doctrine of forcible economic expansion over subject peoples must go."[52] Similarly, under Wall Street Imperialism, the price to be paid for abundance derived from the superexploitation of the colonized world was endless war against "the Idea—against the rising demand of the working classes of the world for better wages, decent housing, regular employment, medical service and schools for all."[53] The ultimate beneficiaries were corporations and investors who owned a large portion of mines in South Africa worked by slave labor, who extracted large profits from Rhodesian copper, and who "sought to dominate China, India, Korea, and Burma."[54]

Here, Du Bois offered a color line–specific analysis parallel to Lenin's "aristocracy of labor" thesis. The latter arose "when the economic circumstances of capitalism ma[de] it possible to grant significant concessions to the proletariat, within which certain strata manage, by means of their special scarcity, skill, strategic position, organizational strength, etc., to establish notably better conditions for themselves than the rest."[55] Drawing on Friedrich Engels's analysis of an "aristocracy among the working class" in England, Lenin argued that in the age of monopoly finance capitalism, there was a "labour aristocracy" in every imperialist country that was bought off by the financial oligarchy that was simultaneously "oppressing, crushing, ruining and torturing the *mass* of the proletariat and semi-proletariat." Like Du Bois, Lenin maintained that this bribery was possible because a handful of powerful countries were parasites that sustained themselves through "the exploitation of Negroes, Indians, etc. keeping them in subjection with the aid of the excellent weapons of extermination provided by modern militarism." However, the labor aristocracy was not sustainable for long because of imperialist wars over division of spoils and because of the struggle of workers who bore the brunt of imperialist wars to overthrow the ruling class.[56]

Also akin to Du Bois's position, Lenin argued that the working class in oppressor nations received "crumbs from the *superprofits*" obtained by the ruling class through the superexploitation of workers in oppressed nations and rose to the "labor aristocracy" and became "straw bosses" in much larger percentages than toilers in oppressed nations. Workers in imperial countries were also politically privileged vis-à-vis those in oppressed nations and were ideologically trained to feel disdain and contempt for "lesser" workers.[57] Ultimately, Lenin held that in the "advanced"—or imperialist—countries the labor aristocracy of industrial workers betrayed the mission of "emancipating mankind from the yoke of capital and from wars" by narrowly focusing on their craft, trade interests, and petty bourgeois material conditions. Such workers had betrayed socialism and were "petty-bourgeois chauvinists and agents of the bourgeoisie within the working-class movement."[58]

Some contemporary Marxist scholars contend the labor aristocracy was, and is, a myth because, among other things, superprofits were not extracted from the colonized world, racialized workers were not superexploited, comparatively higher wages paid to a particular class of workers did not make them more reactionary, and in fact these workers tended to be at the forefront of mass worker uprisings.[59] However, the similar analyses of Du Bois and Lenin on the subject, especially as they relate to the role of war, remain compelling. Ultimately, the role of war in maintaining Wall Street and other imperialisms and in ensuring superprofits rendered peace a crime against US Capitalist Racist Society.

The Black Scare, the Red Scare, and the Punishment of Peace Activism

Wall Street Imperialism and warmongering were entangled with the Black Scare and the Red Scare because when peace was advocated, "every effort is made by secret police, organized spies and hired informers; by deliberate subversion of the fundamental principles of our law, to imprison, slander, and silence such persons and deprive them of earnings and an honest livelihood."[60] The only way to avoid such repression, Du Bois explained in the context of the early Cold War, was to perpetuate the Red Scare—to vow to hate Russia, to oppose socialism and communism, to declare wholehearted support for the Korean War, to advocate endless expenditure on war, to promise to fight any nation the US deemed a threat, to support the use of the atomic bomb and weapons of mass destruction and regard those who oppose them traitors, and to denounce and report on anyone who did not believe these things.[61]

The Black Scare was also instrumental in that freedom for Black people was not possible as long as the United States was committed to fighting, destroying, and killing all around the world to secure enormous profit for big business—and struggle against such commitments were deemed subversive.[62] As *We Charge Genocide* put forth, "Political and economic freedom for the Negro people means increased freedom for the whole American people and the beginnings of a 'political platform' that 'threatens the integrity' of anti-democratic monopoly rule. It also threatens the integrity of super-profits," which were the foundation of anti-Black genocide.[63] War was the means by which Blacks' violent domestic reality would become a global reality if such practices were allowed to persist. Petitioners therefore pushed "not only for an end of the crime of genocide against the Negro of the United States," but also for peace.[64]

Du Bois's peace activism was punished as an anti-American, foreign-inspired threat to national security attributable to the communist "peace offensive" not least because he linked global conflict, armament, and nuclear proliferation with Wall Street Imperialism and capitalist racism and argued that progress and justice could only be realized through international cooperation and peaceful coexistence. The Red Scare constructed counterhegemonic peace activism that was congruent with the Soviet Union's conceptualization of peace and international cooperation as particularly un-American, with the House Committee on Un-American Activities (popularly known as the House Un-American Activities Committee, or HUAC), for example, arguing that "the Communist 'peace' drive [was] . . . calculate[d] to develop a feeling of false security among [Americans] so that the Red military machine c[ould] strike whenever and wherever it please[d]"; thus, "Communist declarations of peace and friendship . . . [aimed] to sap American morale and secure converts to treason."[65] Internationalist peace efforts not only accompanied the spread of communism, but also directly contravened the United States' drive to amass nuclear weapons, police the international system, and neutralize hostility and opposition.

The achievement of radical conceptualizations of peace and progress would undoubtedly endanger US leadership of the world-system since the "military-industrial complex" and defense industries had become essential to Wall Street Imperialist accumulation.[66] Likewise, peace would make it exceedingly difficult for the United States to control dissent directed against capitalist racism. Given this reality, HUAC regarded advocates of disarmament as supporters of communism and the Soviet Union, using as an example the "terrible strikes that delayed U.S. rearmament" during the Molotov-Ribbentrop Pact of 1939–41.[67] As was the case with the prosecution of the IWW during the Great War, to be antiwar, antiaggression, and anti-imperial was to be a threat to national security, and therefore to be un-American. Moreover, the type of peace to which Du Bois and the drafters of *We Charge Genocide* were committed challenged Wall Street Imperialism because peace was the basis of international solidarity and the end of all forms of racialized exploitation. The association of a durable peace with solidarity among oppressed peoples and the socialist reorganization of society challenged the hegemony of the United States as the dominant global political and economic authority. Peace and international cooperation also threatened to hold the United States accountable for its racist, antidemocratic, repressive, and genocidal practices against Black Americans and other minoritized peoples.

In the United States' conception, peace was inseparable from Wall Street Imperialism. It meant a combination of military strength, capitalist prosperity, and the defense of "freedom" and the free market through armament, nuclear buildup, and anti-Soviet aggression. Red Scare logic meant that peace hinged on the eradication of the purported totalitarianism and expansionism of the Soviet Union and containment of the "communist-inspired" radicalization of racialized and colonized populations. Thus, peace became conflated with "anti-communist stability" that was contingent upon a strong military and long-term heightened tensions among the public.[68] Peace became achievable only through willingness and readiness for war. It was in this hostile environment that Du Bois's peace advocacy was violently contested. The US government all but criminalized antiwar activism that dovetailed with USSR policy and practice, listing a number of organizations dedicated to worldwide peace solidarity—including the Du Bois–led Peace Information Center (PIC)— as subversive, communist, and/or communist fronts.[69]

Du Bois was arrested in 1951. His acceptance of the vice chairmanship of the Council on African Affairs (at the request of Paul Robeson); his push for cooperation with the Soviet Union; and his support for the 1948 Progressive Party presidential candidacy of Henry Wallace underscored his peace activism as subversive and dangerous. He began to consistently argue that war undermined rationality, goodwill, and collaboration; that violence and aggression would not resolve differences in ideology; and that war and respect for civil rights were irreconcilable.[70] Furthermore, he rejected the US position on peace because it was entangled with Red Scare repression of civil liberties, Black Scare violation of civil rights, and Wall Street Imperialist abuse of weaker nations.[71] The DOJ filed charges to determine whether the PIC and its octogenarian leader used peace advocacy to act as an agent of a foreign political organization or power, specifically the World Committee of the Defenders of Peace (later the World Peace Council). According to the Attorney General's List of Subversive Organizations, the latter was a communist front. Du Bois was susceptible to US retribution because, despite the hostile environment, he was extremely effective in his antiwar organizing.[72] Along with his wife, Shirley Graham Du Bois, he influenced Americans "from California to Massachusetts" to join the peace cause.[73] He and Paul Robeson, through the Council on African Affairs, were also able to garner international support for peace, especially in Africa and throughout the African diaspora. Moreover, Du Bois provided a critical link between Black and Euro-American antiwar activists by helping to cultivate Black opposition to the Korean War.[74]

The PIC drew the ire of the US government for its circulation of the Stockholm Peace Appeal, also known as the "Ban the Bomb Petition."[75] Circulating the appeal ostensibly made Du Bois an agent of a foreign nation because, according to HUAC, it was a "smoke screen" for communist aggression against South Korea.[76] Because the appeal had the support of the Soviet Union, HUAC conceived of it as an instrument of communist subversion instead of as a genuine demand for the restoration of peaceful cooperation. In reality, the Stockholm Peace Appeal emerged out of an international mass movement that called for the outlawing of atomic weapons, international controls to enforce the measures, and the treatment of any countries that use atomic bombs as war criminals that had committed crimes against humanity.[77] By July 13, 1950, the Ban the Bomb Petition had received over 1.5 million signatures from forty states.[78] Ultimately more than 2.5 million Americans signed it, notwithstanding the fact that many who did were criticized, arrested, physically attacked, and fired from their jobs.

Du Bois's own civil liberties were severely curtailed, and his civil rights were violated in a number of ways, including the denial of a permit by the mayor of New York to hold a peace rally—the first time this had occurred in 150 years.[79] Likewise, his passport was revoked. Despite the slanderous campaign against it, the appeal may have been signed by more people than any other appeal in the history of the United States.[80] The US government saw it as a threat precisely because of the overwhelming international response to it: there were ten million signatories in France, sixty million in China, 115 million in the Soviet Union, and 3.75 million in Brazil.[81] This international coalition posed an enormous challenge to the US administration that had come to understand its prosperity, defense, and security as tied to sustained militarism.

Secretary of State Dean Acheson called the Stockholm Peace Appeal a "propaganda trick in the spurious 'peace offensive' of the Soviet Union."[82] HUAC accused it of condemning the United States to national suicide, and of attempting to confuse and divide Americans.[83] It was maligned as a ploy to undermine resistance to communist aggression, the first step of USSR infiltration and invasion, and a "hoax and fraud" meant to manipulate those "hungry for peace." Thus, for circulating the appeal, Du Bois was accused of committing something akin to treason on behalf of the Soviet Union.[84] By labeling it as communist inspired, the United States attempted to discredit it to legitimate the use of nuclear weapons and aggression, to prevent dissent, and to suppress the international movement for peace.

Du Bois replied to the gross misrepresentation of the Ban the Bomb Petition, and of peace activism more broadly, by arguing that opposition to the appeal, the PIC, and organizations like it was predicated on the lie that they were part of the Soviet peace offensive. This represented the "standard reaction" in US Capitalist Racist Society to demonize challenges to the status quo as communist, and thereby subversive and unpatriotic. This tactic, he argued, had gone too far.[85] In fact, the *actual* threat to stability, tranquility, and prosperity was the United States' disingenuous insistence "that the existence of Socialist and Communist states are in themselves reasons for fear and aggression."[86] US aversion to the Stockholm Peace Appeal revealed that the purported protector of freedom and democracy in reality lacked commitment to peace, real understanding of the horrors and ravages of war, and empathy for those who were impoverished and devastated by such dehumanizing aggression.[87] It was therefore US Capitalist Racist Society, not communism, socialism, internationalism, or even the Soviet Union, that undermined peace and cooperation.

Du Bois was indicted under the Foreign Agent Registration Act of 1938 for operating as an "unregistered foreign agent" and for failing to register the PIC.[88] The DOJ also filed charges against PIC members Kyrle Elkin, Elizabeth

Moos, Abbott Simon, and Sylvia Soloff. Soloff was let go on the last day of the trial, as the judge declared that she was wrongfully indicted because she was never a PIC officer.[89] The DOJ sought to determine "whether or not this organization acted as an agent or in a capacity similar to that of a foreign organization or a foreign political power."[90] Employing Red Scare tactics, the FBI interrogated members that had attended even one PIC meeting, and many were subpoenaed for the trial. The organization was in existence only from April 3 to October 12, 1950, but the trial proceeded even though it had disbanded.[91]

The prosecution used Red Scare rhetoric, the Korean War, and hysteria about the Soviet Union to discredit peace activism. It called as its star witness Oetje John Rogge, a former assistant attorney general and founding member of the PIC. Interestingly, it was Rogge who had invited Du Bois to a conference that aimed to better US-USSR relations, and it was Rogge's home at which the PIC was formed. In his testimony, he claimed that the objective of the PIC was not peace, but rather to enact USSR foreign policy. The turncoat also argued that the purpose of the World Committee of the Defenders of Peace, for which the PIC was alleged to be an agent, was to focus international attention on the United States' use of the atomic bomb to distract the world from Soviet aggression in Korea. Yet in August 1950, Rogge had signed a petition pledging his support to the World Committee and its peace program, and stating that he was one of the first signers of the Stockholm Peace Appeal.[92] The government intended to use this testimony to paint the PIC with the taint of a "Russian and Communist controversy" so that "current popular hysteria could be aroused against [Du Bois and the PIC]."[93]

The PIC was acquitted of all charges on November 20, 1951.[94] The judge announced that the government had failed to support the allegations of the indictment, and that the only way to move forward would be through conjecture as opposed to the conception of law. Despite the acquittal, Elizabeth Moos pointed out that the defendants lost nine months of their lives, peace of mind, and over $35,000. Du Bois lamented, "It had not occurred to us how costly justice in the United States is. It is not enough to be innocent in order to escape punishment. You must have money and a lot of it."[95] Moreover, the defendants had been subjected to Red Scare indignities, harassments, slanderous publicity, and the cloud of criminality, which severely impeded their ability to continue the fight for social justice.[96]

✶

A decade after the acquittal, Du Bois would permanently relocate to Accra, Ghana—after joining the CPUSA—as life in US Capitalist Racist Society proved to be too much to endure for a Radical Black nonagenarian. In doing so, he rejected a society that harnessed the Black Scare and the Red Scare to the extraction of superprofit from the Structural Location of Blackness; the targeting of Radical Blackness—especially its enunciation through the West Indian, Outside Agitator, and Red Black / Black Red—as an existential threat; the malignment and repression of Black self-determination in its manifold forms; the violent expropriation of the African diaspora to shore up capitalist racist accumulation; and the perpetuation of war, warmongering, and militarism to sustain Wall Street Imperialism.

To further explore US Capitalist Racist Society and its internal logic of Wall Street Imperialism during the Black Scare / Red Scare Longue Durée, part 2 takes up anticommunism as a mode of governance; the role of the executive, legislative, and judicial branches of the federal government and state governments in such governance; True Americanism as "legitimating architecture"; and the Countersubversive Political Tradition that gives the society its fascistic character.

PART II

Black Scare / Red Scare Codification: Governance and Legitimating Architecture

7

Theorizing Anticommunism as a Mode of Governance

> Today, with the increasing ascendancy of the world socialist system, imperialism merges with anti-Communism and racism even more closely in its efforts to stave off extinction.
>
> HENRY WINSTON, 1974

More than a political culture, a set of foreign policy concerns, or a brief period of hysteria fomented and flamed by demagogic right-wing politicians and business leaders, anticommunism was a durable mode of governing US Capitalist Racist Society during the Black Scare / Red Scare Longue Durée. Such governance served to manage and criminalize racial and political "others" whose ideas and beliefs, as much as actions, threatened to transform the racialized class order. Anticommunism worked through and with white supremacy to encourage cross-class collaboration that obfuscated economic exploitation and discouraged interracial class solidarity. It operationalized an expansive dragnet that effectively converted the Black Scare and the Red Scare into bills of attainder[1] and forms of licensing[2] to discipline radical challenge and circumvent the empowerment of the most oppressed and exploited groups. It also called into question who was deserving of, and who could be denied, rights and liberties based on beliefs, and thus provided a powerful check on freedom of speech, freedom of the press, freedom of assembly, freedom of association, due process, and protection against self-incrimination. Additionally, anticommunism was maintained through repressive action, intentional inaction, and stifling reaction.

Codifying Anticommunism: State- and Local-Level Governance

Though anticommunist governance at the federal level had the most wide-reaching effects, US states and municipalities passed "innumerable repressive statutes, regulations and ordinances which deal[t] more harshly than the federal government with political dissent and democratic rights." State-level antiradical laws cropped up after the failure to pass national anti-syndicalism and peacetime sedition bills. One reason these bills did not come into fruition was because some senators feared they would give the US government jurisdiction over the crime of lynching. State and municipal laws thus complemented and worked with federal bodies to maintain anticommunism in the face of constraints on the federal legislative branch.[3] The federal government overwhelmingly backed state-level anticommunism. For example, Attorney General A. Mitchell Palmer championed antiradical legislation since none had been enacted by Congress despite his requests and even though there were more than seventy bills before Congress in 1919 alone to criminalize "sedition and seditious utterances and publications . . . whether by an individual or by two or more in conspiracy." He argued that, given their "law-enforcing machinery," the states, at the time, had more power than the federal government to detect and punish sedition. He singled out New York City as being especially effective with its "12,000 policemen, all of who are charged with the duty of investigation" and its "force of over 50 prosecuting attorneys."[4] Palmer held that without federal peacetime legislation to "prevent the dissemination of radical publications by means of which it [was] sought to create a social and industrial revolution and forcibly overthrow the Government of the United States and establish, if possible, a so-called dictatorship of the proletariat,"[5] it was up to the states to do so. As such, the state-level anticommunist offensive picked up after World War I and took off in the 1920s.

Throughout the Black Scare / Red Scare Longue Durée, states required public employees to adhere to mainstream political opinion and barred from employment "dissenters of all kinds." These laws were spurred by the world war, the Russian Revolution, "unsettled conditions" after the war, and unrest caused by the Great Depression. Between 1917 and 1923, twenty-five states enacted anti-syndicalism laws especially in response to the perceived threat of the IWW and Bolshevism in the United States. These laws variously sought to guard against the overthrow by force, violence, injury to person or property, or general strike, of the government; disloyalty or belief in anarchy or other dangerous political doctrines; defiance of the law in relation to the disruption of organized government; inciting people to disorder or breaches of law; and the display of any symbol that supported or promoted Bolshevism, anarchy, or radical socialism. Washington State's anti-syndicalism law is representative in its concern with "any organized or unorganized group of persons who, by their laws, rules, declarations, doctrines, creeds, purposes, practices, or effects, espouse, propose or advocate any theory, principle, or form of government antagonistic to, or subversive of, the constitution, its mandates, or laws of the United States and of this state." Often, even ownership of any paraphernalia that demonstrated such commitments was considered to be criminal, pernicious, and perilous to the public.[6]

In Southern states like Arkansas, laws against "radicals and foreign languages" were particularly aimed at the IWW and other organizations that engaged in interracial labor agitation.[7] By 1939, there were red-flag laws in thirty-one states, criminal syndicalism laws in eighteen states, and anarchy and sedition laws in twenty-six states. Likewise, three Southern states maintained old insurrection and sedition laws—like that used against Angelo Herndon in Georgia—which could only be applied to radical groups. In addition, twenty-one states required loyalty oaths for teachers, and four states had laws barring from the ballot parties or candidates that advocated the overthrow of the government by force or violence or that carried on a program of sedition or treason—meaning communist/socialist parties.[8] In typical fashion,[9] Texas took these laws to the extreme by imposing the death penalty for communists.[10] All told, antiradical legislation of some kind was found in forty-two states; of these, criminal anti-syndicalism laws—largely in place to eradicate the IWW—were the most extreme.[11]

The states combined discourses of insurrection, subversion, "foreign inspired," and disloyalty to beat back worker militancy, Black agitation, and the influence of socialism/communism and other forms of radicalism that could be construed as such. Contrary to the idea that anticommunist crusades were a "laughingstock" or were merely the pursuit of fringe groups and political zealots, anticommunism was an invaluable tool used by state governments to legislate against challenges to US Capitalist Racist Society—and to make ample use of the Black Scare and the Red Scare in the process.[12] State-level antiradical campaigns after World War I, for example, were buttressed by widespread sentiment that the labor unrest resulting from postwar economic conditions was in fact caused by Bolshevik agitation. This misconception helped to hasten the shift from hatred of Germans to hatred of communists, Bolsheviks, and the Soviet Union. Likewise, business associations throughout the country denounced Bolshevism as a danger and menace that needed to be crushed.[13] It was at this time that "the word 'red' came to signify anyone who did not consider the present organization of society as ideal, and became part of [the] national vocabulary."[14]

The New York State Legislature helped to pioneer state-level anticommunism by convening the Lusk Committee, headed by Senator Clayton R. Lusk, in March 1919. Its mission was to investigate radicalism and sedition and to stave off a Bolshevik revolution in the state. The latter was a top priority because Bolshevism was said to be rampant there, especially in New York City, the "Red headquarters."[15] The bipartisan committee was dominated by Archibald E. Stevenson, the assistant counsel who took the lead in directing its activities. Stevenson had a long history of hostility toward radicalism, serving as chairman of the Committee on Aliens, which was part of the Committee on National Defense convened by New York City's mayor. In 1917, he assisted the DOJ in investigating German propaganda and supervised the Military Intelligence Division's indexing of persons who were suspected of harboring pro-German sentiments. On January 21, 1919, he testified before the Overman Committee—the 1919 subcommittee of the US Senate Judiciary Committee that firmly established Germanism and Bolshevism as overlapping forms of subversion—denouncing Bolshevism and pacifism and accusing twenty-six citizens of holding dangerous anarchistic positions.[16] Similarly, as part of the Lusk Committee, Stevenson aimed to save US institutions from foreign philosophy, to disrupt the "very real" plot to violently overthrow the republic, to limit the extension of democracy to industrial management, to prove that socialism and the Socialist Party were foreign and un-American, and to ensure uncritical acceptance of the status quo.[17]

Following Stevenson's lead, the Lusk Committee's massive *Revolutionary Radicalism* report argued that there was no substantive difference between anarchists, socialists, communists, pacifists, and Wobblies. They all purportedly followed the doctrines of the "International Socialist Movement" emanating from the German Revolution of 1848, the ideas of Karl Marx, and the *Communist Manifesto*. The "Third Communist International, founded at Moscow" was but a continuation of those dynamics.[18] Through their propaganda and organizations, these subversives sought to "develop agitators to enter the labor fields, to preach the doctrine of revolt, and to divide the people of the United States into contending classes . . . [to] haste[n] the social revolution."[19] To combat this influence, the Lusk Committee insisted upon leadership in the government and civil society that recognized the urgent need for religious and moral standards and the "American ideals of individual freedom and initiative" to be "the basis of any political and economic program."[20] The implication was that anyone who defied these principles was unfit for leadership, opposed the United States, and ultimately abetted the spread of dangerous and subversive ideas and actions.

Given that the "communist menace" in New York was but a microcosm of the ostensible national threat, on the one hand, and the collaborative nature of anticommunism as a mode of governance, on the other hand, the Lusk Committee worked closely with the BI, procuring aid in conducting investigations and sharing its findings. Additionally, it cooperated with similar bodies in other states, as well as with the DOJ and immigration authorities. The

Lusk Committee provided these bodies with "much valuable information" that had resulted in a large number of deportations and prosecutions.[21] The Lusk Committee and its report thus set the tone for state-level investigations of seditious, subversive, un-American, and insurrectionist activities, in the same way that New York's April 3, 1902, Criminal Anarchy Statute— perhaps the earliest law to criminalize political dissent—modeled the forms of antiradical legislation that would be passed in numerous states following World War I.

As part of its investigation, the committee "procured a number of search warrants against various organizations that were found to be the centers and sources of radical revolutionary propaganda," raided these organizations in a coordinated fashion, seized "revolutionary, incendiary, and seditious written and printed matter," and collected information about the leaders and members of the organizations. They also focused on procuring information about how radical organizations were financed.[22] The purpose of this tactic was not to make arrests, but rather to secure evidence to be turned over to prosecutors for later indictments.[23] The Lusk Committee thus institutionalized foundational technologies of anticommunist repression, not least the conflation of ideas with actions as it related to charges of subversion and revolutionary activity; the establishment of guilt by association in construing as subversive those who had simply received literature from or donated to a targeted organization; the practice of gathering the names and addresses of leaders and members with the intent of indicting them for conspiracy; punishment for belonging to a communist or socialist organization; and imprisonment and deportation for possessing radical literature. The Lusk Committee also modeled a number of techniques of criminalization that would be used by committees like HUAC and the Subversive Activities Control Board (SACB), such as charging witnesses with contempt for declining to answer questions or refusing to disclose the identity of donors to their organization.[24]

It is also noteworthy that, like future state-level and federal countersubversive committees, the Lusk Committee proceeded without any real knowledge of the "enemies" they targeted. This imprecision allowed for blanket charges and maximum repression. One member who resigned from the committee explained that he joined it out of anti-Bolshevik principles, but he immediately became ashamed of himself and others who invested his colleagues with any authority. He claimed that the committee lacked any knowledge or in-depth study of the issues, none were acquainted with the works of Karl Marx and others they deemed dangerous, and their knowledge of political economy was drawn from a few pamphlets and articles. Despite being unskilled and ill-prepared, they nonetheless aimed to combat "such a mighty economic influence as Bolshevism!" He insisted that these ignorant investigators, uniformed committees, and brutish methods would actually encourage the type of popular resentment of which agitators took advantage instead of deterring it.[25]

✶

The Lusk Committee helped to imbricate the Black Scare and the Red Scare as a function of anticommunist governance by emphasizing how radical organizations like the Rand School of Social Science intended to "arm the negroes in the South for bloody revolution."[26] Here, *Revolutionary Radicalism* converged with Attorney General Palmer's November 17, 1919, report to the Senate that included "Radicalism and Sedition among the Negroes as Reflected in Their Publications."[27] "Practically all of the radical organizations in this country," Palmer warned, "have looked upon the Negroes as particularly fertile ground for the spreading of their doctrines. These radical organizations have endeavored to enlist Negroes on their side, and in many respects have been successful."[28] Both the Lusk Committee and Palmer effectively asserted a "Red Scare analysis of the race problem" by positioning Black self-defense, demands for equality, and criticism of the war and the current racial order as evidence that Blacks were embracing Bolshevism and that communism was the culprit "of much of the racial trouble in the United States at the present time."[29] The inclusion of a warning about US Blacks in reports that otherwise largely focused on foreign influence helped to convey Blacks as the most dangerous "others from within," which legitimated casting them out and keeping them down. This antiradical white supremacy[30] helped to conflate militant Blacks, Bolsheviks, Wobblies, and other radicals as indistinct vectors of subversion that could only be subdued through rigorous defense—legal, discursive, and if necessary, physical—of the capitalist racist status quo.

The hefty "Propaganda" subsection of *Revolutionary Radicalism*, almost four hundred pages in length, included a specific chapter on "Propaganda among Negroes"—the only chapter dedicated to a single race or ethnic group. The effort of radicals and revolutionaries to reach African descendants with their propaganda was "the most interesting as well as one of the most important" because it was an appeal to those who had "just cause of complaint"[31] based on their history and experience of oppression, superexploitation, exclusion, violence, and racial terrorism. New York was an important site for examining the spread of radicalism among Black people because opportunities for industrial employment had drawn them in large numbers from the South and from the West Indies. It was argued that while Blacks were treated well in New York, they nonetheless possessed a natural "spirit of resentment" on which "agents and agitators" from radical organizations like the Socialist Party and the IWW capitalized by emphasizing their poor treatment in other parts of the country. On this logic, it was not discrimination and subjection that merited concern, but rather "the marked increase of the activities of radicals in trying to recruit negro followers" to "stimulate race hatred" and to "engender so-called class consciousness in their ranks." In US Capitalist Racist Society, where the Structural Location of Blackness rendered racial hierarchy inextricable from class hierarchy, "race hatred" among Black people was assumed to be a natural outcome of "class consciousness," with race hatred understood as illegitimate Black animus toward whites. This "antipathy" constituted all manner of militant fightback against white supremacy, including opposition to discrimination, belief in racial equality, advocacy of self-defense, and self-assertion rooted in race pride. Both race hatred and class consciousness were machinations of radicals to stir up trouble against which "loyal and thoughtful negroes" needed to organize, and their entwinement placed Radical Blacks of all genres, "nigger lovers," and fellow travelers under the purview of anticommunist governance.[32]

The "Propaganda" subsection contained, in addition, a chapter on newspapers and periodicals and asserted that "the publications from which quotations [were] drawn [were] either frankly revolutionary and seditious, or those which show[ed] an apologetic attitude toward all subversive movements."[33] It included articles about the Negro Question in the periodicals *Novy Mir*, the *One Big Union Monthly*, the *Weekly Industrial Worker*, *Russky Golos*, and *Liberator* to illuminate "the various arguments used to appeal to various classes of society." The implication was that, as an exceptionally vulnerable or susceptible "class of society" that was intentionally targeted by radical elements, Blacks were a natural and necessary focal point of anticommunist governance. Relatedly, the Rand School was singled out because of its relationship with editors of the Black socialist publication the *Messenger*, and because two of the editors, A. Phillip Randolph and Chandler Owen, instructed and lectured at the school. This conveyed to the Lusk Committee that the school "lost no opportunity for preaching the doctrine of class hatred in every conceivable direction," and showed "the existence of an active propaganda among negroes."[34]

However, Randolph, Owen, and the *Messenger*, according to *Revolutionary Radicalism*, were dangerous in their own right given their devotion to internationalism and class struggle, "distinctly revolutionary" politics, commitment to the principles of the Soviet Union, and efforts to organize Blacks for class struggle.[35] An editorial entitled "Thanksgiving" was said to epitomize the spirit of the editors. It thanked the Russian, German, Hungarian, and

Bulgarian revolutions; expressed appreciation for world unrest and labor solidarity; celebrated strikes that had spread throughout the US and especially
the nation's first successful general strike in Seattle, Washington; and cheered
the "oncoming of the new order of society" brought about by the sleeping giant, labor.³⁶ Worse than this, the editorial praised the influence of the "New
Crowd Negro" in every field, "economic, political, social, educational and
physical force." The New Crowd Negro was firmly rooted in socialist politics;
defended his home, life, and family; and upheld "the dignity of the law against
both white hoodlums and the government." The New Crowd Negro—equal
parts Outside Agitator, West Indian, and Red Black / Black Red—had also
eclipsed the influence of "the Old Crowd Negro and white leaders" and was
popular with the masses throughout the world.³⁷ The ascent of the New Negro
was confirmed by the conservative Monroe Work, who asserted in the *Negro
Year Book*:

> Although lacking the personal contact with whites which the old Negro had,
> the new Negro, on the other hand, has developed an individual independence
> and also a confidence in himself, in the race, in race enterprises, and in racial
> understandings which the "old Negro" never had. He has a knowledge of what
> other Negroes are thinking and doing. Self-defense is another characteristic
> which the new Negro has developed.³⁸

The Lusk Committee further contended that the *Messenger* was infecting the
sentiment of white "intellectual liberals" and was fanning the flames of social
unrest.³⁹ Given this unapologetic Radical Blackness and unsavory interracialism, the publication, its editors, its doctrines, and its principles were paramount targets of anticommunist governance.

   Even though a substantial portion of the "Radicalism and Sedition" appendix of the attorney general's letter was likewise devoted to raising the alarm
about the *Messenger*,⁴⁰ it was noted that "no amount of mere quotation could
serve as a full estimate of the evil scope attained by the Messenger."⁴¹ It was
accused of being openly defiant and seditious for, inter alia, its advocacy of a
New Negro rising, its support of the IWW as "the only labor organization in
the United States which draws no race or color line," its advocacy of the general strike, its promotion of physical and economic force to stop lynching, and
its reporting of the reprehensible treatment suffered by Black soldiers.⁴² It was
also deemed noteworthy that the periodical took pride in self-defense, openly
supported "sex equality," and reflected the "wide-spread, if not universal, feeling among the negroes that the negro soldiers punished at Houston, Tex., were
foully murdered by the Army authorities."⁴³ "Radicalism and Sedition" conveyed that anticommunist governance existed to crush enunciations of Radi-

cal Blackness like the *Messenger* because the magazine's insolence, promotion of the "jargon of the ultraradical foreign-born agitator," and of exhibition of the true characteristic of the "Negro type" in its "emotional abandon" was not simply a menace to New York, but to the nation as a whole.[44]

Reading *Revolutionary Radicalism*, the *Attorney General's Report*, and "Radicalism and Sedition" together illuminates how anticommunism as a mode of governance imbricated state-level and federal efforts to construct, control, and condemn forms of unrest and opposition that contravened US Capitalist Racist Society.

Public Authority

At the national level, anticommunism as a mode of governance administered by all three branches of the federal government, fused "public authority" and "societal self-regulation"[45] to penalize, regulate, censure, and criminalize ideas and beliefs that challenged US racial oppression, economic inequality, and class antagonism by labeling them "communist."

Public authority manifested in, inter alia, legislation, court rulings, presidential executive orders, security initiatives by government agencies, and a deluge of federal and state congressional committees. US congressional committees conducted more than 135 antiradical investigations between 1945 and 1955 alone. Investigations prior to 1948 primarily focused on domestic targets like New Deal personnel and agencies and militant labor leaders, while later ones aimed at espionage, subversion, and the ostensible presence of communists in government.[46] Irrespective of the focus, the Black Scare ensured that views on racial equality were used to gauge potential subversion. Each branch of government contributed to the constitution and maintenance of anticommunism. Executive branch entities included the State Department, the Justice Department, the BI/FBI, and presidential initiatives like Executive Order 9835 of 1947 (the "Loyalty Order"), Executive Order 10450, which superseded it in 1953, and the Attorney General's List of Subversive Organizations. The US Supreme Court's role was twofold. It handed down decisions at either end of the Black Scare / Red Scare Longue Durée, including *Schneck v. United States* (1919), *Debs v. United States* (1919), and *Abrams v. United States* (1919), and *American Communications Association v. Douds* (1950) and *Dennis v. United States* (1951). It also refused to rule on particular cases that would ensure the civil rights and liberties of the central victims of anticommunist governance. The legislative branch was perhaps the most active when it came to anticommunist governance, with highly visible participation through congressional committees including the Overman Subcommittee of the Committee on the

Judiciary, the House Un-American Activities Committee (HUAC), the Subversive Activities Control Board (SACB), and the Senate Internal Security Subcommittee (SISS). It also passed a cacophony of legislation, not least the Espionage Act (1917) and the Sedition Act (1918), the Foreign Agents Registration Act (1938), the Act to Prevent Pernicious Political Activities (1939), the Anti-Propaganda Act (1940), the Alien Registration Act (1940), the Labor Management Relations Act (1947), the Internal Security Act of 1950, and the Communist Control Act (1954).[47]

Altogether, this public authority aimed to neutralize, penalize, and outlaw communists, "fellow travelers," and "sympathizers"—broad designations that included "peace activists, civil rights leaders, dissident artists[,] progressive labor organizers of all types,"[48] and manifold others who offered progressive political, economic, and social challenges to US Capitalist Racist Society. Irrespective of which branch of government was dominant at a given moment, and despite the balance between federal regulation and "states' rights," anticommunism institutionalized legal bindingness, sanctions and material regulation, fixed norms, and hierarchical and centralized authority. This authority was complemented by and shared with "big business," which combined force and "soft law" methods of anticommunist rule.[49]

Anticommunism included orders, directives, and legal decisions alongside recommendations, opinions, jurisprudence, and declarations in a mode of governance that might be characterized as a "framework of regulation" in the realm of binding law that was both flexible and coercive.[50] It also encompassed politics, policy, and polity.[51] Anticommunist politics took "place within interorganizational networks characterized by interdependence and resource exchange"[52] between a constellation of actors, the most important of which were federal, state, and local governments; corporations and private firms; and civil society. Anticommunist policy constituted "a system of rules that shape[d] the actions of social actors"[53] through a nexus of hierarchies with capitalist, elite, white, and Americanism at the top and socialism/communism, labor, Blackness, and radicalism at the bottom and on the constitutive outside. Anticommunist polity combined coercion and the manufacturing of consent through "different types of more or less heavy-handed instruments in order to achieve certain societal outcomes: command and control, incentive and supply, information, deliberation and persuasion, as well as all forms of social influence and control."[54]

In effect, anticommunism represented a failure or refusal to contend dynamically with the political and revolutionary realities and expectations confronting the twentieth century, emanating from two world wars and numerous revolutions. As such, it imposed a uniformity on an array of left-wing ideas, ideologies, and practices—reduced to the designation communism—

positioning them as preeminent threats to US national security and societal organization. Such governance encouraged an "international strategy . . . of military containment and rollback."[55] Domestic strategy included repressive opposition to transformative change and imposition of adherence to the status quo, which normalized Black Scare and Red Scare attacks on even reformist ideas and policies like an antilynching bill or the New Deal. Importantly, anticommunism also erased any substantive distinction between acts, intentions, and ideas[56] when the charge was disloyalty, subversion, or sedition.

Societal Self-Regulation

In addition to public authority, anticommunist governance operated through "societal self-regulation," or soft power, insofar as the existence of antiradical laws and censures casted "a shadow far beyond their literal reach," leaving a large swath of the population in fear that their thoughts, beliefs, and opinions would result in disciplining given an atmosphere that had been "poisoned" by the passage of such laws.[57] As Eslanda Goode Robeson noted, anticommunist crusades in the United States undermined progressive struggles, not least the struggle for racial justice, since citizens were plagued by "fear of losing one's job, home, education" and "fear of non-conforming, or of even being accused of non-conforming."[58] In other words, the soft power of anticommunism meant that racially and politically minoritized persons were forced to genuflect to the status quo lest they be exiled, excluded, criminalized, physically attacked, or worse. Likewise, those with access to power—including landlords, private employers, book publishers, and mass media workers—were conditioned by and through anticommunism to be hostile to and prejudiced against communists, militants, and agitators and to act against them.[59] As an article in the progressive Black publication the *California Eagle* claimed, the persecution of communists and their right to free speech had especially dire consequences for Black people, for whom the right to dissent was essential to challenging racism and white supremacy.[60]

Paid informants, stool pigeons, and turncoats also represented the use of soft power for anticommunist ends. These ordinary citizens cooperated with the government and were compensated to insinuate themselves into the organizations and lives of those suspected or accused of radicalism, in order to procure—or to manufacture—information.[61] They were given the tools and incentive to infiltrate organizations, and in turn, they provided intelligence that confirmed suspected subversion and created new targets.

One such example was Julia Clarice Brown, a Black informant who infiltrated numerous communist, Radical Black, and militant civil rights organizations

during the early Cold War. After feeling that she had been "tricked" into joining the Cleveland chapter of the CPUSA and "deceived" about its intent, she
volunteered to become a paid FBI informant in 1951 to expose the communist "conspiracy."[62] She provided extensive information that confirmed the
CPUSA as sinister, dangerous, racially manipulative, and undemocratic, and
testified before HUAC in 1962 to this effect. A consummate anticommunist,
Brown claimed that communism was evil and US-born communists were
enemies because, while they preached "brotherly love," they actually encouraged hatred. Likewise, if the revolution they envisioned came to fruition, the
US would descend into another civil war, and if communists seized control,
they would impose a dictatorship that eliminated civil rights.[63] She also confirmed the government's Black Scare and Red Scare rhetoric about communists using "divide and conquer tactics" to create racial friction. For example,
she insisted that the charge of police brutality was part of the Red attack on
law enforcement agencies because she had never seen law enforcement officers attack a Black person, but she had seen Black people provoke police officers and blame ensuing violence on them for the sake of propaganda. These
provocations, she claimed, were committed "under the instruction" of Reds
who respected neither Blacks nor the law.[64]

Additionally, Brown was particularly active in construing Black and interracial civil rights and labor organizations like the Civil Rights Congress
(CRC), the National Negro Labor Congress (NNLC), and the American Committee for the Protection of the Foreign Born (ACPFB) as communist fronts.[65]
Brown's perfidy was instrumental in the decimation of the Sojourners for Truth
and Justice (STJ), of which she helped to start a chapter in Cleveland, Ohio.
Founded in September 9, 1951, by a national cadre of militant Black women,
including Charlotta Bass, Shirley Graham Du Bois, Dorothy Hunton, Louise
Thompson Patterson, Beah Richards, and Eslanda Goode Robeson, the group
sought to organize wives and mothers "of the legally lynched . . . of those imprisoned and threatened with prison . . . widowed by police brutality . . . [and]
who mourn [their] sons dead in foreign wars." They vehemently critiqued US
Capitalist Racist Society by connecting the insults, humiliations, and indigni-
ties of Jim Crow; the antiradical repression and violence meted out by the
domestic police state; and the US war machine that sent Black men to kill
other racialized persons on behalf of a country that systematically devalued
and disregarded Black life. In response, they organized a sojourn to the DOJ
in Washington, DC, from September 29 to October 1, 1951, to contest lynching,
unemployment, state violence, segregation, and the Korean War.[66]

The FBI insisted that all of the organization's officers were either in the
CPUSA or "front organizations," that STJ was "Communist Party sponsored,"

and that it followed the CPUSA line. Here, it used Red Scare guilt by association to rationalize its surveillance and infiltration. Brown gave credence to these spurious claims in several ways, including by drawing attention to the organization's name. She asserted that naming an organization after a revered American was a "typical tactic . . . [of] deception" used by communists to give their organization legitimacy.[67] She claimed that STJ was a "badly infiltrated" front group, "Communist inspired, . . . initially supported by the Party."[68] Even though the noncommunist members were legitimately working for civil rights, she contended, the Reds sought to wreck the organization because, as an all-Black multi-tendency women's organization, the CPUSA could not fully control it. She blamed the communists for STJ's ultimate demise in 1956.[69]

Brown identified several members of the organization as CPUSA members; provided the FBI with a vast array of information, including who attended STJ meetings and spoke at events, the home addresses of members, and internal debates and disputes; and informed about purported subversives affiliated with STJ, including Paul Robeson, Vicki Garvin, William Patterson, Du Bois, and Claudia Jones. Moreover, she claimed that it was communists who convinced Black Americans that they were "no better off than slaves," to "promote race consciousness and resentment," to engage in demonstrations and protest marches, and to demand massive federal intervention. Because STJ utilized all these strategies, they were indelibly linked to the CPUSA.[70] Brown's "soft power" of informing shows that anticommunist myths were sustained and "perpetrated in the first instance by informers who [were] paid to perpetrate them."[71]

Racial liberalism, especially as espoused by the Black petit bourgeoisie and leadership class, was another form of societal self-regulation that was as much strategic as it was coerced. The intersection of racial liberalism and anticommunism was rooted in the idea that opposition to communism could facilitate Black advancement; that the Negro Question could be resolved through reforms to US political, economic, social, and moral intuitions; and that socialism was not the best means of eradicating racial oppression.[72] This form of Black anticommunism arose largely among the Black buffer—or misleadership—classes. This class character was manifested, on the one hand, in the attack on the failure of the United States to live up to the ideals of equality and justice that were the conditions of possibility for Black bourgeois mobility. On the other hand, it was evident in the excoriation of the "values and lifestyle" of the Black masses that defied mainstream middle-class definitions of respectability—and that rendered them susceptible to unsavory political ideas.[73] Even the Black petit bourgeoisie's most militant protests against forms of racialized violence and exclusion (e.g., debt peonage, disinvestment in Black education, disenfranchisement, lynching) were shot through with class-based strivings to build nuclear families, to attend church, and to receive an education for social advancement.[74]

During the Black Scare / Red Scare Longue Durée, the understanding of racial progress as predicated upon a well-trained capitalist leadership class dovetailed with the aversion to any ideology that promoted radical organization, mass mobilization, or working-class empowerment.[75] The Black church, for example, took up anticommunism to "share fully in [the] bourgeois blessing" of the social order, to protect its middle-class commitment to capitalist accumulation, and to condemn atheism.[76] Political scientist Cedric Robinson wrote that "anti-communism transformed the effective terrain of Black liberal initiatives to an abject dependence on elite self-definitions and stalled Black democratic activity with outright hostility."[77] Likewise, corporate elite striving readily accommodated the "abstract ideals" of liberal anticommunism.[78] The denigration of radical modes of thought and activism that sought to empower the Black masses through interracial solidarity was necessary for "the achievement of autonomy and ability among [petit bourgeois] elements."[79] Hence, as the polarization of the world between the United States and Soviet Union spheres of influence set in, anticommunism as a feature of racial liberalism offered a program of democratic inclusion that repudiated socialism/communism, Radical Black internationalism, and allied sociopolitical, economic, and cultural projects as viable forms of struggle.

Anticommunism was a way for Black people to attack the Black Scare while shielding themselves from the Red Scare—in other words, it was an attempt to disentangle the two. It was also a "quid pro quo" between Blacks and the US state:[80] those on the darker side of the color line would not only avoid, but also attack, communism, in exchange for anticommunist governance pivoting toward the eradication of racial hierarchy. This separation was necessary because, as the labor organizer Coleman Young argued, paranoia about communism mapped seamlessly onto paranoia about civil rights struggles. Communism and civil rights were linked through the discourse of subversion, so it was exceedingly difficult for Blacks and other militants to agitate for civil rights without being labeled a communist or fellow traveler.[81] This convergence meant that advocates of civil rights attempted to navigate the paradox of critiquing racism while defending the US from international attacks on its race problem, not least to avoid being labeled un-American or sympathetic to communism.[82]

Anticommunism as a facet of racial liberalism attempted to undermine the claims of government entities that *any* organizations or individuals who engaged in mass campaigns for equality of opportunity irrespective of race

or class were "agents, conspirators, subversives, and Communists."[83] Insofar as those who fought militantly for Black rights (especially interracially),
against the atomic bomb, and for better wages and working conditions were
construed as communists, racial liberalism attempted to evade this label by
eschewing peaceful coexistence, promoting reformism, taking loyalty oaths,
and expelling actual, accused, or suspected Reds from their ranks.[84] Here,
whether or not communists were treated as equals was seen as immaterial
to whether or not Blacks should be treated as equals.[85] Importantly, racial
liberals' anticommunism generally accommodated socialists, like the Socialist Workers Party, that repudiated the Soviet Union, while singling out the
CPUSA whose real and imagined relationship with the USSR made it the
preeminent (though not sole) target of anticommunist governance.[86]

When compared to Wall Street Imperialism, which had a true political
economic stake in the eradication of communism, the anticommunism of
racial liberalism was more a matter of "expediency" and pragmatism.[87] Racial liberals took up anticommunism as a flexible tactic essential to gaining
concessions from the US government and to extend an olive branch to the
staunchest enemies of Black liberation, that is, white racists. Anticommunism was seen as common ground for these otherwise antagonistic groups:
because white supremacists combined the Black Scare and the Red Scare to
construe racial justice organizations as communists, racial liberals attempted
to repurpose anticommunism to both disprove racists and strengthen their
claim for equal rights.

Even as anticommunism was a key tool of the ruling class, racists, and
antilabor forces alike, racial liberals attempted to distinguish themselves by
linking communism with fascism—including the fascist-like character of Jim
Crow.[88] They claimed that the two biggest threats to liberal democracy were
communism, which eschewed universal civil rights by silencing those who
disagreed with them, and fascism, domestically and abroad, which was likewise opposed to the US "heritage of freedom and equality." Communism and
fascism were allegedly linked in their totalitarian tactics and their attempt to
conceal who they were and what they stood for. Though racial liberals did not
believe in the *special* persecution of communists, they did believe that the US
needed to protect itself from these enemies not only by exposing them and
insisting on disclosure, but also by defending democracy *especially* through
ensuring civil liberties for all except those who could legitimately be proven
dangerous or disloyal. Thus, racial liberals understood anticommunism to
be an important tool that needed to be used judiciously and in a way that
ensured *all* "good responsible Americans" could take up their duty to counter
totalitarians through the equal exercise of rights.[89]

Racial liberals participated in societal self-regulation primarily by upholding the ideological dimensions of anticommunist governance and by
construing racism, along with communism, as incompatible with liberal democracy. For example, Black liberals like Sadie T. Alexander and Channing
Tobias were part of the President's Committee on Civil Rights, which was established by Harry S. Truman in response to massive demonstrations against
mob violence held in Washington, DC, in July–September 1946. The committee produced a report, *To Secure These Rights*, an archetype of the racial
liberalism–anticommunism nexus. It argued that ensuring the right to safety
and security of the person, the right to citizenship and its privileges, the right
to freedom of conscience and expression, and the right to equality of opportunity to all people, not least Blacks, was a moral, economic, and especially
an international imperative.

Quoting Dean Acheson, the acting secretary of state, the committee argued that the oppression of and discrimination against minorities was having
an adverse effect on relations between the US and other countries, as foreign
nations' suspicion and resentment about racial violence within US borders
undermined mutual understanding and trust. Likewise, the US's poor civil
rights record gave "totalitarian critics" and those with "competing philosophies" tools to cultivate anti-American sentiment among particular nations,
races, and religious groups. The communists were especially effective in using
racial violence to undermine the standing of the United States in the world.
For these racial liberals, then, anticommunism grounded their recommendation for, among other things, the strengthening of the Civil Rights Section of
the DOJ, a special unit within the FBI focused on civil rights, the formation
of state-level civil rights agencies, a federal antilynching act, widespread suf-
frage legislation, the elimination of all segregation, and a federal Fair Employment Practices Commission.[90]

The statements of Channing Tobias and other racial liberals at the NAACP
convention in Dallas in 1954, just months after the *Brown v. Board of Education* decision, likewise represent the use of anticommunism to racial liberal
ends. Tobias held that the menace of communism was spreading from Korea
to Guatemala, and the United States could not afford the "expensive luxury"
of racial domination. At the same time, it was incumbent upon US Blacks
to be steadfast in their allegiance to their country as it battled "the enemies
of the free world." Such arguments assumed that anticommunism would
buttress Black struggles for equal rights at home and shore up democracy
abroad. Tobias went on to contend that there was indeed a communist menace within the United States that was attempting to undermine the bedrock
of the society by lying, cheating, and even killing on behalf of their foreign

master—Moscow. These nefarious elements had attempted to infiltrate the NAACP but had been repelled because, as a liberal and loyal organization, it believed in the American system and waged struggle based on American principles and ideals.

Even as other racial liberals like Walter White, Thurgood Marshall, and Constance Motley condemned McCarthyism, they did so by calling for a liberal, as opposed to reactionary, anticommunism. Anticommunism was an objective good, but the conservative and overzealous nature of McCarthyism undermined its merit. On this view, liberal anticommunism, which included conceding racial equality to Black people, would keep communists from being able to take advantage of this beleaguered group's legitimate grievances. Moreover, racial liberals argued that failing to implement the *Brown* ruling aligned Dixiecrats and other racists with the communist position that the court decision was merely a Cold War spectacle. "Good" Americans supported racial equality and integration, they counseled, because it would boost the nation's image and its ability to lead the Free World.[91]

Like paid informants, racial liberals employed anticommunism as a form of societal self-regulation that, while facilitating some nominal gains, especially for the Black buffer classes and organizations like the NAACP, helped to make the denigration of the CPUSA, socialism/communism, and Radical Blackness a prerequisite for racial justice. By extension, it shifted the struggle for Black liberation to civil rights, and legitimated the Red Scare as long as it was dirempted from the Black Scare.

Anticommunism from Above and Below

If the United States' entry into World War I "sacralized" antiradicalism,[92] then the Bolshevik Revolution of 1917 reduced all dangerous radicalism to communism and Bolshevism. The latter became the preeminent bogeyman because the United States was confronting, for the first time, a large and potentially powerful nation ruled by communists who were seen as menaces to foundational US values like liberal democracy, Christianity, and capitalism. Given the enthusiastic support for the rising socialist giant by a not insignificant number of people in the US, the deeply rooted fear of an "ideologically alien foreign power" linked up with a "subversive domestic movement" was ostensibly becoming a frightening political reality for politicians and their constituencies alike. Thus, as a mode of governance encompassing public authority and societal self-regulation, anticommunism was both top-down and bottom-up.

On the one hand, anticommunism was "popular but not populist," emanating from federal and state governments at the helm of US Capitalist Racist Society that made communist, communist inspired, and/or communist infiltrated synonymous with illegal, illicit, and/or criminal.[93] While some laws were addressed exclusively to communism, in the long tradition of US antiradicalism, anticommunism also targeted an array of dissident political beliefs and associations,[94] especially those challenging Wall Street Imperialism and the Structural Location of Blackness. It therefore exceeded the "imperative" of controlling a small minority of communists by harnessing statist technologies to the transformation of counterhegemony and nonconformity into subversion, foreignness, and/or disloyalty.

US Capitalist Racist Society, therefore, was constitutively more repressive than any other Western liberal democracy, implementing legislation that stifled civil liberties and refusing to accommodate any counterhegemonic thought and action. The US government legitimated this reactionary domestic and interventionist foreign policy through aggressive nationalist ideology, coercion of loyalty, compelling anticommunist credentials to hold office or be in positions of leadership, and widespread prosecution or threat thereof.[95] Relatedly, those who were accused, indicted, or found guilty of violating the wide array of anticommunist legislation, dictates, and custom were subjected to loss of work, livelihood, income, freedom, and liberty.

Anticommunism flourished through the blurred distinction between "clear and present danger" and undesirability. Here, the repression of communism was merited because it was "undesirable in the United States" and "the proscription of an undesirable movement" remained in the power of Congress without sustained concern about freedom of speech or the test of clear and present danger.[96] In constructing communism as un-American, communists, fellow travelers, and those who sympathized with them could be denied legal protection not because they were actually violent or dangerous, but because their beliefs were "wrong or immoral."[97] Likewise, "Because Communists posed a fearsome threat to liberties enshrined in the Constitution, it seemed reasonable to restrict those very liberties when claimed by Communists."[98] This Red Scare logic—which informed and was informed by the Black Scare—was foundational to the passage of repressive legislation throughout the Black Scare / Red Scare Longue Durée, and helped to sweep racial militancy, worker agitation, and peace activism into the dragnet of repression. Anticommunism thus transformed into official rule a combination of political manipulation, popular myth, stereotype, and ruling-class propaganda that eschewed social change, especially as it related to race relations, economic democracy, and immigration.[99]

Given the power of the state, popular attitudes followed from those of prominent politicians. These leaders, who linked class antagonism, racism, and religious intolerance to fears of "assault by The Other on their wealth and power" were able to influence "a ready audience among some working-class Americans."[100] The federal government also empowered the business sector, supported by organizations like the National Association of Manufacturers, the chamber of commerce, the National Metal Trades Association, and the National Founder Association, to use anticommunist instruments like loyalty oaths to undermine unions, disempower workers, and preserve a conservative work culture. Moreover, the influence of these organizations, which financed campaigns and endorsed candidates, helped to devolve federal anticommunism into "derivative anticommunist politics at the state and local level." State, and even some municipal, legislatures "responded almost slavishly to the force of federal law" to implement new or reinvigorate old anticommunist laws that had been drawn from the federal government or from other states.[101]

On the other hand, the masses also drove anticommunism. Myriad civil society organizations spanning the racial and ideological spectrum—the Ku Klux Klan, NAACP, American Federation of Labor, American Legion, American Defense Society, National Civic Federation, the Negro Labor Committee—helped to inculcate anticommunism in every facet of society. Far from being simply an "elite-inspired phenomenon [that] trickled down into state and local bureaucracies, private corporations, and civil groups,"[102] a broad "civic culture of anticommunism"[103] existed from the inception of the Black Scare / Red Scare Longue Durée, and included intellectuals, conservatives, countersubversives, religious leaders, and racists. The Black Scare and the Red Scare from below reflected the protracted struggle of the US public to contend with the purported duty of its country to shield the society, and in some cases the world, from the militant expansion of communism.[104]

Key institutions of US Capitalist Racist Society, built and patronized by everyday people, helped to sustain anticommunism. Mass entertainment spread popular anticommunism, churches of all denominations juxtaposed communism and faith, and civic organizations supported widespread education about the nature and dangers of communism.[105] Conservative and liberal anticommunists were united in the view that communism needed to be contained because it was an attack on the American way of life. For conservatives, the focus was religion, patriotism, family, and civil society. For liberals, the concern was intellectual, academic, and artistic freedom; various constitutional guarantees; and individual freedom.[106] Ordinary citizens, especially those in the middle and upper classes, developed fear and anxiety about labor and racial radicalism, not least when it seemed to challenge the idea that rights and privileges were reserved primarily for those who "play[ed] the game respectably" and patiently worked for them.[107] Likewise, from World War I onward, everyday Americans conflated nativism, xenophobia, and racism with the idea that radicalism was alien influenced and the struggle for equal rights was the product of outside—namely, communist—agitation. By 1948, 61 percent of Americans supported a legal ban on the CPUSA, and 77 percent agreed that communists should register with the government. Such antipathy was vehemently expressed at the state and local levels with little "goading or coaxing" from the federal government.[108]

White workers, who derived some benefit from the subjection of Black labor—though little from their superexploitation, which accrued primarily to the white ruling class—also helped to reinscribe anticommunism by employing both the Black Scare and the Red Scare to shore up white supremacy. Vigilantism—an "extralegal enforcement of community mores" predicated on the rights of self-preservation and sovereignty—was a stark manifestation of this. During the Black Scare / Red Scare Longue Durée, the conjunction of vigilantism and anticommunism was used primarily against racial, ethnic, religions, and political minorities.[109] White workers participated in anti-Black and anti-Red violence in part because "psychological and ideological realities of ordinary white folk [were] filtered through the prisms of race, nationalism and white supremacy. The perceived threats, therefore, [were] viewed as threats to white people as a collective and not solely to the economic interests of the nation, or even to specific class interests."[110] The Black Scare was central to undermining interracial labor solidarity because it facilitated a worldview in which whiteness was an alternative to class as the basis of identity. In times of stability and strife, the Black Scare offered a framework through which white workers accepted their exploitation by white employers based on the idea of racial benefit.[111] Yet white workers were not merely pawns of the ruling class.

The Black Scare helped to propel the Red Scare and vice versa through white workers' eschewal of interracial organizing, both because such organizing disrupted the idea of white privilege and because it was dangerous. This danger was firmly rooted in the Red-baiting of individuals and organizations who espoused racial equality, insofar as being Red invited violence almost as much as being Black. As such, white workers often chose to protect their superordinate structural position vis-à-vis Black labor by affirming Jim Crow policies, abandoning or brutalizing Black workers, and struggling on behalf of race instead of class. Unsurprisingly, the unions most likely to be interracial were those that had a high number of communists and/or strong communist leadership, so the attack on white dominance and Black subordination by those often construed as "Nigger lovers" or fellow travelers became appended to communism. Anticommunism ensured that those who avoided the most radical forms of labor organizing—that which fought for Black and white labor rights on equal footing—were rewarded, and those who crossed the color line for economic equality suffered huge penalties at the hands of private employers and the state, including unemployment, arrest, physical assault, and social ostracism.[112] The American Federation of Labor was instructive in its notorious rejection of interracial unionism, commitment to segregation, and staunch anticommunism—attributes that allowed it to be touted by government officials as quintessentially American and the antidote to radicalism.[113]

One means by which anticommunism upheld the Black and Red scares from below was through leftists' rejection of the special character of the Structural Location of Blackness in US Capitalist Racist Society. The view that Black workers were an appendage to the white working class positioned those who did take superexploitation and the right to self-determination seriously, especially Radical Blacks, as divisive agitators, outsiders, and by extension, deserving targets of anticommunism. One example of this is so-called Debsianism, named after Eugene V. Debs, perhaps the most influential leader in the Socialist Party during the first two decades of the twentieth century. He held that class was the singular basis of the Negro Question in the United States, and that class struggle, the overthrow of capitalism, and the realization of socialism were its resolutions.[114] In other words, the Negro Question was simply a class question, so US Blacks needed no special attention or remedy.[115] An article titled "There is No Race Problem," published in *New Solidarity* in 1919, summed up the position:

> For the purpose of keeping the workers divided, the employers want all workers to believe that there is a race problem. . . . The problem of the workers is not a race problem. . . . All have but one problem to solve, and that is the problem of how to overthrow the system of slavery under which all are bound to the employing class. When this one problem is solved there will be no race problems.[116]

Likewise, Debsianism tended to conflate exploitation and oppression, reducing the question of social equality to a specter raised by racist whites to maintain Black subordination. "The Negro, given economic freedom," Debs held, "will not ask the white man any social favors; and the burning question of 'social equality' will disappear like mist before the sunrise."[117] This position misrecognized how the genocidal logic of capitalist racism included both superexploitation and social subordination.

The idea that economic exploitation could be separated from racialism, that the race problem was simply the machination of bosses, and that "social equality" was less important than economic emancipation denied that Black workers "were still victims of a rigid and brutal system" that rendered them "an inferior servile class at the bottom of capitalist society, exploited, degraded, and persecuted by the white imperialist master class *and by prejudiced whites of all classes*."[118] Even as Debsianism asserted an "emancipationist view that the Civil War had placed black and white workers on equal terms as 'wage slaves,'"[119] the failure to recognize the peculiarity of Black workers' subjection and the racially informed radical struggle against capitalist racism it required lent power to the idea that "a worker was simply a worker, and a Black worker who faced racism and Jim Crow required no more from socialism than the white worker who got double his salary and the choice of jobs from which his Black brother was barred."[120] This gave credence to theories like the BBNT as foreign inspired and Radical Blackness as undue agitation, thereby legitimating Black Scare and Red Scare logic and a form of anticommunist that provided some level of cover for individuals, ideas, and organizations whose left ideas were safe by comparison.

A related, but perhaps more complicated, means of upholding anticommunism from below was the position held by Black anticommunists like Ben Fletcher, Marcus Garvey, and A. Philip Randolph, whose experiences with the CPUSA and misgivings about Soviet foreign policy colored their position that communism was antithetical to Black freedom. Fletcher despised communists and was part of the faction of the IWW that refused the support of the Soviet Union because it did not align with the principles of syndicalism.[121] Even though he had been imprisoned for his left-wing politics and organizing, he held fast to his belief that communism was antithetical to achieving a democratic and equitable society through interracial industrial unionism.[122] He claimed that around 1920, Moscow gave orders to "American agents" to attempt to control the IWW and bring it into the communist camp.[123] He also blamed communists for the ultimate disintegration of Local 8 in 1922, which had been plagued by white supremacist violence after an employer lockout undermined the local's interracial solidarity. He asserted that because the CPUSA could not absorb Local 8, its communist members took advantage of the turmoil to liquidate it. Fletcher's characterization of the CPUSA as under foreign influence, manipulative, disruptive, destructive, and insincere employed Red Scare discourse without its Black Scare counterpart—not unlike Black racial liberals—a unique feature of this iteration of grassroots anticommunism.

Marcus Garvey's hostility to the CPUSA was twofold. First, he considered communism to be a white man's creation, conceived of by a white man— Karl Marx—who knew very little about Africa's sons and daughters. As such, Marxism was rooted in the interests of white people and sought to empower "the most ignorant, prejudiced and cruel class of the white race." Garvey found the capitalist system to be superior in that it gave "the Negro a chance for employment competitive with the working classes of whites for the purpose of extracting profit from labour, irrespective of the colour of labour." By contrast, communists desired for Blacks to lose the "good will" of the capitalist employer so that they would become unemployed, thereby eliminating competition with the white worker. Further, communism was a "vile and wicked" scheme to conscript Blacks into a party in which they would exert no control and would be subjected to the dictates of common white men who were the most vicious and ignorant in the United States and in the colonized world. Garvey counseled Black people to let the communists wage their own fight and to take advantage of the opportunities presented by the struggle of "class against class" without joining a fight in which the darker race would bear the brunt of the battle without any guarantee of better conditions. In fact, the plight of Blacks under communism would be "objectively worse" because that system would wrest power from the most "cultured" and "intelligent" whites and transfer it to the most backward of that group.[124]

Second, like Fletcher, Garvey opposed the CPUSA based on the latter's efforts to capture the UNIA. Garvey claimed that W. A. Domingo, an early editor of *Negro World*, attempted to impose a communistic view on the membership even though they were disinclined toward it, and after leaving the association, he had linked up with other "red Socialists" like Cyril Briggs to sabotage Garvey's Black Star Line Corporation.[125] Garvey also stated that communists had done Blacks a great deal of harm by attempting to capture his organization of four million, and by slandering him with virulent propaganda when they failed. They engaged in both of these actions because their work among Blacks was a thin plot to link up the powerful Black minority group with other discontented groups of the world to overthrow the extant system and impose universal communism. Not only was communism as oppressive as any other system, according to Garvey, but it was also antithetical to peace.[126] The historian Tony Martin agreed that several Black communists had indeed infiltrated the UNIA, and communist publications like the *Daily Worker* made plain their aim to convert Garveyism into a joint movement of Black and white workers under communist leadership. In fact, the organization of the ANLC in 1925 and the adoption of the 1928 BBNT resulted from the party's inability to make inroads with Garveyites.[127]

Likewise, the one-time communist George Padmore confirmed that the CPUSA attempted to bore into the UNIA, which Garvey swiftly rebuffed, denouncing Black communists at "Red Uncle Toms" and race traitors. The white communists, according to Padmore, had made a tactical error in attacking Garvey and his movement before gaining the confidence of Black workers and proving that the CPUSA was distinct from the Democrats or Republicans. Garvey was effectively successful in blocking the communists from making inroads in Black organizations, which they were only able to do after he was imprisoned and deported. Padmore also affirmed that the Communist International decided to push for the establishment of a Black state in the US South to turn Black workers away from Garvey's brand of Black Nationalism.[128] Garvey's anticommunism thus came from his grassroots organizing, and his anticommunist "tirades," "half-truths, vilification, and thuggery" were especially effective in normalizing anticommunism among ordinary Black folk. At the same time, anticommunist governance from above did color Garvey's position in that "savage" Red Scare repression of white communists incentivized the UNIA to disassociate from those who were being "ruthlessly suppressed and deported."[129]

Finally, A. Philip Randolph—an early target of anticommunist governance during World War I because of his editorship of *Messenger* magazine—staunchly supported the Red Scare repression of the CPUSA. In the NNC, founded in 1936, a feud ignited between this influential socialist, labor leader, and founder of the Brotherhood of Sleeping Car Porters and members of the party. During this "Popular Front" era, the CPUSA abandoned its "class against class" position and attacks on the Black petit bourgeoisie, which allowed for Blacks from all walks of life to come together and fight for economic and social justice in the NNC. Randolph was appointed its president, and things ran fairly smoothly until 1939 when communist members attempted to use the organization as a forum to support the Molotov-Ribbebtrop Pact, a nonaggression agreement signed between the USSR and Germany. As a result, the CPUSA pushed the line that the conflict brewing in Europe was an imperialist war in which racialized people should take no part. John P. Davis, the NNC executive secretary, condemned the Roosevelt administration for providing aid to countries resisting Nazism and declared that Black people would not support the United States or other imperialist powers in a war against the Soviet Union.

Incensed and dismayed, Randolph resigned in 1940, claiming that the CPUSA was controlled by a foreign power, was antithetical to the interests of the United States and Black people, and that Blacks should unequivocally reject Reds. He further contended that, because the NNC was funded by communists, it was effectively run by them and had ceased to be useful for the Black masses. He opposed not only the "domination" of the NNC by the communists but also the communists themselves, who were a danger to Black people and to labor because of their "disruptive tactics in the interest of the Soviet Union."[130] He argued that the USSR repressed freedom of speech, assembly, and the press; was undemocratic; and was a dictatorship akin to Nazi Germany—and, the CPUSA served this authoritarian, alien master.[131]

Randolph's vitriol was not new; he had condemned the CPUSA almost twenty years earlier for attempting to confuse and undermine the New Negro liberation movement. But after his break with the NNC, Randolph embraced Red Scare rhetoric with greater intensity—despite its disproportionate effect on Black people given its imbrication with the Black Scare. In 1943, he barred communists from the March on Washington Movement (MOMW)—which was nonetheless targeted and Red-baited by the FBI during World War II—in part by limiting its membership to Black people only. Not unlike government officials, he continued to claim that the CPUSA would sacrifice Black people for Soviet Russia, that communists were enemies of Black people, and that the communists used Blacks to their own ends. While he claimed to be against the "fascist" tactics of the FBI and HUAC, his employment of their discourse and his cooperation with them effectively merged his anticommunism from below with that from above. Moreover, his grassroots anticommunism was especially impactful because of his extensive influence as a labor leader.[132]

✶

Fletcher, Garvey, and Randolph did not share the Black Scare aims of anticommunism as a mode of governance and were, in fact, "race men" who dedicated themselves to the Black struggle. However, among ordinary Black people, their anticommunism from below, as a form of societal self-regulation, gave legitimacy to the public authority of anticommunist governance from above. This governance was facilitated, through coordinated action and strategic inaction, by the executive, judicial, and legislative branches of the US federal government.

Loyalty, Criminality, and "Clear and Present Danger": The Anticommunist Governance of the Executive and Judicial Branches

We hear so much about loyalty today. Loyalty, as I understand it, is not something that is demanded of one. Loyalty is recognition of the truth and the determination to follow it. It is loyalty to principles, to ideals, and to the fulfillment of those ideals in our daily lives. This to me is the real loyalty, certainly something altogether different from the loyalty oath business that we see today being used to make this country of ours into a nation of panic-driven sheep.

DOROTHY HUNTON, 1952

During the Black Scare / Red Scare Longue Durée, anticommunist governance was the means by which the executive, judicial, and legislative branches of the US government entangled the Black Scare with the Red Scare because "the rights of the Negro people have always been akin to the rights of labor and political minorities, so that an attack upon one invariably is followed by an attack on the others."[1] While the effort of all three branches of government would be necessary to guarantee rights to Black people, and by extension "labor and political minorities," such coordination had, to the contrary, historically worked to abrogate or limit those rights, directly and indirectly. This was because the ruling class and "business used its government, Federal and state, of 'three equal parts' as the instruments with which to do the job" of maintaining US Capitalist Racist Society through anticommunist governance.

Since 1876, the executive branch could have ended Jim Crow and segregation in its departments and in the armed forces, and could have directed the State Department to outlaw the Ku Klux Klan and other white terrorist organizations. Instead, the attorneys general chose to rely on the argument that the Justice Department did not have the power to defend Black life and property. The Supreme Court had numerous cases before it through which it could have protected "the fundamental rights of Negroes." Instead, the court "always evade[d] basic issues of the people." For example, regarding the "legal lynchings" of Blacks, instead of rectifying these "frame-ups," the Supreme Court "always remanded such cases for retrial before the lyncher's tribunal of death." This failure to protect Blacks inevitably resulted in the failure to protect other minoritized and oppressed peoples. The legislative branch could have created and legally utilized an un-American activities committee to investigate and punish those who violated the Fourteenth and Fifteenth Amendments; instead, it used this entity to illegally "terrorize the progressives" in the United States.[2] Likewise, it could have easily passed constitutionally sound laws to ensure the citizenship rights of Blacks and radicals just as it had passed "the unconstitutional Smith Act, McCarran Law and the infamous Taft-Hartley Measure."[3]

There were rare exceptions. The LaFollette Civil Liberties Committee was formed in the context of the passage of the Wagner Act, the formation of the Congress of Industrial Organizations, attacks on New Deal legislation, and workers' struggles in rural and industrial settings. In existence from 1936 to 1940, the committee investigated employers' undermining of civil liberties and labor rights, especially the ability of workers to unionize. Specifically, it sought to interrogate the violation of free speech and assembly manifested in the unlawful interference with the right of labor to organize and collectively bargain.[4]

In the main, however, "the entire apparatus of government—its legislatures, its judiciaries, its executive branches" perpetuated superexploitation in the South, anti-Black discrimination in the North, and antiradical repression of those who dared to challenge it.[5] In a general sense, the executive branch used its police powers to protect and implement the interests of the ruling elite to exploit Black laborers and other oppressed peoples. The courts handed down opinions to legitimate the actions of the other branches of government and private policy. And, instead of protecting Black people, legislatures enacted laws to deny them political rights and took little action when private institutions denied them social and economic rights.[6] The same held for political minorities, especially communists. On the one hand, each branch of government refused to check another in its violation of constitutional rights or liberties that were supposed to extend to racial and political minorities, and, on the other hand, each worked to mitigate or nullify other branches' rare protection of Blacks or radicals.[7] This was the cornerstone of anticommunism as a mode of governance.

The Executive Branch

The executive branch of the US federal government is responsible for the execution and enforcement of laws and policies and the administration of public affairs. Its participation in anticommunism as a mode of governance was multifaceted and wide-ranging throughout the Black Scare / Red Scare Longue Durée. In particular, this branch of government played a leading role in conflating radicalism with criminality. These measures were instrumental in embedding the Black Scare and the Red Scare in US Capitalist Racist Society in ways quotidian and exceptional. While the more extreme aspects of anticommunism might be condemned at certain moments in history, the idea that radicalism—whether socialism, communism, anarchism, racial assertion, or worker militancy—was not just dangerous but criminal, remained constant, thus ensuring that repressive measures could be called on at any time. For example, one argument against government overreach in the targeting of radicals was not that it was immoral and wrong to criminalize persons for their ideas and associations, but rather that such violations would, in fact, breed more radicalism. The position that suppression, ruthlessness, and deliberate violations of US ideals of the rule of law and decency fomented revolution[8] maintained radicalism as crime, danger, and threat; antiradicalism as the objective good; and repression as an important tool as long as it did not deliberately violate rights of those who deserved them.

The president, the BI/FBI, the attorney general, and the DOJ harnessed anticommunism to the violation of the constitutional rights of accused subversives. The president issued executive orders and granted powers to other units to enforce anticommunism by any means necessary. The BI/FBI helped to shore up the link between criminality and radicalism by implanting "agent provocateurs" in dissident organizations to encourage unlawful practices, from instigating criminal acts to luring persons to meetings to arrest them. The attorney general levied propaganda against radicals and attempted to prejudice the press and public opinion against them to legitimate repression.[9] The DOJ imposed excessive bail in violation of the Eighth Amendment, made arrests without warrant and engaged in unreasonable search and seizure in violation of the Fourth Amendment, and compelled persons to be witnesses against themselves in violation of the Fifth Amendment.[10] Even groups that "made no argument in favor of any radical doctrine as such"[11] confessed that the overreach of the executive branch was doing more than any radical propaganda to create revolutionary sentiment. As such, this branch of government not only engaged in illegal acts to criminalize radicalism, but also engaged in forms of repression that inspired more radicalism in US Capitalist Racist Society, which, in turn, rationalized more repression.

During the early Cold War, collaboration within the executive branch and with the legislative branch in anticommunist governance was manifested in the Attorney General's List of Subversive Organizations (AGLOSO). President Harry S. Truman issued Executive Order 9835 on March 21, 1947, "Prescribing Procedures for the Administration of an Employees Loyalty Program in the Executive Branch of the Government," which included the provision for the AGLOSO. Truman's action was a response to Republican insistence that he was soft on communism. In 1946, the Republican congressional majority prompted Truman to create the Temporary Commission on Employee Loyalty (TCEL) to determine "loyalty standards and procedures to remove or disqualify 'any disloyal or subversive person'" from federal service. The TCEL report argued that if even one federal employee was found to be disloyal, then the comprehensive federal loyalty was justified. It proposed that loyalty be determined based on one's beliefs regarding "sabotage, espionage, and related activities," "treason or sedition," "advocacy of illegal overthrow of the government," "intentional and unauthorized disclosure of confidential information," "serving a foreign government" over the US, and "membership in, affiliation with or sympathetic association with any foreign or domestic organization, association, movement, group or combination of persons designated by the attorney general as totalitarian, fascist, communist, or subversive."[12] These broad recommendations were overwhelmingly adopted by the Truman administration in the creation of the federal loyalty program. This program thus helped to sustain the conflation of fascism and communism—with the latter receiving the brunt of discipline and punishment—and to make "subversive" capacious enough to include militant organizing for Black equality.

This blacklist of organizations deemed subversive by the acting attorney general was an important instrument that cultivated and continued anticommunism between the Truman and Nixon administrations.[13] Since past or present association with any organization listed on the AGLOSO abrogated the civil rights and liberties of the accused, it molded an entire generation of US citizens who were afraid to join organizations, sign petitions, consume particular literature, or express their views in other ways. Signaling collaboration within the executive branch, the AGLOSO provided the FBI with the opportunity to engage in extensive and expansive surveillance of political organizations and activities in the United States.[14]

The AGLOSO built upon previous lists compiled by the executive branch. A few months before the December 1941 attack on Pearl Harbor, Attorney General Francis Biddle used stipulations of the Act to Prevent Pernicious Political Activities, or the Hatch Act, passed in 1939 to create a list outlining which organizations were deemed subversive enough to warrant the detainment and possible deportation of aliens affiliated with them. Nearly in tandem, the DOJ secretly drafted a list detailing "groups viewed as predominantly composed of alien radicals" that could be construed as anarchistic, subversive, or seditious. The list would determine who would be eligible for trial by the Alien Enemy Hearings Board. Taken together, these lists were virtually all-encompassing, with the DOJ's list targeting the general civilian population while Biddle's list was used to evaluate federal employees.[15] As would be the case throughout the Black Scare / Red Scare Longue Durée, the importance of fascist groups paled in comparison to communist and ostensible communist front groups. The lists included major organizations with communist members as well as those with little or no relationship to the CPUSA, such as the NNC and the National Federation for Constitutional Liberties.[16] This focus conveyed that communism was considered far more subversive, un-American, and criminal than fascism.

Importantly, the AGLOSO aided in the expansion of federal anticommunist power anchored in the executive branch during the early Cold War, with DOJ records informing the list's compilation, and the loyalty program granting the FBI expansive authority to conduct limitless investigations of individuals and organizations that defied US Capitalist Racist Society. This power went virtually unchecked since there was no effective oversight entity to ensure that organizations actually belonged on the list. Therefore, manifold groups targeted by the Black Scare and the Red Scare, from labor to civil rights to anticolonial organizations, were added "without any accompanying write-ups" and with little ability to contest their placement on the list.[17]

President Truman's executive order was instrumental to the development of the AGLOSO into a key anticommunist technology insofar as it sanctioned *allegations* of membership in, affiliation with, or sympathy for organizations as a legitimate source of evidence confirming disloyalty and subversion. This solidified the practice of making allegations and association central foci of antiradical investigations, with persons who had attended only one meeting of, donated to, or were affiliated with someone in an organization on the list being swept into the dragnet of repression.[18] In the final analysis, since there was rarely any criminal activity to be found, the AGLOSO's target became "wrong thinking," ideas, and guilt by association, especially since determination of association only required allegations.[19] These were staples of anticommunism and the executive branch's criminalization of radicalism.

✳

At the helm of executive branch anticommunism was the BI/FBI. As the preeminent law enforcement agency, it was central to suturing radicalism and criminality through the Black and Red Scares. Because repression was a mainstay of anticommunist governance, this agency converted itself into a colossal and well-funded political police force that superseded any other in the world.[20] Starting around 1919, Hoover continually asserted that it was the ignorant and the violent criminal elements that believed in and proffered the communist doctrine and sought to thrust the nation into anarchy, lawlessness, and immorality.[21] He argued that communism was a method of implanting distrust of freedom, the government, and law and order and of turning the people against established authority.[22] Communists especially worked to "shackle" the BI/FBI, to undermine effective law enforcement, and to malign "progressive" police departments by invoking the protection of civil liberties to conceal their nefarious ends.[23] Since the BI/FBI was the supreme law enforcement agency, Hoover was keen to castigate any critique of law enforcement and construe such critiques as criminal and subversive.

This focus on the criminality of dissent was a pillar of anticommunist governance that brought together the Black Scare and the Red Scare insofar as disregard for law and order was something levied at Blacks and radicals alike to legitimate state violence, the use of extraordinary police force, disregard for basic civil rights, and extralegal repression. Hoover asserted, "Disrespect for law and order [was] a fundamental cornerstone of communist tactics. Charges of 'police brutality,' 'illegal arrest,' and 'persecution' have long echoed in the Party press. These false communist charges, unfortunately, have been taken up by other groups whose basic purpose is to destroy law and order and to create chaos."[24] Here, it was the link between Black and Red that was of particular concern, insofar as communists purportedly worked to inculcate and exacerbate Black hostility toward policemen to foment racial antagonism.[25] A key technique of the CPUSA, Hoover claimed, was to rankle race relations by charging police brutality to discredit law enforcement, to exacerbate racial issues, and to create the conditions for riots and other disorder.[26] They did so through their mass agitation tactics aimed at garnering maximum publicity for political and social issues "real or imagined or invented."[27] The perfidy of this approach lay in the fact that the communists' interest in Black suffering was insincere and lacked a true desire to aid and uplift this oppressed group. Rather, the aim of communism was to undermine Americans', and especially Black people's, faith in government and belief in law and order.[28]

At the same time, the BI/FBI criminalized Black agitation by linking it to communism. The agency claimed that the CPUSA exploited anti-Black racial oppression to transform Blacks into vectors of communist subversion.[29] By the same token, in the struggle for civil rights, Red Blacks / Black Reds, or Black people who espoused anything that could be construed as communism, were "dangerous opportunists and morally corrupt charlatans . . . [attempting] to advance their own prestige."[30] On this logic, the understanding of race struggle as a function of class struggle, the demand for economic redistribution as a central aspect of racial justice, or the argument that racism was endemic in capitalism could be criminalized as a communist plot to exploit racial tension, to foster disunity by dividing Blacks and whites into warring factions, to undermine established authority, to encourage and/or ignite racial strife and rioting, to turn Black sentiment against law and order, and/ or to foster belief that it was only the communists who were willing or able to improve the conditions of Blacks and other oppressed groups.[31] As well, Black critique of established authority was accused of being outright communist, communist inspired, sympathetic to communist influence, or abetting the spread of communism to link it to illegality and criminality.

The bureau mobilized criminalization as an instrument of anticommunism through the discourse of conspiracy. It argued that, since the Bolshevik Revolution, the United States was the obsessive target of international communism.[32] This was because communism was not simply an economic system or a form of social organization, but rather a way of life, a false materialistic religion that stripped men of their belief in God and love of freedom and mercy, and a system aimed at reducing the masses to twentieth-century slaves.[33] In other words, Marxist-Leninism was a "materialist atheistic conspiracy dedicated to overthrowing the institutions of [US] society."[34] This was not simply an affront to the American way of life, but rather a *criminal conspiracy* to upend it, inasmuch as communism was totalitarian and authoritarian and thereby against established freedoms of the US variety and absolutely incompatible with liberal democracy. Communist conspirators sought to weasel their way into every stratum of life through hypocrisy, deception, duplicity, and by "making calumny respectable, deceit a virtue, and downright falsehoods the unimpeachable truth."[35]

Under Hoover's leadership, the BI/FBI shaped methods of surveillance, infiltration, counterintelligence, and discipline around the idea that communists were anti-American and therefore were foreign inspired and influenced, subversive, and threatening to national security—and thereby criminals. One could not be a communist and loyal to the United States at the same time, and unity with communists was impossible because they were enemies of the American way of life and sought to destroy US institutions. Communism meant the criminal destruction of the US form of government, US democracy, and free enterprise.[36] As long as communism remained a worldwide movement, the presence of the CPUSA, and anything linked or sympathetic to it, was a threat to internal security.[37] Simply put, "As the history of the communist movement in the United States proves, the Communist Party, USA, has been inspired and completely controlled by the fountainhead of world communism, the Soviet Union. Every major phase has been determined, not by any factor indigenous to the United States, but rather by the exigencies of communist imperialism."[38] In these ways, Hoover conflated criminality, disloyalty, foreign inspiration, and threat to national security through anticommunist governance.

For the BI/FBI, communist agitation was little more than exploitation of societal issues to "divide, weaken, and confuse" the anticommunist offensive and to exacerbate class warfare and racial hatred to accelerate revolution. Their partial and immediate demands were merely tactics to create the conditions for revolutionary action, to make agitation against the free-market economy ongoing, and to promote unrest and discontent in an effort to radicalize the masses—that is, transform them into subversives and criminals.[39] The communist distortion of every struggle into class and race struggle[40] threatened property, profit, and elite domination—the hallmarks of US Capitalist Racist Society. The BI/FBI's raison d'être for anticommunist governance was the exposure and criminalization of the clandestine and "diabolical" purposes of communism and all that was influenced by it,[41] including its "defiance of the law," "disrespect for authority," and disregard for (the racial and economic) order, which underscored its conspiratorial nature.[42]

*

The case of Marcus Garvey illustrates the expansive ways executive branch anticommunist governance disciplined the UNIA leader as an undesirable alien, distorted his aims by linking them with Bolshevism, and engendered a rightward shift in his politics as he attempted to shield himself from repression.

The "ideological signatures" of anticommunist governance—"the emergence of the problem of the 'New Negro,' the fear of social radicalism and revolution, the targeting of the alien radical"—were all inscribed in the rabid attack on Garvey throughout the 1920s.[43] Despite the fact that, by 1921, the DOJ found the UNIA to be in disarray, financially struggling, and of questionable effectiveness, it nonetheless prosecuted Garvey because he "had been giving the Department of Justice endless trouble for years."[44]

Not unlike Bolshevism, Garvey's Black Nationalism was treated as a catalyst for the spread of radicalism throughout the United States and the colonized world, especially in places where Wall Street Imperialism had spread its tentacles—like in the Panama Canal Zone. There, Garvey's influence was accused of fomenting strikes throughout 1920. As such, his ideas as much as his actions menaced the ability to accumulate along racialized lines. Relatedly, throughout the British West Indies, *Negro World* was deemed seditious because it incited race consciousness, "racial hatred," and labor unrest among the natives.[45] British officials encouraged the US government to suppress the paper at the source—within its borders—before it arrived in the colonies where "the black population [was] several times that of the whites" and "prominent [Black] persons such as officials, lawyers, doctors, and ministers" were developing a radical political consciousness.[46]

The United Fruit Company also demanded that the Costa Rican government ban *Negro World* in the interest of public safety.[47] That those concerned about Radical Blackness abroad were following with great interest "conditions in America, particularly the Southern States," attested to how the anti-communist governance of US Capitalist Racist Society influenced the rest of the world as the US rose to global hegemony.

Taking their cue from Uncle Sam, colonial officials connected the Black Scare and the Red Scare in their belief that worldwide unrest, especially racial uprisings, derived not from racism, but rather from socialist doctrines of equality preached to Blacks by agitators throughout the United States. There, New York City was the "fountainhead" of Black radicalism, and those responsible for the spread of dangerous unrest were Black socialists and their organizations like the National Association for the Promotion of Labour Unionism among Negroes, militant Black veterans and their League for Democracy, the IWW with their promotion of interracial labor militancy, and Garvey's UNIA. Of these, the UNIA was the most concerning because it had the largest following while articulating the same dangerous challenges to racial oppression and exploitation as the other organizations.

The UNIA supported Black self-determination; excoriated the treatment of Black soldiers during World War I and after; claimed that Blacks were equal—or even superior to—whites; and asserted the right and responsibility of Black people to self-defense. It thus encouraged Blacks off the "beaten path" of conciliation they normally followed, and "under these circumstances [the Negro was], perhaps, the most radical of all radicals, his trend of thought swinging from one extreme to the other."[48] Though the UNIA leadership as a whole purportedly lacked the intelligence of the Black socialists, Garvey, equal parts West Indian and Outside Agitator, was considered to possess the "intellectual equipment" to effectively influence his "ignorant" following away from the "beaten path."

Moreover, like the Bolsheviks, the UNIA, with its largely "foreign" West Indian membership, practiced a dangerous form of internationalism that forged connections with "prominent coloured men in foreign countries . . . such as Africa, India, China, Japan, and the West Indies" that had the potential to establish "a closer relationship between the coloured races of the world."[49] As was the case with US anticommunism, British officials linked growing race consciousness and manipulation of the "colour question" by revolutionary agitators as twin dangers that could potentially lead to two entwined catastrophes: the linking up of Black and other racialized peoples throughout the world and the "breakdown of the Capitalist system." The Outside Agitator "radiating from the United States" was the culprit cultivating racial solidarity among Blacks by connecting local grievances and transforming them into an internationalist race militance.[50] It was here that Garvey, his Black Nationalism, and the UNIA posed an immense threat.

Heading up the executive branch's attack on Marcus Garvey, J. Edgar Hoover, as head of the General Intelligence Division (GID) of the Justice Department, made his first move on September 15, 1919. Hoover used Black informants to try to indict Garvey under the Mann Act—encouraged by the BI's first Black agent, James Wormley Jones—based on their initial belief that his secretary, Amy Jacques, was a white woman. When that plot failed, they planned to charge him with various financial crimes. Between 1917 and 1924, Hoover demonstrated his fear and hatred of Radical Blackness and his willingness to use illegal tactics to extinguish it by reserving the types of counterintelligence operations that led to Garvey's arrest almost exclusively for Black agents, who primarily infiltrated the UNIA and the ABB.[51]

The efforts to arrest and deport Garvey illuminated the instrumental role of the Black Scare and the Red Scare in anticommunist governance. Early on, the BI warned the US Shipping Board "of Garvey's menace"[52] and tried to convince it not to sell the Black Star Line the SS Orion because the UNIA was a front for the Communist Party and was thus affiliated with the Soviet government. The BI also claimed that Garvey was a racial agitator who associated with anarchists and who advocated and taught the overthrow of the US government by force or violence. Based on these allegations, the shipping company delayed the sale of the SS Orion by six months and charged an exorbitant $450,000 performance bond.[53] Ultimately, the negotiations collapsed, and the US Shipping Board retained the Black Star Line's $22,500 deposit. This financial penalty for purported radicalism was common under anticommunist governance, and those subjected to the Black Scare and the Red Scare quite literally paid dearly.

All of these attempts to criminalize Garvey hit paydirt on January 12, 1922, when a complaint was filed against him by the assistant United States attorney general based on the testimony of Post Office Inspector Oliver B. Williamson. He testified that Garvey had "unlawfully, willfully, and knowingly devise[d] and intended[ed] to devised a scheme and artifice to defraud" based on the inducement, solicitation, and procurement of money and property from "victims" to purchase stock in the Black Star Line and to become members of the UNIA. Garvey was also accused of fraudulently selling stock by faking ownership and control of the Phyllis Wheatley steamship and claiming that it was in good enough condition to make voyages to Africa that could be purchased for a stated sum.[54] It was the BI, of course, that had made the post office inspector aware of Garvey's ostensible crimes. The bureau wrote in late

1921, "As you are well aware, this Bureau for many months past has been investigating Marcus Garvey, an alien Negro who, for more than two years has
been living lavishly off the meager savings of poor Negroes throughout the
United States. The investigation so far discloses violations of several federal
statutes not the least in importance being the violation of the Postal laws."[55]
Garvey's indictment was thus made possible by several departments and
individuals within the executive branch. The same day of Williamson's testimony, on February 15, 1922, Garvey and three Black Star associates, Elie
Garcia, George Tobias, and Orlando Thompson, were formally indicted on
twelve counts of using the mail for fraudulent purposes.[56]

Throughout the trial, which began on May 21, 1923, after a fifteen-month delay, the prosecution presented flimsy evidence about the defendants' fraud and
the use of the mails to effect it. Nonetheless, Garvey was convicted on June 18,
1923, and received the maximum sentence: five years in prison, a $10,000 fine
plus court costs, and no bail.[57] The prosecutor used Black Scare and Red Scare
logic to deny bail, arguing that Garvey was a danger to the community because UNIA members were amassing weapons to violently defend him and
help him evade justice.[58] This charge was eerily similar to the "attempting to
overthrow the government by force or violence" charge consistently levied
at the CPUSA. Despite this maneuvering, Garvey was ultimately released on
bond in September. On February 2, 1925, the US Circuit Court of Appeals
rejected his appeal of the mail fraud conviction, and he was immediately sent
to federal prison in Atlanta, Georgia. On March 23, 1925, the Supreme Court
refused to review the case.[59] When Garvey attempted to attain a presidential
pardon, officials across the US government agreed that he was an undesirable
alien agitator to whom poor, Black "ignorant followers" were devoted. Thus,
commuting his sentence would be an affront to US Capitalist Racist Society.[60]

To guard against Garvey's freedom, the BI prepared to launch a case
against him based on "radical statements" that potentially violated the alien
anarchist provision of the Immigration Laws. He was also indicted for a second time by a federal grand jury on August 18, 1924 for perjury and fraud in
the filing of his 1919 and 1921 income taxes.[61] Despite this Black Scare and
Red Scare maneuvering to keep Garvey imprisoned, Attorney General John G.
Sargent eventually recommended the commutation of the UNIA leader's
sentence—but only if he was swiftly deported. President Calvin Coolidge
complied on November 18, 1927. This recommendation was not based on a
feeling that Garvey's conviction or sentence had been unjust, but rather, in
part, on the growing unrest that was developing among Black people "as a
class" who regarded the sentence as "an act of oppression of the race in their
efforts in the direction of race progress and of discrimination against Garvey

as a negro." Garvey's Radical Blackness ensured that the BI and the Immigration Bureau wasted no time in deporting him. He was ousted from the United States on December 2, 1927.[62]

That the US government was punishing Garvey for his Radical Blackness was evidenced by the fact that while he was found guilty on one count of mail fraud, specifically of sending promotional material through the mail to Benny Dancy who then purchased Black Star Line stock, the three codefendants in the case were acquitted of any complicity or wrongdoing even though they were far more involved in selling stock.[63] As well, the special attack on Garvey because of his race militancy, as he saw it, became clear in that he had received the maximum sentence though this was rarely the outcome in mail fraud cases. This demonstrated that someone deemed subversive because of their foreign origin *and* "foreign" beliefs could not get a fair trial in the US judicial system. "I was convicted . . . because I represented, even as I do now, a movement for the real emancipation of my race," Garvey claimed.[64] Though he blamed his Black enemies and not the government or whites for his conviction and claimed that the higher court would not "mingle prejudice and justice and condemn a man simply because he is Black," he did so in an attempt to shield himself from the Red Scare that, along with the Black Scare, was the source of his repression.

Such attempt was to no avail. Hoover, through his work in the GID, and later the BI, did much to conflate the UNIA and the CPUSA to strengthen his case for Garvey's deportation. Indeed, he saw Blacks demanding equal rights "as one more radical group—like the anarchists, labor militants, or the immigrant communists." In his job as chief of the BI's Radical Division, "he would open a broad investigation on 'negro activities' and keep particular tabs on Marcus Garvey, a rising New York–based agitator whose newspaper, *Negro World*, seemed to Edgar to preach Bolshevism . . . behind it all, he saw Reds."[65] Through the Red Scare crescendo in 1919, Garvey was seen as a threat equal to "Black sharecroppers . . . organizing, Black Detroiters attending an IWW school, Black longshoremen [striking], and middle-class Blacks espousing socialism." However, when those modes of Black militancy linked to broader forms of radicalism were interrupted by mass deportation and intimidation, "the Justice Department and Immigration Bureau began to pursue Garvey, who had already won their displeasure and whose alien status made him vulnerable" to anticommunist governance.[66]

As Robert Hill argued, Garvey had become more conservative in his rhetoric to curry favor with Hoover and the US government after authorities had tried to prevent him from reentering the United States in 1921 after a speaking tour in Jamaica. Garvey's trip lasted five months instead of the planned thirty days in part because he was having trouble securing a reentry visa. He was only able to return in June 1921 after William Matthews, the UNIA's New York City assistant counselor general, bribed a member of the State Department.[67] Given the Justice Department's attempt to effectively deport Garvey by denying re-entry, he began to talk about the United States as the cradle of liberty and to assert his organization's loyalty. Garvey pursued this patriotic rightward course with the same fervor and determination that had characterized his radical phase in which he spoke positively of the Bolshevik Revolution. This race to the right, though, did not insulate him from political repression or make him acceptable in the eyes of J. Edgar Hoover or the anticommunist state apparatus. In fact, Hoover was more intent than ever to punish Garvey since the UNIA leader had bested him by gaining re-entry into the United States. Garvey did not take seriously the "political factors"—the Black Scare and the Red Scare—that precluded the government from accepting a Black, foreign, subversive agitator.[68]

Garvey's rightward shift included the development of a vehement anticommunist position; as such, the charge of Bolshevism was grossly inaccurate. However, his disdain for the Reds did not save him—nor did his condemnation of Black leaders' promotion of social equality, that he reduced to a desire for amalgamation,[69] which resonated with Black Scare hysteria about "social equality" and parroted Red Scare anti-interracialist discourse. By contrast, Garvey inadvertently affirmed the very tools of anticommunist governance used to punish him. His employment of some of the very logics of the Black Scare and the Red Scare did nothing but encourage the dragnet of anticommunism. For example, the accusation that Garvey had committed fraud, while attributed to personal gain during his trial, was in fact rooted in Black Scare and Red Scare fears that if he could convince ignorant Blacks to give up their meager savings, he could also imbue them with subversive ideas, from antiwhite hatred to Black self-determination. This was conveyed in the fact that "the prosecution, from the U.S. attorney's office in New York to the Bureau of Investigation in Washington, applauded the judgment and anticipated deporting Garvey because of his agitation." This anticommunist aim was concealed by the government's claim of "alleged deception."[70]

To be fair, Garvey's use of Black Scare and Red Scare logics in an attempt to evade government repression was not unlike the cooperation of communists like Cyril Briggs and socialists like Hubert Harrison with the state to prosecute and deport Garvey. In doing so, they too negotiated the terms of their political immiseration. For example, Briggs's encouragement of the US Postal Inspection Service to prosecute Garvey for his "fraudulent" Black Star Line mailers did not insulate him or the ABB from being targeted by anticommunism. In fact, "agents searched for a way to indict Briggs, too. Co-operation brought no immunity."[71] Garvey's patriotic and conservative talking points emanated from the exigencies of engaging in Radical Black struggle while attempting to evade the Black Scare and the Red Scare. Nonetheless, the executive branch was committed to the anticommunist prosecution and persecution of the race man whose advocacy of Black self-determination, autonomy, and independence made him irrevocably radical, dangerous, and undesirable.

The Judicial Branch

The judicial branch of the US federal government has the authority and responsibility to interpret the law, decide which federal laws are constitutional, and to resolve disputes about them. This branch significantly relies on the other two, as federal judges are appointed by the president and confirmed by the Senate. The Supreme Court is the only part of the judicial branch specifically stipulated in the Constitution. This branch is supposed to be apolitical, but it nonetheless played a significant role in anticommunist governance during the Black Scare / Red Scare Longue Durée.

From World War I onward, the US judicial system became engulfed by anticommunist hysteria, abandoning its responsibilities to protect the rights and liberties of communists and progressives.[72] One interpretation holds that between 1919 and 1927 and 1950 and 1956, the Supreme Court largely rendered "bad faith interpretations of clear and present danger," but in the era spanning 1927–47, "the Court's speech decisions consistently expanded freedom to communicate and correlatively restricted governments' power to suppress that communication."[73] However, when both the Black Scare and the Red Scare are taken into account, the criminal legal system, the judicial branch, and the Supreme Court can be seen as active participants in anticommunist governance. Especially as the United States began its rise to global hegemony, "there was little tolerance in America for speech that threatened polite society, let alone the security of the state."[74]

The judiciary tended to evade "aggressive enforcement of personal rights" and even after World War I "when the Supreme Court 'incorporated' the provisions of the First Amendment into the Fourteenth Amendment and made them binding on state actors," such freedom, especially as it applied to "dissidents" continued to be left largely to the discretion of "local preference" and "state constitutional safeguards." Demonstrating its commitment to maintaining US Capitalist Racist Society, the reluctance to enforce individual liberties regarding free speech stood in sharp contrast to the "vigorous enforcement of liberty of contract, allegedly enshrined within the due process clauses of the Fifth and Fourteenth Amendments."[75] Much of the Supreme Court's hostility to protecting radical speech—and its relationship to militant acts—had to do with the role of labor in pushing for such protection.[76] It preferred to protect and uphold employers' rights and contractual freedom and to uphold anti-worker convictions for criminal conspiracy, vagrancy, violation of assembly laws, and injunctions against strikes, boycotts, and labor organizing.[77] Thus, in overwhelmingly siding with capital over laborers, radicals, and Blacks, the Supreme Court, the federal courts, and the criminal legal system at the state and local levels played an instrumental role in anticommunist governance.

The several cases of Angelo Herndon affirm this reading of the Supreme Court as effectively anticommunist, even as *Herndon v. Lowry* was ultimately decided in his favor in 1937. *Herndon v. Lowry* was consequential because it was the first time the Supreme Court had reviewed a sedition conviction from the South, the first time it reviewed a sedition case in which the defendant was Black,[78] and the first civil liberties case argued before it in which a Black "dissident" sought the protection of the First Amendment.[79] Moreover, the only two Supreme Court cases during the Great Depression that considered the "clear and present danger" doctrine were those that dealt with Herndon's conviction.[80] Even though *Herndon v. Lowry* was the first time the Supreme Court had used the "clear and present danger" test to uphold civil liberties, its impact was undermined by the other branches of the federal government and state governments, which were enacting various forms of antiradical repression.[81]

Furthermore, prior to the *Lowry* decision, Herndon's appeal was denied by the Georgia Supreme Court on May 24, 1934, the first appeal to the Supreme Court was denied on May 20, 1935, and the Supreme Court turned down the initial petition for a rehearing on October 13, 1935. That denial resulted in an order for Herndon to surrender himself to the Georgia authorities within twenty days to begin serving his sentence of twenty years on a chain gang. Herndon's cases convey that anticommunism was not reducible to "Southern justice." The hostility toward and criminalization of interracial cooperation, Black self-determination, and the Red Black / Black Red were national phenomena.[82]

The experience of Angelo Herndon in the criminal legal system—or criminal punishment system—from his initial indictment to his case's final resolution by the Supreme Court is an archetypal example of how anticommunist governance brought together the Black Scare, the Red Scare, and efforts to preserve US Capitalist Racist Society. In a general sense, the courtrooms, cases, and trials he endured were transformed into sites to condemn, criminalize, and punish Radical Blackness. As Herndon understood his trial, the

Southern whites who were more refined than the brute white supremacists, but who were no less hostile to Blacks, communists, and the Red Black / Black Red, "were determined that no 'impudent' and 'uppity' nigger should get away with insulting the white upper class of Georgia . . . they were going to make an example of me for all those 'damn Red' and Yankee 'nigger lovers'!"[83]

During his first trial, when his Black lawyer, the future Smith Act defendant Benjamin J. Davis Jr., moved to have the case dismissed on the grounds that the anti-insurrection law was unconstitutional, that the indictment was too vague, and that Blacks had been excluded from the jury, his motion was denied outright. Any evidence that would have helped Herndon was dismissed as "irrelevant and immaterial," and when Davis vigorously protested the use of "nigger" when referring to Herndon because it would prejudice the jury, the judge overruled him.[84] After a witness for the prosecution referred to Herndon as a "darkey," Davis moved for a directed verdict because the racism exhibited throughout the trial precluded it from being fair for his client. The judge overruled the motion. These objections were made not because he thought the racist judge would rule in his favor, but rather with appeal to higher courts in mind. Davis knew Herndon would not receive justice in the heart of the Southern Black Belt.[85]

The assistant state solicitor of Georgia made liberal use of both the Black Scare and the Red Scare. He emphatically argued, "The Communists must be put down or civilization will fail."[86] Such failure of civilization was linked to intermarriage, worker militancy, and Black self-determination. The prosecutor constantly used the threat of intermarriage to stoke fear about the communist platform, particularly the idea of Black self-determination.[87] In his closing statement, he dramatically enjoined: "You have heard the defendant lay down his [intent to] defy to the State of Georgia. He is a confirmed revolutionist . . . send this damnable anarchistic Bolsheviki to his death by electrocution . . . and the daughters of the state officials can walk the streets safely. Stamp this thing out now with a conviction."[88] Every opportunity was taken to resort to mythologies about deviant Black sexuality, particularly the Black male rapist, in the effort to criminalize and crush CPUSA-led, Radical Black–inflected worker organizing.

Prosecutor Hudson balanced the threat Herndon ostensibly posed to the racial order[89] with heavy doses of the Red Scare because the racial order in the South was fundamentally an economic one. The prosecution pressed Herndon on a number of issues concerning what they perceived to be the dangers of worker empowerment and Black equality. These included whether employers and the government should pay unemployment insurance to jobless workers, if Blacks should have complete equality with whites, if Black people should have self-determination in the Black Belt, and if white landlords and government officials should be overthrown in that territory.[90] This anticommunist line of questioning used the twin scares to convey that the beliefs and actions of a poor, Radical Black worker menaced the extant social and political economic order.

According to one legal historian, "while the court's opinion in *Herndon v. Georgia* claim[ed] to be and appear[ed] to be about radical politics, it [was] in fact best understood as a case about the politics of race."[91] However, in all of Herndon's cases the courts employed anticommunism to manage race *and* radicalism in US Capitalist Racist Society. Herndon's indictment and ultimate conviction under Georgia's insurrection law in 1933 was a function of his assertive Blackness, his membership in the CPUSA, and his interracial organizing. Individually, all of these things were an affront to the Southern economic and racial order; brought together, they were downright subversive. This was exacerbated by the involvement of the CPUSA-adjacent International Labor Defense (ILD) in Herndon's case. Given the racist nature of Herndon's case—manifested, for example, in the complete exclusion of Blacks from the jury—the ILD audaciously selected two young Black lawyers, Ben Davis and John H. Greer, to take the lead even though they were relatively inexperienced. The ILD's efforts to draw national attention to and garner mass support for the case also carried the stench of subversion.[92] They held that the "class essence of capitalist justice" required them to wage struggle not only in the courtroom, but also through mass protest to put pressure on the state to release Herndon who, as a "class war" prisoner, was also a political prisoner.[93] Hence, the ILD lawyers were quintessential Outside Agitators defending a dangerous Red Black / Black Red and mobilizing "nigger lovers" and fellow travelers in his defense.

Herndon's initial conviction and appeals drew attention to the ways the Southern states used the judiciary to crush radical political activity, challenges to the racial and economic status quo, and any adjacent dissent or protest.[94] As such, the ILD, with the support of several organizations, waged the "Free Angelo Herndon" campaign against this attempted "legal lynching," which quickly gained national support. The campaign sought to make the case a cause célèbre for illuminating the repressive conditions in the South, sustained by white supremacy, anti-Black racial oppression, and staunch anticommunism. The protest campaign built up by the ILD around the push to free first the Scottsboro Nine and then Angelo Herndon demonstrated "the virtues of direct action and militant struggle," which was a significant achievement in the South—and a significant menace to its sociality.[95]

The Scottsboro case provided a precursor for the combination of mass organizing and legal action as a strategy for combating legal lynchings. Nine

Black boys—Andy Wright, Roy Wright, Haywood Patterson, Eugene Williams, Clarence Norris, Charles Weems, Ozie Powell, Olen Montgomery, and Willie Roberson—were accused of rape by two young white women, Ruby Bates and Victoria Price, on March 25, 1931. After Patterson got into a physical altercation with a group of white boys on a train car, the "Scottsboro Boys" were arrested in Paint Rock, Alabama. Though they were initially charged with assault and attempted murder, they were soon accused of raping the two former textile mill workers. That night, three hundred Klansmen attempted to break into the jail and lynch the boys; only the arrival of the Alabama National Guard saved them.

On March 31, the Scottsboro Nine were indicted by a grand jury for rape in Gadsden, Alabama, and faced the death penalty. The trial opened on April 6, and Bates and Price reiterated that they had been raped by the defendants six times over a three-hour time period. Equally damning, Clarence Norris accused Charlie Weems of raping Price. All nine defendants were ultimately found guilty. Given that death sentences were handed down, the ILD took on the case, appealing their convictions and launching an international campaign for their freedom. Through appeals and mass protest, the ILD was able to win postponement of the executions. For its part, the NAACP used persuasive legal argument to save the boys' lives. Conflict between the ILD and the NAACP hampered efforts to save the boys, but ultimately *Powell v. Alabama* established the right to counsel in 1932; Ruby Bates recanted the rape charges and began testifying for the defense that same year; and protests escalated and petitions circulated worldwide. By the time *Lowry* was handed down, four of the defendants were freed, and over the next decade all but Patterson would be released.[96]

Underscoring the threat of mass-based action to ruling-class power that had been effective in saving the lives of the Scottsboro Boys, Atlanta officials and vigilantes engaged in a campaign of relentless terrorism to undermine the popular movement organized for Herndon's freedom. The state raided homes and offices and moved to outlaw left-wing and progressive organizations; the Klan burned crosses on the lawns of workers supporting the Herndon effort; and a white mob accosted Ben Davis and threatened to lynch him.[97] The ultimate terrorism, however, was meted out by the court when Herndon was convicted of insurrection on January 18, 1933.

The ILD immediately appealed to the Georgia Supreme Court. The ruling in *Herndon v. State* on May 24, 1934, was as follows:

> The trial court had been wrong in its charge [to the jury in considering Herndon's conviction]: Section 56, the court said, did not require that violence

should follow Herndon's words immediately, or even at all (nor, presumably, that he violent consequences be "serious" or "widespread"); rather, it "would be sufficient that [Herndon] intended [violence] to happen *at any time*, as a result of his influence, by those whom he sought to incite."[98]

The Georgia Supreme Court refused to overturn Herndon's conviction, but it did issue a stay of sentence pending appeal so Herndon was not immediately sent to the chain gang. Bail was set at the exorbitant sum of $15,000; if it was not paid in twenty-three days, he would be forced to begin serving over two decades of arduous free labor.[99] The money was ultimately raised, and Herndon was released on bail on August 4, 1934.[100]

Next, the ILD, in collaboration with a team of progressive white lawyers, appealed the case to the US Supreme Court, specifically challenging the constitutionality of Georgia's insurrection law. The case took on new importance because on March 14, 1935, the Hartsfield-Almand sedition bill passed the Georgia House of Representatives unanimously, and then the Senate soon after. The bill was meant to supplement the insurrection law because it was claimed that a variety of attempts were being made to spread sedition among Georgians. Not unlike what had been argued in Herndon's case, the bill defined sedition as the possession of or attempt to circulate writings, publications, or ideas that encouraged the use of force against the government, with possession of five or more copies of such material counting as evidence of intent to circulate.[101] Additionally, exactly one week later, an anti-CPUSA act was passed, which aimed to "discourage, regulate, and control communistic activities in Georgia by prohibiting the recognition of political parties advocating communism or similar theories." It declared that no political party advocating the overthrow of the government or that carried out a seditious or treasonous program would be afforded a place on election ballots.[102] Though Governor Herman Talmadge vetoed the bill for political reasons, his statement that the "purpose of the bill[s] were good" demonstrated his ultimate investment in the Red Scare even as he stymied that particular legislation.[103]

In this dangerously hostile milieu, the ILD attempted to attack Herndon's conviction on the grounds that Georgia's insurrection law was unconstitutional; in doing so, they offered up a test case to probe whether attempts to legislate antiradicalism across the country were compatible with the US Constitution. On April 12, 1935, the lawyers argued that the insurrection law restricted free speech and failed to conform with the "clear and present danger" test. The State of Georgia argued that because the communists sought to establish a "Negro Nation" in the Black Belt, the insurrection law in this case did not violate the Constitution and did pass the "clear and present danger test."

This side also argued that the issue of constitutionality had not been raised at the proper time and therefore the Supreme Court did not have jurisdiction.[104]

On May 20, 1935, the Supreme Court ruled 6–3 that the issue had not been properly argued in Herndon's initial trial, which meant that the Supreme Court did not have jurisdiction.[105] Here, it can be argued that the court's refusal was politically motivated, or, more accurately, a reflection of its fidelity to anticommunist governance. That three of the nine justices dissented attests to the dubiousness—and highly political nature—of this decision. The Supreme Court declined jurisdiction, in essence deferring to "states' rights" instead of asserting federal power. The anticommunist overtone of this decision was manifested in the way that the court refused to properly acknowledge Herndon as a victim of Southern racial violence and terrorism as it has done in cases like *Powell v. Alabama*. "Of the Court's decisions from this period that invalidated the convictions of African-American defendants on constitutional grounds, *all except Herndon* followed *Powell's* rhetorical strategy with respect to the politics of race."[106] As a militant Black labor organizer who was also a member of the Communist Party, Herndon was not the same type of defendant as the poor and illiterate Scottsboro Boys who were railroaded through charges of rape. By contrast, Herndon's case was the first time the Supreme Court had to directly deliberate about a political "crime" when the alleged criminal was a Red Black / Black Red.[107] In effect, the court was ambivalent about ruling on free speech in the case of a Black communist,[108] so it built on its history of evading a ruling on a complicated matter by "dispos[ing] of a case on other grounds."[109]

Here, the Supreme Court not only encouraged legal and extralegal methods of preventing Blacks and radicals from asserting their constitutional rights, but also the implementation of criminal statutes designed to "defeat the exercise of civil liberties." The Supreme Court's refusal reflected anticommunism as a means of maintaining the status quo in its "avoid[ance of] the necessity of formulating a standard according to which sedition legislation might be tested," thus leaving the rights of political and racial minorities to the whims of "the forces working for their suppression."[110] The *University of Pennsylvania Law Review's* condemnation of the ruling as an attack on free speech and the rights of minorities[111] and the *Columbia Law Review's* characterization of the decision as "a flagrant and inexcusable miscarriage of justice" and a failure of the court to "uphold the constitutional rights of Negroes who attempt to assert them in the struggle against their miserable economic and social status"[112] illuminated how the Supreme Court tacitly lent support to the Black Scare and the Red Scare by participating in anticommunist governance through inaction.

An ILD pamphlet, *20 Years on the Chain Gang?*, argued that the Supreme Court's refusal to hear *Herndon v. Georgia* on a technicality could be considered the Dred Scott decision of the twentieth century. Not unlike how *Dred Scott v. Sanford* affirmed the power and authority of slaveholders in 1857, the refusal to reverse Herndon's conviction based on specious grounds likewise represented the genuflection of the federal government generally, and the Supreme Court particularly, to the Southern elite.[113] However, the decision more accurately reflected how refusal to act—in this instance, to hear the case—was a key instrumentality of anticommunist governance used by all three branches. The pamphlet argued that, in not hearing the case, the Supreme Court was complicit in upholding the ruling class's "most outspoken declaration of fascism yet made in America" insofar as it deemed that membership in a radical organization and possession of literature aimed at raising the consciousness of the working class were crimes punishable by death—or crimes for which mercy was ruthless and brutal labor on a chain gang.[114]

The relationship between the court's anticommunist refusal and its affirmation of the capitalist racism that undergirded Herndon's indictment and conviction was summed up in a newspaper article that analyzed the national significance of the Herndon case. Georgia officials had admitted in no uncertain terms that if the Supreme Court upheld Herndon's conviction, they would use the insurrection statute against anyone who advocated Black equality or the right of whites and Blacks to organize in the same union. This demonstrated that the race question was central in the struggle to organize Southern workers and sharecroppers, and maintenance of the color line was an invaluable tool in the attack on labor. Herndon's conviction thus laid the groundwork for the open drive to decimate new labor and sharecropper organizations through the use of "old slave laws" in Georgia, Arkansas, and throughout the Black Belt. The whole standard of living in the South would then be lowered, according to the article, which would also threaten the standards and conditions of Northern labor and manufacturing. The fight to free Herndon, then, was a fight to free Southern laborers and farmers, and this fight would also free Northern labor from the low wages and the violent measures used to maintain them.[115] In refusing jurisdiction, the Supreme Court effectively upheld states' rights to criminalize agitation for Black equality, labor rights, and interracial unionism; confirmed the legitimacy of anti-Black and antilabor policy; and sanctioned the use of anticommunism as a means of continuing these forms of oppression, exploitation, and repression.

The Supreme Court doubled down on its refusal on October 14, 1935, by denying the ILD's petition for a rehearing. The case was thus remanded back to Georgia, and Herndon was returned to prison.[116] Herndon was released after a judge ruled in November 1935 in a habeas corpus hearing that the Georgia insurrection law was unconstitutional because it was indeed too vague and indefinite to "provide a sufficiently ascertainable standard of guilt." Here, the problem with the insurrection law was its vagueness, not its intent. As such, the judge was quick to advise the passage of a new law that was both constitutional and effective in combating insurrection. He acknowledged the role of the Supreme Court in upholding such anticommunist governance by stating, "Many of our states have laws that have been upheld by the Supreme Court of the United States which give ample protection against doctrines such as Herndon was advocating."[117]

That statement, as much as the ruling, encouraged the State of Georgia to argue in its January 25, 1936, appeal of the decision to the Georgia Supreme Court that every communist was violent and Herndon was especially so because he sought to overthrow the government and to set up a Black republic in the South. On June 13, 1936, the higher court reversed the lower court's decision and upheld Herndon's conviction. In doing so, it justified the Black Scare and Red Scare persecution of ten white and eight Black radicals who were arrested in the midst of the decision on Herndon's case on May 28, 1936, and charged with attempting to incite an insurrection.[118]

The ILD was more successful in its second appeal to the Supreme Court. In a precursor of what was to come three months later, the Supreme Court issued an ambivalent affirmative ruling in *De Jonge v. Oregon*. The high court overturned the conviction of Dirk de Jonge who had been convicted under Oregon's criminal syndicalism law for his role in convening a peaceful protest—a conviction that very much resonated with Herndon's. In de Jonge's case, "the state's logic was brutally simple. The Communist Party advocated violence and sabotage; de Jonge was a Communist and obeyed the party's dictates; therefore he too must advocate violence and sabotage. The state never bothered to provide further evidence of de Jonge's guilt." The Supreme Court offered a unanimous but very narrow ruling that peaceful assembly was not a crime. However, it did not challenge the constitutionality of Oregon's anti-syndicalism law, and in fact acknowledged that it appeared to be constitutional. In other words, while the Supreme Court ruled that the law was erroneously applied to de Jonge, it refused to establish a rule or test for evaluating state-level legislation related to syndicalism, sedition, or the legality of Communist Party doctrines.[119]

On April 26, 1937 in *Herndon v. Lowry*, the court finally struck down the Georgia insurrection law as construed and applied to the Herndon case because it violated freedom of speech and freedom of assembly. In the 5–4 decision, the court also held that the political-crimes statute in Georgia was unconstitutional because it did not furnish a reasonable standard of guilt.[120] Even here, the court's decision left ample room for Black Scare and Red Scare maneuvering in specifying that Herndon's conviction was not valid because he had not been *caught* circulating the literature and advocating subversion of the government. Here, it was a question of proof, not of the law's ultimate aim or purpose. Likewise, it was ruled that the insurrection law did not stipulate that membership in or recruitment to the Communist Party was prohibited, and yet it had been applied in this way in Herndon's case at the discretion of a jury. The court did not rule that it was illegal to codify such prohibition in law. The vagueness of the insurrection law was also a point of contention. As Justice Owen Roberts argued in the majority opinion, "as construed and applied [the law] amounts to a dragnet which may enmesh anyone who agitates for a change of government if the jury can be persuaded that he ought to have foreseen his words would have some effect in the future conduct of others."[121] Thus, those seeking to enact legislation to shore up anticommunism need only be precise and specific, as was the case with laws then under consideration in the Georgia legislature and in effect throughout the nation.

In the dissenting opinion, Justice Willis Van Devanter reflected prevailing Black Scare and Red Scare views in defending the applicability of the insurrection law to Herndon's case. Blacks' "past and present circumstances," he maintained, made them particularly susceptible to, and a target of, the communist position, which was violent and advocated forcible resistance. Likewise, Herndon, as a Black communist seeking to recruit more Black communists, had dangerously encouraged revolution and was thus guilty under the insurrection law.[122]

The Supreme Court's *Herndon v. Lowry* decision did nothing to counter the idea that "clear and drastic measures [must] be taken to protect the state and Federal Government from these radical assaults," and did not deter it from stabilizing anticommunist governance by equivocating on settling fundamental social issues and evading permanent enforcement of the Thirteenth, Fourteenth, and Fifteenth Amendments. The court merely "frown[ed] upon," but did not forcefully prevent, states from violently repressing radical politics or dissident attitudes.[123]

While the executive and judicial branches of the federal government played an invaluable role in upholding anticommunist governance, it was the legislative branch, with its dizzying array of antiradical legislation and witch-hunt committees, that fortified and spectacularized it.

9

Sedition, Subversion, and National Security: The Anticommunist Governance of the Legislative Branch

The McCarran Act does more to undermine American justice than anything we or anyone else can say against it. Our country is already notorious for its class justice against the poor, and its lynch justice against the Negro. It needs the McCarran Act like it needs a hole in the head.

BENJAMIN J. DAVIS JR., 1962

The legislative branch of the federal government consists of the US Congress and has the singular authority to enact legislation and declare war, the duty of confirming or rejecting most presidential appointments, and, of keen importance, substantial investigative powers. This branch principally engaged in anticommunist governance through the passage of antiradical laws and through convening investigative committees in both the Senate and the House of Representatives.

During the Black Scare / Red Scare Longue Durée, a number of federal "laws which either on their face or as applied by the government, the courts or administrative authorities" were passed to preserve US Capitalist Racist Society and to "punish or restrain speech, membership or thought, wholly apart and independent of any actions which threaten[ed] the security of the state."[1] These laws tended to proliferate as war—World War I, World War II, the Cold War, the Korean War—intensified. Culminating during the early Cold War, the combined aim of these numerous laws was to effectively ban the CPUSA outright and to dismantle organizations that were ostensibly communist fronts or infiltrated by communists and thus equally subversive. This dragnet of legislation directly impacted individuals and groups that had any overlap with communist programs, propaganda, or party lines, like peace, opposition to nuclear armament and testing, protection of labor rights, advocacy of social welfare, and, importantly racial equality. Antiradical laws and committee investigations were particularly potent because they were vaguely defined so as to be broadly applied to manifold forms of dissent and independent thought.[2] They were also extended through conspiracy statutes that allowed for mass indictments and trials and "maximum repressive effect from a single proceeding."[3]

Anticommunism emanating from the legislative branch generally fell into four classes: imposition of criminal penalty on speech, press, or assembly; punishment of political dissent through the loss of benefit, right, privilege, or access to occupation; requirement of registration by individuals or organizations that amounted to a confession of danger or threat based on belief or association; and subjection to congressional investigations that were designed to harass, injure, or destroy individuals through "one-sided, savage interrogations." Some laws and policies combined these classes. Criminalization for perjury or contempt often accompanied the anticommunist governance emanating from the legislative branch.[4]

The Espionage Act and the Sedition Act against Radicalism and Black Militancy

The Espionage Act was passed on June 15, 1917, just as the US entered World War I. Among other things, it criminalized any interference with the operations or success of the military and naval forces through false reports or false statements; the promotion of the success of enemies of the US; and, while the US was at war, the willful cause or attempt to cause "insubordination, disloyalty, mutiny, or refusal of duty" in the armed forces or the obstruction of recruitment or enlistment. The punishment was a fine of up to $10,000 and up to twenty years in prison, or both. Moreover, any "letter, writing, circular, post card, picture, print, engraving, photograph, newspaper, pamphlet, book, or other publication, matter, or thing" that violated those provisions, or that contained "any matter advocating or urging treason, insurrection, or forcible resistance to any law of the United States" was declared nonmailable.[5] Its twin legislation, the Sedition Act, was passed on May 16, 1918, and expanded the government's control over freedom of expression and ability to punish activities and publications that were critical of the war. Such criticism was construed as detrimental to the war effort. The act imposed up to $10,000 in fines and twenty years of imprisonment for speaking, printing, writing, or publishing "disloyal, profane, scurrilous or abusive language" about the US government, Constitution, military or naval forces or their uniforms, or encouraging "contempt, scorn, contumely, or disrepute" against these.[6]

Together, the Espionage and Subversion Acts animated, and were animated by, the Black Scare and the Red Scare. They laid the basis for the prosecution of an array of radicals, including antiwar activists, members of the IWW (Wobblies), anarchists, and socialists who were considered "a lawless and malignant few" and "a menace to organized society."[7] That the Espionage Act brought together these scares is evident in the fact that a Black labor organizer, Joe Dennis, was the first person to be convicted under its purview. His crime was urging a strike for better working conditions, and he was charged with interfering with the movement of troops.[8]

These draconian laws aimed to push the nation to uncritically back involvement in the war. They swept aside First Amendment rights in targeting dissidents of all types, including the militant labor organizers, liberal free speech advocates, antiwar activists, and Blacks agitators for racial equality. This repression intensified after the Bolshevik Revolution, as the Euro-American ruling classes reacted with outrage and panic. The wave of militant strikes and rising spirit of Black resistance to white terrorism brought that panic to new heights in the United States.[9]

Signaling the collaboration of all three branches of government in anti-communist rule, these acts gave power to the BI to target individuals and organizations considered to be hampering the war effort and empowered the DOJ to use legal tactics that would "cripple an organization by subjecting its leaders to costly and protracted court proceedings."[10] Likewise, the acts created the precedent for "national security" to become the basis for convicting dissidents with scant evidence. The trials emanating from the Espionage and Sedition Acts laid the groundwork for Cold War prosecutions that likewise had little to no evidence that defendants actually committed seditious acts. Instead, they were charged based on their militant words and writings. At both ends of the Black Scare / Red Scare Longue Durée, protection of freedom of speech was relaxed to enable convictions on scant and spurious evidence.[11]

The passage of the Espionage and Sedition Acts coincided with both the assertive mood of US Blacks that would soon explode into the New Negro movement and with an uptick in the Black Scare, as Black enlistment in the Great War, Black refusal to enlist, Black migration out of the South, and other forms of Black assertion filled white Americans, across class, with dread. Repression of dissent coupled with pro-war propaganda between 1917 and 1918 propelled the idea that enemies of the United States would exploit divisions in the society. As a result, whites were filled with fear at the prospect of Black men being inducted into the army, armed, and trained to fight, and "suspicion and dread welled up to create a 'black scare' of unprecedented proportions."[12] Whites were hysterical about the possibility of Black domination, and their fear resulted in the revival of the Ku Klux Klan and increased racial violence as Blacks more consistently fought back against racial terror.

The Black Scare ensured that Blacks' indignation and new fighting spirit, flowing from being armed and trained in the military, would be blamed for increased race hostility—not their mistreatment. In other words, Black assertion was deemed a threat to national security while white terrorism and white supremacy were not.[13] Some government officials went so far as to blame both the increase in lynching and Black demands for better treatment on aggravation and intrigue by German spies.[14] Thus, Black challenge to racial hierarchy and mob violence was transformed into a form of radicalism and potential subversion equal to that of communists, socialists, and anarchists. Additionally, it was assumed that misinformation about the war would spread more easily among Black people given the ever-present issue of whether Blacks, whose citizenship was questionable at best, would readily join "real and imagined enemies" of the United States.[15]

These misgivings were coupled with the widespread rumors that German agents were encouraging migration to Mexico to cripple the Southern economy and that Mexicans were coaxing Blacks to do the same by promising them peace, luxury, land, education, and a new life south of the border.[16] In this milieu, Black migration was looked upon with suspicion and in some cases was considered a form of subversion. The Espionage and Sedition Acts gave the legal architecture for both the prosecution and intense BI surveillance of Blacks because of their suspected disloyalty, susceptibility to foreign influence, and manifold forms of action that were potentially dangerous or seditious.[17]

Such fear emanated from a rumored plot, the San Diego Plan, which first came to the attention of US authorities in February 1915. This plan involved Mexico, Germany, and Japan and called for Mexicans and Mexican Americans to rise up against the US government and declare independence. It also suggested "a subsequent annexation of six additional states of the Union, these to be turned over to the 'Negroes,' who were expected to form their own independent republic."[18] The San Diego Plan would include "a provisional directorate, composed of the nine signatories [that] would provide political leadership, while a Liberating Army of Races and Peoples made up of Mexican-Americans, blacks and Japanese fighting under a red and white flag bearing the legend 'Equality and Independence' would wage implacable warfare." While it was unclear whether this plan was real or apocryphal, it succeeded in causing racial tension throughout the nation.[19]

During and after World War I, radical publications like *Crusader* and the *Messenger*, and radicals like Hubert Harrison and Cyril Briggs, would be rendered subversive for advocating the type of solidarity among colored peoples that was outlined in the San Diego Plan. The fear of Black susceptibility to foreign influence, especially German influence, was thus firmly implanted in the minds of members of the US government and the broader society by the time the United States entered the Great War. The effect was twofold. The first was the "weaving together of Germany and Negro grievances," which had "allowed some members of the US government to blame Germany for its 'Negro problem.'"[20] The second was surveillance and punishment of potential, suspected, and concocted Black disloyalty. The latter was manifested, for example, in NAACP leader Major Joel Spingarn calling for a nationwide counterintelligence program within the Black community, which W. E. B. Du Bois, who had earlier come out against the war, reluctantly supported.[21]

It is important to note that there was a seamless transition from fear of Black-German alliance during World War I to fear of Black-Bolshevik alliance shortly thereafter in part because of US hostility to interracialism. This linkage was manifested in the Overman Committee, an ad hoc subcommittee of the Senate Judiciary Committee, authorized on September 19, 1918. During the hearings on "Bolshevik Propaganda," in February through March 1919, it was claimed that "the Bolsheviki movement [was] a branch of the revolutionary socialism of Germany. It ha[d] its origin in the philosophy of Marx and its leaders were Germans." Likewise, "The Bolsheviki [were] simply the modern manifestation of official German socialism, to which has been added some of the principles and tactics of syndicalism."[22] Relatedly, German socialists who came to the United States after 1848 were much more amenable to interracial organizing and socializing and were often more hostile to Jim Crow than were other European groups.[23]

Both Germans and communists/Bolsheviks were hated because of their perceived defiance of racial hierarchy and antiracist appeals to Black people. This interracialism, on the one hand, and hatred by the government, on the other hand, also linked Germans and Bolsheviks to the IWW, an organization that was also maligned by the Overman Committee.[24] As such, irrespective of the lack of mass appeal of socialism/communism among Blacks, the defiance of the racial order through interracialism exacerbated the threat of Blackness, radicalism, and Radical Blackness and made them dangerous and un-American. Interracialism was thus a strong bridge between anti-Germanism and anti-Bolshevism and the Black Scare and the Red Scare.

★

During World War I, the IWW was targeted and harassed incessantly by the government; in fact, the "Great Wobbly Trials of 1918" represented the pinnacle of federal wartime repression.[25] Virtually since its inception, the IWW had been hated by capitalists and imperialists, and its general opposition to war provided an excuse for the government to exterminate it through legal means.[26] Not only did the organization possess a number of immigrant workers, including the hated Germans, but it also allowed Black workers to join on an equal footing—"the *only* labor organization in the second decade of the twentieth century which stood squarely for the organization of Negro workers on the basis of complete equality" and that never in its history organized a segregated local.[27] As NAACP cofounder Mary Ovington White argued, the IWW had systematically "attack[ed] Negro segregation" and "stood with the Negro."[28] In fact, its chapter in Chicago was instrumental in the meatpacking and steel industry union-organizing drives that recruited an "unprecedented" number of Black and immigrant workers into the labor movement. They were successful in doing so because, like the CPUSA would do later, the IWW opposed any Jim Crow approach to organizing workers.[29]

The IWW's broad-based approach was described by Wilfred A. Domingo thus: "these intrepid evangels of industrial unionism made special appeals to the migratory farm worker of the West, the ignorant white man of Louisiana, and the despised negro. . . . In recognizing the importance of reaching negroes with their gospel the IWW are showing statesmanlike farsightedness."[30] Despite the fact that the IWW did not have broad appeal among the Black masses because it organized in industries in which Black workers were not largely represented[31]—and because it tended to reduce the race question to the class question—the danger of this organization was in its interracialism, in its willingness to defy the racial hierarchy that structured US Capitalist Racist Society.[32] If "the reason why the Negro had not been admitted to membership in the trade unions [was] on account of that distinguished slogan: Americanism,"[33] then the IWW's acceptance of Blacks and the interracial solidarity it engendered was decidedly un-American.

Philadelphia's Local 8, "the most stable East Coast IWW organization" led by the Black longshoreman Ben Fletcher—whom one BI agent described as a "very black Negro"[34]—was composed of mostly Blacks who held at least half of the leadership positions. It also had a system of rotating chairmen, with Black and white chairmen alternating each month.[35] Local 8 exemplified the ability of Blacks and whites to work, live, and conduct affairs in close proximity without conflict and to work out the race problem among themselves.[36] Such interracial organizing, the *Messenger* claimed, was superior to the race reductionism of the UNIA and, most importantly, was a bulwark against capitalist exploitation: "When the workers, in America, are able to build Local 8's in every section of the country, the 100 per centers, the Open Shoppers, the combined manufacturers and capitalists of America, will not dare to institute an assault upon labor in the guise of the 'American Plan.'"[37] As such, the IWW generally, and Local 8 particularly, threatened to be "a revolutionary force for both racial and economic justice."[38] This, coupled with its promotion of strikes, which the Woodrow Wilson administration construed as "seditious interference in war production,"[39] positioned the IWW as the preeminent domestic threat to the war effort; as such they were placed under surveillance by the DOJ and naval intelligence.[40]

Since Local 8 wielded tremendous power over the Philadelphia port, the US government did not attempt to eradicate it altogether.[41] Instead, it used the Espionage Act to stamp out its radical spirit by targeting four of its leaders, including Fletcher, "the color of blackest ebony and the only Negro indicted in the lot,"[42] and the broader organization as a whole, as subversives.[43] Two mass trials all but eliminated their leadership and severely crippled Local 8, though the union carried on in a diminished form after the war.[44] Its headquarters was raided on September 5, 1917, and federal agents confiscated mounds of records, including correspondence, dues books, meeting minutes, and publications. Later that month, arrest warrants were issued for Fletcher and 165 other IWW leaders and members for violating the Espionage Act. Underscoring the objective of anticommunist governance to protect capitalist accumulation (and the partnership between the US government and private enterprise constituting Wall Street Imperialism), the Wobblies were also charged with "violating the constitutional rights of employers executing government contracts."[45]

For the US government, the IWW's opposition to capitalism was inextricable from its alleged pro-German leanings, and amounted thus treason. The defense noted, however, that that the trial was not about national security, but rather, "it [was] the purpose of this prosecution to destroy the organization with which these men are connected and to break the ideal for which their organization stands."[46] The IWW's actual "crime" was its organization of exploited workers and inclusion of superexploited Blacks that had been largely marginalized by American Federation of Labor (AFL) unions.[47]

Though the Sedition Act of 1918 was repealed on December 13, 1920, much of the Espionage Act remained and was reenacted as another imperialist war enveloped Europe and pulled the rest of the world into the conflict. As well, persons convicted under their purview continued to serve their jail sentences well into the 1920s. As the Bolshevik Revolution helped to transfer hatred from Germans to communists, and as the 1917 and 1918 acts solidified the "federalization of intelligence," the legislative branch worked alongside its executive and judicial counterparts to target radicalism and Radical Blackness through illiberal legislation and witch-hunt committees.

Congressional Committees and the Amplification of the Black and Red Scares

Given the failure to pass a peacetime sedition bill, individual states largely took over the passage of legislation and the convening of committees to curb

antiradicalism throughout the 1920s. However, the federal government re-
gained its leadership in this realm during the Great Depression. These anti-
subversive committees were particularly pernicious because they were a
source of intimidation that, unlike legislation, was not beholden to any standard of constitutionality.[48] The 1930 Congressional Committee to Investigate
Communist Activities, chaired by New York representative Hamilton Fish,
was established by a vote of 201–18. The Fish Committee, as it was called,
represented a resurgence of the federal legislative branch in anticommunist
inquisitions. It followed from a public charge made by the president of the
AFL, Matthew Woll, that the USSR was funding the spread of propaganda
in the United States to the tune of $1.25 million. The committee was also a
product of "forged anti-Soviet documents by former Police Commissioner
Whalen of New York."[49]

Fish's anticommunism was robust, construing "communist" to mean not
only members of the CPUSA, but also "revolutionary, militant, and dissatisfied workers generally" and those who organized against the "present situation" of "unemployment, hunger and privation, speed-up, long hours, child
labor, low wages, injunctions, arrests, persecutions, war."[50] In order to generate jobs for loyal workers, he claimed, communists needed to be deported.
Thus, a spate of publications and organizations controlled by or allied with
the CPUSA, from the *Daily Worker* to the ILD, were subjected to investigation in addition to "parlor Pink" and "near-'Red'" groups. Left-wing groups
organizing for relief, against imperialism, for the protection of the foreign-
born, for peaceful relations with the Soviet Union, and for youth organizing
were included on the list of those to be examined. Likewise, the Trade Union
Unity League—and its Negro and women sections—were to be investigated.
The committee was allotted "unlimited finances" not only to conduct open
hearings, but also to procure experts and carry out inquiries into "Moscow's
machinations" in the United States, Canada, and Latin America. Moreover,
attesting to anticommunist collaboration between the three branches of government, the committee relied upon the FBI to conduct clandestine investigations. The ILD, which would go on to defend the Scottsboro Nine and
Angelo Herndon shortly after the Fish Committee was organized, likened
these sneaky methods to those used during the 1919–20 Palmer Raids, which
indicated "preparation of a drive against militant workers' organizations."[51]

Typical of the Black Scare / Red Scare Longue Durée, a key expert and witness for Fish Committee investigations was J. Edgar Hoover, who by then had
become the unequivocal powerhouse of the BI. As he had been doing since
World War I, Hoover brought together the Red Scare and the Black Scare in
his claim that the CPUSA aimed to stir up "class and racial" disturbances by

sowing discontent among unemployed workers and inciting "racial antagonism" among US Blacks. Especially dangerous, according to Hoover, was the CPUSA's organization of "a special committee to incite revolutionary activities among the Negroes, and to send selected Negroes to Moscow for special communistic training for world revolution." Such actions were predicated upon foreign influence, insofar as the CPUSA was acting under the direction of Moscow and the Third International and used its propaganda not only to influence Blacks, but also to undermine American values embodied by organizations like the Boy Scouts, the American Legion, and the AFL.[52]

Fish exposed the important role of the AFL in perpetuating anticommunism from below in his proclamation that "great credit should be given to the American Federation of Labor for combatting and exposing the aims of the communists to undermine our republican form of government and destroy our industries." Indeed, without their defense, communism would be an even more serious threat to US industry. Maine representative John E. Nelson infused this praise with antiforeignness,[53] arguing that the communist movement was largely made up of the foreign-born, whose ideas "native-born" Americans did not respect given their commitment to "American ideals and institutions."[54] The AFL's anticommunism was complemented by its racism; unlike the Congress of Industrial Organizations, founded in 1935, AFL unions maintained Jim Crow shops—if they admitted Blacks at all.[55] They did not share the "treachery" of the communists, who were making headway with Blacks, especially in the South, through the promise of "full social equality."[56]

Though Nelson found communism to be dangerous, pernicious, and a virus, unlike Fish, he did not find any immediate national threat or occasion for hysteria since organizations like the AFL had kept communism at bay. Additionally, many of the people who were labeled communists were "simply seeking to improve their own working conditions and [knew] nothing and care[d] less of the theories of Marx and Engels."[57] Nelson's dissent illuminates that, since communism posed no physical threat, it was the very existence of their ideas and beliefs that challenged the social order. Nelson also showed that these committees, and the Red Scare more broadly, were as committed to manufacturing communists as they were to identifying them.

The Fish Committee report maintained that times of economic crisis and social suffering created ideal conditions for the spread of communism, and it proposed "drastic legislation" to eradicate it and "subversive activities" more broadly. The report suggested anticommunist collaboration between all three branches of government, including a spy service in the DOJ, the deportation of alien "Reds," a federal sedition act, and the suppression of communist literature through the Postal Service.[58] One conclusion to be drawn from this contrast—the negligible influence of communism, on the one hand, but the recommendation of broad-based measures to crush its influence, on the other hand—is that because US Capitalist Racist Society was predicated on the very conditions conducive to the spread of radicalism, anticommunism aimed to repress opposition to racial and class antagonism instead of transforming oppressive and exploitative conditions. The alternative to repression, but the other side of the same coin, was a compulsory commitment to the pedagogy of the US state, antiforeignness, and emphasis on "economic freedom for the individual." Here, open shops led by "American citizens supporting our American institutions" would combat radicalism, nullify the influence of the Third International, and expose those committed to it. A more inclusive capitalist racism, under the guidance of legislators and industrialists, was the best defense against "communistic ideas," which were "germs in the body politic." On this logic, "economic justice" meant class collaboration aimed at eliminating radical or communist ideas.[59]

Moreover, the Fish Committee highlighted the synergy between federal and state anticommunism in its support of state-level Red Scares, including the indictment of six labor organizers under the insurrection law in Atlanta, Georgia; sedition charges against nine workers in Newark, New Jersey; and the sentencing of seven Gastonia, North Carolina, strike leaders to 117 years in prison.[60]

After the Fish Committee, congressional investigative committees reached new heights. In 1938 the Special Committee on Un-American Activities, or the Dies Committee, was formed. Texas congressman Martin Dies proposed the formation of this committee to identify communists in the Franklin D. Roosevelt administration. It was approved by a vote of 191 to 41.[61] This committee was noteworthy not only because it intensified the inquisitions of the Fish Committee, but also because it perfected most of the techniques originated by the Lusk Committee and later associated with Senator Joseph McCarthy and the eponymous era of repression. The Dies Committee was supported by conservatives and faced little opposition from liberals, some of whom began to invoke the committee positively in their campaigns for reelection.[62] By 1943, when the committee was given new life by Representative John Rankin of Mississippi, it was a bastion of Black Scare and Red Scare repression—and a complement to FBI's *RACON* report.

Rankin was the personification of anticommunism and its attack on democracy given his slander of Blacks, Jews, and the foreign-born; his hatred of and efforts to weaken organized labor; and his use of "parliamentary skill" and political power to block all measures aimed at broadening the freedom and economic security of the masses.[63] For example, Rankin called Ben Davis,

Angelo Herndon's former lawyer, to testify before the committee, weaponizing the BBNT in an attempt to prevent him from being reelected to the New York City Council as the Communist Party's candidate.[64] Though Rankin's racist interrogation of Davis ultimately helped instead of hurt the Harlem congressman's campaign, the Dies Committee's use of "Davis's theses on Black Liberation . . . to generate the Red Scare" demonstrated its commitment to crushing radicalism, Blackness, and Radical Blackness.[65]

That these inquisition bodies were essential to the legislative branch's anti-communist governance was demonstrated in the fact that an August 2, 1946, statute transformed the Dies Committee from a special committee into the notorious HUAC. Now a permanent standing committee, HUAC aimed to

> make from time to time investigations of (i) the extent, character, and objects of un-American propaganda activities in the United States, (ii) the diffusion within the United States of subversive and un-American propaganda that is instigated from foreign countries or of a domestic origin and attacks the principle of the form of government as guaranteed by our Constitution, and (iii) all other questions in relation thereto that would aid Congress in any necessary remedial legislation.[66]

In reality, HUAC and committees like it sought to malign and discredit all individuals and organizations who earnestly sought and fought for progressive reforms in the areas of labor, race relations, and monopoly through "smear" campaigns, lies, assumptions, and other forms of propaganda "reminiscent of fascist techniques."[67]

By design, HUAC hearings were extralegal because they "were immune from the due process requirements that accompanied criminal prosecutions." The hearings discouraged appeals to the First and Fifth Amendments by assigning guilt to those who exercised their protections. Not only were these hearings adept at avoiding due process, but they were rigged to extract information by any means necessary, in turn always harming people brought before the committee. Even cooperative parties faced adverse social and financial consequences.[68] And, given the extralegality of the committee, those who were summoned had no recourse for the negative consequences they suffered from either the outcome of the interrogation or from having to testify in the first place.[69]

The important role of the legislative branch in authorizing anticommunism was demonstrated in the fact that thirteen states and multiple municipalities adopted their own HUACs with identical tactics, subjecting even more Americans to Red Scare and Black Scare pressures. Additionally, the close relationship between the FBI and HUAC, with the former providing the latter with classified files and testimonies from informants, conveyed the branches' essential collaboration in anticommunist governance. This relationship prompted HUAC to be described by a journalist as "almost an adjunct of the FBI" that was being used by Hoover for his personal agenda.[70] The FBI also had a strong relationship with the SISS, the upper house's version of HUAC formed in 1951, with the two trading files on "disloyal" groups or individuals.

HUAC's formulation and promotion of draconian laws was crucial to entrenching anticommunism. For example, it proposed the Subversive Activities Control Act of 1948, or the Mundt-Nixon Bill, an extraordinarily repressive piece of legislation that signaled the arrival of the Cold War. It reflected HUAC's tendency to not only attack communism, but also to "stamp 'subversive' all those whose opinions it found unpalatable" based on a refusal "to tolerate those whose estimate of our current problems [did] not match its own."[71] The Mundt-Nixon Bill was meant to "expose communists and their fronts by requiring them to register publicly with the Attorney General and plainly label all their propaganda as their own; forbid Communists passports or government jobs; make it illegal for ANYBODY to try to set up in this country a totalitarian dictatorship having ANY connection with a foreign power."[72] Though it did not pass the Senate, it provided many of the provisions of the Internal Security Act of 1950, and as documentary practice, it created the conditions for the slippage between attempting to set up a totalitarian dictatorship and an allegiance to a foreign power and any form of mobilization that challenged the US state, especially if it could be Red-baited as communist. More generally, it was an effort to use legislative sanction to force all opinion and "into the channels of conformity."[73]

Antiradical Legislation and the Codification
of Anticommunist Governance

From the 1930s onward, investigative committees and repressive antiradical legislation were mutually reinforcing. The Foreign Agents Registration Act of 1938, commonly known as the McCormack Act, required those considered to be agents of foreign principals to register with the US attorney general and to fill out a detailed survey about which organizations, activities, and publications they were involved with. This act was used to misconstrue activities of radical organizations as instituted by a foreign power—generally the Soviet Union—even when they were purely national in origin. Violation of this law could result in fines up to $10,000, up to five years in prison, and deportation for noncitizens.[74] It was under this 1938 law that W. E. B. Du Bois and the PIC

were indicted in 1951 for circulating the Stockholm Peace Appeal. The Voo-
rhis Anti-Propaganda Act, enacted on October 17, 1940, strengthened the
McCormack Act, requiring "the registration of every organization subject to
foreign control which engages in political activity" or advocating the overthrow of the government by force or violence.[75] These acts "served as a partial
precedent for the Communist registration section of the McCarran Internal
Security Act of 1950."[76]

The Act to Prevent Pernicious Activities, or the Hatch Act of 1939, was
the foundation of the loyalty programs and the AGLOSO that took off under
Harry S. Truman's administration. Its primary aim was to curtail the political
activities of federal employees, especially those of a radical variety. The act
forbade anyone who advocated the overthrow of the US government, broadly
construed, to work in government agencies.[77] It created the conditions for
more than half of US states after World War II to enact laws seeking to bar
from public employment persons who advocated the violent overthrow of the
government or who belonged to such organizations.[78]

Completing the trifecta of countersubversive acts, the Alien Registration
Act, commonly known as the Smith Act, was enacted on June 28, 1940. It was
designed to "prohibit certain subversive activities" and, among other things, "to
amend certain provisions of the law with respect to the admission and deportation of aliens." Reminiscent of the 1918 Sedition Act, it criminalized those who
"knowingly and willingly advocate[d], abet[ted], advise[d] or [taught] the
duty, necessity, desirability, or propriety of overthrowing or destroying any
Government of the United States by force or violence"; the drafting, publishing, circulation, editing, distributing, and selling of such ideas; and organizations, groups, and societies that encouraged them. Those found guilty of the
latter offenses would be imprisoned, fined, and deported.[79]

While the earliest Smith Act victims were members of the Socialist Workers Party, by the end of World War II the CPUSA was its unequivocal target. In the Smith Act trials throughout the late 1940s and 1950s, this group
was charged with conspiracy of insurrection based on books, writings, and
membership, which made it easy to understand why radicals "discerned an
aroma of fascism."[80] The 1948 trial of eleven CPUSA leaders—Eugene Dennis,
Gus Hall, Henry Winston, Ben Davis, John Williamson, Robert Thomas, Gil
Green, John Gates, Jack Satchel, Carl Winter, and Irving Potash—charged the
defendants with teaching and advocating the overthrow of the US government by force or violence though no actions were submitted as evidence. In
1951, Claudia Jones, Pettis Perry, and sixteen other working-class communists were arrested on the same trumped-up charges. Jones's specific "crime"
was "writing an article which described the forward movement of Negro and

white women in opposition to the fascist bent world domination of US foreign policy."[81] This crusade against those who advocated economic equality,
racial justice, and socialist democracy in their speeches, and writing conveyed that "McCarthyism [was] American fascism."[82]

Over the next ten years, more than one hundred top leaders of the CPUSA
across the nation were indicted based on a "reactionary statute under which
progressive fighters [were] convicted and jailed not for committing any overt
act, but merely for their ideas."[83] The indictment and trial of top party leadership was a "classic frame-up based on a statute ultimately viewed as unconstitutional,"[84] and attested to the US government's use of the Smith Act to
criminalize radical ideas in an effort to regulate and discipline opposition.

These "frame-ups," according to Perry, were an assault on the American
people as a whole because the conviction of political minorities put the rights
and liberties of all Americans in mortal danger. In an address to the court in
1951, Perry held that depriving communists of their right to write, speak, assemble, and publish abrogated those rights for all Americans. Likewise, outlawing ideas, which was the primary goal of the Smith Act, was the first step
on the path to fascism. Here, he conveyed that anticommunism as a mode
of governance meant that US Capitalist Racist Society toed the line between
fascist-like and outright fascist, and legislation like the Smith Act pushed
them over the edge. He lamented, "The very fact that this trial, a trial of ideas
and books, can take place in our country shows how far the Wall Street rulers
have taken our country down the disastrous path of fascism." He urged the
court to curtail this drive toward fascism.[85] Indeed, the Smith Act was referred to by many of its targets as a form of thought control not least because
it was primarily applied to punish radical *ideas* and to construe them as *acts*
of force and violence.

The Smith Act was especially repressive because it allowed for the conflation of counterhegemonic ideas with dangerous and subversive acts to circumscribe freedom of speech and freedom of the press. Furthermore, as the
case of the Chicago Black communist Claude Lightfoot conveyed, the Smith
Act also criminalized freedom of association. Unlike previous cases, when
Lightfoot was captured by the FBI and put on trial in 1954, he was charged
under the membership clause of the Smith Act that declared membership
in the CPUSA was evidence enough to confirm that communists might attempt to overthrow the government by force and violence. Stated differently,
membership in the CPUSA automatically meant conspiracy of insurrection.
For Lightfoot, the judge and jury in his case were called upon, for the first
time in US history, "to examine the contents of people's minds" to determine
guilt or innocence. This was a powerful reason why targets of the Smith Act

considered it a fascist curtailment of free speech and thought.[86] This "thought control law," charged Sojourners for Truth and Justice cofounder Dorothy Hunton, placed unconstitutional constraints on freedoms of speech and political association to punish people for their ideas, especially those deemed distasteful by the US government because they challenged the status quo. Additionally, because it aimed to punish those who acted together to combat war, economic hardship, and white supremacy, among other things, "the first victims to be tried and convicted were the top Communist leaders, among whom were two Blacks."[87]

Since anticommunism targeted "all genuine fighters for Negro rights,"[88] the Smith Act gave potency to its Black Scare and Red Scare criminalization of Radical Black leaders. The Smith Act trials, it was argued, aimed to intimidate Black people who had any affiliation with communists or who took a militant approach to racial justice. As the Smith Act defendant Ben Davis contended, "Actually it was the purpose of the court in giving me the maximum sentence to intimidate and terrorize all militant Negroes, to serve notice that a fight for free and equal citizenship would be met with severe reprisal."[89] This was true for others whose thoughts, speeches, and associations were criminalized because they fought for Black freedom and rallied against forms of violence endemic in US Capitalist Racist Society. As well, it was no accident that the first prosecutions under the Smith Act membership clause involved those who fought for racial justice; this was a form of browbeating meant to "halt the advances being made by Negro people as a result of their efforts . . . in the struggle for freedom and democracy."[90]

Moreover, the roundup of communists under the Smith Act was a Red Scare attempt to crush those who understood the intersections of racism, capitalism, and war. After Jones was convicted in 1953, she queried in her speech to the court, "Is all this [the trial and conviction] no further proof that what we were also tried for was our opposition to racist ideas, an integral part of the desperate drive by men of Wall Street to war and fascism?"[91] This provocative question dovetailed with Dorothy Hunton's contention that the Red Scare converged with warmongering to conceal the real threat to world peace: "the oppression of the darker races,"[92] which further sutured it to the Black Scare. This deceit transformed the Smith Act into a tool of not only mind control, but also white supremacy and creeping fascism.

A potent instrumentality of legislative branch anticommunist governance was the Internal Security Act of 1950, or the McCarran Act. Even more carceral than the Smith Act, it was commonly referred to as *the* anticommunist law. It laid "the foundation for immigration checks, deportation, harassment of African Americans, and even 'authorized concentration camps for emergency situations.' In section 22 of this far-reaching act . . . a variety of aliens [were] identified as inadmissible or deportable for offenses such as teaching revolutionary information." Expanding and revising the Immigration Act of 1917 and invoking the Sedition Act of 1918, the McCarran Act, in tandem with the Smith Act, provided the basis for state-sanctioned surveillance and the machinations of HUAC especially during the early Cold War.[93] Reflecting and deepening the terroristic nature of anticommunism, the McCarran Act also authorized the loss of American citizenship for naturalized citizens based solely on their political beliefs or activities; annual registration for noncitizens; arrest without a warrant and denial of bail for noncitizens; and the deportation of noncitizens, no matter how long they had resided in the country, for any political opinion deemed threatening to the government. This "gestapo pass system for noncitizens" deprived them of all rights and liberties while severely circumscribing the rights and liberties of citizens, too.[94]

Underscoring the ways investigative committees and repressive legislation worked together in the legislative branch, the McCarran Act required all communists to register with the SACB; the specific penalties for not registering outright communist organizations or those that were purported to be communist fronts, communist infiltrated, communist dominated, communist supported, or communist inspired included five years imprisonment and a $10,000 fine for every day unregistered.[95] This effectively meant that "if one decided to stand up for a principle that person could be jailed for life" or expelled from the country.[96] Relatedly, the "labeling" section of the act required "Communist-action" and "Communist-front" organizations to label any materials sent through the mail as deriving from such organizations. Such labeling, it was argued, aimed to curtail freedom of information by inviting persecution and harassment to persons who received these mailings. It also imposed a "malignant form of censorship" based on the allegedly "dangerous or harmful character . . . of the publisher or distributor."[97] Particularly damaging, because the act specifically defined a communist organization as advocating subversion, espionage, violence, and sabotage, labeling compelled organizations like the CPUSA to accept that mischaracterization. This was tantamount to self-defamation.

Another frightening aspect of the McCarran Act was the provision that the president could take control of all government institutions and put people in jail without trial during a national emergency. This threat was made all the more realistic given evidence that concentration camps were being constructed within US borders.[98] Thus, the McCarran Act expanded the power of all three branches of the federal government to target the most vulnerable populations, not least Blacks, Jews, and the foreign-born, as well as US-born persons whose radical ideas positioned them "foreign," dangerous, and subversive.[99]

Claudia Jones, the West Indian Ferdinand Smith—a communist sailor and union leader—and four others imprisoned on Ellis Island under the Mc-Carran Act sent a letter to the United Nations Social, Humanitarian, and Cultural Committee in November 1950 to protest their pending deportations. They warned that the Smith and McCarran Acts effectively criminalized any progressive ideas and activism, so everyone committed to justice or equality was a potential target. They argued, "If we can be denied all rights and incarcerated in concertation camps, then trade unionists are next; then the Negro people, the Jewish people, all foreign-born, and all progressives who love peace and cherish freedom will face the bestiality and torment of fascism. Our fate is the fate of all opponents of fascist barbarism, of all who abhor war and desire peace."[100] Here, the McCarran Act worked through and with the Black Scare and the Red Scare by denying human rights to radicals not because they posed a physical threat, but because their fight on behalf of labor, Black rights, and true democracy threatened to subvert the status quo. Likewise, the capaciousness of anticommunist governance meant that repression of one group of "others" could quickly spread to all groups of "undesirables." Finally, the state of perpetual siege and war in which repression flourished was becoming normalized in the United States, and values like peace and freedom were being distorted into threats to national security to legitimate racialized carcerality and expulsion.

In describing her personal experience of harassment, incarceration, and deportation, Jones offered some of the most insightful analysis of the Black Scare and Red Scare aspects of the McCarran Act and of anticommunist governance more broadly. Shortly after she had been deported, she explained that she had been targeted by those who were committed to the "official pro-war, pro-reactionary, pro-fascist line of the white ruling class of that country."[101] Further, in US Capitalist Racist Society, to be radical was anathema, and to be a Radical Black was even worse, since the government tended to believe that Black populations were inclined toward communism—meaning prone to subversion. Worse still was to be a "Negro woman Communist of West Indian descent," whose rights and liberties were forfeited, according to the government, if one struggled to end Jim Crow, to unite white and Black workers, to empower women, and to push US domestic and foreign policy to the side of durable peace.[102] Additionally, Jones believed her application for American citizenship had been rejected in 1938 because she urged spending for social welfare instead of arms and prosecution of lynchers instead of communists, and because she continually noted that it was "financiers and war mongers" who were the "real advocates of force and violence in the U.S.A."[103]

Two further pieces of legislation passed in 1952 and 1954, respectively, underscored the instrumental role of the legislative branch in anticommunist governance. The Immigration and Nationality Act of 1952, commonly known as the McCarran-Walter Act, combined the Black Scare and the Red Scare through antiforeignness. It implemented quotas from foreign countries on a "purely racist basis" and permitted the attorney general and other consular officers to prevent aliens from coming to the United States if they were suspected of having dissident political views. The McCarran-Walter Act also broadened the scope of deportation to include not only those who were communists, but also "persons affiliated with organizations declared by biased and reactionary official bodies to be subversive." Noncitizens could be deported for both current "objectional" political views and for those they may have held in the past. Moreover, it authorized a daunting process of registration for all noncitizens, whether or not they were politically suspect; imposed criminal punishment upon citizens who aided or cooperated with aliens suspected of dissidence; and authorized that an individual's naturalization could be revoked if they joined a suspect organization within five years of receiving it. It also rendered ineligible for naturalization members of the CPUSA, members of organizations advocating goals similar to the CPUSA, members of organizations required to register with the SACB, and anyone who had been a member of a proscribed organization within a ten-year period of applying for naturalization. If there was no country to which a dissident alien could be deported, they were to be held in a special detention center or concentration camp.

Jones noted that this law was "widely known for its special racist bias towards West Indians and peoples of Asian descent." These groups were targeted because their progressive ideas were the most threatening to the conservative foundations of the US state. "This law which came into being as a result of the whole reactionary drive against progressive ideas in the United States," she continued, "encourage[d] immigration of fascist scum from Europe but restrict[ed] West Indian immigration once in their thousands annually to the United States, to 100 persons per year, from all Caribbean islands."[104] Elsewhere, she argued that the "racially-based McCarran-Walter Immigration Act" aimed to protect the "white 'races' purity'" and to promote Anglo-Saxo supremacy.[105] In perceptively pinpointing not only the restriction on the immigration of racialized people, but also the welcoming of white "fascist scum," Jones conveyed that fascism and white supremacy were compatible with anticommunist governance while racial equality and justice were threats to it.

Finally, the Communist Control Act of 1954 was an amendment to the McCarran Act that outlawed the CPUSA. It also provided thirteen broad standards to determine membership in the CPUSA, which included making a financial contribution to the party, participating in any work or organization affiliated with the CPUSA, and conferring with its officers.[106] As such, "anyone who ha[d] shown sympathy or support for the Communists, even though he himself may be a non-Communist or even and anti-Communist" could be found guilty. The act contained a further provision directed at trade unions that denied recognition to those that were found to be communist infiltrated—a provision that would ultimately lead to its dissolution.[107] Unsurprisingly, the unions accused of being Communist infiltrated tended to be interracial and to advocate racial equality.

∗

The McCarran Act destroyed the peace and happiness of the foreign-born; the Smith Act killed freedom of speech; and "repressive labor legislation" like the Labor Management Relations Act, commonly known as the Taft-Hartley Act, destroyed freedom, harmony, and equality in the labor movement and was a step toward stripping workers of gains made during World War II. Passed in 1947, Taft-Hartley required trade union officials to file an affidavit swearing they were neither members nor supporters of the CPUSA and resulted in numerous jailings of prominent trade unionists through convictions of perjury or conspiracy to commit perjury.[108]

These laws, along with the McCarran-Walter Act and the Communist Control Act, used the Black Scare and the Red Scare to imperil the rights and citizenship of, strip rights and citizenship from, or deny rights and citizenship to those who believed in, advocated, or struggled for an alternative to US Capitalist Racist Society. Other legislation like the Espionage and Sedition Acts, the McCormack Act, and the Hatch Act, along with the bevy of congressional inquisition committees, attested not only to the legislative branch's invaluable role in upholding anticommunist governance, but more importantly, to a long Countersubversive Political Tradition undergirding US Capitalist Racist Society that, as Jones, Perry, Hunton, and others noted, gave the United States a fascistic character.

The Countersubversive Political Tradition
and the Threat of US Fascism

We fought to destroy Hitlerism—but its germs took root right here. I look about me, at my own people, at all colored peoples all over the world. I can see the men who lead my government supporting oppression of the colored peoples of the earth who today reach out for the independence this nation achieved in 1776.

CHARLOTTA BASS, 1952

During the Black Scare / Red Scare Longue Durée, the "Countersubversive Political Tradition"[1] was articulated through anticommunist governance, and this gave US Capitalist Racist Society its fascistic character. The Countersubversive Political Tradition "extended back at least to the Alien and Sedition Acts of the 1790s,"[2] a set of repressive laws to which anticommunist legislation like the Smith Act and the McCarran Act were often compared. In his veto of the latter, for example, Harry S. Truman held that "the application of the registration requirements to so-called Communist-front organizations can be the greatest danger to freedom of speech, press, and assembly since the Alien and Sedition Laws of 1798."[3] Referencing the same law, Claude Lightfoot concurred, "The nation had not experienced a period like this since the days of the Alien and Sedition Laws."[4] As he was being interrogated before HUAC and accused of being a communist, Paul Robeson likewise chided, "You are like the Alien Sedition Act, and Jefferson could be sitting here, and Frederick Douglass could be sitting here and Eugene Debs could be sitting here."[5] In naming Jefferson, Douglass, and Debs, Robeson illuminated how the Countersubversive Political Tradition targeted dissidents, Blacks, labor militants, *and* those who spoke up on their behalf. This broad-based silencing and discipling that extended back to the United States' founding contributed to the fascistic character of US Capitalist Racist Society.

A genre of fascism unique to the United States became evident with the maturation of monopoly finance capitalism in the 1920s because "the germ of fascism inhere[d] in the division of labor in the epoch of monopoly-finance capitalism and imperialism. In the end, this is what ma[de] fascism the dictatorial rule of capitalism over American society."[6] The Palmer Raids between

1919 and 1920, for example, were efforts of "Government, in tandem with Big Business," to crush worker insurgency by launching an offensive to rid US Capitalist Racist Society of public enemies, especially anarchists and communists who were identified as the source of radical ideas among rebellious workers.[7] Here, anticommunism informed Black Scare and Red Scare tools and techniques businessmen used in their countersubversive offensive to subdue immigrants who infected "old Stock" Anglo-Saxon workers with foreign ideas and "uppity" Blacks who defied their lowly status in the racial hierarchy.[8] Throughout the 1920s and 1930s, anticommunist governance worked through and with the "terrorist and non-terrorist rule of Big Business" to "totalize the powers of capital over all aspects of material life and consciousness."[9] The aim of monopolists and their government partners was to narrate the "United States [as] the great bulwark of democracy against the rising menace of international communism"[10] while harnessing anticommunism "to maintain its rule over society by eviscerating liberal democracy" and "snuff out working-class radicalism and a socialist alternative."[11]

The Black Scare, the Red Scare, and the Countersubversive Political Tradition

The Countersubversive Political Tradition was born out of the United States as a "settler society, and expanding, domestic imperial power" and was animated by a discourse of "alien conspiracies" that allowed the government to blame problems, issues, and unrest in US Capitalist Racist Society "on forces operating outside it." The United States cultivated and sustained a fear of alien ideologies and the "foreigners" who ostensibly held and spread them by interpreting these exogenous thoughts and beliefs as invading the ideals and organization of the republic. This hostility was linked to the idea of internal racial, ethnic, and religious enemies who were allied with, sympathetic to, or could be easily duped by minacious external forces.[12] The suppression of those cast outside the "normal political system" was construed as a condition for the freedom and security of the people who properly belonged to it.[13]

Given the settler colonial origins of the United States, the Countersubversive Political Tradition could be traced back to the "original Red Scare"[14] against Indigenous populations. They were the first to embody disorder, lack of civilization, and "alien" control. Differences between "Reds" and whites rendered the former culturally unassimilable, on the one hand, and dangerous, on the other hand. Settler colonialism, conquest, and dispossession became legitimate violence against these inhabitants and created the conditions for the invaders' use of force against alien groups. Peaceful coexistence thus became unnecessary and even an impediment to white rule.[15] Sioux American studies scholar Nick Estes argues that respecting the peaceful existence and political autonomy of Indigenous people was a political impossibility for the US settler colonial state.[16] Both the treaties themselves and their disavowal were methods of denying the self-determination and sovereignty of Indigenous nations by creating a framework for "land cessation and eventual incorporation."[17] The result was the reservation upon which Indigenous peoples were confined through ongoing removal. This racial segregation[18] existed alongside protracted and brutal military campaigns following the Civil War, federal expropriation of Indigenous lands, and twenty years of Indigenous land allotment. These Red Scare practices were codified in the 1883 Dawes Act, which inaugurated the appropriation of Indigenous lands to whites, on the one hand, and forced Indigenous people to accept individual parcels of land as a "civilizing" process, on the other hand. The 1903 *Lone Wolf v. Hitchcock* Supreme Court decision then gave Congress power over Indigenous land rights, thereby stripping Indigenous nations of control and proscribing their political power.[19]

Subsequent Red Scares that engulfed the United States, stripping dissidents of their rights, power, and belonging, had their roots in the founding—and ongoing—anti-Indigenous Red Scare. As Joanne Barker explains, "the Red Man and communism and socialism were made indistinct from one another in state discourses of terrorism." Further, "as Indigenous groups . . . addressed the principles of 'communal land-holding' or community-based governance"—direct challenges to anticommunist governance—"associations between the Indigenous and the communist became normalized." Indigenous people were targeted as "the original communists, outright collaborators, or the unwitting dupes of infiltrators welcoming communists into their communities."[20] Moreover, insofar as "the life and history of Afro-American and Indian peoples are closely interwoven in their contribution to the development of America. . . . The plantation and the reservation are twin institutions of social control and 'containment,'"[21] the original Red Scare, like its subsequent iteration, was inseparable from the Black Scare.

Fear of Indigenous populations was displaced onto other enemies from within. Blackness, labor relations, and radical dissent became the "major loci" of political suppression.[22] Anticommunism inflated, stigmatized, and criminalized these "political foes" by counterposing US citizenship and identity "against racial, ethnic, class, and gender aliens" from within and from without.[23] A political culture was created from above and below in which the public was primed to stay vigilant about endogenous and exogenous menaces to US Capitalist Racist Society. This countersubversive vigilantism included identifying and reporting on "conspiratorial" meetings in which un-American activities were taking place, naming names, and becoming experts on the particulars of subversion. In conflating radicalism with danger and political dissent with crime and contagion, anticommunism encouraged the rise of a national security state[24] through which the government "shared its monopoly over legitimate force with corporations" and private groups to deprive dissenters of their rights to organize, assemble, publish, and speak freely.[25] In short, as the crucible of the Countersubversive Political Tradition during the Black Scare / Red Scare Longue Durée, anticommunist governance transposed militant challenges to the status quo and antagonism between subordinate and superordinate groups into problems of national security and existential threats to capital, property, and national identity.

Radical Blackness and the Countersubversive Political Tradition

Radical Blackness was a focal point of anticommunist governance during the Black Scare / Red Scare Longue Durée because it traversed the shift in the Countersubversive Political Tradition "from visibility to invisibility, from the body to the mind, and from the American individual to the national-security state." The "invisibility" of subversives, who blended in with mass society despite being foreign inspired, committed to a foreign ideology, and/or working on behalf of an alien power, required constant and coordinated anticommunist surveillance, and that put the burden of proof on the accused to establish that they were indeed loyal.[26] This burden was particularly onerous for Radical Blacks because the "visible" aspect of their subversion and disloyalty—their Black skin, "the badge of slavery"—remained constant and could not be sufficiently disproven. Likewise, their subversive Black bodies were exacerbated by their disloyal minds, which, either because of inherent ignorance or uppity education, were susceptible to foreign influence and outside agitation. In effect, every aspect of Radical Blackness legitimated the countersubversive efforts of anticommunist governance.

J. Edgar Hoover was instrumental in constructing Radical Blackness as the embodiment of old and new iterations of the Countersubversive Political Tradition. In his role at the helm of the executive branch's investigative bodies from World War I onward, he combined "criminal detection and political surveillance in a single agency," imbricated political countersubversion and law enforcement, severed any distinction between crime and radical dissent, and positioned racial and economic militancy as mutually constitutive dangers. While Hoover's endeavors were often coordinated with the other branches of the federal government and with state and local authorities, he and his agencies were at the forefront of "punishing dissenting political speech, [ideas,] and action" and in developing "countersubversive instruments."[27]

One such instrument was *RACON*. This surveillance of Black individuals, organizations, publications, and actions during World War II brought together the idea that foreign groups generally, and the CPUSA particularly, were instilling, inspiring, and exploiting un-American ideologies and activities among the disaffected on the dark side of the color line. As such, the FBI was a "key bulwark defending the ascendancy of Southern Jim Crow power in national politics" and expressed "particularly where African Americans were concerned, all the values of the resurgent South in opposing the struggle to put an end to racial discrimination both during and after World War II."[28] *RACON* linked Black agitation for civil rights, dignified work, and an end to Jim Crow to foreign influence and to the CPUSA, even as it acknowledged that much of Black discontent came from extant economic and social conditions. In other words, the Black Scare and the Red Scare were key to leveraging anticommunism to maintain racial inequality by Red-baiting strivings for civil rights and Black-baiting struggles for socialist redistribution thereby allowing Hoover to "undermine and discredit both simultaneously by smearing one with the other and vice versa."[29] The danger Hoover and the FBI ascribed to racial unrest was manifested in the deluge of intelligence reports submitted to the Roosevelt administration between 1939 and 1945 and the pickup in FBI surveillance of this group around 1941.[30]

RACON's coverage of A. Phillip Randolph's March on Washington Movement (MOWM) illuminates how the Countersubversive Political Tradition facilitated the close connection between the Black Scare and the Red Scare to ascribe danger to Black militant organizations, especially those that ostensibly encouraged antiwhite sentiment, and to construct proximity to communism even when it was vehemently rejected. Randolph's organization was considered to cause "much unrest and discontent" given its "effective and influential" focus on "alleged discrimination" and the denial of rights that tended to enlarge the impact "beyond the alleged incident."[31] Though the organization was categorized as "independent and unaffiliated," the FBI's surveillance of it demonstrated how Radical Black advocacy for racial equality or justice inexorably linked it to communism because the latter also supported this idea. Importantly, "in local areas, some of the [independent] organizations [were] reported to be Communist infiltrated."[32]

RACON described the MOWM as a recently formed all-Black organization that had threatened numerous times to organize Black workers to invade Washington, DC, if its demands were not met.[33] It was said to be most active in New York, Chicago, Saint Louis, Detroit, Cincinnati, and Washington, DC, where its focus was increased Black employment in the defense industry and government agencies and the end of Jim Crow in the armed forces.[34] Likewise, the organization was committed to "non-violent direct action" to upend Jim Crow, segregation, and restrictive covenants. For the FBI, this translated to a gross violation of law and order during a time that commanded national unity. The MOWM had held several meetings throughout 1942 in the East and Midwest that were attended by majority-Black crowds numbering between eight thousand and eighteen thousand attendees.[35] Based on its aims and scope, the organization was "of course, being closely followed."[36]

The MOWM was also characterized as "a militant anti-communist Negro organization"[37] and a "a reportedly anti-communist group of Negroes" that had separated from the NNC, a "reported Communist front organization."[38] As previously discussed, the split had taken place in late April 1940 when Randolph refused to accept the presidency of the organization and resigned when the convention passed a resolution of nonintervention in World War II. Randolph and a group of anticommunist Black members went on to form the MOWM.[39] The organization sought to "stop the exploitation of the grievances of the Negro by Communists and other subversive elements"[40]; denounced members of the CPUSA as insincere; worked to purge communists, fellow travelers, and sympathizers from its ranks; and passed a resolution in September 1942 "opposing any cooperation with the Communist Party or Communist front organizations."[41] Importantly, though, Trotskyists belonging to the Socialist Party, who shared Randolph's hatred of the CPUSA and the Soviet Union, were involved in the organization.[42] That hostility toward communism did not curry favor with the US government attests to the fact that the Black Scare and the Red Scare cannot—or would not—be easily separated.

Thus, though the MOWM engaged in anticommunism from below, the Countersubversive Political Tradition articulated through the Black and Red Scares meant that critiques of discrimination in the armed forces, the denial of equal opportunity in employment, disenfranchisement, misrepresentation and slander in the media, segregation and housing restriction, Jim Crow in public and private accommodations, and routine lynching and mob murder eliminated any substantive political distinction from the CPUSA. The MOWM, like the CPUSA, demanded an end to all of these realities, and went on record with its goal of "economic equality, political equality, social equality and racial equality for ultimate attainment" and the immediate goal of extirpating discrimination and segregation.[43] Drawing attention to these issues and threating militant action, especially in times of war, was a form

of subversion. Likewise, Randolph and crew were potentially subversive because their methodology of struggle was inspired by Fellowship of Reconcili-
ation, a "militant pacifist group . . . devoted to strict and utter pacifism . . .
the promotion of conscientious objection to war, inter-racial matters, [and]
negotiated peace."[44]

Additionally, Randolph—a paradigmatic Outside Agitator since the World
War I era—was accused of articulating talking points that echoed that of the
communists. On July 4, 1943, he argued that World War II was an imperialist
war aimed at maintaining white supremacy; that "the cause of freedom [was]
in full retreat and the Allies may win but democracy [would] lose"; that Blacks
were unfree and had been so because of extant inequalities in US society; and
that Blacks continued to be segregated in all social, economic, and political
fields in the United States.[45] Randolph's statements did in fact dovetail with
those made by the communist Esther V. Cooper, a member of the Southern
Negro Youth Congress, the youth wing of the NNC Randolph had abandoned
that included CPUSA members in its ranks. In a speech on April 19, 1942, at
the Fifth All-Southern Youth Conference, Cooper maintained that the Allied
effort in the war was undermined by persistent police brutality against Black
people in the South, the inability of Black people to seek protection in the Bill
of Rights, the continuation of lynching, disenfranchisement, segregation in
the armed forces, and the abuse of Black soldiers.[46]

In a meeting on June 26, 1942, it was further reported in *RACON*, MOWM
member Charles Wesley Burton stated that he knew there were FBI agents
present, which he welcomed and wished the attorney general would also attend.[47] This hostility toward the FBI and law enforcement, commonly attributed to communists, entwined the two organizations in the logic of the FBI.

Aware of the mutual antipathy between the MOWM and the CPUSA,
RACON reported that the latter formed its own organization, the Negro Labor Victory Committee (NLVC), in May 1942 under the auspices of the Negro
Commission of the CPUSA National Committee. It did so to combat the influence of Randolph's formation, of its attendant "Black Nationalism" that endangered the CPUSA's united front policy, and of the Socialist Party.[48] *RACON*
reported that the NLVC attempted to poach members from Randolph's organization by holding meetings in close proximity and distributing handbills
"to confuse the people and to attract them to the Communist-inspired meeting away from the March on Washington Movement Meeting."[49] Because
the Countersubversive Political Tradition lumped together all threats from
"aliens" and "others from within," the clear animosity between the CPUSA
and the MOWM was not enough to convince the FBI that the organization
was free of communist influence. *RACON* insisted, "as it ha[d] been said by

confidential informants . . . that various local units of the organization have Communist influence in them" and "attempts ha[d] been and [would] be made to obtain control in local units."

It was immaterial, moreover, that the CPUSA opposed the MOWM, because the Reds allegedly attempted to bore from within to take control of the organization.[50] As such, the MOWM was suspect because it was susceptible to such infiltration. The Detroit and Chicago chapters, for example, purportedly had members who either sympathized with or were members of the CPUSA.[51] The Washington chapter had also ostensibly been infiltrated by communists.[52] The Chicago chapter of the CPUSA was said to have supported the June 26, 1942, MOWM meeting held there to gain leadership of it and to obtain new members, with the party reportedly supplying money to hold and publicize the meeting.[53] Likewise, the NLVC had voted to support the MOWM parade, meeting, and petitions on July 25, 1942, in New York City.[54] The ability of the CPUSA to infiltrate the MOWM meant the all-Black anticommunist formation was nonetheless a conduit of communism, even if unwitting or unwilling.

The Countersubversive Political Tradition shaped the FBI's obsessive focus on the relationship between the MOWM and the CPUSA. In the *Daily Worker*, *RACON* documented, Ben Davis, a CPUSA leader, wrote about a MOWM mass meeting that took place on June 16, 1942. He characterized it as a "high point in the militancy and aggressiveness of the Negro people for their just demands of equal integration in the war effort and complete citizenship in the United States" and an expression of Black people's strong antifascism that conveyed their loyalty and devotion to the USA. Davis then criticized the MOWM for exploiting the grievances of Black people and acting against their best interests.[55] *RACON* also reported on an article written in the *Daily Worker* on July 23, 1943, by CPUSA doyen James W. Ford that was typical of the Reds' condemnation of the MOWM and Randolph. Ford excoriated Randolph's exclusion of whites to avoid communist infiltration, which, according to Ford, conveyed that white CPUSA members were at the forefront of the fight for Black rights. Ford also held that Randolph's sectarianism was actually antithetical to the struggle for Black equality.[56] The dispute between the MOWM and the CPUSA was interpreted through Black Scare and Red Scare logic that subversive organizations were jockeying for the "hearts and minds" of Black people because they were susceptible to ideas and activities that undermined national security.

RACON's scrutiny of the MOWM brought into sharp relief that the FBI's participation in anticommunist governance extended the Countersubversive Political Tradition into World War II by inextricably linking Blackness and communism in its understanding of subversion, disloyalty, un-Americanism, and threat to national security. It was this uncritical and unrelenting linkage between anti-Black and anti-Red, and its accompanying repression and violence, emanating from a long history of racialized superexploitation, expropriation, and war-driven accumulation, that gave US Capitalist Racist Society its fascistic character.

Anticommunism and Fascistic Character of the United States

According to the militant Black author, journalist, and historian Joel Augustus Roger, the "American spirit" was "already largely fascistic," especially in the US South.[57] *We Charge Genocide* captured this "largely fascistic" character of US Capitalist Racist Society, which had persisted in the US "for more than three hundred years." However, during the Black Scare / Red Scare Longue Durée, anticommunist governance intensified its "sinister implications for the welfare and peace of the world."[58] Adolf Hitler, the petition reminded, had demonstrated how domestic genocide often became international in scope and was intimately linked to "predatory war." In a similar fashion, US genocide of Black people was deeply engrained in not only the government, but the civilization writ large, and as such, imperiled world safety. The externalization of racialized, imperialist violence was fascistic.

The fascistic character of US Capitalist Racist Society was also manifested in the economic foundations of genocide. "There [were] billions to be gained through jim-crowism and segregation at home," *We Charge Genocide* explained. "But there [were] added billions to be drained from the blood of the more than a billion colored peoples of the East. War, for the rulers of the USA is but an enlargement of legal and illegal lynching. There is money in both. They are trying to sell war as the only means of protecting their American way of life."[59] Relatedly, the violence, repression, and even murder on the basis of race and radical beliefs were "sanctified" through anticommunist governance and upheld by those who ostensibly fought for free elections abroad while killing their fellow citizens who demanded the freedom to exercise the franchise at home.[60] Akin to the fascist regimes that arose between the 1920s and 1930s, those at the helm of the US government, irrespective of the party, were mongers of racist hatred, lynch terrorism, and white supremacist chauvinism, and their distorted history rooted in racist mythologies and exceptional violence produced a form of fascistic nationalism and accompanying "murderous militarism."

The Black Scare emanated from the relentless struggle of Black people against the arrogance, dehumanization, and indignity of those who genocidally maintained their structural location. Likewise, the capitalist oligarchy mirrored the philosophies, language, and rapacious and murderous programs of the worst fascists in their white supremacy and atomic warmongering that harnessed the Red Scare to the production of legislation like the Smith Act and the McCarran Act.

William Patterson, the architect of *We Charge Genocide*, explicated how the fascistic character of US Capitalist Racist Society manifested most prominently in unpunished government, police, and civilian violence against Black people. What he called "monopoly's way of life and death" constituted linked forms of fascistic terror including "pogroms" in Columbia, Tennessee, Monroe, Georgia, and Groveland, Florida; the "legal lynchings" of the Martinsville Seven, Willie McGee, Edward Honeycutt, Milton Lewis Wilson, Rosa Lee Ingram, the Trenton Six, Robert Mallard, and Wesley Robert Wells; the Black Scare and Red Scare repression of W. E. B. Du Bois, William Patterson, Benjamin J. Davis, Pettis Perry, and Claudia Jones; the attempt to first murder Paul Robeson in Peekskill, New York, then to cancel his passport rights; and insults and indignity such as those hurled at the phenomenal Black artist Josephine Baker in a club frequented by J. Edgar Hoover. These were not the crimes of individuals, but rather of the government and the powerful men who used their political power to the end of repression. Such violence, constitutive of the Countersubversive Political Tradition, permeated the "administrative, judicial and legislative branches of city, state and federal governments," which "deliberately and in concert" employed anticommunist governance in a fascistic manner to protect US Capitalist Racist Society at all costs.[61]

We Charge Genocide demonstrated the fascistic character of the society in its argument that those in charge of governing, upholding the law, and representing the people readily employed the Black and Red Scares to thwart political, economic, and social progress. Judges, law enforcement, mob terrorists, senators, and governors worked to demoralize and divide the entire nation through speeches, writings, political resolutions, and racist laws that rivaled those of Hitler and Goebbels.[62] The rise of the Dixiecrats was notable in this regard. This proudly racist wing supported blatant and aggressive methods of oppression.[63] The other "wing" of the Democratic Party, represented by Harry Truman, embraced a policy that permitted anti-Black racial oppression while proclaiming that anti-Black genocide was on the decline through the extension of democracy to this subjected group. These factions represented two articulations of anticommunist governance insofar as both made liberal use of the Red Scare and were committed to the maintenance of racial and economic hierarchy, but the Dixiecrats more blatantly employed the Black Scare, which, in turn, ensured that Truman and his faction upheld a more liberal "method of oppressing the Negro people."[64]

The Dixiecrats were overtly white supremacist and their candidates openly attempted to invite direct and indirect violence against Blacks and anyone sympathetic to them—especially those Red-baited as communists.[65] These "states' rights Democrats" argued that race equality was un-American and a plot of Moscow.[66] The Dixiecrats' *States Rights Information and Speakers' Handbook* plainly stated that racial equality was a "communistic theory" and that legislation like the Fair Employment Practices Commission "was patterned after a Russian law written by Joseph Stalin about 1930, [and was] suited to the Russian form of government." It would not work in any "free" country, least of all the United States, where the dignity and worth of the individual was respected.[67] Dixiecrats also claimed that Blacks, as the preeminent subversives from within, were "non-supportive of the government" and were rightfully screened out by the poll tax and other methods of disenfranchisement; that nothing was more un-American than antilynching laws; and that desegregating the armed forces threatened the safety of the country.[68]

These caustic positions allowed the Truman faction to evade any real structural change by being less overt, making incremental or inconsequential progress seem substantial by comparison to the blatantly racist Dixiecrats. In other words, Truman could be lackadaisical in his support for, and not actually move on, federal antilynching legislation, abolishing the poll tax, ending segregation and discrimination, creating an FEPC, and enforcing federal law in the South because of the Dixiecrats' staunch opposition to these.[69] In fact, "bills providing for the implementation of the civil rights guaranteed Negroes by the Constitution . . . [had] been introduced again and again in successive Congresses. And again and again they have been defeated, shelved, or filibustered to death."[70] This was done through the "Gentleman's Agreement" between those who disagreed in theory but who agreed in practice to stymie any legislation providing for full citizenship rights for Blacks. As such, Blacks were reduced to "voiceless automaton[s] whose function was only to contribute to monopoly's profits." The absolute subordination of Black people was fascistic in nature.[71]

These factions of the Democratic Party came together both in their refusal to pass any protections for Black people and political minorities and in their passage of repressive legislation that fortified the subjection of these beleaguered groups. "The passage of the McCarran Act," for example, "would make the very advocacy of civil rights a crime." In supporting it, Congress "took a major step in denying the Negro people and their white allies the right even to petition for civil rights in the future. Thus the record of the legislative branch of government in 1950 was actually one of attack on the fights and lives of the Negro masses."[72] Anticommunist governance maintained the capitalist racist status quo by one group of politicians advocating blatantly fascist views, especially as they related to Black people, while another group espoused antifascist politics and lofty ideals to obfuscate their unwillingness to undo fascistic social relations.

The Black Scare, the Red Scare, and the Peculiar Character of US Fascism

In his study of fascist regimes in Germany, Indonesia, Italy, Spain, and several Latin American countries, Lawrence W. Britt identified fourteen characteristics of fascism: powerful and continuing nationalism, disdain for human rights, the construction of enemies/scapegoats as a source of unification, military supremacy, rampant sexism, controlled mass media, obsession with national security, lack of separation between government and religion, the aggressive protection of corporate power, the suppression of labor, disdain for intellectuals and artists, obsession with crime and punishment, ubiquitous cronyism and corruption, and fraudulent elections.[73] Claudia Jones identified a number of these characteristics in her 1951 Smith Act trial, and by extension in US Capitalist Racist Society.

In a statement before her sentencing in 1953, Jones began by arguing that the US government had doubled down on its peculiar brand of nationalism, which was predicated on denying democratic rights to Black second-class citizens.[74] The disenfranchisement of the Black population meant support for fraudulent elections since the votes of those on the darker side of the color line were excluded. The government's disdain for human rights was manifested in "the obscenity of this trial of ideas," built on the "concocted lies" of "stool pigeons and informers." She excoriated, "For me to accept the verdict of guilty would only mean that I considered myself less than worthy of the dignity of truth, which I cherish as a communist and as a human being." In other words, the railroading of communists—who had become enemies and scapegoats to rationalize what was fast becoming a fascistic police state—was an assault on human rights.[75] Jones further argued that she was being found guilty of struggling against military supremacy, specifically to "end the bestial Korean war, to stop 'operation killer,' to bring our boys home, to reject the militarist threat to embroil us in war with China."[76] Her position highlighted "the desperate drive by the men of Wall Street to war and fascism" and the government's callous protection of corporate power over and against the interests of the masses of the world.[77]

Jones's persecution was also tinged with sexism insofar as her original indictment was based on her article "Women in the Struggle for Peace and Security," in which she urged Negro and white mothers and women to join their

218

CHAPTER TEN

antifascist sisters throughout the world to put pressure on the US government in the cause of peace. This flew in the face of the Truman administration's "fascist triple-K (*Kinder-Küche-Kirche*)" ideology. This emphasis on "Children, Kitchen, and Church" was deeply antiwoman and aimed to hamper women's social participation and progressive politics. As such, it especially penalized Black and working women and that worsened their economic status.[78] In the same article, Jones argued that progressive labor forces didn't always glean how the ideological attack on women, couched in terms of her femininity, womanliness, and pursuit of family happiness, was rooted in capitalist racism. "Big capital" levied this ideological offensive against Black and working women to discredit their drive for peace and their "pressing economic and social demands.[79] Here, she emphasized that the interrelationship between patriarchal, sexist, and misogynistic denigration of women; superexploitation of Black women; and suppression of working women as a function of dominating labor and the working class more broadly was characteristic of anticommunist governance—and of fascism.

Moreover, Jones's prosecution conveyed the intersection of anticommunist governance and fascism in the government's desire to control the press, since she was indicted on the basis of published articles in periodicals deemed subversive; the government's emphasis on crime and punishment, insofar as communist and progressive ideas were being criminalized and those who espoused them were being incarcerated, deported, and otherwise harassed; and the government's obsession with national security in that counterhegemonic ideas were being punished as attempts to overthrow the government by force or violence.

While sharing the above characteristics with other fascist regimes, there were distinctive features embedded in US Capitalist Racist Society that gave it a fascistic character. Perhaps the most glaring was antiblack genocide and the concomitant Black Scare, with fascistic measures generally meted out to Black people in a much more intense and protracted fashion than to other groups.[80] The most visceral articulation of this was white supremacist violence in the form of lynching, race riots, and generalized racial terrorism against veterans and civilians alike meant to maintain racialized economic hierarchies.

In 1943, when the United States was aiding in the struggle against fascism abroad, fascistic race riots, "one of Hitler's most deadly weapons on the home front," were rampant at home. Antiblack mob violence in Mobile, Alabama, injured at least eighty and hampered wartime production. Whites attacked Mexican American and Black workers at an aircraft center in Los Angeles, California. Black workers were brutalized by a white mob in Beaumont, Texas, resulting in two deaths, sixty injuries, and halted production. Shortly there-after, Blacks were attacked at a shipyard in Chester, Pennsylvania, and in a war production center in Newark, New Jersey. And, in Detroit, Michigan, a bloody and deadly race riot erupted in the industrial center, with twenty Jewish and Black workers killed and hundreds more seriously injured. All of these racist attacks happened in the span of four weeks.

These riots were accompanied by serious racial conflicts at army camps throughout the nation, and especially in the South, with three in Georgia alone at Camp Stewart, Fort Benning, and Augusta. A Black man was also lynched in Marianna, Florida, after his death sentence was overturned by the state supreme court. These were not random or isolated race conflicts, but rather a wave of genocidal violence accompanying Black Scare propaganda that engulfed the nation in an astonishingly short span of time. It was no coincidence that this racist brutality accrued around army camps and key industrial centers where Blacks had an increased presence due to the war. This made US Capitalist Racist Society appear deeply fascistic in character not least because each anti-Black attack was deliberately incited, organized, and accompanied by "systematic rumor campaigns" meant to encourage rac-ist vitriol to spark unrest.[81]

In *We Charge Genocide* parlance, these rumor campaigns were "direct and public incitement to commit genocide" not unlike that which permeated Nazi Germany.[82] The Black communist Doxey Wilkerson explained, "Hitler bragged, years ago, that he would foment race conflict of precisely the type that has beset our nation during the past four weeks. These riots . . . waged against us from within our own nation . . . are [part] of a much broader con-spiracy."[83] This "broader conspiracy" was the Black Scare that legitimated widespread attacks on Black people to keep them subordinated at any cost. Moreover, this heightened racial violence coincided with the passage of the draconian Smith-Connally Anti-Strike Act—reminiscent of the World War I Espionage and Sedition Acts—which led directly to the brutal suppression of labor unrest, attacks on price and rent control, and efforts to destroy the National Resource Planning Board.[84] Moreover, as the war drew to a close, anti-Black terrorism intensified, including the lynching of two veterans in Monroe, Georgia—among forty others that had occurred by the end of the summer of 1946. This gave US Capitalist Racist Society the feeling that it was hurling from fascistic to fully fascist.

The reality of Wall Street Imperialism meant that the Black Scare within the United States tended to mirror its foreign policy toward the darker na-tions. For example, the United States was essentially unconcerned about the

plight of Ethiopia when it was invaded by fascist Italy in 1935 because Wall
Street Imperialism had few investments in the Horn of Africa at that time.
The United States' refusal to defend Ethiopia reflected the government's accommodation of domestic racial terrorism. Likewise, the complicity of American industrial capitalists like Henry Ford in supplying economic aid to Benito
Mussolini was an international manifestation of the way Northern big business
maintained the Structural Location of Blackness through its investments and
monopolies in the US South. Though the United States officially declared neu-
trality and imposed embargos on both Italy and Ethiopia, the economic support provided to Italy by American corporations represented the state's tacit
alignment with fascists.[85]

The Black Scare informed and was informed by the second fascistic aspect of US Capitalist Racist Society, the Red Scare and its peculiar construal
of diverse progressive and militant politics as communist or communist-
adjacent and therefore illicit. The Red Scare was a means of criminalizing
radical thought through the "Hitlerian Big Lie" about foreign agents, foreign
influence, and foreign domination of progressive groups, spread by the prac-
titioners of anticommunist governance.[86] These same forces explicitly and
implicitly supported the fascistic treatment of Black, oppressed, and exploited
peoples, because "instead of prosecuting the Ku Klux Klan, the anti-Semites,
and the reactionaries, the government [arrested] anti-fascists."[87] As Claudia
Jones charged about her deportation: "I was a victim of McCarthyite hysteria
against independent political ideas in the U.S.A., a hysteria which penalizes
anyone who holds ideas contrary to the official pro-war, pro-reactionary line
of the white ruling class of that country." Likewise, as a Black communist
woman, she was targeted by the government for opposing Jim Crow and for
urging the prosecution of white supremacists instead of communists.[88] Pettis Perry, Jones's co-defendant in the 1951 Smith Act trial, contended that the
Red Scare prosecution of communists solely on the basis of their ideas sought
"to bring into being fascism in the United states in its American variety."[89] In
effect, the "Hitler-like anti-communist hysteria" brought together the "fascist,
anti-Semitic, and anti-Negro forces in the country," and threatened democracy, freedom, and standards of living in the United States.[90]

A particularly pernicious event that demonstrated the entanglement of the
Red Scare, the Black Scare, anti-Black genocide, and the fascistic character of
US Capitalist Racist Society was the Peekskill riot. On August 27, 1949, Paul
Robeson was scheduled to sing at a concert organized by the Harlem chapter
of the CRC in Peekskill, New York. As soon as he arrived, white World War II
veterans paraded in opposition and barricaded the roads leading to the concert grounds. A vicious mob then assaulted the men, women, and children in

attendance and yelled anti-Black and anti-Semitic insults. They also burned a five-foot cross on the concert grounds. Anti-Robeson sentiment had been mounting since he delivered an angry speech at the World Peace Conference in Paris earlier that year in which he excoriated US Capitalist Racist Society, not least its warmongering and racism. Press reports indicated that he found it unthinkable that American Negroes would go to war for a country that had historically oppressed them (the United States) against a country that treated African Americans with full dignity (the Soviet Union). In the context of the Cold War and increasing Red Scare hysteria, he was construed as disloyal, traitorous, and a "stooge" of Moscow.

After being terrorized and beaten at the August 27 concert, twenty-five thousand Robeson supporters refused to submit to Black Scare and Red Scare terror and gathered on September 4, 1949, to hear him sing. Again, they were attacked when leaving the concert: their cars and buses were pelted with rocks and clubs, windows were smashed, and some cars were overturned. Over two hundred people were injured. More than nine hundred police officers on the scene sided with, aided, and encouraged the attack. On September 14, in typical Red Scare fashion, New York governor Thomas Dewey blamed the violence and lawlessness on the victims by construing the concert as a "communist plot."

On October 12, officers of the Council on African Affairs, the radical anticolonial organization that would fold a few years later due to the anticommunist pressures, submitted a letter to President Harry Truman in response to the violence and Dewey's ignominy. Robeson, Du Bois, Alphaeus Hunton, Louise Thompson Patterson, and others wrote: "A criminal assault was made against the American people and their rights at Peekskill, New York, on the night of August 27, 1949. The criminal attack was repeated a week later on Sunday, September 4, in the same locality." They charged that Governor Dewey and his lackeys had failed to protect the lives, rights, and property of American citizens. As such, he was unfit to hold office. They demanded an investigation by the attorney general and the Civil Rights Department and prosecution of those responsible. They also linked the riot to earlier attacks on Robeson, to the repression of other Black leaders, and to cases of police brutality for which no one was held accountable. The letter underscored the fascistic character of the Black and Red Scares in US Capitalist Racist Society by arguing that "Peekskill demonstrated what this mounting anti-Negro violence and contempt for human rights may develop into unless speedily checked. Peekskill was a reminder of Hitlerite Germany where fascism got its start with organized mob assaults, with official sanction, against the Jewish people in the name of German 'patriotism' and 'anticommunism.'"[91]

US Capitalist Racist Society's third fascistic characteristic was the use of war and the threat of war in the service of reaction and counterrevolution. During World War II, Doxey Wilkerson argued, a "powerful clique of American pro-fascists and imperialists," worked to preserve the fascist governments in Germany and throughout Europe in order to forestall "the democratic upsurge of liberated peoples throughout the world which the destruction of fascism would surely bring." The support for fascism by particular segments of the US ruling class during the war, Wilkerson claimed, aimed to curb anticolonialism and self-determination in the Third World in much the same way that the Red Scare worked in a fascistic manner to undermine struggles for racial justice. Such wartime commitment to imperialism and colonialism abroad was complemented by opposition to the progressive policies of the Roosevelt administration domestically. This cabal of Wall Street Imperialists, warned Wilkerson, would "try to establish an oppressive fascist regime here in America" to overturn the gains made by labor, Blacks, and other minoritized groups and to crush progressive dissent.[92] Worse still, given the realities of anti-Black genocide and its legitimation through the Black Scare, Black people would suffer most if the "real threat of a fascist America" came to fruition in that they would be "forced back into a slavery far worse than their forefathers ever knew."[93] Because the fascistic character of the United States particularly threatened Black people, Wilkerson held that the extension of democratic rights and equality to Black people—along with other exploited and oppressed populations—was essential to the protection of the nation as a whole.[94]

As the Cold War ascended, so too did US militarism and warmongering, including nuclear buildup, the waging of "hot" wars in Asia and Africa, and the drive toward World War III. The perpetual march toward war was one of the ways that the US government rationalized Black Scare and Red Scare policing of thought and action. The "demagogic slogan" of "national unity" imposed during wartime was a way of uniting the ruling class against the people "to make profits, by starvation, by clamping down on the civil rights of the people, on the basis of war."[95] Relatedly, the fascistic bipartisan war drive, the Truman-Acheson warmongering, the "repressive and death-dealing measures carried through . . . by Wall Street's puppets in Marshallized Italy, in fascist Greece and Spain," and the "Marshall-Plan-financed war . . . against the heroic Vietnamese" paved the road to "monopoly oppression" and actually-existing fascism.[96]

In effect, the US government and big business used war and the threat of war to entrench Wall Street Imperialism by using the "sons of American mothers as 'blue chips' in [the] vicious plot of world conquest, fascism . . .

and death." Likewise, war and the threat of war normalized the "militarization of youth," the disruption of families, labor shortages, land dispossession, shrinking incomes, and the undermining of workers who already occupied precarious economic positions—namely, women and Blacks.[97] Moreover, as building blocks of fascism in US Capitalist Racist Society, war and the threat of war were inextricably linked to the Black Scare and the Red Scare. As the Black communist New York City councilman Benjamin J. Davis Jr. fumed, Truman could "cook up a red-baiting pretext to send Negroes 10,000 miles away to die, but he can't find a single way to get the anti-lynch, anti-poll tax or FEPC bills passed."[98]

Wall Street Imperialism was the final fascistic feature of US Capitalist Racist Society. The US capitalist elite, a wealthy financial community that created and controlled the prevailing political climate, equated the nation's welfare with their ability to freely accumulate wealth. This imperialistic control, which drained profit from all parts of the world, was constitutively racist in that the original base of their "Wall Street superprofits" was the Structural Location of Blackness, which during Black Scare / Red Scare Longue Durée amounted to a larger profit source than any single foreign country.[99] Capitalist accumulation was connected organically from its inception to the fascistic logics of white supremacy and anti-Black racial oppression, with Wall Street Imperialism continuing the subjugation, emanating from racial slavery, of Black people in the US South. The Black Scare, as an expression of capitalist racism, was "integrally related to the jingoism of imperialism" that appeared viciously in the conquest of Cuba, Puerto Rico, Hawaii, and the Philippines and occurred simultaneously with and for the same reason as the national oppression of Blacks in the US South.[100] In effect, Wall Street Imperialists "unfurled the banner of Anglo-Saxon fascism"[101] in their drive to establish racially codified world domination for the purpose of capital accumulation.[102]

★

During the Black Scare / Red Scare Longue Durée, the fascistic character of US Capitalist Racist Society was manifested in the confluence of the Countersubversive Political Tradition articulated through anticommunist governance, the nexus of anti-Black genocide and the Black Scare, the Red Scare and its attack on radical thought and organizing, war and the threat of war as sources of political repression, and Wall Street Imperialism's racialized plunder domestically and abroad. This fascistic character worked through and with the "legitimating architecture" of "True Americanism." True Americanism both rationalized and obfuscated the violent material processes that facilitated accumulation and extraction along racialized lines by positioning US Capitalist

Racist Society as fundamentally democratic, equal, and fair, on the one hand, and political economies and social orders that challenged it as dangerous, illegitimate, and criminal, on the other hand. True American discourses, narrations, doctrines, ideologies, and customs made this double move by harnessing the Black Scare and the Red Scare to the codification of oppositional ideas, ideologies, individuals, organizations, and movements as un-American, subversive, seditious, disloyal, foreign, foreign inspired, threatening to internal security, and otherwise undesirable.

True Americanism: The Legitimating Architecture of US Capitalist Racist Society

The national scene is basic. If they believe abroad in the equality of races, the solution is not for us to adopt this un-American principle of race equality but for them to adopt the white supremacy of "True Americanism."

WE CHARGE GENOCIDE, 1951

If anticommunism was the mode of governing US Capitalist Racist Society, then "True Americanism" was the legitimating architecture. Legitimating architecture includes rationalizing discourses, political narrations, reigning ideology, legal instrumentalities, and social practices that normalize and codify US Capitalist Racist Society and Wall Street Imperialism. It proffers very particular narrations or presentations of society that obfuscate and conceal, even as they authorize and give meaning to the material reality. During the Black Scare / Red Scare Longue Durée, "subversion," "un-American," "sedition," "disloyalty," "foreign," and "threat to national security" were key discourses of True Americanism and its constitutive Black Scare and Red Scare. These worked to position capitalist racism as the preeminent system of political, economic, and social organization to which any challenge was dangerous, illicit, and illegitimate. This legitimating architecture sustained US Capitalist Racist Society by identifying which peoples, organizations, ideas, and political formations were dangerous to the status quo, and therefore must be controlled and neutralized. As well, True Americanism was the antithesis of Radical Blackness, which was undeserving of civil rights and liberties and the rightful target of incarceration, indictment, deportation, surveillance, coercion, and/or manifold forms of extreme and quotidian physical and structural violence.

During the World War I era, there arose the dialectic between the ascent of the United States to global capitalist hegemony and the unprecedented rise of "big business," on the one hand, and the shift in race relations in response to global agitation, the growth of the Black press, Southern Black and West Indian migration to industrial cities and urban centers, and the return of Black veteran, on the other hand.[1] Likewise, the global upheaval caused by

World War I cast doubt on the white civilization narrative that positioned Euro-America as the arbiter of culture, rationality, and reason, and "the end of the First World War witnessed, amidst the larger turbulence that engulfed American social and political life, the dramatic appearance of the twentieth-century's first expression of Black radicalism on a significant mass scale."[2] This coincided with the successful Russian Revolution that portended the split of the world into capitalist and socialist camps, the emergence of the Communist International as an adversary of Wall Street Imperialism, the Bolshevik support for self-determination in colonized territories, and the bourgeoning radicalization of Black people nationally and internationally. These developments precipitated for the US government an urgent need for the "conservation, development, and absorption of American ideals of national, civil, and social life, particularly among the [foreign], with the end in view of securing a United America."[3]

Democracy as the "American Way of Life"

True Americanism was the means by which the "great need" to "secure" the nation was addressed in accordance with the demands of US Capitalist Racist Society. Discourses of democracy, freedom, citizenship, and equality obfuscated the race and class antagonism that constituted the society while also employing the Black and Red Scares to normalize them. Through True Americanism, "democracy" was reduced to and conflated with the "American way of life." The American way of life, in turn, was inextricable from "the free-enterprise system" as the "bulwark and guarantor of a democratic society; that is, a society where official policies and values [were] realistically within the free choice of a majority of ordinary citizens."[4] Here, business interests, or the interests of the white ruling class, became synonymous with US interests, and the ability to satisfy those interests became interchangeable with democracy. This chain of signification positioned ideas, ideologies, and forms of political and economic organization, like socialism, communism, and Black self-determination, that challenged or rejected the foundations of US Capitalist Racist Society, as un-American, authoritarian, and unfree, and thus diametrically opposed and inferior to True Americanism.[5]

Democracy took on the additional meaning of choice and availability in the marketplace and "the strength of America's competitive economic system with the individual's right to own property, to buy and sell in the free market, and to earn a fair profit for his efforts."[6] True Americanism was codified by these capitalist norms of individual ownership, profit, and rights that facilitated the narration of US Capitalist Racist Society as "a partnership of all men who believe in equality of opportunity, in the abolition of class distinctions, and in the sweeping aside of racial prejudice."[7] In this way, True Americanism concealed, obfuscated, and distorted the material realities of the society with abstract ideals that trivialized the distinctions between the ruling class and the exploited, the powerful and the disempowered, and the privileged and the oppressed. The result was a form of enforced belonging and participation, on the one hand, and violent exclusion and abjection, on the other hand, that rendered challenges to racial and economic hierarchy foreign, subversive, un-American, and dangerous.

If democracy meant that all citizens, irrespective of class or status, enjoyed equality, freedom, and ability in the marketplace, then demands for economic redistribution, racial remediation, and the attenuation of elite power and privilege were undemocratic and thereby un-American. True Americanism, then, normalized an array of reactionary ideas, illiberal actions, and practices of intolerance that were applied to real or imagined defiance of the status quo. The result was the direct or indirect stifling of progress for the masses. Like anticommunist governance, True Americanism was furthered from above by state and federal governments and from below by civil society.[8] In other words, it was "not a monolith but a coalition"[9] of federal, state, and local government and civil society legitimating architecture that constructed loyalty to the United States in direct opposition to "foreign" radicalism. The latter presented a threat to national security by endangering the organization of society rooted in capitalist exploitation and racial hierarchy. Likewise, the capacious nature of "foreign" and the vague specification of "loyalty" produced a highly variable "common threat" that could and should be combated in numerous ways. As we have seen, government entities spearheaded both ideological and material assaults on anything considered proximal to an external threat.

Relatedly, True Americanism illuminated the co-constitutionality of legitimating architecture and political economy in US Capitalist Racist Society by operating as a form of (de-)valuation in three key ways. First, it added or withheld value based on willingness and ability to conform. Second, it articulated the preeminence of US institutions and the inferiority or illegitimacy of other forms of organization, which overvalued US citizenship and devalued those who were cast outside of it through law and discourse. Finally, it articulated a set of value-added duties, obligations, and privileges predicated on the idea of a "common country," the eschewal of which could be devalued as foreign or foreign inspired.[10]

Americanization against Radicalism and Revolution

In the years following the Great War, federal and state governments imposed True Americanism through a broad, if uneven, project of Americanization, which was "the process which the foreign undergo in orienting [themselves] to American ideals and traditions, as well as to the custom and manners of this country."[11] Fundamental ideals, traditions, customs, and manners of US Capitalist Racist Society included the entanglement of responsibility and privilege, progress as predicated on self-reliance and individual initiative, and justice and good government rooted in "enlightened" and "patriotic" participation in public life.[12] Such principles aimed to produce loyal citizens and efficient workers to stave off foreign inspiration, especially Bolshevism, which was codified as the "revolutionary keynote" of the class war–driven hate and distrust that had ruined Russia and would destroy the rest of the world if given the chance.[13]

Radicalism was both dangerous and incompatible with True Americanism as it harped on discontent and promoted an "unreasonable state of mind" among workers that was amenable to subversion.[14] Americanization was a method of bringing the foreign into alignment with the nation's ideals and steering them away from "propaganda of a seditious nature" propagated by the immigrant and Black press, street corner agitators,[15] and other subversive forces. These dissidents took advantage of the highly segregated nature of immigrant and Black life to gather large audiences, to increase their membership through local organizations and to facilitate the spread of their propaganda.[16] Thus, Americanization was deemed vital not only for national defense,[17] but also to weaken alien influence that caused disorder.[18]

True Americanism and its concomitant process of Americanization were positioned as the antidote to revolution, revolutionary change, or revolutionary struggle. According to the secretary of the interior in 1919, True Americanism meant that "we have evolved for ourselves machinery by which revolution, as a method of changing our lives, is outgrown and outlawed."[19] Here, "outgrown" connoted that those who advocated revolution were backward, uncivilized, and immature, as were those who were susceptible to revolutionary ideas. Outlawing revolution, by contrast, was the signal of a mature, functioning, secure society. Ideas that articulated revolutionary—that is, transformative—change to US Capitalist Racist Society were antithetical to the modern social order.

Reiterating True Americanism's conflation of democracy and the "American way of life," the secretary contended, "one of the meanings of democracy is that it is a form of government in which the right to revolution has been lost by giving the government wholly to the people. Revolution means revolt. Against who are we to revolt in the United States excepting the people of the United States?"[20] This specification of "the people" was set against those foreclosed from True Americanism and for whom revolution-as-structural-transformation was essential. Revolt was an affront to the government and the people and was not only criminal but un-American insofar as "no man can be a sound and sterling American who believes that force is necessary to effectuate popular will."[21] The coupling of "force" with those who could not be "sound and sterling Americans" obfuscated the force and violence endemic in US Capitalist Racist Society that precipitated the necessity of revolt. Moreover, the role of the government and its partnership with business, the secretary argued, was to protect "the possessors from non-possessors who would dare seize it through violence of other means" and to ensure that propertyless workers or their political representatives could not take control and sweep away the capitalist order in the name of socialism—or racial equality.[22]

In addition to being the process of staving off revolution, Americanization also aimed to bludgeon foreign influence. It was an imperative that, while spearheaded by "private enterprise" prior to World War I, traversed the public and private sectors thereafter and cultivated a close relationship between them. The rise of big business meant that this sector did much to shape and impose True Americanism and its legitimation of the domination of capital and business over all aspects of society as an objective good. True Americanism was animated by American business theory and its promotion of social hierarchy, with large business owners at the top; its aim to bind and subsume labor to capital; its defense of selfish individualism as central to advancing public good; and its advocacy of businessmen serving their communities and the nation through politics, especially local politics, to eradicate the influence of radicals, organized labor, and the masses.[23] Thus, businessmen were the preeminent defenders of democracy from "mob rule." Likewise, because businessmen were the most affluent and therefore the most deserving of power, they also had the responsibility to protect society from "agitators" who were the enemies of True Americanism. Such responsibility translated into an outsized influence in shaping the legitimating architecture of US Capitalist Racist Society.

True Americanism was operationalized as the only means by which the foreign could protect themselves against exploitation and fraud. On the one hand, True Americanism, and the acceptance of ruling-class ethics it engendered, was the prerequisite for avoiding the hard and dangerous work, abysmal living conditions, exclusion from vital US institutions, and subjection to mob violence that characterized the lives of the foreign who lacked the access of native white workers.[24] It is important to note here that, because the native worker was always-already white, Black laborers, especially recent migrants from the South, were lumped in with immigrants as "foreign." The implication was that exploitation flowed from an antagonistic relationship with the state and capital, not from the social relations of capitalist racism, so adopting True Americanism, not unionizing, organizing, or protesting, was the answer. On the other hand, those who rejected True Americanism for foreign ideas and ideologies were either frauds or exploiters, abetted them, or were vulnerable to them. The exploitation of foreigners was thus the provenance of other foreigners or radicals who had "acquired a working knowledge of American conditions and turned that knowledge to the exploitation of their fellows," which in turn prejudiced these exploited foreign workers against the US industrial system.[25] This was the logic inculcating the prosecution of Ben Fletcher, who belonged to an organization overrun by foreigners that supported the enemies of the United States; Marcus Garvey, the West Indian rabble rouser; and Angelo Herndon, who belonged to the most despicable foreign-inspired organization: the CPUSA. Each of these men was guilty of exploiting the foreign and downtrodden with their ideas, practices, and action. In effect, US Capitalist Racist Society, which by design oppressed, exploited, and repressed persons based on race, class, origin, and political orientation, was not the culprit; rather, it was those on the constitutive outside of True Americanism who were both victims and perpetrators.

The US Chamber of Commerce (COC)—the paramount organization of the employing class[26]—and the National Association of Manufacturers (NAM) were at the forefront of Americanization. These business organizations helped to fund, and thereby shape the discourse of, civil society organizations like the National Security League, the American Defense League, the National Civic Federation, and the American Legion. Backed by large corporations and businessmen like J. P. Morgan and John D. Rockefeller, these entities linked the sanctity of private property, "economic conservatism," and hostility to organized labor with "a new spirit of American patriotism" to combat Bolshevism and "Red radicalism."[27] Similarly, through its Americanization work, the COC underscored True Americanism as fidelity to the status quo by suturing US citizenship to nationalism and loyalty, and failure to take up the "obligations" of US citizenship to "social and political danger" and "un-American" customs.

For the COC, True Americanism meant speaking English, the common national language; uniting under one flag; maintaining the "American standard of living"; displaying understanding of and love for the United States; demonstrating a desire to remain and have a home in the US and to support its institutions and laws; and embracing the necessity of war, closing ranks, and helping to win the war. All of this meant avoiding anything un-American and disloyal.[28] Moreover, Americanization meant uncritical acceptance of a linear progress narrative that American institutions, ideals, traditions, and standards were striving toward the abolition of race prejudice and discrimination. Importantly, the COC asserted Americanization in wartime and peacetime as an industrial matter on which business and industry should take the lead. Insofar as "the American employer must always be the strategic influence in Americanization," True Americanism was, at is core, the legitimation of capitalist racism, and by extension, other hierarchal arrangements in society, as objectively good. This meant that the subordination of labor to capital was the American way, and that socialism/communism and mandated racial equality were not only bad, but were quintessentially anti-American. Moreover, in keeping with the legitimacy of hierarchy and True Americanism as a form of (de-)valuation, the COC contended that there should be an economic incentive for Americanization—namely, a higher wage for those who had Americanized than for those who refused.

The NAM, which organized the COC in 1912, aimed to promote the industrial interests of the United States, secure better relations between employer and employee, educate the public in the principles of individual liberty and the ownership of property, and support legislation to further those principles and oppose legislation that undermined them. As such, it was one of the leading forces in shaping True Americanism, not least through its opposition to labor unions and its promotion of "industrial peace" and the "open shop"—aptly named the "America Plan." The latter did much to sustain the Red Scare. It aimed to construe union militancy as "subversive, Bolshevistic and alien to basic American values" in contradistinction to the equality, democracy, and freedom of the open shop. Unionism that sought to empower workers and challenge the authority of bosses was disguised "Sovietism," while capitulation to the capitalist class was True Americanism. This mischaracterization helped to reduce labor organizing to unlawful agitation, to encourage government surveillance, and to discredit and malign radicalism more broadly.[29]

For example, in 1923 NAM argued that the employer was the natural leader of workers because he owned the means of production and could inculcate correct thinking and loyalty to the "common enterprise" through instruction, example, and fairness.[30] Here, capitalist economic organization, hierarchy, and ideology were normalized as "right" thinking, and loyalty was understood as dedication to both free enterprise and to the capitalist leadership. Furthermore, during the Great Depression, and in opposition to the New

Deal, NAM worked in earnest to articulate True Americanism through "the economic objectives, the ideals, and the program of the business community as a whole" and "complete government coordination with the needs, interests, and social outlooks of business."[31] NAM also opposed both organized labor and liberal social legislation like the New Deal. It fomented opposition through "educational literature" aimed at disseminating True Americanism in "every nook and cranny of American life, economic, political, social, and cultural."[32]

The role of not only the Red Scare, but also the Black Scare, in codifying True Americanism was evident in that business leaders advocated the coordination of political policies in alignment with the requirement of monopoly-oriented business and demanded the use of government to suppress groups antagonistic to its interests.[33] These elements included political radicals and militant Black workers. On this view, the indispensable role of government was to control and disappear the national and ideological influence of detractors.[34] In effect, NAM was formative in the identification of "free enterprise"—"state subsidized private power with no infringement on managerial prerogatives"—as True Americanism that needed to be defended against subversives and un-Americans, including the foreign, communists, anarchists, and Blacks.[35]

The COC and NAM were highly successful throughout the Black Scare / Red Scare Longue Durée in attacking communists and other radicals by forcefully asserting the virtues of capitalist enterprise through True Americanism. These private sector juggernauts, alongside federal and local governments, appended the Black Scare and the Red Scare to the denigration of legislation and social programs that helped to protect workers and consumers against exploitation; to the maligning of militant unionism as "creeping socialism," and thus un-American; and to the legitimation of political repression as "just" and "necessary."[36]

Black and Red Threats to True Americanism

True Americanism conscripted diverse peoples and ideas into the narrative of the nation or, through the Black Scare and the Red Scare, positioned them on the constitutive outside of, and as dangerous to, US Capitalist Racist Society.[37] This was not least because "U.S. world-ordering aspirations were explicitly legitimated by claiming the virtues of *internal* democracy, or the harmonious cooperation of different groups within the vast national body, and the broad toleration of cultural, religious, ethnic, and racial differences in America."[38] Such "internal democracy" and "toleration" were predicated on a deep suspicion of the "foreign," a broadly conceived category operationalized to render suspect anyone and anything that was ignorant of, hostile to, or critical of True Americanism. On this logic, "foreign" was that which threatened destabilization. Thus, True Americanism meant disavowing foreign politics, customs, and "allegiance" to a foreign ruler; actively demonstrating a desire to belong to the nation; and accepting the official discourse of the society and expressing a unity of purpose with it. "Toleration" both obfuscated and standardized the structural intolerance of ideas, politics, and ways of being that could not easily be accommodated to US Capitalist Racist Society. In this way, True Americanism was a means of defending the status quo against the foreign-as-destabilizing, including economic redistribution, popular franchise, the union movement, and racial equality.[39]

True Americanism rendered predominant the ideological dimensions of US ideas and values and made these interchangeable with American identity.[40] "We know that this country is bound together by an idea," wrote Eleanor Roosevelt during World War II. "The citizens of this country belong to many races and many creeds. They have come here and built a great Nation around the idea of democracy and freedom. . . . The present crisis challenges us to preserve what this country was founded to be, a land where people should have the right to life, liberty, and the pursuit of happiness, regardless of race creed or color."[41] It was this "idea"—or legitimating architecture—that overdetermined actually-existing inequality and repression and set democracy, freedom, and equality to work in defense of US Capitalist Racist Society.[42] As such, the Red Scare helped to cast Marxist intellectual and political traditions, and anything adjacent them, as anathema to True Americanism, while True "'Americanism' . . . created the special conditions that had blocked the development of an American Marxist" tradition.[43] More than this, True Americanism was rooted in the intentional criminalization and disciplining of this tradition through the Black Scare and the Red Scare.

Roosevelt's enunciation of True Americanism, in which the ideas of democracy, freedom, and citizenship distorted and rationalized the realities of capitalist racism, was the complement to FBI director J. Edgar Hoover's use of it to construct challenge to US Capitalist Racist Society as a foreign menace. While Roosevelt conscripted citizens into True Americanism through the elevation of ideas-as-identity that harbored capitalist racism, Hoover hardened the boundaries of True Americanism by outlining the dangers to it. He made this point very strongly in a speech before HUAC on March 26, 1947. He argued that because radicalism, particularly communism, was a "malignant way of life" and a "disease that spread like an epidemic" that threatened to infect the entire nation,[44] the primary responsibility of HUAC and

committees like it was to publicly disclose, expose, and spotlight this social
and political ill so it could be "quarantined" and "do no harm."[45]

Likewise, Hoover insisted that it was only through True Americanism
that Red "doublespeak," which concealed un-American aims, could be un-
covered. When Reds used the term "democracy," for example, what they actually meant was authoritarianism, and when they critiqued capitalist racism,
they were really attempting to impose a foreign social and political system to
undermine US democracy.[46] Here, Hoover employed True Americanism to
circumscribe the meaning of democracy by transforming it into danger when
it was articulated by those deemed enemies of the state. Based on Hoover's
position, radical demands for democracy, which included racial equality and
justice, the transformative redistribution of wealth and resources, and world
peace, were little more than "Red fascism" and attempts to subvert the US order. In this way, Hoover created the conditions for any critique of or mobilization against the extant social order, domestically and globally, to be treated
as a "menace to freedom, to democratic ideals, [and] to the worship of God"
that threatened the "American way of life."[47]

The best defense against subversion, according to Hoover, was unrelenting vigilance through "vigorous, intelligent, old-fashioned"[48] True Americanism, which meant uncritical allegiance, conformity, and surveillance. As such,
organizations committed to social change, "hundreds" of which, Hoover
claimed, had been infiltrated by, or organized to accomplish, the interests
of the USSR, the CPUSA, and communism within the United States, had to
be particularly aggressive in identifying and exposing Reds and their supporters, and in avoiding any political aims that aligned with them. Moreover,
drawing on the Black Scare, Hoover considered groups that focused on the
exploitation of US Blacks to be especially suspect,[49] which allowed him to link
advocacy of Black equality and political minorities with un-Americanism.[50]
Hoover's speech codified "foreign" as the antithesis of True Americanism
through dichotomies including loyalty/disloyalty, American/un-American,
and conformity/subversion—dichotomies aimed at preserving US Capitalist
Racist Society.[51]

*

A cornerstone articulation of True Americanism appeared in the Lusk Committee's 1920 report *Revolutionary Radicalism*. It established the preeminence
of US Capitalist Racist Society, the dangers posed to it by radical ideas and
movements, and the role of True Americanism in cultivating and maintaining order and crushing dissent. Instructively, the first part of the report meticulously documented "revolutionary" and "subversive" movements abroad

and their establishment in the United States, and documented that the propaganda of radical, revolutionary, and "seditious" groups was "extremely effective" in foreign populations, especially in industrial centers, because radicalism thrived upon "ignorance" and a lack of appreciation for the United States and its institutions.[52] The bulk of attention was reserved for socialism/communism; nearly five hundred pages were dedicated to its European origins, the development of the "Russian Soviet Regime," the impact of the Bolshevik Revolution, and the Third International. An additional 350 pages examined the development of socialism in the United States, with particular focus on the left-wing section of the Socialist Party, the Communist Party of America, the Communist Labor Party, and the Socialist Labor Party. That comparatively less attention was given to "Anarchism" and "Revolutionary Industrial Unionism" conveyed two important points. First, socialism/communism, and especially Bolshevism, was the preeminent threat to US Capitalist Racist Society because it ostensibly permeated and infected other radical movements. A lengthy subsection was dedicated to the spread of socialism in "educated circles through pacifist, religious, [and] collegiate societies."[53] Second, communism and Bolshevism ultimately became shorthand for radicalism more broadly.

Demonstrating the entanglements of the Black Scare and the Red Scare, one of the longest and most detailed chapters in *Revolutionary Radicalism*, titled "Propaganda among Negroes," provided excerpts from numerous texts, including periodicals, pamphlets, speeches, and conference resolutions, that were considered dangerous, inflammatory, and subversive in their efforts to stimulate race hatred or to "engender so-called class consciousness in their ranks."[54] Relatedly, as previously mentioned, the socialist Rand School of Social Science was construed as the headquarters for US Bolsheviks not least because it ostensibly aimed to propagandize Blacks, financially support Black radical speakers and publications, and play up acts of racial injustice to incite Black resistance. The Rand School was considered exceptionally subversive because of its inclusion of and emphasis on Blacks.[55]

This focus on Black people as a dangerous vector of "revolutionary radicalism," and hostility toward organizations and institutions that included them in their praxis, was rooted in the foreclosure of Blacks, like other "foreigners," from True Americanism. This rendered them suspicious as an always-already audience for radicalism, especially susceptible to radicalism, and exceedingly dangerous as radicals. Here, *Revolutionary Radicalism* built upon A. Mitchell Palmer's 1919 report and its appendix "Radicalism and Sedition among the Negroes as Reflected in Their Publications," in which he employed the Black Scare and the Red Scare to condemn hostile Black reactions to race riots, Black retaliation for lynching, militant demands for social equality, open identification with and support of the IWW and Bolshevism, and the disdain Blacks exhibited toward the federal government and the racialism of the US South.[56] *The Attorney General Report* meticulously documented the link between Blacks and other subversive organizations. For example, Exhibit XVIII, an excerpt from the *Messenger* titled "Why We Must Organize," argued that Blacks and the IWW had "interests not only in common, but interests that [were] identical" and encouraged disenfranchised Blacks to link up with white workers who also lacked political rights. The excerpt stated: "The Negro who is disenfranchised must join other voteless workers. The Negro, who is largely the unskilled workers in industry, must join that organization in which the workers are organized upon the basis of industry, thereby giving the skilled and unskilled equality of rights."[57] This advocacy of interracial solidarity, militant unionism, and labor equality conveyed the subversive nature of the *Messenger*, the IWW, and any entity that promoted such radicalism among Blacks. These entities were foreclosed from, and an affront to, True Americanism.

Thus, both *Revolutionary Radicalism* and *The Attorney General Report* conveyed hysteria about the connection between Black and Red, but for different reasons. The former was preeminently concerned with Blacks becoming vectors of socialism in the United States and linking up with the international Bolshevik movement, while the latter expressed concern about rising Radical Blackness and its threat to US Capitalist Racist Society, especially through assertions of social equality and Black self-defense. The Lusk Committee conveyed anxiety about Blacks as Reds, while Palmer "displayed more fear of Blacks as Blacks."[58] Nonetheless, both reports "were alive to the dangers from subversion" and articulated Blacks as an outstanding area of concern. Hence, the harnessing of the Black Scare and the Red Scare to the ends of True Americanism at the federal and state levels was "cast in the same mold."[59]

Part 2 of *Revolutionary Radicalism* documented "Constructive Movements in America," and a substantial portion—the entirety of section 3, nearly two thousand pages—focused on "Americanization Work," also called "Citizenship Training." Here, it was acknowledged that repressive measures against subversive and revolutionary organizations and movements must be accompanied by "constructive action." However, from World War I onward, repressive action was the foundation of True Americanism precisely because Americanization was coercive and rooted in the construction of insiders and outsiders. In fact, the order in which information was presented in *Revolutionary Radicalism* underscored that True Americanism was quintessentially about identifying, defining, and eradicating all that was politically, economically, and socially abhorrent to US Capitalist Racist Society. True Americans were those who were *willing and able* to "acquaint themselves with the forces which play upon the people with less favored circumstances, to become acquainted with facts as they are" and do their part in combating foreign influence and subversion in their communities.[60]

Black "Foreignness" and Foreclosure from True Americanism

Related to True Americanism's manufacturing of insiders and outsiders, the discourse about illiteracy and ignorance in *Revolutionary Radicalism* employed the Black Scare and the Red Scare in a way that established Blackness as a genre of "foreign" alongside immigrants. Foreignness as it related to Blackness designated not only those without US origins, but also those whose ignorance, ideas, affiliations, and/or susceptibility to foreign influence undermined or negated their status as citizen. In other words, foreign applied not only to those who came from elsewhere, but also to those whose *ideas*, and very existence, endangered the organization of society and were thus "alien." As foreignness, Blackness was that which could never quite be truly American, and thereby required scrutiny, control, and containment.

Illiteracy was "a matter of serious concern . . . because it appear[ed] to have a direct bearing upon susceptibility to attack by radical agitators."[61] This was true for "aliens" and Blacks—especially those who had migrated from the rural South.[62] Southern Blacks were said to do "extraordinarily little reading of newspapers" and to "take information through the ear." This, coupled with the fact that they were more "isolated" than whites and therefore more gullible, meant that "enemy agents and agitators had good success in proportion to small effort among Negroes."[63] Illiterates were also a threat to capitalist accumulation in that they cost the US $825 million annually in diminished productivity and could not adequately inhabit True Americanism because they could not keep personal or business accounts. Likewise, they were effectively or potentially disloyal because they did not make effective soldiers and could not fully comprehend the meaning and importance of war, which made them less willing to contribute their "life, or property, or liberty."[64] Illiteracy was an impediment to absorbing the ideals and the ethics of US Capitalist Racist Society, which left this population open to foreign influence.

Equally concerning, illiterates and the ignorant could not properly adhere to True Americanism because they could not read "a bulletin on agriculture, a farm paper, a food-pledge card, a Liberty loan appeal, a newspaper, the Constitution of the United States, or their Bibles" and they could not comprehend

mainstream public opinion. This made them "fertile soil for seeds of radicalism and incendiary propaganda."[65] Illiteracy as a marker of foreignness was
particularly intractable for Blacks given that such illiteracy and ignorance
were inextricable from the Structural Location of Blackness and the forms of
social oppression, including subpar education, it engendered.

At the same time, the Black Scare positioned Black education as equally
threatening to US Capitalist Racist Society, given that it encouraged Radical
Blackness, especially Outside Agitators. Both Black illiteracy as a potential
vector for foreign influence and Black education as a potential vector for militant agitation against the status quo positioned Blackness in opposition to
True Americanism and codified the intractability of their potential danger,
disloyalty, and subversion. Given this contradiction, *Revolutionary Radicalism* was replete with concerns about the convergence of Red propaganda and
Black receptivity and the ways various organizations might capitalize on the
Negro Question to sow discontent. That Blacks were the only racial group
subjected to such scrutiny in the report underscored both their foreignness
and the role of the Black Scare and the Red Scare in constructing it.

Black "foreignness" also flowed from the "strict despotism" that was required to rule Blacks.[66] The forms of brute control to which they were subjected placed them outside of True Americanism's spirit of capitalist democracy, individualism, and freedom. This naturalized abrogation of Black
autonomy through force, compounded by their "untutored" nature, was assumed to prime them for "authoritarian"—that is, socialist/communist—
propaganda. This susceptibility, coupled with foreignness, rendered Black protests against the status quo indistinguishable from outside agitation. According
to *Revolutionary Radicalism*, "The very fact that the negro has many just causes
of complaint adds to the seriousness of the propaganda . . . which cannot
but lead to serious trouble if [radicals] are permitted to continue the propaganda which they now disseminate in such large volume."[67] Blacks were suspect because their long history of white domination made them amenable to
foreign control, their structural location foreclosed them from True Americanism, their "causes of complaint" were the very foundation of US Capitalist
Racist Society, and challenge to the status quo was construed as radicalism
and subversion.

True Americanism and the Danger of Black Agitation

Like *Revolutionary Radicalism* after WWI, *RACON* documented the convergence of the Black Scare and the Red Scare in the codification of Black militancy, agitation, and unrest as antithetical to True Americanism and danger-

ous to US Capitalist Racist Society during WWII. On July 11, 1942, Hoover claimed: "There is widespread action among Negroes in all sections of the country which indicates that several sources are purposely creating unrest among the negro element which is believed to be against the best interests of this country."[68] Of particular concern was the Black press as the "outstanding agitational force" that reported on "sensational" and "inflammatory" matters like "alleged instances of discrimination" and white brutality against Blacks. Especially problematic was its promotion of the "Double V" campaign that claimed Blacks were denied democracy at home even as they were fighting for it abroad.[69] This was subversive because it contravened True Americanism's conflation of democracy with the American way of life and the racial linear progress narrative. This disposition of the Black press, like Red "double speak," bastardized democracy.

The FBI treated "widespread action" among Blacks as a form of outside agitation despite the fact that local elements were organizing against and protesting their immediate conditions. As one FBI official put it, "the apparent forces responsible for this situation [Negro unrest and dissatisfaction] are entirely national in scope."[70] In the North, agitation was primarily linked to labor issues, inadequate housing, overcrowding, and discrimination. The catalyst in the South was ongoing lynching, labor difficulty and antagonism between white and Black workers, the presence of Northern Black personnel, and fights over segregation. Racial conflict in the West resulted from the mere presence of Black soldiers, discrimination in employment, lack of recreational facilities, and improper and unsanitary living conditions. Discrimination in industry, lack of housing and recreational facilities, and segregated union locals precipitated Black unrest on the Pacific Coast.

Even though Black people were responding to experiences of racist subjection, exclusion, and depravation, their mobilization against capitalist racism in its numerous manifestations was nonetheless "against the best interest of the United States." Blacks were un-Americans instead of True Americans because their dissent presented a militant challenge to the economic and racial order, thus creating a potential opening for outside subversive influence to take hold. They were disloyal instead of patriotic because they critiqued the status quo at a time when loyalty meant closing ranks. Because True Americanism not only accommodated, but was also a means of legitimating, the economic, political, and social conditions to which Black people were responding, Black protest was construed as unsympathetic and antagonistic to the war effort—and to US Capitalist Racist Society writ large.[71]

Concomitantly, despite the reality that Black agitation was directly linked to the structural and material conditions of Wall Street Imperialism, it was continually attributed to foreign influence, especially Japanese and communist intrigue. In Baltimore, for example, complaints poured in about Blacks favoring a Japanese victory in the war, and this was linked to allegations that "large groups of Negroes" were arming themselves.[72] Likewise, organizations including the Moorish Science Temple of America, the Peace Movement of Ethiopia, the Ethiopian Pacific Movement, and the UNIA were labeled as pro-Japanese and, according to one FBI special agent, "leaders of some of the organizations [had] already been incarcerated as a result of violations on their part of the Sedition and related Statutes."[73]

More than the Japanese, though, it was the Communist Party that was considered to have the most expansive "un-American activity among the Negroes."[74] For instance, in Detroit it was claimed that "outside of economic and social forces and influence, the Communist Party and its various elements are believed to be by far the most responsible of all subversive groups" for Black unrest.[75] *RACON* transformed Black discontent into a magnet for communist subversion in numerous ways, including the argument that the Communist Party seized upon Black protests of lynching and other forms of racial discrimination to cause considerable unrest.[76] The Red Scare implication was that communist activity influenced a change of attitude among Blacks that made them "arrogant, dissatisfied," and disrespectful. The Black Scare logic was that Black people were both incapable of protesting their abysmal conditions without outside influence, and they were so suggestible that such influence caused a change in their collective disposition. The Communist Party and purported communist front organizations like the Southern Negro Youth Congress and the NNC were implicated by FBI informants as key factors in "racial disturbances," "racial problems," "race rivalry," and "subversive activities" in areas including Birmingham, Boston, Charlotte, and Chicago.[77]

Though it was widely reported that Blacks were "in general loyal to the United States," their "bitterness and resentment"[78] nonetheless drew suspicion of disloyalty, and the Black Scare and the Red Scare positioned this discontent as a harbinger of subversion.[79] In effect, "what the FBI's World War II investigation of Blacks show[ed] [was] that it was designed and executed from its inception as a measure aimed at halting the African-American challenge to Jim Crow"[80]; and, more than that, it showed that because True Americanism rationalized anti-Black racial oppression and linked forms of superexploitation, agitation against it was un-American.

True Americanism was an instrumentality for the imbrication of the ideational and material; the demarcation of which ideas, individuals, and institutions are valid and which must be "exorcised"; and the casting of those who sought to transform the racial or economic makeup of society as dangerous, unbelonging, criminal, and punishable. As legitimating architecture, True Americanism offered up discourses and narrations of subversion, un-Americanness, sedition, disloyalty, and foreignness that were codified in law and politics by all three branches of the federal and state governments, weaponized by big business and the capitalist elite, and acculturated in civil society. Ideologically, it was an expression of the Countersubversive Political Tradition, the method of concealing the fascistic character of US Capitalist Racist Society, and the means of normalizing the Structural Location of Blackness. In effect, in concert with Wall Street Imperialism and anticommunism as a mode of governance, True Americanism was pivotal to the inscription of the Black Scare and Red Scare in US Capitalist Racist Society.

EPILOGUE

Black Scare / Red Scare is a history of the present. It offers a lexicon, analytical framework, and field of reference for understanding our contemporary reality. The Black Scare and the Red Scare, codified in and through Wall Street Imperialist internal logic, anticommunist governance, and True American legitimating architecture, continue to structure US Capitalist Racist Society beyond the Black Scare / Red Scare Longue Durée. For example, on April 18, 2023, the African People's Socialist Party (APSP), an African internationalist, socialist, anti-imperialist organization founded in 1972 "in the tradition of Marcus Garvey, Kwame Nkrumah, and Malcolm X," was indicted by the US government. A federal grand jury in Tampa, Florida, charged members of the APSP and its solidarity network with working on behalf of the Russian government in concert with the Russian Federal Security Service (FSB) to facilitate a foreign malign influence campaign in the United States over several years. They were further accused of illegally acting on behalf of and being funded by Russian agents to foment anti-American dissent and spread pro-Russian propaganda.[1]

The harassment started in July 2022 when the APSP's headquarters were raided by the FBI based on alleged ties to a Russian national, Aleksandr Ionov, who was indicted by the Justice Department for failing to register under the 1938 Foreign Agents Registration Act. The FBI simultaneously raided the home of APSP chairman Omali Yeshitela, the Uhuru Solidarity Center in Saint Louis, Missouri, and the Uhuru House in Saint Petersburg, Florida, searching for evidence that Ionov had provided financial support, funneled from the Russian Federation, to the APSP to develop relationships that would allow him to evade registering under the McCormack Act. The APSP was thus suspected of facilitating and participating in the spread of Ionov's "foreign and malign influence campaign against the United States," including causing dissension and spreading secessionist ideologies. As if drawing from the playbook of the early Cold War era, the US government cited as evidence the APSP's petition to the United Nations charging the United States with genocide, which was accused of being under Ionov's direction.

While some expressed surprise at the FBI's focus on "fringe, bit players on the American political scene," others connected the raids to the Counterintelligence Program (COINTELPRO) operations that decimated Black liberation movement organizations in the 1960s and 1970s, and still others aptly identified this repression as "reminiscent of McCarthyist witch hunts that targeted and criminalized workers, immigrants, and colonized people who organized domestically and internationally against capitalist imperialism."[2] However, *Black Scare / Red Scare* illuminates how the targeting of a Radical Black organization like the APSP is part of a durable discourse of foreign influence and outside agitation that took off during the Black Scare / Red Scare Longue Durée. Such charges were levied at Black members of the IWW, Radical Black periodicals like the *Messenger*, the UNIA, Black members of the CPUSA organizing for self-determination in the Black Belt, Black insurgents against white terrorism and superexploitation during World War II, and individuals and organizations who analyzed the genocidal and fascistic conditions of the United States. In effect, the APSP is the latest casualty of the Black Scare and the Red Scare, which has taken on new life in the aftermath of the racial justice rebellions that exploded in the summer of 2020.

Persons and organizations who espouse, agitate on behalf of, or struggle for racial and economic egalitarianism are still viewed with suspicion or derision, while the steady march of neofascist and white nationalist elements is feared but, in many ways, tolerated and abetted. One instance of such toleration in the narrowing of the Select Committee to Investigate the January 6th Attack on the United States Capitol Report to focus almost exclusively on Donald Trump as the culprit of the January 6, 2021, Capitol riot instead of offering a more robust assessment of the threat of neofascism and white supremacy in law enforcement and in US society.[3]

Because Black self-determination and socialism continue to be seen by the United States as the biggest challenges to peace, prosperity, and security, untold resources are dedicated to smashing these "threats" instead of those that unite the right wing from Ukraine to the United States, Brazil to Belarus. Though the world is rapidly evolving toward multipolarity, the United States remains a military superpower with outsized influence in supranational organizations like the United Nations Security Council, the North Atlantic Treaty Organization, and the Organization of American States, so even as its warmongering and aggressive "diplomacy" continue to lose credibility, its construction of racialized and socialist enemies continue to have catastrophic material consequences for these beleaguered populations within and beyond its borders. That white supremacist authoritarianism, intensified economic subjection within and among nations, and the threat of nuclear annihilation are real possibilities is directly predicated on continued hostility and violence toward nation-states, organizations, individuals, and ideas that directly confront these realities.

Police forces in the United States replicate the violence of Africa Command (AFRICOM) and Southern Command (SOUTHCOM) against Black and racialized populations whose poverty marks them as criminal, and whose organized and spontaneous struggles for livable lives render them savage and subversive. Critiques of the United States because of its imperialist practice, war-driven expropriation, and intolerance for ways of living that defy its authority are deemed anti-American and therefore dangerous and destabilizing. State-level laws criminalizing racial justice protesters are seldom replicated to prevent or punish neo-Nazi–infused attacks on the Capitol or antivaccine mandate convoys, and antifascist and antiracist protesters are brutalized and murdered by law enforcement and vigilantes while white nationalist hooligans, from Buffalo to Colorado Springs, survive police encounters even when they attack or aggressively confront officers. Black activists are stained as looters while white insurrectionists are said to be engaging in legitimate political discourse.

A trillion dollars for social legislation and policy that would have an outsized impact on racialized and poor people is said to be too expensive and inflationary, while a trillion dollars for "lethal aid" and "defense" that ensure aggression in international relations, and for bank bailouts that effectively amount to the redistribution of wealth upwardly, garners little debate or pushback. The explosion of homelessness that disproportionately impacts marginalized populations is seen as an unfortunate side effect of capitalism while petty crime resulting from extreme poverty is seen as an affront to the fabric of society that must be met with swift action. Those in the executive and legislative branches of government rush to find common ground with their right-wing colleagues, while their left-leaning party members—many of whom are Black and Brown—are berated, ignored, and blamed for the failures of the party. (And even those "left-leaning" Democrats support US imperialist foreign policy.) Meanwhile, the US Supreme Court systematically upends protections for the most marginalized groups in society while strengthening the power of corporations.

Racial liberals double down on imperialist domestic and foreign policy to shore up identity reductionism and empty representation and to evade any real commitment to radical transformation. On this logic, a Black woman vice president or Supreme Court justice counteracts the explosion of incarceration, homelessness, AIDS, and maternal mortality among their poor and exploited counterparts. If the world is a ghetto and the United States is a prisonhouse, then Blacks, radicals, Radical Blacks, and other constructed enemies sustain, legitimate, and obfuscate this reality. The targeting of the APSP is just one example of how the Black Scare and the Red Scare underwrite these continuities and contradictions.

Black Lives Matter in the Age of Neoliberalism

The continued articulation of the Black Scare and the Red Scare is especially true regarding Black Lives Matter (BLM), which took off in 2012 in the context of neoliberalism. The neoliberal phase of US Capitalist Racist Society has been characterized by "free-market reform, the rollback of social spending, and cuts in taxes for corporations and the wealthy [that has] produced social inequality on a scale unseen since at least the" Great Depression.[4] As a regime of capitalist racism, neoliberalism constitutes the normalization of containment as the replacement for the state's welfarist function, the criminalization of poverty, and policing and punitive justice as the primary means of managing economic crisis.[5] Punitive conceptions of social order have taken hold, with "legislation, regulation, monitoring, surveillance, and the ambiguous 'target' and 'control' cultures" employed through a version of liberal authoritarianism meant to manage race and class hierarchies.[6]

In the United States, starting in the 1980s, the Reagan administration's law-and-order agenda in general, and the "war on drugs" in particular, dovetailed with the criminalization of the Black liberation movement and facilitated the hyperincarceration of Black males and the increased incarceration of racialized and poor people more broadly. The undeniable link between state policy toward crime, the private sector, prison industries, and disparities in the criminal legal system—the prison industrial complex—wreaked havoc on Black people.[7] Such criminalization spread from the United States and became a multinational project, with Black people, Indigenous populations, and women becoming overrepresented in a rapidly expanding prison industrial complex transnationally. Privatization and incarceration became increasingly entangled as the necessity of warehousing surplus labor produced by neoliberal policies grew. Prison privatization was legitimated on the grounds that it would be more cost effective, curb overcrowding, and reduce human rights violations.

Globally, with the few exceptions of socialist nations like Venezuela, Cuba, and China, private prisons became transformed into significations of modernization and development, welfare policies were replaced with a war on drugs and crime that complemented wars waged in the Global South for strategic resources and spheres of influence, law-and-order policies reigned, and programs geared toward income redistribution and poverty alleviation were replaced

with programs aimed at strengthening criminal legal systems. The criminalization of oppressed, disproportionately Black, nonunionized, exploited workers,
who had been systematically immobilized and disenfranchised, was directly
predicated upon their growing position as redundant labor. Sites of production, manufacturing, and farming came to be converted into prisons and jails
to satisfy the growing demand for incarceration created by neoliberalization.[8]

In this context, and in response to police murder within these conditions,
BLM, a number of national and international organizations primarily focused
on the issues of Black poor people, exploded. The historian Barbara Ransby argues that BLM is rooted in the idea that "if we liberate the black poor, or if the
black poor liberate themselves, we will uplift everybody else who's been kept
down."[9] Likewise, as BLM was consolidating, the radical journalist and organizer Glen Ford contended, "the Black Lives Matter movement consciously
draws on this authentic—and still deeply honored—radical tradition, seeking
to put it into practice under 21st century conditions" not least by resisting the
criminal legal system, prioritizing social and economic transformation, and
demanding global peace.[10] As a grassroots movement about racial and economic justice, it challenges US Capitalist Racist Society in its attempt to destabilize inequality and create "new possibilities" for all who suffer under the
yoke of US imperialism.[11] Political theorist Siddhant Issar concurs that BLM
is a site of knowledge production about racial capitalism as the basis of anti-
Black racial oppression, or in the language of *Black Scare / Red Scare*, about
capitalist racism as the foundation of the Structural Location of Blackness.

"A Vision for Black Lives," prepared by the Movement for Black Lives, a coalition of organizations, issued six demands aimed at combating this reality:
the end of the war on Black people, reparations, invest-divest, economic justice, community control, and political power. Such demands expand the idea of
Black self-determination that spanned the UNIA and the CPUSA in their analyses and rejections of "the interlinked systems of white supremacy, imperialism, capitalism, and patriarchy" and in their illumination of the ways that "racial domination structures the capitalist economy."[12] Moreover, these demands
are a critique of Wall Street Imperialism and the ways the partnership between
the government and big business, along with other institutions like academia,
continue to benefit from the oppression and exploitation of Black people, from
transatlantic enslavement, to redlining, to mass incarceration, to food deserts.[13]

That the phrase "Black Lives Matter" emanated from a hashtag popularized in 2012 by three queer Black women organizers, Alicia Garza, Opal To-
meti, and Patrisse Cullors, has remained significant insofar as the various
organizations, actions, and movements that constitute BLM have been intentional about lifting up femme and queer leadership. This "unapologetic in-

tersectional analysis" is meant to offer a corrective to forms of discrimination and marginalization that existed within previous Black movements.[14] #BlackLivesMatter, according to Garza, came about after the extrajudicial killing of Trayvon Martin on February 26, 2012, by George Zimmerman and the latter's subsequent acquittal. This "political and ideological intervention" moved from "social media to the streets" in a big way after the murder of eighteen-year-old Michael Brown in Ferguson, Missouri, on August 9, 2014, by police officer Darren Wilson and the massive uprising that followed.[15] As Black studies scholar Keeanga-Yamahtta Taylor described, in the ten months spanning summer 2014 and fall 2015, mass protests exploded across the United States in response to the police murder of Brown, bringing global attention to the ubiquity of racist police violence in the heart of empire. When police snuffed out Freddie Gray eight months later in Baltimore, Maryland, these uprisings only intensified.[16]

Though BLM is often invoked in protests of extrajudicial killings by police officers and vigilantes—some of the most well-known being Rekia Boyd in March 2012, Eric Garner in July 2014, Laquan MacDonald in October 2014, Tamir Rice in November 2014, Sandra Bland in July 2015, Freddie Gray in July 2016, Philando Castile in July 2016, Alton Sterling in July 2016, Korryn Gaines in August 2016, Charleena Lyles in June 2017, Stephon Clark in March 2018, Botham Jean in September 2018, and Atatiana Jefferson in October 2019—it is not reducible to this phenomenon. More broadly, the movement's mission is, in part, to challenge the structures that led to these scores of killings, not least the "Black Mass Incarceration State" and its concomitant stigmatization, enforced unemployment, and subjection of the Black and oppressed communities to armed occupiers in the form of the police.[17] The massive protests that take place under the banner of BLM are effectively protests against US Capitalist Racist Society and its predatory policing, overpolicing, and racialized police torture that facilitate resource expropriation in the form of fees and fines. It is a movement flowing from the Structural Location of Blackness; labor superexploitation; expropriation by domination; ongoing primitive accumulation; and the continuing forms of state, private, and intracommunal violence and repression that accrue around these. As well, like *We Charge Genocide*, BLM directly confronts the state, the ruling class, and the agents of force that protect them and place a particular burden on poor and racialized women, queer people, trans people, immigrants, and disabled people.[18]

Black Identity Extremism

Akin to earlier government responses to Black militancy during the Black Scare / Red Scare Longue Durée, the police responded to BLM uprisings by repressing and punishing the beleaguered but incensed population that de-fied its authority.[19] The treatment of these protesters was not unlike that of the Black Wobbly Benjamin Harrison Fletcher, and the IWW leadership more broadly, when the Espionage Act of 1917 and the Sedition Act of 1918 provided the legislative underpinning for the punishment of radicalism and Black agitation.

An important FBI document that emerged in the context of BLM insur-gency was *Black Identity Extremists Likely Motivated to Target Police Officers*.[20] Issued on August 3, 2018, by the counterterrorism division, this "intelligence assessment" found that Black "perceptions" of police brutality were a catalyst for premeditated, retaliatory deadly violence against law enforcement and would continue to be a justification for these assaults. These findings were based on six incidents. Zale H. Thompson "attacked" four white officers with a hatchet in New York City in October 2014. A man was arrested for and convicted of purchasing explosives in Ferguson, Missouri, in November 2014 ostensibly intended for use after the grand jury verdict in the Brown case was released. Micah Johnson "ambushed" eleven, and killed five, officers in Dal-las, Texas, in July 2016. Gavin Eugene Long allegedly "ambushed" and shot six police officers in July 2016 in Baton Rouge, Louisiana, before being killed by police. In September 2016, a man in Phoenix, Arizona, struck two officers with his car. Finally, a man identifying himself as a Moor allegedly shot at an Indianapolis, Indiana, police station on two occasions in October 2016 and made "antiwhite" statements.

This purported onslaught of ideologically driven deadly force, the FBI as-sessment claimed, emanated from the police murder of Michael Brown in August 2014 and the subsequent failure of the grand jury to indict Darren Wilson.[21] This assessment of Black militancy as subversive was not unlike that in the federal *Attorney General Report* and the Lusk Committee's *Revo-lutionary Radicalism*. Both conveyed Black self-defense and self-assertion as un-American while ignoring the context of white terrorism and state repres-sion that provoked Black and radical fightback. Relatedly, in the FBI memo, Black Identity Extremists (BIEs) are defined as "individuals who seek, wholly or in part, through unlawful acts of force or violence, in response to per-ceived racism and injustice in American society . . . [to establish] a separate Black homeland or autonomous Black social institutions, communities, or governing organization within the United States."[22] This recourse to "force or violence" also recapitulated the discourse of *Revolutionary Radicalism* and *The Attorney General Report*. Additionally, the emphasis on a "separate Black homeland" and Black autonomy as encompassing threats to the US govern-ment drew on similar legitimating architecture used throughout the 1920s to deport Marcus Garvey and to demonize the CPUSA's Black Belt Nation Thesis. The insistence, moreover, that ideology, as opposed to "alleged" acts of police abuse, motivated BIE action was reminiscent of claims during the Black Scare / Red Scare Longue Durée that those who defied True American-ism were susceptible to un-American, foreign, and/or outside ideologies like communism, socialism, and Black Nationalism, and were therefore actually or potentially subversive.

Black Identity Extremists connects uprisings against, and isolated attacks on, police officers during the BLM era to a "history" of violence against law enforcement generally, and to "extremist" acts during the 1960s and 1970s particularly, especially attacks by the Black Liberation Army (BLA), a revolu-tionary Marxist-Leninist organization decimated by federal and state authori-ties. Such "extremism" happened against the backdrop of "political dissent, turbulence, and violence" that served as the pretext for the extraordinary repression and "law and order" legitimating architecture aimed at crushing opposition to the Vietnam War, Black militancy, and the ubiquitous youth counterculture.[23] Likewise, the offensive of newly decolonized nations and their willingness to cooperate with socialist powers—or refusal to align with either pole of the Cold War—represented an international challenge to US Capitalist Racist Society.[24]

Despite the fact that there was never an attempt to overthrow the US gov-ernment, that violence was not the prevailing force in widespread protests, and that FBI and police informants were heavily involved in inciting violent incidents, the Black Scare and the Red Scare continued to construe urban re-bellions, militant Black organizations, and struggles against the draft and the war as a menace to the prevailing order. The result was "a calculated campaign by high-ranking officials in the executive branch and by Congress to intimi-date and repress dissident activity."[25] The consensus at this time was that "any excess was permissible in the name of forestalling 'black revolution,'"[26] espe-cially given the continued discourse of communist plots to undermine the US war effort, communist aggression, "communist and extremist elements," and close links between "foreign communists and domestic dissidents." J. Edgar Hoover continued to be at the forefront of Red-baiting and Black-baiting, claiming that "communists and subversives and extremists strive ceaselessly to precipitate racial trouble and to take advantage of racial discord in this country."[27] This was a repetition of the arguments made in *The Attorney General Report, Revolutionary Radicalism*, and *RACON* that also overdeter-mined challenges to the racial and economic status quo with discourses of outside agitation, foreign inspiration, and subversion. On the local level, nearly five hundred local "Red Squads" operated as a potent political force against "radicalism, student demonstrations, and black power" and gathered "political intelligence." This attests to the continued influence of the Black Scare and the Red Scare in creating policy aimed at neutralizing Black rebellion.[28]

As has been widely documented, the most notorious articulation of the Black Scare and the Red Scare during this era was the FBI's COINTELPRO, which employed illegal wiretapping; bugging; break-ins; frame-ups; and informant infiltration, harassment, and disruption campaigns to address "the threats from militants of the 'New Left' as it had those from the Communists in the 1950s."[29] The BLA, along with the Black Panther Party (BPP) and several other Radical Black organizations, was decimated by COINTELPRO. The attack on the BLA and its leaders harkened back to the extraordinary violence meted out against the Red Black / Black Red Angelo Herndon. His case(s) revealed how Radical Blackness meant that the civil rights, civil liberties, and safety of individuals and organizations could be violated by the state. Dhoruba bin Wahad, cofounder of the BLA, explained that he had been "targeted as 'a Black extremist' and put into the U.S. government's 'Agitator Index' and 'Black Extremist' files," which "target[ed] certain leaders and spokespersons of the Black struggle for human rights" to be "neutralized and otherwise taken out of circulation."[30]

"BIEs have historically justified and perpetrated violence against law enforcement," *Black Identity Extremists* claimed,

> which they have perceived as representative of the institutionalized oppression of African Americans, but had not targeted law enforcement with premeditated violence for the nearly two decades leading up to the lethal incidents observed beginning in 2014. BIE violence peaked in the 1960s and 1970s in response to changing socioeconomic attitudes and treatments of blacks during the Civil Rights Movement. BIE groups, such as the [BLA], which was created in the early 1970s "to take up arms, for liberation and self-determination of black people in the United States" . . . targeted law enforcement officers without regard to their race.[31]

By contrast, bin Wahad explained that brutal police repression was the motivation for the BLA's formation. The clandestine formation was responding to "the murder of Black youth by police and the ongoing racist police brutality" that stalked Black communities and to the legalization of repressive violence against the Radical Black organizations generally, and the BPP particularly. In effect, "repression [bred] resistance. And the more vicious and physical the repression, the more intense and physical the resistance."[32] Police brutalization of the BLA was manifested in the treatment of one of its members, Assata Shakur, after a shootout with New Jersey police on May 2, 1973. They shot her twice, kicked her, and dragged her by her hair; encouraged the ambulance to leave her for dead; and tortured her while she was in the hospital, beating and choking her whenever doctors left the room. Likewise, "the state, the police, the DA's office, [and the] FBI did everything possible to frustrate [her] recovery" thereafter.[33] As the BLA explained, discourses of "domestic reform," "law and order," and a "return to traditional American values" served as the legitimating architecture of this police violence—a function of the "undeclared war" against Black people and the domestic arm of Wall Street Imperialism in Vietnam and throughout the Third World.[34] This was True Americanism in updated form.

Furthermore, the emphasis in *Black Identity Extremists* on the *perception* of racism, injustice, and police brutality in US Capitalist Racist Society as the basis for BIE violence was akin to the FBI's claim that reports of white violence and discrimination that led to Black protests and racial unrest during World War II and after were overblown. In other words, the contention that Black grievances resulted from *feelings* of oppression as opposed to its *structural reality* allowed the government to blame tensions on outside subversive influences instead of addressing the root problem. *RACON*, for example, conveyed that no matter how oppressed and superexploited Blacks are in US Capitalist Racist Society, their protests of these conditions are easily construed as illegitimate, subversive, and against the interests of the US state. Likewise, the misrecognition of anti-Black racial oppression and injustice not as features of social relations with real material consequences, but as a perception that led to reactive and violent Black behavior, was a continuation of the psychoanalytic turn during the early Cold War era. The US State Department repurposed psychoanalysis to construe critiques of US Capitalist Racist Society as Marxist or communist inspired and therefore un-American and illegitimate. The emphasis on behavior was a form of legitimating architecture that promoted the understanding of sociopolitical problems as personal and individual maladjustments that could be remedied through proper coping skills and behavior modification rather than societal transformation.[35] However, as convincingly analyzed in *We Charge Genocide*, the dire straits of Black people in US Capitalist Racist Society absolutely require social and political transformation—and agitation for it. The petition revealed why Radical Black analysis and action were necessary to combat True Americanism that served "the interests of the state by encouraging adjustment and accommodation in opposition to activism"[36] and "undermined the potential for political activism and reinforced the chilling effects of anticommunism and the Cold War consensus."[37] In an identical fashion, the FBI's usage of "perceived racism and injustice" in *Black Identity Extremists* positions the interpretations and actions of BIEs as pathological threats to law and order. Even worse, this "perception" could "lead to an increase in BIE group members, collaborations among BIE groups, or the appearance of additional violent lone offenders motivated by BIE rhetoric."[38] The *perception* of police brutality and abuse trumped its actuality as a dangerous motivator of Radical Black violence. We are reminded here of Black Scare discourse during the Great War that construed defense against white terrorism, but not lynching or mob violence, as disloyal to and subversive of the war effort.

Black Identity Extremists created an unbroken lineage of Black subversion and insurrection that provided cover for the use of extraordinary repression and subjection. The continuity between the Black Scare and the Red Scare in the moment of BLM and in the Black Scare / Red Scare Longue Durée is striking. The FBI's assessment of BIE reasserts Wall Street Imperialist policy and practices by criminalizing BLM protests as assertions of self-determination that catalyze police murder; challenges to superexploitation and expropriation from Ferguson to Baltimore; and calls to end the warlike attacks on protesters by militarized police. The counterterrorism division of the FBI reinscribed True Americanism's legitimating architecture by transforming those who opposed racist police violence, considered the US criminal legal system to be patently unjust, supported Black self-determination, and defended Black life into a threat to law enforcement, and by extension, national security. Additionally, *Black Identity Extremists* reifies anticommunism as a contemporary mode of governance enunciating the Countersubversive Political Tradition by articulating BLM and BIEs as enemies from within, constructing them as threats to local police forces and the national polity, and establishing the convergence of interests between federal and state governments and law enforcement.

From Black Identity Extremism to "Wokeism"

A resurgence of BLM in 2020 resulted from the vigilante and police murders of Ahmaud Arbery in February, Breonna Taylor in March, and George Floyd in May. The latter case in particular led to the largest Black movement in US history since the Garvey movement. There were, however, many other factors, not least the global COVID-19 pandemic and the economic, political, and social havoc it wrought globally; the chaotic reelection campaign of Donald J. Trump; the contested election of Joseph R. Biden; the January 6, 2021, right-wing attack on the US Capitol; catastrophic US foreign policy, from the ongoing neocolonial occupation of Haiti that undergirded the assassination of Haiti's deeply unpopular US-allied president Jovenel Moïse to

the poorly executed withdrawal of US troops from Afghanistan that effectively ended the longest and most expensive war in US history; the NATO-
provoked war in Ukraine; national and global labor strikes and union drives
that convey a newly reinvigorated workers' offensive; and the deeply polar-
ized economic and political situation that has elicited widespread talk of im-
pending fascism.[39]

The Black Scare and the Red Scare permeate this cacophonous reality
animating contemporary US Capitalist Racist Society and its refashioning
of Wall Street Imperialism, anticommunist governance, and True Americanism. Old and new specters of un-Americanism, subversion, outside agitation,
foreign inspiration, and dangerous Radical Blackness are being invoked. For
example, "cultural Marxism" is a recent variation of the old socialism and
communism bogeymen,[40] while "wokeism" is a new phenomenon. Wokeism
is a shorthand for anything and everything considered to challenge True
Americanism, not least identity politics, "Critical Race Theory," calls to de-
fund or abolish the police, and "cancel culture." The most recent articulation
of True Americanism, in turn, is "America First," which has been articulated
by Donald J. Trump since 2015. The former president, who still wields considerable influence in the Republican Party and is planning another presidential run in 2024, combined the idea that the United States had saved the
world from "totalitarianism and communism" by winning the Cold War with
the claim that under Barack Obama, US jobs were stolen and the military
and economy were weakened, to put forth a program that combined unilat-
eralism, brute force or the threat of it, xenophobic nationalism, anti-China
hawkishness, a renewed commitment to Israel, punishing and humiliating
Iran, and ideological and military struggle akin to that which predominated
during the Cold War.

Likewise, in America First discourse, the US nation-state and its citizens
outweighed all other concerns, and this was counterposed against radical and
social justice activists, who threatened US security, and against socialism, which
Trump called the "wrecker of nations and destroyer of societies."[41] As was the
case with True Americanism during the Black Scare / Red Scare Longue Durée,
America First is the ideological enunciation of the Countersubversive Political
Tradition, counterposing the safety and prosperity of the United States against
others from within, especially radicals and social justice activists, and from
without, not least socialism and China. The America First characterization of
wokeism spans the typical Black Scare / Red Scare gamut, from un-American
to subversive, and is a frequent target of moderate and right-wing politicians,
scholars, journalists, and civil society organizations with the ultimate goal
of distracting from the structural and material conditions—unemployment,

houselessness, stagnant wages, unchecked COVID-19 spread, police violence, all disproportionately affecting Black people—that continue to induce social unrest.[42]

On December 15, 2021, Florida governor Ron DeSantis, who is also running for president in 2024, intensified the attack on, and scapegoating of, "wokeism" with his proposed Stop WOKE (Wrongs against Our Kids and Employees) Act,[43] which would allow parents to sue teachers for teaching radical ideas like "Critical Race Theory," and would ban "racist" diversity training in the corporate sector.[44] The Black Scare and Red Scare nature of this bill becomes more stark in relationship to Florida's HB1 bill, signed into law by DeSantis in April 2021. The "Anti-Riot Law" targeted protesters—implied to be radical and Black—in the aftermath of the nationwide 2020 uprisings. It criminalized protests that turn violent and made it easy to deem protests "mob intimidation" (a first-degree misdemeanor with a penalty of up to one year in prison) or a "riot" (a second-degree felony that could send protesters to prison for up to fifteen years). Property damage generally, and destruction of historical property particularly, was classified as a third-degree felony, with a penalty of up to five years in prison. Moreover, the law disallowed protesters bailing themselves out before making an initial court appearance, and protected drivers who assault or kill protesters with their vehicles by "granting them affirmative defense, excusing them from civil or criminal liability." Though the law was blocked by a federal judge for being overly vague, the legal battle over its implementation is ongoing.[45]

The "Anti-Riot Law," in turn, reflects the swiftness and viciousness with which Radical Black protest is condemned and criminalized when compared with racist and right-wing uprisings. On January 6, 2021, a mob of white supremacist, white nationalist, and neo-Nazi elements—including the Oath Keepers, the Three Percenters, the Proud Boys, and the Boogaloo Boys—stormed the Capitol in an attempt to undermine the 2020 election results and the transfer of power from the Donald J. Trump administration to that of Joseph R. Biden. These events have been variously described as a coup, an insurrection, a riot, a violent protest, and treason.[46] The attack was, in part, a response to the return of power to the Democratic Party, which has a more diverse and progressive base that reflects the changing demographics of US society. In true cross-class collaborationist fashion, the event was financially supported by members of the "one percent," including the wife of Supreme Court Justice Clarence Thomas, hedge fund heiress Rebecca Mercer, and Julie Jenkins Fancelli of the Publix supermarket chain. Protesters included a wide array of law enforcement officers and current and former military personnel. As the joint session of Congress convened to count the electoral votes, insurrectionists entered the US Capitol complex and shortly thereafter, police began evacuating Capitol office buildings due to this rioting. Police then locked down the Capitol and evacuated lawmakers and staff as insurrectionists stormed buildings. Chaos ensued.

Hearings conducted by the US House of Representatives Select Committee to Investigate the January 6th Attack on the United States Capitol offered details that reveal collusion at many levels of government, dereliction of duty, and the participation of scores of officers and elected officials from around the country. Yet the punishment of those who stormed the Capitol pales in comparison to the widespread and harsh repression of protesters who participated in the 2020 racial justice uprisings and BLM protesters more broadly. A potential exception is the recent verdict in the case of two members of the Oath Keepers, who were found guilty of seditious conspiracy and face up to twenty years in prison, and three others who were convicted of obstructing an official proceeding.[47] Only fifty-two people were arrested on January 6, 2021, itself, for example, whereas "between May 30 and June 2, 2020, the height of the racial justice protests, 427 'unrest-related' arrests were made in D.C., including 24 juveniles."[48] Further, dozens of people involved in the protests sparked by George Floyd's murder were charged with serious federal crimes and sent to prison, while only a fraction of the seven hundred people arrested in relationship to the January 6 insurrection had received punishment as of August 30, 2021, and only three had been sentenced to jail time. The vigor with which William Barr, the attorney general during the time of the 2020 uprisings, pushed federal prosecutors to target and prosecute racial justice protesters was not replicated in the pursuit of Capitol rioters. In fact, dozens of the insurrectionists have been charged only with misdemeanors or have pleaded to a single count of demonstrating at the Capitol based on a standardized plea deal.[49]

Relatedly, the comparisons of the 2020 uprisings to the attack on the Capitol—despite the fact that 93 percent of the former were peaceful protests against state repression and violence—convey that Black and interracial militancy in the service of racial justice are, in the eyes of the US government, constitutively riotous, potentially subversive, and anathema to America First/ True Americanism. This idea was all but confirmed when Kyle Rittenhouse, a white vigilante, was acquitted of murdering two white Black Lives Matters protesters and wounding another. Though he was indeed an "Outside Agitator," having traveled from Illinois to Kenosha, Wisconsin, to counterprotest, it was found that the killings were in self-defense.[50] Likewise, despite the fact that "in these two different instances [BLM protests and the Capitol riot], you ha[d] people without power who [were] trying to advance this project of

America for equality for all and those who already ha[d] the power trying to make sure that they suppress[ed] any political opinion that differs from their own," the struggles of the oppressed were ultimately deemed more dangerous and subversive than the attempts of insurrectionists to overturn an election.[51]

*

The Black Scare and the Red Scare endure. Their permutations continue to encourage the "invention of witchwords," as Du Bois put it, from "Black identity extremist" to "terrorist" to "Critical Race Theory" to "wokeism." They also ossify and reintroduce old enemies of the state, like "Marxist," "communist," and "nigger." The Black Scare and the Red Scare still undergird the transformation of radical organizers, activists, and scholars into boogeymen to rationalize racial, economic, police, military, and ideological violence—in other words to maintain and reproduce US Capitalist Racist Society.

Acknowledgments

The process of conceptualizing, writing, and revising (revising, revising) this book has been arduous but rewarding. Throughout this journey, I have been fortunate to have the support, guidance, and input of many; this has been a collective, dialogical project since its inception.

Research for the book would not have been possible without several generous research fellowships and travel grants, including the Postdoctoral Scholar Fellowship with the Race and Capitalism Project and Political Science Department at the University of Chicago; the Elledge Faculty Development Fellowship and Hildebrant/Higinbotham Fund for Faculty Development Grant from Carleton College; the Agnes N. Haury Travel Grant for research at the Tamiment Center for the United States and the Cold War; the C. L. R. James Research Fellowship from the African American Intellectual History Society; and the Du Bois Visiting Scholar Fellowship at the University of Massachusetts Amherst. Relatedly, I am grateful for the warm and effective assistance from the archivists at the Tamiment Institute, Bobst Library, New York University; the Schomburg Center for Research in Black Culture; the W. E. B. Du Bois Library at the University of Massachusetts Amherst; and the Stuart A. Rose Manuscripts, Archive, and Rare Book Library at Emory University. I am also thankful that LaShawn Harris, Le'Trice Donaldson, Winston James, and William J. Maxwell shared invaluable primary and archival documents with me.

Editing and revising were instrumental to getting this book to publication. I am indebted to my University of Chicago Press editor, Timothy Mennel, and my developmental editor, Bill V. Mullen, for their careful reading and suggestions. I also benefited from a manuscript workshop in which Robin D. G. Kelley, John Munro, Juliet Hooker, and Adom Getachew provided an excellent critical assessment. I am grateful to Eloy Toppin, a graduate student at the University of Chicago, for taking diligent notes throughout the workshop. Several other scholars read parts of the manuscript in its embryonic and later stages, provided helpful comments, and guided me in intangible ways, including Vaughn Rasberry, Martha Biondi, Nitasha Sharma, Michael J. Allen, Jonathan Fenderson, Gerald Horne, Peter James Hudson, Aaron Kamugisha, and Minkah Makalani.

Much of this manuscript was drafted as the COVID-19 pandemic took off in March 2020—a time during which virtual writing groups were a lifeline. My cowriters, Sandy Placido, Jarvis Givens, Gavriel Cutipa-Zorn, Brian Kwoba, Kimberly Ann Harris, Sheena Sood, Tiffany Barber, and Anwar Uhuru, among many others, provided accountability and community in a time of profound uncertainty. As well, aspects of the book were shared with a junior faculty working group that provided thoughtful and extraordinarily helpful feedback. These interlocutors included Ashley Farmer, Adom Getachew, J. T. Roane, Takiyah Harper-Shipman, Jesus G. Smith, Randi Gill-Sadler, and Shamara Wyllie Alhasan. In addition, the latest revisions of the manuscript took place as another writing group took off, which included dear colleagues and friends Amani Morrison, Layla Brown, Amanda Joyce Hall, Dara Walker, Mahasan Chaney, Ashley Dennis, and Danya Pilgrim.

A project of this magnitude also benefits from interpersonal support and informal conversations. Here, my mother, Elizabeth Burden; my coach, Katie Linder; my dissertation adviser, Percy C. Hintzen; my best friend and comrade, Layla Brown; Ula Y. Taylor; Harvey Neptune; Sandy Placido; Destin Jenkins; Jemima Pierre; Constanza Ocampo-Raeder; Michael Dawson; Ianna Hawkins Owen; and Alex Adamson, among many others were invaluable. It is also vital to name my organization, Black Alliance for Peace, and key members therein—Ajamu Baraka, Margaret Kimberly, Erica Caines, Jaribu Hill, Dedan Waciuri, Noah Tesfaye, Tongo Eisen-Martin, Djibo Sobukwe, Rafiki Morris, and Paul McLennan—whose comradeship and political education have made me a better scholar-activist.

To anyone whom I have failed to acknowledge, charge it to my head not my heart. When so many people contribute, in ways big and small, to a project of this magnitude, very important people unfortunately fall through the cracks. However, I am profoundly thankful to the many collectives and communities, named and unnamed, who nurtured and believed in this project.

Notes

Introduction

1. Testimony of W. E. B. Du Bois, August 11, 1949, W. E. B. Du Bois Papers (MS 312), Special Collections and University Archives, University of Massachusetts Amherst Libraries (hereafter Du Bois Papers). Retrieved from https://credo.library.umass.edu/view/full/mums312-b124-i109, 1–2.

2. Testimony of W. E. B. Du Bois, August 11, 1949, Du Bois Papers. Retrieved from https://credo.library.umass.edu/view/full/mums312-b124-i109, 1–2. The secretary to which Du Bois was referring was James Francis Byrne; the general may have referred to George C. Marshall, though he actually graduated from Virginia Military Institute and never attended West Point; and the baseball player, Jackie Robinson.

3. Testimony of W. E. B. Du Bois, August 11, 1949, Du Bois Papers. Retrieved from https://credo.library.umass.edu/view/full/mums312-b124-i109, 1–2.

4. Testimony of W. E. B. Du Bois, August 11, 1949, Du Bois Papers. Retrieved from https://credo.library.umass.edu/view/full/mums312-b124-i109, 3.

5. Testimony of W. E. B. Du Bois, August 11, 1949, Du Bois Papers (MS 312). Retrieved from https://credo.library.umass.edu/view/full/mums312-b124-i109.

6. See Michael Ralph and Maya Singhal, "Racial Capitalism," *Theory and Society* 48, no. 6 (2019): 857, 858, for a comprehensive discussion of the scholarship on racial capitalism in the past ten years.

7. James E. Turner, *The Next Decade: Theoretical and Research Issues in Africana Studies* (Ithaca, NY: Africana Studies and Research Center, 1984), vi.

8. Reiland Rabaka, *W. E. B. Du Bois and the Problems of the Twenty-First Century* (Lanham, MD: Lexington Books, 2007), 9–10.

9. Rabaka, 2. Likewise, *Black Scare / Red Scare* embodies Africana Critical Theory by "avoiding the obsessive economism of many mainstream modern and postmodern Marxists" and lifting up "the power of ideological critique; the primacy of politics; the political economy of race (especially 'the black race') in a white supremacist world; the racist nature of colonialism *and* capitalism; the political economy of patriarchy and the need for women's decolonization and women's liberation; the politics of leadership and liberation." Reiland Rabaka, *Africana Critical Theory: Reconstructing the Black Radical Tradition, from W. E. B. Du Bois and C. L. R. James to Frantz Fanon and Amilcar Cabral* (Lanham, MD: Lexington Books, 2009), x–xi.

10. Rabaka, *Africana Critical Theory*, xi.

11. Raya Dunayevskaya, *American Civilization on Trial: Black Masses as Vanguard* (Detroit: News and Letters, 1983), 53.

12. Wilson Jeremiah Moses, *Classical Black Nationalism: From the American Revolution to Marcus Garvey* (New York: New York University Press, 1996), 2.

13. Wilson Jeremiah Moses, *Modern Black Nationalism: From Marcus Garvey to Louis Farrakhan* (New York: New York University Press, 1996), 14.

14. Oliver Cromwell Cox, *Capitalism and American Leadership* (New York: Philosophical Library, 1962), 231.

15. Quoted in National Popular Government League, *Report upon the Illegal Practices of the United States Justice Department* (Washington, DC: National Popular Government League, May 1920), 65.

16. James E. Bristol et al., *Anatomy of Anti-Communism: A Report Prepared for the Peace Education Division of the American Friends Service Committee* (New York: Hill and Wang, 1969), 26.

17. Bristol et al., 27–29.

18. Robbie Lieberman, "The Long Black and Red Scare: Anti-Communism and the African American Freedom Struggle," in *Little Red Scares: Anti-Communism and Political Repression in the United States, 1921–1946*, ed. Robert Justin Goldstein (London: Routledge, 2014), 271n31.

19. Antiforeignness is a key aspect of True Americanism. Also see Charisse Burden-Stelly, "Constructing Deportable Subjectivity: Anti-foreignness, Antiradicalism, and Antiblackness during the McCarthyist Structure of Feeling," *Souls: A Critical Journal of Black Politics, Culture, and Society* 19, no. 3 (2017): 342–58.

20. To date, while there is ample literature on anti-Blackness, especially with the rise of the Afropessimist tradition, there is no full-length monograph, journal article, or essay that comprehensively defines and theorizes the Black Scare. "Black Scare" is named and given some attention in several works, including Robert A. Hill's "'The Foremost Radical among His Race': Marcus Garvey and the Black Scare, 1918–1921," *Prologue* 16, no. 4 (Winter 1984): 215–31; Mark Ellis's *Race, War and Surveillance: African Americans and the United States Government during World War I* (Bloomington: Indiana University Press, 2001); and Robbie Lieberman's "The Long Black and Red Scare." There is also passing reference to the "Black Scare" in a number of historian Gerald Horne's works in relation to different eras, including the American Revolution, the Haitian Revolution, and the 1960s. Relatedly, the phrase "black and red scare" appears in James Goodman's *Stories of Scottsboro* (New York: Vintage, 1994) to describe the context in which the conviction of one of the Scottsboro Nine, Haywood Patterson, was overturned in 1933. Goodman argued that there was widespread fear, even among the educated classes, that communists were active in urban and rural settings, inspiring Blacks to meet in secret and to cavort with white women. Rumor had it that Blacks were receptive and eager to heed this advice, and that if they were arrested for assault, the would be shielded by the International Labor Defense—the organization that was instrumental to defending and saving the lives of the Scottsboro Boys. Given this white unease, every Black gathering was suspected to be communist in nature, so whites organized to spy on, terrorize, and intimidate Blacks and to beat and shoot anyone who was suspected of subversion. More recently, in *Spider Web: The Birth of American Anticommunism* (Urbana: University of Illinois Press, 2016), Nick Fischer mentions the "civil-rights era marriage of the Red and Black scares" that had been practiced on figures like Marcus Garvey and later perfected on leaders like Paul Robeson, on whom the Federal Bureau of Investigation

(FBI) and State department had waged war for more than ten years. While Goodman captures the modes of repression that accompanied real or imagined communist influence on Blacks, his description tends to convey the Black Scare as a function of the Red Scare; and even though Fischer notes the "marriage" of the two scares, he likewise understands the Black to follow from the Red. He held, for example, that throughout Hoover's fifty-year rule of the FBI, he and his allies in police forces, the military, and the legislative branch relied on Red-baiting to justify the surveillance of Blacks and their organizations.

21. Michael Cohen, " 'The Ku Klux Government': Vigilantism, Lynching, and the Repression of the IWW," *Journal for the Study of Radicalism* 1, no. 1 (Spring 2007): 43.

22. C. M. D. Ellis, " 'Negro Subversion': The Investigation of Black Unrest and Radicalism by Agencies of the United States Government, 1917–1920," vol. 1, PhD thesis (University of Aberdeen, 1984), 421.

23. Ellis, 422.

24. Laurence Todd, "The Washington Scene," *Federated Press Washington Weekly Letter,* Sheet 2, No. 3068, June 10, 1930.

25. Joint Legislative Committee Investigating Seditious Activities, *Revolutionary Radicalism: Its History, Purpose and Tactics with an Exposition and Discussion of the Steps Being Taken and Required to Curb It* (Albany, NY: J. B. Lyon, 1920), 1476.

26. Tony Martin, *Race First: The Ideological and Organizational Struggles of Marcus Garvey and the Universal Negro Improvement Association* (Baltimore: Black Classic Press, 2020 [1976]), 14.

27. Doxey Wilkerson, "Race Riots—Hitler's Weapon on the Home Front," radio address, June 27, 1943, Doxey A. Wilkerson Papers (MG 386), Schomburg Center for Research in Black Culture, Manuscripts, Archives and Race Books Division, New York Public Library, New York (hereafter Doxey Wilkerson Paper), Box 19, Folder 3.

28. Robert Hill, ed., *The FBI's RACON: Racial Conditions in the United States during World War II* (Boston: Northeastern University Press, 1995), 29.

29. Claudia Jones, "On the Right to Self-Determination of the Negro People in the Black Belt," in *Claudia Jones: Beyond Containment*, ed. Carole Boyce Davies (Boulder, CO: Lynne Reiner Publishers, 2011), 61.

30. Claudia Jones, "International Women's Day and the Struggle for Peace," in *Claudia Jones: Beyond Containment*, ed. Carole Boyce Davies (Boulder, CO: Lynne Reiner Publishers, 2011), 94.

31. Jones, 104.

32. Federal Bureau of Investigation (FBI), *Black Identity Extremists Likely Motivated to Target Police Officers*, Counterterrorism Division, August 3, 2018, https://www.documentcloud.org /documents/4067711-BIE-Redacted.html (accessed January 30, 2018).

33. Black Alliance for Peace, "Black Alliance for Peace Condemns FBI Attack on the African People's Socialist Party," July 30, 2022, https://blackallianceforpeace.com/bapstatements /bapsolidaritywithapsp.

34. Florida House of Representatives, "CS/HB 1," https://www.flsenate.gov/Session/Bill/2021 /1/BillText/er/PDF.

35. "Governor DeSantis Signs Legislation to Protect Floridians from Discrimination and Woke Indoctrination," *Ron DeSantis 46th Governor of Florida,* April 22, 2022, https://www.flgov .com/2022/04/22/governor-ron-desantis-signs-legislation-to-protect-floridians-from-discrimination -and-woke-indoctrination/.

Chapter One

1. "Every frontier in American progress has, and will always be, opened up by the joint enterprise of business and government." Alphaeus Hunton, *Decision in Africa: Sources of Current Conflict* (New York: International Publishers, 1960), 80.

2. Siddhant Issar, "Theorising 'Racial/Colonial Primitive Accumulation': Settler Colonialism, Slavery and Racial Capitalism," *Race & Class* 63, no. 1 (April 2021): 37.

3. Claudia Jones, *Ben Davis, Fighter for Freedom* (New York: National Committee to Defend Negro Leadership, 1954), 37, 39.

4. Harry Haywood, *Negro Liberation* (Chicago: Liberator, 1976), 46–48.

5. Clarence J. Munford, *Production Relations, Class, and Black Liberation: A Marxist Perspective in Afro-American Studies* (Amsterdam: BR Gruner, 1978), 62.

6. Combahee River Collective, "The Combahee River Collective Statement," in *Homegirls: A Black Feminist Anthology*, ed. Barbara Smith (New Brunswick, NJ: Rutgers University Press, 1983), 264–69.

7. Eugene Gordon and Cyril Briggs, *The Position of Negro Women* (New York: Workers Library Publishers, 1935), 5.

8. Gordon and Briggs, 5.

9. Gordon and Briggs, 10.

10. Claudia Jones, "An End to the Neglect of the Problems of the Negro Woman!," *Political Affairs* 28, no. 6 (June 1949): 56.

11. William Patterson, ed., *We Charge Genocide* (New York: International Publishers, 1951), 151–52.

12. Mark Solomon, *The Cry Was Unity: Communists and African Americas, 1917–1938* (Jackson: University of Mississippi Pres, 1998), 61, 99.

13. Patterson, *We Charge Genocide*, 141.

14. Issar, "Theorising 'Racial/Colonial Primitive Accumulation,'" 38–39.

15. Gerald Horne, *The Apocalypse of Settler Colonialism: The Roots of Slavery, White Supremacy, and Capitalism in Seventeenth Century North America and the Caribbean* (New York: Monthly Review Press, 2018), 22.

16. Manu Karuka, *Empire's Tracks: Indigenous Nations, Chinese Workers, and the Transcontinental Railroad* (Oakland: University of California Press, 2019), 170, 183, 174–75. Further, "the origins of property rights in the United States are rooted in racial domination. . . . The [super-exploitation] of Black labor was accomplished by treating Black people themselves as objects of property. Race and property were thus conflated by establishing a form of property contingent upon race—only Blacks were subjugated as slaves and treated as property. Similarly, the conquest, removal, and extermination of Native American life and culture were ratified by conferring and acknowledging property rights of whites in Native American land. Only white possession and occupation of land was validated and therefore privileged as a basis for property rights. These distinct forms of [ongoing racial/colonial primitive accumulation] each contributed in varying ways to the construction of whiteness as property." Cheryl Harris, "Whiteness as Property," *Harvard Law Review* 6, no, 8 (June 1993): 1716.

17. Alyosha Goldstein, "On the Reproduction of Race, Capitalism, and Settler Colonialism," in *Race and Capitalism: Global Territories, Transnational Histories* (Los Angeles: UCLA Luskin Institute on Inequality and Democracy, 2017), 45.

18. Harris, "Whiteness as Property," 1716.

19. Cox, *Capitalism and American Leadership*, 4.

20. Cox, 3–4.

21. Pettis Perry, "U.S. Emerging as an Imperial Power," Pettis Perry Papers (MG 354), Schomburg Center for Research in Black Culture, Manuscripts, Archives and Race Books Division, New York Public Library, New York (hereafter Pettis Perry Papers), Box 4, Folder 10, 1.

22. Victor Perlo, *American Imperialism* (New York: International Publishers, 1951), 9.

23. Cox, *Capitalism and American Leadership*, 5.

24. Perlo, *American Imperialism*, 10.

25. Perlo, 8.

26. Oliver C. Cox, *Capitalism as a System* (New York: Monthly Review Press, 1964), 136, 141, 66.

27. James Ford, *The Communists and the Struggle for Negro Liberation: Their Positions on the Problems of Africa, of the West Indies, of War, of Ethiopian Independence, of the Struggle for Peace* (New York: Harlem Division of the Communist Party, 1936), 19.

28. Vijay Prashad, "Du Bois before Lenin," *People's World*, November 14, 2003, https://www .peoplesworld.org/article/du-bois-before-lenin/.

29. Vladimir I. Lenin, "Imperialism, The Highest Stage of Capitalism: A Popular Outline," in *Lenin: Selected Works in Three Volumes*, vol. 1, *1897 to January 1917* (New York: International Publishers, 1967), 685–97.

30. W. E. B. Du Bois, "The African Roots of War," *Atlantic Monthly* 115 (May 1915): 707–14.

31. *Production Relations, Class, and Black Liberation: A Marxist Perspective in Afro-American Studies*, 101.

32. W. E. B. Du Bois, *Darkwater*, 137–38.

33. Perlo, *American Imperialism*, 14.

34. According to the radical economist Victor Perlo, "The owners of banks, railroads, steel, and oil seized the lands of the Indians, foreclosed the homesteads of farmers, and absorbed the barbaric economy of the southern slaveowners. They imported workers from Europe by the millions . . . [and] used hundreds of thousands of Mexicans, Chinese, and Filipinos to build the railroads and capitalist farms of the Southwest, employing them within the boundaries of the United States, but at colonial wage standards and conditions of work. Above all, American capitalists built their early fortunes on the suffering of millions of Negro slaves kidnapped from Africa, and on their sons and daughters for succeeding generations." Perlo, 8.

35. For a critique of the misapplication of caste to the United States, see Charisse Burden-Stelly, "Caste Does Not Explain Race," *Boston Review*, December 15, 2020, https://bostonreview .net/articles/charisse-burden-stelly-tk/.

36. *Production Relations, Class, and Black Liberation: A Marxist Perspective in Afro-American Studies*, 60.

37. Oliver C. Cox, "The Modern Caste School of Race Relations," *Social Forces* 21, no. 4 (December 1942): 224.

38. Herbert Aptheker, *The Negro People in America: A Critique of Gunnar Myrdal's An American Dilemma* (New York: International Publishers, 1946), 62–63.

39. Aptheker, 45.

40. Hubert Harrison, "Socialism and the Negro," *International Socialist Review* 13 (July 1912): 72.

41. Harrison, 72.

42. Du Bois, *Crisis*, August 1921, 151.

43. Du Bois, *Darkwater*, 115.

44. Harrison, "Socialism and the Negro," 73.

45. Harrison, 76.

46. Rayford W. Logan, "The Negro Wants First Class Citizenship," in *What the Negro Wants*, ed. Rayford Logan (Notre Dame, IN: University of Notre Dame Press, 2001 [1944]), 4.

47. "The Specter of Slavery Still Stalks the Land," Interview with Gerald Horne, April 19, 2018, https://antidotezine.com/2018/04/19/the-specter-of-slavery-still-stalks-the-land/.

48. Gerald Horne, *Negro Comrades of the Crown: African Americans and the British Empire Fight the US before Emancipation* (New York: New York University Press, 2012), 197–98.

49. Logan, "The Negro Wants First Class Citizenship," 5.

50. Perlo, *American Imperialism*, 83.

51. See, e.g., Michael Goldfield, *The Southern Key: Class, Rae, and Radicalism in the 1930s and 1940s* (New York: Oxford University Press, 2020), 1–2.

52. Cox, *Capitalism and American Leadership*, 277, 230.

53. Logan, "The Negro Wants First Class Citizenship," 11.

54. William L. Patterson, ed., *We Charge Genocide: The Historic Petition to the United Nations for Relief from a Crime of the United States Government against the Negro People* (New York: Civil Rights Congress, 1951), 136–37.

55. Gordon and Briggs, *The Position of Negro Women*, 11.

56. Harold M. Baron, *The Demand for Black Labor: Historical Notes on the Political Economy of Racism* (Somerville, MA: New England Free Press, 1971), 20. According to Du Bois, "this migration is apparently a mass movement and not a movement of the leaders. The wave of economic distress and social unrest has pushed past the conservative advice of the Negro preacher, teacher, and professional man, and the colored laborers and artisans have determined to find a way for themselves." "The Migration of Negroes," *Crisis* 14, no. 2 (June 1917): 65.

57. Baron, *The Demand for Black Labor*, 20.

58. James R. Grossman, "The White Man's Union: The Great Migration and the Resonance of Race and Class in Chicago, 1916–1922," in *The Great Migration in Historical Perspective: New Dimensions of Race, Class, and Gender*, ed. Joe William Trotter Jr. (Bloomington: Indiana University Press, 1991), 85.

59. According to historian Darlene Clark Hine, "By 1920, almost 40 percent of Afro-Americans residing in the North were concentrated in eight cities . . . Chicago, Detroit, Cleveland, Cincinnati[,] Columbus, Ohio . . . New York, Philadelphia, and Pittsburgh. These eight cities contained only 20 percent of the total Northern population. Two peaks characterized the first phase of the Great Black Migration: 1916–1919 and 1924–1925. These dates correspond to the passage of more stringent anti-immigration laws, and the years in which the majority of the approximately 500,000 blacks relocated northward." Hine, "Black Migration to the Urban Midwest: The Gender Dimension, 1915–1945," in *The Great Migration in Historical Perspective: New Dimensions of Race, Class, and Gender*, ed. Joe William Trotter Jr. (Bloomington: Indiana University Press, 1991), 128.

60. Baron, *The Demand for Black Labor*, 20.

61. Baron, 20.

62. Hine, "Black Migration to the Urban Midwest," 130.

63. Logan, "The Negro Wants First Class Citizenship," 6.

64. Sterling D. Spero and Abram Harris, *The Black Worker* (New York: Atheneum, 1968 [1931]), 385.

65. Baron, *The Demand for Black Labor*, 23.

66. Baron, 24.

67. Baron, 24.

68. Baron, 22.

69. Spero and Harris, *The Black Worker*, 128.

70. Spero and Harris, 129–31.

71. Spero and Harris, 131.

72. Theodore Kornweibel Jr., *Investigate Everything: Federal Efforts to Compel Black Loyalty during World War I* (Bloomington: Indiana University Press, 2001), 52.

73. Philip S. Foner, *Organized Labor and the Black Worker, 1619–1973* (New York: International Publishers, 1976), 146.

74. Robert Whitaker, *On the Laps of Gods: The Red Summer of 1919 and the Struggle for Justice That Remade a Nation* (New York: Three Rivers Press, 2009), 47.

75. According to Historian Claudrena Harold, "Whenever the life or property of a Negro who had moved into a white section was threatened, the Negro masses rose up to protect him. In the Washington, East Saint Louis, and Chicago race riots, which were to a large degree caused by competition between Negroes and whites for jobs and houses, the Negro masses demonstrated very clearly that they would meet violence with violence. This determination of the Negro masses to fight back . . . was the expression of a spirit of revolt that accompanied the migrations." Harold, *New Negro Politics in the Jim Crow South* (Athens: University of Georgia Press, 2016), 30.

76. Harold, 30.

77. Baron, *The Demand for Black Labor*, 18.

78. Harry Haywood, "The Struggle for the Leninist Position on the Negro Question in the USA," *Communist* (September 1933): 889.

79. Haywood, 889.

80. Baron, *The Demand for Black Labor*, 17, 18.

81. Baron, 699.

82. Patterson, *We Charge Genocide*, 228.

83. Patterson, 55–59.

84. Patterson, 231.

85. Patterson, 228.

86. Patterson, 229.

87. Patterson, 229.

88. Patterson, 229–30.

89. Patterson, 230.

90. Patterson, 232.

91. Patterson, 232.

92. "Report of Comrade Minor on the Negro Question," n.d., Papers of the Communist Party of the United States of America (TAM.132), Tamiment Library and Robert F. Wagner Labor Archive, Elmer Bobst Library, New York (hereafter CPUSA Papers), Box 145, 2.

93. Aptheker, *The Negro People in America*, xx.

94. Angelo Herndon, *Let Me Live* (Ann Arbor: University of Michigan Press, 2007 [1937]), 40–49.

95. Herndon, 40–49.

96. Herndon, 57.

97. Goldfield, *The Southern Key*, 9–10.

98. Herndon, *Let Me Live*, 58.

99. Herndon, 67.

100. Herndon, 62.

101. Herndon, 63.

102. Herndon, 97.

103. Herndon, 101.

104. Herndon, 29.

105. Premilla Nadasen, "Domestic Worker Organizing: Storytelling, History, and Contemporary Resonance," *Souls* 18, no. 1 (2016): 156.

106. Lydia Lindsey, "Black Lives Matter: Grace P. Campbell and Claudia Jones—An Analysis of the Negro Question, Self-Determination, Black Belt Thesis," *Africology: The Journal of Pan-African Studies* 12, no. 10 (March 2019): 117.

107. Gordon and Briggs, *The Position of Negro Women*, 2.

108. Esther Victoria Cooper, "The Negro Woman Domestic Worker in Relation to Trade Unionism," MA thesis (Fisk University, 1940), 6.

109. Louise Thompson Patterson, "Toward a Brighter Dawn," *Woman Today* (April 1936), 14.

110. Jones, "An End to the Neglect," 7.

111. Cooper, "The Negro Woman Domestic Worker in Relation to Trade Unionism," 15.

112. Gordon and Briggs, *The Position of Negro Women*, 6.

113. Cooper, "The Negro Woman Domestic Worker in Relation to Trade Unionism," 2.

114. Gordon and Briggs, *The Position of Negro Women*, 6.

115. Marvel Cooke and Ella Baker, "The Bronx Slave Market," *Crisis* 42 (November 1935): 330–31, 340.

116. Cooke and Baker, 330.

117. Cooke and Baker, 340.

118. Patterson, "Toward a Brighter Dawn," 14.

119. Cooper, "The Negro Woman Domestic Worker in Relation to Trade Unionism," 5.

120. Cooper, 7.

121. Gordon and Briggs, *The Position of Negro Women*, 7.

122. Jones, "An End to the Neglect," 5–6.

123. Gordon and Briggs, *The Position of Negro Women*, 7.

124. Gordon and Briggs, 2–4.

125. Patterson, "Toward a Brighter Dawn," 1.

126. Gordon and Briggs, *The Position of Negro Women*, 11.

127. Gordon and Briggs, 11.

128. Gordon and Briggs, 13.

129. Gordon and Briggs, 14.

130. Jones, "An End to the Neglect," 5.

131. Patterson, "Toward a Brighter Dawn," 1.

132. Gordon and Briggs, *The Position of Negro Women*, 14.

133. Jones, "An End to the Neglect," 6.

134. Marvel Cooke, "The Bronx Slave Market Part I," *New York Compass*, 1950.

135. Jones, "An End to the Neglect," 6.

136. Gordon and Briggs, *The Position of Negro Women*, 8.

137. Gordon and Briggs, 10.

138. See, e.g., Howard Botwinick, *Persistent Inequality: Wage Disparity under Capitalist Competition* (Chicago: Haymarket Books, 2018).

139. Hill, *RACON*, 255.

140. Hill, 346.

141. Hill, 594.

142. National Negro Congress, *Resolutions of the National Negro Congress held in Chicago, Ill., February 14, 15, 16, 1936* (Washington, DC: The Congress, 1936), 15.

143. National Negro Congress, 4.

144. National Negro Congress, 14.

145. National Negro Congress, 31.

146. National Negro Labor Council, *"Get on Board the Freedom Train": Proceedings of the Founding of the National Negro Labor Council held in Cincinnati, October 28, 1951* (photocopy pamphlet), 31.

147. National Negro Labor Council, 32.

148. National Negro Labor Council, 36.

149. National Negro Labor Council, 39.

150. National Negro Labor Council, 74.

151. National Negro Labor Council, 79.

152. Cooke and Baker, "The Bronx Slave Market," 340.

153. Cooper, "The Negro Woman Domestic Worker in Relation to Trade Unionism," 27–28.

154. Cooper, 99.

155. Cooper, 103–5.

156. Jones, "An End to the Neglect," 12.

157. Marvel Cooke, "The Bronx Slave Market: I Was Part of the Bronx Slave Market," *New York Compass*, January 8, 1950, 1.

158. Cooke, 1.

159. Marvel Cooke, "The Bronx Slave Market: Some Ways to Kill the Slave Market," *New York Compass*, January 12, 1950, 6.

Chapter Two

1. See, e.g., Michael Goldfield, *The Color of Politics: Race and the Mainsprings of American Politics* (New York: New Press, 1997); David Roediger, *The Wages of Whiteness: Race and the Making of the American Working Class* (London: Verso, 2007); and Gerald Horne, *The Apocalypse of Settler Colonialism: The Roots of Slavery, White Supremacy, and Capitalism in Seventeenth Century North America and the Caribbean* (New York: Monthly Review Press, 2018).

2. William Patterson, "The Battle for America: Unity in Struggle: Key to the People's Victory," n.d., CPUSA Papers, Box 147, 3–4.

3. Perry, "U.S. Emerging as an Imperial Power," Pettis Perry Papers, Box 4, Folder 10, 1.

4. Perlo, *American Imperialism*, 28–29.

5. Perlo, 32.

6. Patterson, *We Charge Genocide*, 32, 33.

7. Patterson, 16.

8. Patterson, 4.

9. Patterson, 42, 44.

10. William Patterson, "We Charge Genocide," speech to launch the publication of the book, November 12, 1951, CPUSA Papers.

11. National Negro Congress, *A Petition to the United Nations on Behalf of 13 Million Oppressed Negro Citizens of the United States*, June 1946, 8.

12. Patterson, *We Charge Genocide*, 5.

13. Patterson, 27.

14. Patterson, "We Charge Genocide," speech.

15. Civil Rights Congress National Office, "Chapter Bulletin," January 4, 1952, CPUSA Papers, Box 146, 2.

16. Patterson, *We Charge Genocide*, 27.

17. Patterson, 120–21.

18. Hill, "'The Foremost Radical among the Race': Marcus Garvey and the Black Scare, 1918–1921," 215.

19. Chad Williams, "Vanguards of the New Negro: African American Veterans and Post–World War I Racial Militancy," *Journal of African American History* 92 (2007): 348.

20. Williams, 168.

21. Williams, 167.

22. *Crisis* is a case in point; because of accusations in the first half of 1918 that it was inciting pro-German sentiment among Blacks, it was thereafter associated with "enemy-inspired race subversion of American race relations." Ellis, "'Negro Subversion,'" 197.

23. Ellis, 197.

24. Carole Boyce Davies, "Deportable Subjects: U.S. Immigration Laws and the Criminalization of Communism," *South Atlantic Quarterly* 100, no. 4 (Fall 2001): 955.

25. Davies, 951.

26. George Yancy, *Black Bodies, White Gazes: The Continuing Significance of Race* (Lanham, MD: Rowan and Littlefield Publishers, Inc., 2008), 80.

27. Yancy, 168.

28. Yancy, 161.

29. Mary Dudziak, "Desegregation as a Cold War Imperative," *Stanford Law Review* 41 (1988): 122.

30. Regin Schmidt, *Red Scare: The FBI and the Origins of Anticommunism in the United States* (University of Copenhagen: Museum Tusculanum Press, 2000), 20.

31. A. C. Ratshesky, "Americanization Is Cure for Bolshevism," *New York Times*, November 24, 1918.

32. Albert E. Kahn, ed., *McCarthy on Trial* (New York: Cameron and Kahn: 1954), 19–20.

33. Ellen Schrecker, *The Age of McCarthyism: A Brief History with Documents*, 3rd ed. (Boston: Bedford/St. Martin's, 2017), 2.

34. Kahn, *McCarthy on Trial*, 19–20.

35. Kahn, 19–20.

36. Nancy Stepan Leys, "Race and Gender: The Role of Analogy in Science," in *Anatomy of Racism*, ed. David Theo Goldberg (Minneapolis: University of Minnesota Press, 1990), 44.

37. Davies, "Deportable Subjects," 958.

38. Stepan, "Race and Gender," 44.

39. Stepan, 42.

40. Stepan, 42.

41. Stepan, 45.

42. Davies, "Deportable Subjects," 959–60.

43. Yancy, "The Return of the Black Body: Seven Vignettes," 90.

44. Stepan, "Race and Gender," 48.

45. Stepan, 92.

46. Stepan, 67.

47. Davies, "Deportable Subjects," 955.

48. Davies, 69.

49. Charisse Burden-Stelly, "W. E. B. Du Bois in the Tradition of Radical Blackness: Radicalism, Repression, and Mutual Comradeship, 1930–1960," *Socialism and Democracy* 32, no. 3 (2018): 191–92.

50. Quoted in *American Civilization*, 65.

51. Penny Von Eschen, "Challenging Cold War Habits: African Americans, Race, and Foreign Policy," *Diplomatic History* 20, no. 4 (October 1996): 635.

52. J. E. Spingarn to Capt. John Geary, July 17, 1918; Kornweibel, *Investigate Everything*, 29.

53. Mark Ellis, " 'Closing Ranks' and 'Seeking Honors': W. E. B. Du Bois in World War I," *Journal of American History* 79, no. 1 (June 1992): 106.

54. W. E. B. Du Bois, "To the Board of Directors," July 2, 1918, https://credo.library.umass.edu/view/full/mums312-b012-i224.

55. W. E. B. Du Bois, "A Momentous Proposal," *Crisis* 16, no. 5 (September 1918): 215–16.

56. David Levering Lewis, *W. E. B. Du Bois: Biography of Race, 1868–1919* (New York: Henry Holt and Company, 1993), 553–54.

57. Kornweibel, *Investigate Everything*, 35.

58. Kornweibel, 35.

59. Kornweibel, 36.

60. Ellis, " 'Closing Ranks' and 'Seeking Honors,' " 102.

61. Erik McDuffie, "Black and Red: Black Liberation, the Cold War, and the Horne Thesis," *Journal of African American History* 96, no. 2 (Spring 2011): 237.

62. David Krugler, *1919, The Year of Racial Violence: How African Americans Fought Back*, (Cambridge: Cambridge University Press, 2014), 198.

63. Hill, "The Foremost Radical," 216.

64. Hill, 198n7.

65. Hill, 200.

66. The Espionage Act was passed on June 15, 1917, and included the criminalization of any interference with the operations or success of the military and naval forces through false reports or false statements; the promotion of the success of enemies of the US; and, while the US was at war, the willful cause or attempt to cause "insubordination, disloyalty, mutiny, or refusal of duty" in the armed forces or the obstruction of recruitment or enlistment. The Sedition Act was passed on May 16, 1918, and expanded the government's control over freedom of expression and ability to punish activities and publications that were critical of the war.

67. Peter Cole, *Ben Fletcher: The Life and Times of a Black Wobbly* (Oakland, CA: PM Press, 2021), 131.

68. Cole, 153–54.

69. Cole, 153.

70. Cole, 64.

71. Cole, 67.

72. Cole, 83.

73. Cole, 83–84.

74. Cole, 84.

75. Cole, 89.

76. Cole, 100, 101.

77. See, e.g., Khalil Gibran Muhammad, *The Condemnation of Blackness: Race, Crime, and the Making of Modern Urban America* (Cambridge, MA: Harvard University Press, 2019), and

Tommy Curry, *The Man-Not: Race, Class, Genre and the Dilemmas of Black Manhood* (Philadelphia: Temple University Press, 2017).

78. Cole, *Ben Fletcher*, 26.

79. Cole, 102.

80. Cole, 103.

81. Cole, 99.

82. Cole, 104–5.

83. Cole, 29.

84. Cole, 33.

85. Cole, 33.

86. Cole, 33.

87. Cole, 34.

88. Cole, 35–36.

89. Cole, 50.

90. Hill, *RACON*, 255.

91. Hill, 357.

92. Hill, 372.

93. Hill, 15.

94. Hill, 15.

95. Kahn, *McCarthy on Trial*, 26.

96. Dorothy Hunton, *Alphaeus Hunton: The Unsung Valiant* (Richmond Hill, GA: D. K. Hunton, 1986), 51.

97. Davies, "Deportable Subjects," 957–58.

98. Pettis Perry, "Further Strengthening the Fight against White Chauvinism," 1951, Pettis Perry Papers, Box 4, Folder 1, 4.

Chapter Three

1. Dennis Forsythe, "West Indian Radicalism in America: An Assessment of Ideologies," in *Ethnicity in the Americas*, ed. Frances Henry (Stuttgart: Walter de Gruyter, 2011), 302; Ira Reid, "Negro Immigration to the United States," *Social Forces* 16 (1937–38): 221.

2. W. A. Domingo, "Gift of the Black Tropics," in *The American Negro*, ed. Alain Locke (New York: Arno, 1968), 346; Perry Mars, "Caribbean Influences in African-American Political Struggles," *Ethnic and Racial Studies* 27 (2004), 574; Forsythe, "West Indian Radicalism," 301.

3. Mars, "Caribbean Influences in African-American Political Struggles," 573.

4. Carole Boyce Davies, ed., *Claudia Jones: Beyond Containment* (Boulder, CO: Lynne Rienner Publisher, Inc., 2011), 18.

5. Walter T. Howard, *We Shall Be Free! Black Communist Protest in Seven Voices* (Philadelphia: Temple University Press, 2013), 2.

6. Domingo, "Gift of the Black Tropics," 346; Mars, "Caribbean Influences in African-American Political Struggles," 573, 574; Forsythe, "West Indian Radicalism," 301, 302; Reid, "Negro Immigration to the United States," 221.

7. C. Lorenzo, "The Negro Liberation Movement," in *American Communism and Black Americans: A Documentary History, 1919–1929*, ed. Philip S. Foner and James S. Allen (Philadelphia: Temple University Press, 1987), 15.

8. Foner and Allen, *American Communists and Black Americans: A Documentary History, 1919–1929*, 17.

9. Robert A. Hill, ed., *The Crusader*, vol. 1, *September 1918–August 1919* (New York: Garland Publishing Inc., 1987), xxviii.

10. Robert A. Hill, ed., *Marcus Garvey Life and Lessons: A Centennial Guide to the Marcus Garvey and Universal Negro Improvement Association Papers* (Berkeley: University of California Press, 1987), 206–10.

11. Michael Newton, *The FBI Encyclopedia* (Jefferson, NC: McFarland and Company, Inc., 2003), 345.

12. "Emergency Conference on Deportations," March 1948, Du Bois Papers.

13. George W. Crockett, "Rights of the Foreign Born," 1951, Du Bois Papers.

14. Forsythe, "West Indian Radicalism," 304.

15. Buzz Johnson, *"I Think of My Mother": Notes on the Life and Times of Claudia Jones* (London: Karia Press, 1985): 129.

16. Robert A. Hill, ed., *The Marcus Garvey and Universal Negro Improvement Association Papers*, vol. 2, *August 1919–August 1920* (Berkeley: University of California Press, 1983), 10.

17. Hill, 72.

18. Hill, 541.

19. Hill, 10.

20. Hill, 219.

21. Hill, 221.

22. Hill, " 'The Foremost Radical among the Race': Marcus Garvey and the Black Scare, 1918–1921," 221.

23. Judith Stein, *The World of Marcus Garvey: Race and Class in Modern Society* (Baton Rouge: Louisiana State University Press, 1986), 186.

24. Stein, 206.

25. Stein, 208.

26. Cyril Briggs, "The Decline of the Garvey Movement," *Communist*, June 1931.

27. W. E. B. Du Bois, "Marcus Garvey," *Crisis*, December 1920, 60.

28. Hill, *Marcus Garvey*, 547.

29. Hill, 61.

30. Hill, 546.

31. Jones, " 'Brightest Africa' in the New Negro Imagination," 42.

32. According to one scholar, "Garvey used the term *redeem* to mean the rescue of Africans from European 'unrighteousness' *and* from their own 'backwardness.' In declaring himself provisional president of Africa, he argued that Africans lacked the culture, education, and civilization at that time to assume leadership over the continent. In this sense, Europeans were guilty of the 'inhuman, unchristian, and uncivilized behavior in Africa,' contributing to the darkness emanating from the continent." Jeanette Eileen Jones, " 'Brightest Africa' in the New Negro Imagination," in *Escape from New York: The New Negro Renaissance beyond Harlem*, ed. Davarian L. Baldwin and Minkah Makalani (Minneapolis: University of Minnesota Press, 2013), 43.

33. Marcus Garvey, "An Answer to his Many Critics," in *Marcus Garvey and the Vision of Africa*, ed. John Henrik Clarke (New York: Vintage Books, 1974), 252.

34. Marcus Garvey, "Negro Progress Postulates Negro Government," *Blackman*, April 23, 1929.

35. E. Franklin Frazier, "Garvey: A Mass Leader," *Nation* 123 (August 1926): 147–48.

36. Richard B. Moore, "The Critics and Opponents of Marcus Garvey," in *Marcus Garvey and the Vision of Africa*, ed. John Henrik Clarke (New York: Vintage Books, 1974), 215.

37. Du Bois, "Marcus Garvey," 58–60.

38. Marcus Garvey, "Why the Black Star Line Failed," in *Marcus Garvey and the Vision of Africa*, ed. John Henrik Clarke (New York: Vintage Books, 1974), 149.

39. *New York Times*, July 28, 1919.

40. Patrick S. Washburn, *A Question of Sedition: The Federal Government's Investigation of the Black Press during World War II* (New York: Oxford University Press, 1986), 5.

41. *New York Times*, July 28, 1919.

42. *New York Times*, July 28, 1919.

43. *Investigation Activities of the Department of Justice: Letter from the Attorney General Transmitting in Response to a Senate Resolution of October 17, 1919, a Report on the Activities of the Bureau of Investigation of the Department of Justice against Persons Advising Anarchy, Sedition, and the Forcible Overthrow of the Government*, Senate Document No. 153 (Washington, DC: Government Printing Office, November 17, 1919); Washburn, *A Question of Sedition*, 27.

44. Washburn, *A Question of Sedition*, 27.

45. "Radicalism and Sedition among the Negro as Reflected in Their Publications," in *The Attorney General Report on the Activities of the Bureau of Investigation of the Department of Justice against Persons Advising Anarchy, Sedition, and the Forcible Overthrow of the Government*, 162.

46. "Radicalism and Sedition," 162.

47. Joint Legislative Committee Investigating Seditious Activities, *Revolutionary Radicalism*, 1520.

48. "Radicalism and Sedition," 187.

49. "Radicalism and Sedition," 172.

50. Joint Legislative Committee Investigating Seditious Activities, *Revolutionary Radicalism*, 1312.

51. *New York Times*, November 23, 1919.

52. "Radicalism and Sedition," 162.

53. The report erroneously listed "William H. Domingo" as the second editor.

54. "Radicalism and Sedition," 164.

55. "Radicalism and Sedition," 163–65.

56. "Radicalism and Sedition," 165.

57. "Radicalism and Sedition," 168–71.

58. "Radicalism and Sedition," 184.

59. Martin Duberman, *Paul Robeson* (New York: Alfred A. Knopf, 1988), 373.

60. "precisely at a time . . . ," Pettis Perry Papers, Box 4, Folder 4/16.

61. Gerald Horne, *Black Liberation/Red Scare: Ben Davis and the Communist Party* (Newark: University of Delaware Press, 1994), 218.

62. "precisely at a time . . . ," Pettis Perry Papers, Box 4, Folder 4.

63. Ellis, "'Negro Subversion,'" 182, 189.

64. Oliver Cromwell Cox, "The New Crisis in Leadership among Negroes," *Journal of Negro Education* 19 (1950): 464.

65. Herndon, *Let Me Live*, 87.

66. Herndon, 144.

67. Committee on Un-American Activities, US House of Representatives, "100 Things You Should Know about Communism in the U.S.A." (Washington, DC: Government Printing Office, 1949), 15.

68. Committee on Un-American Activities, US House of Representatives, "100 Things You Should Know about Communism in the U.S.A.," 15.

69. Committee on Un-American Activities, US House of Representatives, "100 Things You Should Know About Communism in the U.S.A.," 101.

70. Herndon, *Let Me Live*, 42.

71. Herndon, 51.

72. Herndon, 43–44.

73. Herndon, 71.

74. Herndon, 94.

75. Horne, *Black Liberation / Red Scare*, 207.

76. Herndon, *Let Me Live*, 100.

77. Herndon, 100–101.

78. Herndon, 146.

79. Herndon, xii.

80. Herndon, 115.

81. Herndon, 114.

82. Herndon, 110.

83. Herndon, 117.

84. Herndon, 122.

85. Herndon, 148–54.

86. Herndon, 161.

87. Kendall Thomas, "*Rouge et Noir* Reread: A Popular Constitutional History of the Angelo Herndon Case," *Southern California Law Review* 65 (1992): 2663.

88. Thomas, 2662.

89. Quoted in the introduction.

90. Herndon, *Let Me Live*, 405.

91. Herndon, 189–92.

92. Herndon, xxii.

93. Herndon, xxi.

94. Charles H. Martin, "Communists and Blacks: The ILD and The Angelo Herndon Case," *Journal of Negro History* 64, no. 2 (Spring 1979): 131–32.

Chapter Four

1. Nell Irving Painter, *The Narrative of Hosea Hudson: His Life as a Communist in the South* (Cambridge, MA: Harvard University Press, 1979), 103.

2. Kornweibel, *Investigate Everything*, 177.

3. Kornweibel, 177; James R. Grossman, "Black Labor Is the Best Labor: Southern White Reactions to the Great Migration," in *Black Exodus: The Great Migration from the American South*, ed. Alferdteen Harris (Jackson: University Press of Mississippi, 1991), 58.

4. Kornweibel, *Investigate Everything*, 120.

5. Ellis, " 'Negro Subversion,' " 160.

6. Kornweibel, *Investigate Everything*, 177; Grossman, "Black Labor Is the Best Labor," 58.

7. Grossman, "Black Labor Is the Best Labor," 64.

8. Grossman, 51.

9. Whitaker, *On the Laps of Gods*, 49, 50.

10. Philip S. Foner, *Organized Labor and the Black Worker, 1619–1973* (New York: International Publishers, 1976), 146.

11. "When a Negro Is a Bolshevist," *Pittsburgh Courier*, October 25, 1919, in Robert T. Kerlin, *The Voice of the Negro, 1919* (New York: E. P. Dutton and Company, 1920), 150–51.

12. John Riddell, ed., *Toward the United Front: Proceedings of the Fourth Congress of the Communist International, 1922* (Chicago: Haymarket Books, 1922), 803; Jacob A. Zumoff, *The Communist International and US Communism, 1919–1929* (Chicago: Haymarket Books, 2014), 299–300.

13. Lieberman, "The Long Black and Red Scare: Anti-Communism and the African American Freedom Struggle," 267.

14. Theodore Kornweibel Jr., ed., *Federal Surveillance of Afro-Americans (1917–1925): The First World War, the Red Scare and the Garvey Movement* (Frederick, MD: University Publications of America, Inc., 1986), ix.

15. Lieberman, "The Long Black and Red Scare: Anti-Communism and the African American Freedom Struggle," 264.

16. "Bolshevist!!!," *Crusader*, October 1930, in Kerlin, *The Voice of the Negro, 1919*, 151.

17. "Not Bolshevism—Just American Injustice," *Cleveland Advocate*, October 18, 1919, in Kerlin, *The Voice of the Negro*, 1919, 155.

18. Bishop George C. Clement, quoted in Kerlin, *The Voice of the Negro, 1919*, 156.

19. "Uncle Sam Angers Colored Folks," *Searchlight*, August 23, 1919, in Kerlin, *The Voice of the Negro, 1919*, 152.

20. "Negroes Stead and Pause," *Denver Star*, September 27, 1919, in Kerlin, *The Voice of the Negro, 1919*, 156.

21. Lieberman, "The Long Black and Red Scare: Anti-Communism and the African American Freedom Struggle," 266.

22. Kerlin, *The Voice of the Negro, 1919*, 87.

23. Robert Justin Goldstein, ed., *Political Repression in Modern America from 1870 to 1976* (Urbana: University of Illinois Press, 2016 [2001, 1978]), 150; "Systematic Robbery Cause of Riots, Arkansas Negroes Had Not Planned Massacre," *Savannah Tribune*, October 23, 1919, in Kerlin, *The Voice of the Negro, 1919*, 89.

24. Goldstein, *Political Repression in Modern America from 1870 to 1976*, 150; Kerlin, *The Voice of the Negro, 1919*, 92.

25. Goldstein, *Political Repression in Modern America from 1870 to 1976*, 150.

26. "Race Clash in Phillips Co.," *Hot Spring Echo*, October 4, 1919, in Kerlin, *The Voice of the Negro, 1919*, 87–88.

27. "Systematic Robbery Cause of Riots, Arkansas Negroes Had Not Planned Massacre," 88.

28. "Systematic Robbery Cause of Riots, Arkansas Negroes Had Not Planned Massacre," 89.

29. Joint Legislative Committee Investigating Seditious Activities, *Revolutionary Radicalism*, 2292.

30. Joint Legislative Committee Investigating Seditious Activities, 1143.

31. W. F. Elkins, "'Unrest among the Negroes': A British Document of 1919," *Science & Society* 32, no. 1 (Winter 1968): 68.

32. Elkins, 75.

33. Joint Legislative Committee Investigating Seditious Activities, *Revolutionary Radicalism*, 1225.

34. Joint Legislative Committee Investigating Seditious Activities, 1264.

35. Joint Legislative Committee Investigating Seditious Activities, 1312.

36. Joint Legislative Committee Investigating Seditious Activities, 1422.

37. Joint Legislative Committee Investigating Seditious Activities, 1478–79.

38. Joint Legislative Committee Investigating Seditious Activities, 1479.

39. Joint Legislative Committee Investigating Seditious Activities, 1483.

40. Joint Legislative Committee Investigating Seditious Activities, 1483.

41. Joint Legislative Committee Investigating Seditious Activities, 1512, 1519.

42. Joint Legislative Committee Investigating Seditious Activities, 1519–20.

43. "Radicalism and Sedition," 172–79.

44. "Radicalism and Sedition," 182.

45. "Radicalism and Sedition," 172.

46. *The Attorney General Report*, 13.

47. *The Attorney General Report*, 162.

48. *The Attorney General Report*, 162.

49. *The Attorney General Report*, 12.

50. *The Attorney General Report*, 162.

51. *The Attorney General Report*, 13.

52. *The Attorney General Report*, 11.

53. *The Attorney General Report*, 13.

54. *The Attorney General Report*, 2.

55. James S. Allen, *Negro Liberation* (New York: International Publishers, 1938), 13–14; Haywood, *Negro Liberation*, 11–13.

56. B. D. Amis, "For a Strict Leninist Analysis of the Negro National Question in the United States," in *B. D. Amis, African American Radical: A Short Anthology of Writings and Speeches*, ed. Walter T. Howard (Lanham, MD: University Press of America, 2007), 38.

57. Riddell, *Toward the United Front*, 811.

58. Riddell, 803.

59. Riddell, 801.

60. Riddell, 949.

61. Vladimir I. Lenin, "The Socialist Revolution and the Right to Self-Determination (Theses)," in *Lenin on the National and Colonial Questions: Three Articles* (Peking: Foreign Languages Press, 1967), 21.

62. Zumoff, *The Communist International and US Communism, 1919–1929*, 321.

63. Amis, "For a Strict Leninist Analysis of the Negro National Question in the United States," 39.

64. Amis, 40.

65. Harry Haywood, *Black Bolshevik: Autobiography of an African-American Communist* (Chicago: Liberator Press, 1978), 229–30.

66. Haywood, 222–35.

67. Minkah Makalani, "An Apparatus for Negro Women: Black Women's Organizing, Communism, and the Institutional Spaces of Radical Pan-African Thought," *Women, Gender, and Families of Color* 4, no. 2 (Fall 2016): 265.

68. Keith Griffler, *What Price Alliance? Black Radicals Confront White Labor, 1918–1938* (New York: Garland Publishing Inc., 1995), 65.

69. Solomon, *The Cry Was Unity*, 70–72.

70. Makalani, "An Apparatus for Negro Women," 266.

71. Hakim Adi, *Pan-Africanism and Communism: The Communist International, Africa and the Diaspora, 1919–1939* (Trenton, NJ: Africa World Press, 2013), 51–58.

72. Adi, 56.

73. Minkah Makalani, *In the Cause of Freedom: Radical Black Internationalism from Harlem to London, 1917–1939* (Chapel Hill: University of North Carolina Press, 2011), 152–53.

74. Foner and Allen, *American Communism and Black Americans*, 181.

75. Harry Haywood, "The Negro Problem and the Tasks of the Communist Party of the United States," *Die Kommunitische Internationale*, September 5, 1925, 2253–63, in Foner and Allen, *American Communism and Black Americans*, 174.

76. Haywood, "The Negro Problem and the Tasks of the Communist Party of the United States," 177.

77. Haywood, 66–67.

78. Haywood, 67–68.

79. Harry Haywood, "Against Bourgeois-Liberal Distortions of Leninism on the Negro Question in the United States," *Communist*, August 1930, 701.

80. *RACON*, 554.

81. B. D. Amis, "To the Exploited and Oppressed Toilers: Close Ranks! Join the Communist Party!," in *B. D. Amis, African American Radical: A Short Anthology of Writings and Speeches*, ed. Walter T. Howard (Lanham, MD: University Press of America, 2007), 13.

82. Haywood, "Against Bourgeois-Liberal Distortions of Leninism on the Negro Question in the United States," 695.

83. Amis, "To the Exploited and Oppressed Toilers: Close Ranks! Join the Communist Party!," 40.

84. Amis, 41.

85. Zumoff, *The Communist International and US Communism, 1919–1929*, 361.

86. Robin D. G. Kelley, *Hammer and Hoe: Alabama Communists during the Great Depression* (Chapel Hill: University of North Carolina Press), 16.

87. Kelley, 32, 44–45, 34–56.

88. Kelley, 93.

89. Glenda Gilmore, *Defying Dixie: The Radical Roots of Civil Rights, 1919–1950* (New York: W. W. Norton and Company, 2008), 101.

90. Irving Howe and Lewis Coser, *The American Communist Party: A Critical History, 1919–1957* (Boston: Beacon Press, 1957), 441–51.

91. Howe and Coser, 64.

92. Howe and Coser, 65.

93. Howe and Coser, 66.

94. Howe and Coser, 62.

95. Howe and Coser, 62.

96. Hamilton Fish, "The Menace of Communism," *Annals of the American Academy of Political and Social Science* 156 (July 1931): 8.

97. Herndon, *Let Me Live*, 228.

98. Herndon, 312.

99. "The Communist Party and the Negro," i.

100. Hill, *RACON*, 635.

101. Hill, 203.

102. Hill, 55.

103. Hill, 552.

104. Hill, 555.

105. Hill, 556–57.

106. Hill, 558–59.

107. Hill, 561.

108. Hill, 562.

109. Hill, 586.

110. Hill, 591.

111. Hill, 592.

112. Hill, 593–94.

113. Hill, 591.

114. See, e.g., Margaret Stevens, *Red International and Black Caribbean: Communists in New York City, Mexico and the West Indies, 1919–1939* (London: Pluto Press, 2017), 155–58; Solomon, *The Cry Was Unity*, 190–91; Joyce Moore Turner, *Caribbean Crusaders and the Harlem Renaissance* (Urbana: University of Illinois Press, 2005), 188–90; Haywood, *Black Bolshevik: Autobiography of An Afro-American Communist*, 343–47, 439–40.

115. Makalani, *In the Cause of Freedom*, 90–97.

116. Makalani, 100.

117. Adi, *Pan-Africanism and Communism*, 25.

118. Makalani, *In the Cause of Freedom*, 120–21.

119. Adi, *Pan-Africanism and Communism*, 35–38.

Chapter Five

1. Perlo, *American Imperialism*, 59.

2. Hubert Harrison, "Hands across the Sea," *Negro World*, September 10, 1921, in *A Hubert Harrison Reader*, ed. Jeffrey B. Perry (Middletown, CT: Wesleyan University Press, 2001), 238–39.

3. Perlo, *American Imperialism*, 201–2.

4. Harrison, "Hands across the Sea," 238–39.

5. Peter James Hudson, *Bankers and Empire: How Wall Street Colonized the Caribbean* (Chicago: University of Chicago Press, 2017), 5.

6. Hudson, 7.

7. Hudson, 152.

8. Hudson, 206–8.

9. Hudson, 21.

10. Hudson, 13–14.

11. Hudson, 7.

12. Richard B. Moore, "Statement at the Congress of the League against Imperialism and for National Independence, Brussels, February 1927," in *Richard B. Moore: Caribbean Militant in Harlem; Collected Writings, 1920–1972*, ed. W. Burghardt Turner and Joyce Moore Turner (Bloomington: Indiana University Press, 1988), 145, 146; originally printed in the July 1927 issue of the *Crisis* magazine, the official publication of the National Association for the Advancement of Colored People.

13. James W. Ford, "The Negro Question: Report to the 2nd World Congress of the League against Imperialism," *Negro Worker*, August 1929, 3.

14. Ford, 3.

15. Ford, 2.

16. Harrison, "Hands across the Sea," 239.

17. Hudson, *Bankers and Empire*, 100.

18. James Weldon Johnson, *Self-Determining Haiti: Four Articles Reprinted from The Nation Embodying a Report of an Investigation Made for the National Association for the Advancement of Colored People* (New York: The Nation, 1920), 20.

19. George Padmore, *The Life and Struggle of Negro Toilers* (Hollywood, CA: Sundance Press, 1971 [1931]).

20. This article read: "No one, unless he is Haitian, may be a holder of land in Haiti, regardless of what this title may be, nor acquire any real estate." After the forced revision of the constitution in 1918, Article 5 read: "The right to hold property is given to foreigners residing in Haiti, and to societies formed by foreigners, for dwelling purposes and for agricultural, commercial, industrial, or educational enterprises. This right shall be discontinued five years after the foreigner shall have ceased to reside in the country, or when the activities of these companies shall have ceased." Johnson, *Self-Determining Haiti*, 38.

21. Padmore, *The Life and Struggle of Negro Toilers*, 65.

22. Johnson, *Self-Determining Haiti*, 34–37; Padmore, *The Life and Struggle of Negro Toilers*, 65.

23. Hudson, *Bankers and Empire*, 107.

24. Johnson, *Self-Determining Haiti*, 5.

25. Hudson, *Bankers and Empire*, 101.

26. Walter Rodney, "The Imperialist Partition of Africa," *Monthly Review* 21, no. 11 (April 1970): 113.

27. Hudson, *Bankers and Empire*, 108–9.

28. Johnson, *Self-Determining Haiti*, 18.

29. Johnson, 18.

30. Hudson, *Bankers and Empire*, 109.

31. Johnson, *Self-Determining Haiti*, 13–14.

32. Hudson, *Bankers and Empire*, 109; Johnson, *Self-Determining Haiti*, 14; Jeffrey B. Perry, ed., *A Hubert Harrison Reader* (Middletown, CT: Wesleyan University Press, 2001), 236.

33. Perry, *A Hubert Harrison Reader*, 236.

34. Padmore, *The Life and Struggle of Negro Toilers*, 66.

35. Johnson, *Self-Determining Haiti*, 21.

36. Hubert Harrison, "The Cracker in the Caribbean," *Negro World* (?), 1920, in *A Hubert Harrison Reader*, ed. Jeffrey B. Perry (Middletown, CT: Wesleyan University Press, 2001), 237.

37. Hudson, *Bankers and Empire*, 113.

38. Johnson, *Self-Determining Haiti*, 9.

39. Hudson, *Bankers and Empire*, 83.

40. Hudson, 101, 111.

41. Hudson, 100.

42. Hudson, 114–15.

43. Johnson, *Self-Determining Haiti*, 19. Also see Stevens, *Red International and Black Caribbean*, 49–68, 253–74.

44. Rodney, "The Imperialist Partition of Africa," 113.

45. Padmore, *The Life and Struggle of Negro Toilers*, 75.

46. Hunton, *Decision in Africa: Sources of Current Conflict*, 93; Perlo, *American Imperialism*, 186.

47. Hunton, *Decision in Africa: Sources of Current Conflict*, 94.

48. Perlo, *American Imperialism*, 182.

49. Padmore, *The Life and Struggle of Negro Toilers*, 68–70.

50. Padmore, 71.

51. Hunton, *Decision in Africa: Sources of Current Conflict*, 102.

52. Hunton, 103.

53. Hunton, 80–81.

54. Hunton, 106–8.

55. Martin, *Race First: The Ideological and Organizational Struggles of Marcus Garvey and the Universal Negro Improvement Association*, 13.

56. Hill, "'The Foremost Radical among His Race,'" 221.

57. Hill, 224.

58. Hill, 226.

59. "British Colonial Office Report on the UNIA," *The Marcus Garvey UNIA Papers*, vol. 5, 560.

60. Elkins, "'Unrest among the Negroes': A British Document of 1919," 74.

61. Amy Jacques Garvey, ed., *Philosophies and Opinions of Marcus Garvey* (Mansfield Centre, CT: Martino Publishing, 2014), 353–54.

62. Elkins, "'Unrest among the Negroes': A British Document of 1919," 74.

63. Garvey, *Philosophies and Opinions of Marcus Garvey*, 364.

64. Hill, "'The Foremost Radical Among His Race,'" 226.

65. Garvey, *Philosophies and Opinions of Marcus Garvey*, 365.

66. Martin, *Race First: The Ideological and Organizational Struggles of Marcus Garvey and the Universal Negro Improvement Association*, 124.

67. "Elie Garcia, UNIA Commissioner to Liberia, to Marcus Garvey and the UNIA," August 1920, *The Marcus Garvey and UNIA Papers*, vol. 2, 673n10.

68. "Elie Garcia, UNIA Commissioner to Liberia, to Marcus Garvey and the UNIA," August 1920, *The Marcus Garvey and UNIA Papers*, vol. 2, 669, 670.

69. Martin, *Race First: The Ideological and Organizational Struggles of Marcus Garvey and the Universal Negro Improvement Association*, 126.

70. Hill, "'The Foremost Radical among His Race,'" 229.

71. "Elie Garcia," 667.

72. "Elie Garcia," 123.

73. "Elie Garcia," 668.

74. Martin, *Race First: The Ideological and Organizational Struggles of Marcus Garvey and the Universal Negro Improvement Association*, 125.

75. Ibrahim Sundiata, *Brothers and Strangers: Black Zion, Black Slavery, 1914–1940* (Durham, NC: Duke University Press, 2003), 77–78.

76. Quoted in Sundiata, 80.

77. "*New York World* Advertisement," June 25, 1924, *The Marcus Garvey and UNIA Papers*, vol. 5, 610.

78. "Report by Special Agent John E. Amos," August 7, 1924, *The Marcus Garvey and UNIA Papers*, vol. 5, 682; "Report by Special Agent Joseph G. Tucker," August 9, 1924, *The Marcus Garvey and UNIA Papers*, vol. 5, 689.

79. "Enclosure: Statement for the Press," *The Marcus Garvey and UNIA Papers*, vol. 5, 775n2.

80. "Enclosure," 774.

81. "Report by Special Agent John E. Amos," 689; "Report of the UNIA Delegation to Liberia," August 27, 1924, *The Marcus Garvey and UNIA Papers*, vol. 5, 797; "Convention Report," August 28, 1924, Report of the UNIA Delegation to Liberia," August 27, 1924, *The Marcus Garvey and UNIA Papers*, vol. 5, 805, 806.

82. "Report of the UNIA Delegation to Liberia," August 27, 1924, *The Marcus Garvey and UNIA Papers*, vol. 5, 788.

83. "Report of the UNIA Delegation to Liberia," 800n7.

84. Amy Jacques Garvey, *Garvey and Garveyism* (Baltimore: Black Classics Press, 2018 [1963]), 153.

85. Martin, *Race First: The Ideological and Organizational Struggles of Marcus Garvey and the Universal Negro Improvement Association*, 13.

86. Garvey, *Garvey and Garveyism*, 171.

87. Garvey, 171–72.

88. Garvey, 172.

89. Garvey, 172–73.

90. Garvey, 173.

91. Perlo, *American imperialism*, 183.

92. Perlo, 183.

93. Hunton, *Decision in Africa: Sources of Current Conflict*, 85.

94. Perlo, *American Imperialism*, 185.

95. Alphaeus Hunton, *Africa Fights for Freedom* (New York: Council on Africa Affairs, 1950), 5.

96. Perlo, *American Imperialism*, 187.

97. Hunton, *Africa Fights for Freedom*, 10.

98. Eslanda Goode Robeson, "Introduction," in *Africa Fights for Freedom*, 3–4.

99. Perlo, *American imperialism*, 201–2.

100. Hunton, *Decision in Africa: Sources of Current Conflict*, 221–23.

101. Eslanda Good Robeson, "Unrest in Africa Due to Oppression," in *Organize, Fight, Win: Black Communist Women's Political Writing*, eds. Charisse Burden-Stelly and Jodi Dean (London: Verso, 2022), 254.

102. Richard Nixon, "The Emergence of Africa," in *The Department of State Bulletin* 36, no. 930, (Washington, DC: Government Printing Office, April 22, 1957), 640.

103. Nixon, 636.

104. Nixon, 636–37.

105. Patterson, *We Charge Genocide*, 173.

106. Patterson, "We Charge Genocide" speech.

107. Paul Robeson, *Here I Stand* (Boston: Beacon Press, 1988 [1958]), 75.

108. Nixon, "The Emergence of Africa," 638.

109. Nixon, 639–40.

Chapter Six

1. Perlo, *American Imperialism*, 13.

2. Doxey Wilkerson, "The Historic Fight to Abolish School Segregation in the United States," Pettis Perry Papers Box 4, 4. Also see Julian Go, *American Empire and the Politics of Meaning* (Durham, NC: Duke University Press, 2008).

3. Perlo, *American Imperialism*, 24.

4. Perry, "U.S. Emerging as an Imperial Power."

5. Perlo, *American Imperialism*, 27.

6. Perlo, 27–28.

7. Perlo, 25–26.

8. Perlo, 14.

9. Domonique Pinsolle, "Sabotage, the IWW, and Repression: How the American Reinterpretation of a French Concept Gave Rise to a New International Concept of Sabotage," in *Wobblies of the World: A Global History of the IWW*, ed. Peter Cole, David Struthers, and Kenyon Zimmers (London: Pluto Press, 2017), 44.

10. "The Sedition Act of 1918," *Supreme Court History: Capitalism and Conflict*, December 2006, https://www.thirteen.org/wnet/supremecourt/capitalism/sources_document1.html. Accessed March 28, 2023.

11. Cole, *Ben Fletcher*, 27.

12. Cole, 28.

13. Pinsolle, "Sabotage, the IWW, and Repression," 44.

14. Joyce L. Kornbluh, ed., *Rebel Voices: An IWW Anthology* (Oakland, CA: PM Press, 2011), 35.

15. Pinsolle, "Sabotage, the IWW, and Repression," 45.

16. Pinsolle, 45.

17. Pinsolle, 45.

18. Cole, *Ben Fletcher*, 104.

19. *Messenger*, December 1919; August 19, 1919; July 28, 1921, 213.

20. George Robertson, "'Speak Out Now When Others Grow Silent': The *Messenger*, the IWW and Debates over New Negro Radicalism," Harry Bridges Center for Labor Research, University of Washington, 14–15, https://files.libcom.org/files/Speak%20Out%20Now.pdf. Accessed March 30, 2023.

21. Ben Fletcher, "The Negro and Organized Labor," in Cole, *Ben Fletcher*, 194.

22. Fletcher, "The Negro and Organized Labor," 194.

23. Philip S. Foner, "The IWW and the Black Worker," *Journal of Negro History* 55, no. 1 (January 1970): 58.

24. Miscellaneous Political Records, Political Prisoners, Department of Justice Files, December 10, 1921, TAF/c2c, National Archives, Washington, DC, in Foner, "The IWW and the Black Worker," 50.

25. *We Charge Genocide*, 8.

26. *We Charge Genocide*, 27.

27. *We Charge Genocide*, 58, 10, 13, 60, 70, 71, 73, 226.

28. Adriane Lentz-Smith, *Freedom Struggles: African Americans and World War I* (Cambridge: Harvard University Press, 2011), 19.

29. Mia Bay, *The White Image in the Black Mind: African American Ideas about White People, 1830–1925* (New York: Oxford University Press, 2000), 203.

30. Patterson, *We Charge Genocide*, 26.

31. Patterson, 1.

32. Patterson, 7.

33. Paul Robeson, "Genocide Stalks the USA," in *Paul Robeson Speaks*, ed. Philip S. Foner (Secaucus, NJ: Citadel Press, 1978), 311.

34. "The Marcantonio–Du Bois Television Program," April 3, 1953, Du Bois Papers.

35. "Statement by Dr. W. E. B. Du Bois," July 12, 1950, Du Bois Papers.

36. "The Marcantonio–Du Bois Television Program," Du Bois Papers.

37. Dorothy Burnham, "American Women Join World Peace Crusade," in *Organize, Fight, Win: Black Communist Women's Political Writing*, ed. Charisse Burden-Stelly and Jodi Dean (London: Verso, 2022), 259.

38. John Pittman, "The Struggle for Peace," *Masses and Mainstream* (February 1952): 37–43.

39. Ellis, " 'Negro Subversion,' " 66.

40. Patterson, *We Charge Genocide*, 27.

41. Patterson, 144.

42. Civil Rights Congress Chapter Bulletin, January 4, 1952, CPUSA Papers.

43. Patterson, *We Charge Genocide*, 120–21.

44. W. E. B. Du Bois, *I Take My Stand for Peace* (New York: Masses and Mainstream, Inc., 1951), 7.

45. Du Bois, 7.

46. Du Bois, 9–10.

47. Du Bois, 10.

48. Du Bois, 11–12.

49. Du Bois, "African Roots of War," 709.

50. Du Bois, 709.

51. Du Bois, 709–10.

52. Du Bois, 714.

53. Du Bois, "I Take My Stand for Peace," 12.

54. Du Bois, 13.

55. Eric Hobsbawm, "Lenin and the 'Aristocracy of Labor,' " *Monthly Review* 21, no 11 (April 1970): 50.

56. V. I. Lenin, "Imperialism and the Split in Socialism," in *V. I. Lenin: Collected Works*, vol. 23, *August 1916–March 1917* (Moscow: Progress Publishers, 1974 [1964]), 113, 116–17.

57. V. I. Lenin, "A Caricature of Marxism and Imperialist Economism," in *V. I. Lenin: Collected Works*, vol. 23, *August 1916–March 1917* (Moscow: Progress Publishers, 1974 [1964]), 55–56.

58. V. I. Lenin, "Preliminary Draft of Theses on the Agrarian Questions for the Second Congress of the Communist International," in *V. I. Lenin: Selected Works in Three Volumes*, vol. 3 (New York: International Publishers, 1967), 428.

59. Charles Post, "The Myth of the Labor Aristocracy, Part I," 2006, https://www.marxists .org/history/etol/newspape/atc/128.html; Post, "The 'Labor Aristocracy' and Working-Class Struggles: Consciousness in Flux, Part 2," 2006, https://www.marxists.org/history/etol/newspape /atc/129.html.

60. Du Bois, "I Take My Stand for Peace," 6.

61. Du Bois, 14.

62. Du Bois, 15.

63. The genocidal conspiracy against Black people was as follows: "We find written law, wage scales and other economic facts, the legal opinions of courts, the incitements of officials, the policies and measures of government, legislative acts and failures to act, the deliberate use of the police and the courts, the discriminatory practices of Big Business, discrimination and segregation by federal, state, and county governments, all combining over a long period of years to one invariable result—the systemic institutionalized genocidal oppression of the Negro people of the United States for profit. Such a massive result is not possible without a prior concurrence or agreement. This conspiracy is synchronized so skillfully that not only do the acts of the judicial,

legislative, and executive branches of the Federal Government sustain each in contributing to the desired end, but Federal acts mesh with the similar acts of the subordinate governmental groups on state, county, and municipal levels. The constant and invariable result is discrimination in employment, low wages, bad housing, denial of medical treatment, enforced living in ghettoes, denial of equality of accommodations and services as well as equality in courts, enforced by a combination of genocidal terror and racist law, the whole contributing to the giant profits of monopoly. . . . It is the result of the actions of human beings willfully acting together to write and physically, economically, and judicially sustain racist law that deprives the Negro people of the right to vote or to organize for their political and economic advancement. It is the result of a conspiracy, we repeat, to commit genocide for profit, a conspiracy engineered and directed by monopoly and executed by its state power." Patterson, *We Charge Genocide*, 134.

64. Patterson, 196.

65. Committee on Un-American Activities, US House of Representatives, *Report on the Communist "Peace" Offensive: A Campaign to Disarm and Defeat the United States* (Washington, DC: Government Printing Office, 1951), 2–3.

66. James L. Clayton, "The Impact of the Cold War on the Economies of California and Utah," *Pacific Historical Review* 36, no. 4 (November 1967): 449–73; Ann Markusen, "Dismantling the Cold War Economy," *World Policy Journal* 9, no. 3 (Summer 1992): 389–99.

67. Committee on Un-American Activities, US House of Representatives, "100 Things You Should Know about Communism in the U.S.A.," 89.

68. Robbie Lieberman, "Does That Make Peace a Bad Word? American Responses to the Communist Peace Offensive, 1949–1950," *Peace & Change* 17, no. 2 (April 1992): 201–3.

69. These include the American League for Peace and Democracy: "The largest of the Communist 'front' movements in the United States, [it] . . . contends publicly that it is not a Communist-front movement, yet at the very beginning Communists dominated it. Earl Browder was its vice-president. . . . An examination of the program of the American League will show that the organization was nothing more nor less than a bold advocate of treason"; American Peace Crusade: "part of Soviet psychological warfare against the United States . . . seek[ing] to paralyze America's will to resist Communist aggression by idealizing Russia's aims and methods, discrediting the United States, spreading defeatism and demoralization"; National Labor Conference for Peace: "The Communists' 'peace' movement in the United States also made special efforts to drum up support in the vital field of American labor. In this phase of the campaign, Communist-controlled unions and Communist labor figures played an important role. With their aid a new, nation-wide 'peace' front was organized—the National Labor Conference for Peace"; Northern California Peace Crusade: "All of these misnamed 'peace' organizations continue to have a common objective: The dissemination of Communist propaganda aimed at discrediting the United States and promoting a dangerous relaxation in the ideological and military strength of our country"; and the World Peace Congress: "Cited as being among Communist 'peace' conferences which 'have been organized under Communist initiative in various countries throughout the world as part of a campaign against the North Atlantic Defense Pact.'" Committee on Un-American Activities, US House of Representatives, *Organized Communism in the United States* (Washington, DC: Government Printing Office, 1954), 13–96.

70. Gerald Horne, *Black and Red: W. E. B. Du Bois and the Afro-American Response to the Cold War, 1944–1963* (Albany: State University of New York Press, 1986), 137.

71. Robbie Lieberman, "'Another Side of the Story': African American Intellectuals Speak Out for Peace and Freedom during the Early Cold War Years," in *Anticommunism and the*

African American Freedom Movement: Another Side of the Story, ed. Robbie Lieberman and
Clarence Lang (New York: Palgrave MacMillan, 2009), 17–50.

72. Horne, *Black and Red*, 128.

73. Elizabeth Moos, "Report on W. E. B. Du Bois's Indictment and Trial," December 1951,
Du Bois Papers.

74. Moos, "Report on W. E. B. Du Bois's Indictment and Trial."

75. Quoted in Marcus Anthony Hunter and Zandria F. Robinson *Chocolate Cities: The Black
Map of American Life* (Berkeley: University of California Press, 2018), 164.

76. Committee on Un-American Activities, US House of Representatives, *Organized Communism in the United States* (Washington, DC: Government Printing Office, 1954), 95.

77. Horne, *Black and Red*, 126.

78. David Levering Lewis, *W. E. B. Du Bois: The Fight for Equality and the American Century,
1919–1963* (New York: Henry Hold and Company, 2002), 546.

79. Horne, *Black and Red*, 134.

80. Horne, 126, 133.

81. Horne, 128.

82. Martha Biondi, *To Stand and Fight: The Struggle for Civil Rights in Postwar New York City*
(Cambridge, MA: Harvard University Press, 2003), 160-61.

83. Committee on Un-American Activities, US House of Representatives, *Report on the
Communist "Peace" Offensive: A Campaign to Disarm and Defeat the United States.*

84. Lieberman, "Does That Make Peace a Bad Word?," 213–14.

85. W. E. B. Du Bois, *The Autobiography of W. E. B. Du Bois: A Soliloquy on Viewing My Life
from the Last Decade of Its First Century* (New York: International Publishers, 1968), 358–59.

86. Manning Marable, "Peace and Black Liberation: The Contributions of W. E. B. Du Bois."
Science and Society 47, no. 4 (1983/1984): 402.

87. Lewis, *W. E. B. Du Bois: The Fight for Equality and the American Century, 1919–1963*, 547.

88. *New York Daily Mirror*, February 10, 1951; *Amsterdam News*, April 21, 1951.

89. Moos, "Report on W. E. B. Du Bois's Indictment and Trial."

90. Du Bois, *The Autobiography of W. E. B. Du Bois*, 389.

91. Horne, *Black and Red*, 151.

92. Moos, "Report on W. E. B. Du Bois's Indictment and Trial."

93. "Rogge Testifies for Govt. in DuBois Trial," *National Guardian*, November 21, 1951.

94. Moos, "Report on W. E. B. Du Bois's Indictment and Trial."

95. Du Bois, *The Autobiography of W. E. B. Du Bois*, 375; Hunter and Robinson, *Chocolate
Cities: The Black Map of American Life*, 218.

96. "Peace Information Center VINDICATED," *National Guardian*, December 5, 1951. Moos
wrote that it was improbable that the jury would have convicted them, given that there were eight
Negroes and four whites on the jury. Two Negro jurors told them after the trial, "We could see the
government didn't have anything on you." Moos, "Report on W. E. B. Du Bois's Indictment and Trial."

Chapter Seven

1. "An Open Letter to the President of the United States," CPUSA Papers, Box 31.

2. James Jackson, "The First Amendment or the Last Liberty," CPUSA Papers, Box 31.

3. Eldridge F. Dowell, *A History of Criminal Syndicalism Legislation in the United States* (Baltimore: Johns Hopkins University Press, 1939), 109.

4. *Investigation Activities of the Department of Justice: Letter from the Attorney General Transmitting in Response to a Senate Resolution of October 17, 1919, a Report on the Activities of the Bureau of Investigation of the Department of Justice against Persons Advising Anarchy, Sedition, and the Forcible Overthrow of the Government*, Senate Document No. 153. (Washington, DC: Government Printing Office, November 17, 1919), 8–9.

5. *Investigation Activities of Department of Justice*, 12.

6. Dowell, *A History of Criminal Syndicalism Legislation in the United States*, 14–16.

7. Joey McCarty, "The Red Scare in Arkansas: A Southern State and National Hysteria," *Arkansas Historical Quarterly* 37, no. 3 (Autumn 1978): 268.

8. Dowell, *A History of Criminal Syndicalism Legislation in the United States*, 14–16.

9. On the long history of Texas's antiradical and anti-Black policy and practice, see Gerald Horne, *The Counterrevolution of 1836: Texas Slavery and Jim Crow and the Roots of US Fascism* (New York: International Publishers, 2022).

10. Gus Hall-Benjamin J. Davis Defense Committee, "Anti-Communism in the United States," CPUSA Papers, Box 31, Folder 23, 2.

11. Dowell, *A History of Criminal Syndicalism Legislation in the United States*, 16.

12. William M. Wiecek, "The Legal Foundations of Domestic Anticommunism: The Background of *Dennis v. United States*," *Supreme Court Review* 2001, no. 8 (2001): 393.

13. Legislative Committee of the People's Freedom Union, *The Truth about the Lusk Committee* (New York: Nation Press, Inc., 1920), 7.

14. Legislative Committee of the People's Freedom Union 7.

15. Legislative Committee of the People's Freedom Union, 8.

16. Legislative Committee of the People's Freedom Union, 3–4.

17. Legislative Committee of the People's Freedom Union, 5–6.

18. *Revolutionary Radicalism*, 11.

19. *Revolutionary Radicalism*, 17.

20. *Revolutionary Radicalism*, 14.

21. *Revolutionary Radicalism*, 28.

22. Legislative Committee of the People's Freedom Union, *The Truth about the Lusk Committee*, 21.

23. *Revolutionary Radicalism*, 20–21.

24. *Revolutionary Radicalism*, 27.

25. Legislative Committee of the People's Freedom Union, *The Truth about the Lusk Committee*, 17–18.

26. Legislative Committee of the People's Freedom Union, 22.

27. *Investigation Activities of Department of Justice*.

28. *Investigation Activities of Department of Justice*, 13.

29. Mark Ellis, "J. Edgar Hoover and the 'Red Summer' of 1919," *Journal of American Studies* 28, no. 1 (April 1994): 53–54.

30. Ellis, 55.

31. *Revolutionary Radicalism*, 1476.

32. *Revolutionary Radicalism*.

33. *Revolutionary Radicalism*, 1145.

34. *Revolutionary Radicalism*, 1463.

35. *Revolutionary Radicalism*, 1476–77.

36. *Revolutionary Radicalism*, 1479–80.

37. *Revolutionary Radicalism*, 1480.

38. *Negro Year Book*, 55–56.

39. *Revolutionary Radicalism*, 1481.

40. *Investigation Activities of Department of Justice*, 172.

41. *Investigation Activities of Department of Justice*, 184.

42. *Investigation Activities of Department of Justice*, 172–79.

43. *Investigation Activities of Department of Justice*, 180, 181, 183.

44. *Investigation Activities of Department of Justice*, 179.

45. Oliver Treib et al., "Modes of Governance: Toward a Conceptual Clarification," *Journal of European Public Policy* 14, no. 1 (January 2007): 5.

46. Robert Griffith, "American Politics and the Origins of McCarthyism," in *The Specter: Original Essays on the Cold War and the Origins of McCarthyism*, ed. Robert Griffith and Athan Theoharis (New York: New Viewpoints, 1974), 13–14.

47. See Burden-Stelly, "Constructing Deportable Subjectivity: Antiforeignness, Antiradicalism, and Antiblackness during the McCarthyist Structure of Feeling," 342–58.

48. Barbara Ransby, *Eslanda: The Large and Unconventional Life of Mrs. Paul Robeson* (New Haven, CT: Yale University Press, 2013), 224.

49. Treib et al., "Modes of Governance," 6.

50. Treib et al., 15.

51. Treib et al., 15–16.

52. Treib et al., 3.

53. Treib et al., 4.

54. Treib et al., 4.

55. Bristol et al., *Anatomy of Anti-Communism*, 2.

56. Bristol et al., 33, 36.

57. Gus Hall-Benjamin J. Davis Defense Committee, "Anti-Communism in the United States," 4.

58. Eslanda Robeson, "A Citizen's State of the Union," *Daily Worker*, March 19, 1953.

59. Gus Hall-Benjamin J. Davis Defense Committee, "Anti-Communism in the United States," 2.

60. Charlotta Bass, *Forty Years: A Memoirs from the Pages of a Newspaper* (Los Angeles: C. A. Bass, 1960), 134.

61. Gus Hall-Benjamin J. Davis Defense Committee, "Anti-Communism in the United States," 4.

62. Julia Brown, *I Testify: My Years as an FBI Undercover Agent* (Boston: Western Islands Publishers, 1966), 29.

63. Brown, 29.

64. Brown, 160–61.

65. Brown, 129–44.

66. Erik McDuffie, *Sojourning for Freedom* (Durham, NC: Duke University Press, 2011), 160.

67. Brown, *I Testify: My Years as an FBI Undercover Agent*, 135.

68. Brown.

69. Brown, 137.

70. Committee of Un-American Activities, House of Representatives, *Communist Activities in the Cleveland, Ohio, Area, Part I* (Washington, DC: Government Printing Office, 1962).

71. Gus Hall-Benjamin J. Davis Defense Committee, "Anti-Communism in the United States," 5.

72. Jelani Cobb, "Antidote to Revolution: African American Anti-Communism and the Struggle for Civil Rights, 1931–1954," PhD diss. (Rutgers, The State University of New Jersey, 2003), 5.

73. Evelyn Brooks Higginbotham, *Righteous Discontent* (Cambridge, MA: Harvard University Press, 1993), 15.

74. Higginbotham, 18.

75. For analyses and critiques that support my argument, see, e.g., National Committee to Defend Negro Leadership, "An Appeal in Defense of Negro Leadership, 1952," Du Bois Papers; Civil Rights Congress, *The "Crimes" of Claude Lightfoot and Junius Scales* (New York: Civil Rights Publication, 1955); and Bass, *Forty Years: A Memoirs from the Pages of a Newspaper*, 134. On the government's aversion to Black radicalism, see, e.g., Committee on Un-American Activities, US House of Representatives, *The American Negro in the Communist Party* (Washington, DC, 1954), 1–13.

76. Manning Marable, *How Capitalism Underdeveloped Black America* (Chicago: Haymarket Books, 1983), 206.

77. Cedric Robinson, *Black Movements* (New York: Routledge, 1997), 124.

78. Adolph L. Reed Jr., "Black Particularity Reconsidered," *Telos* 39 (1979).

79. Reed.

80. Cobb, "Antidote to Revolution: African American Anti-Communism and the Struggle for Civil Rights, 1931–1954," 6.

81. Quoted in Richard Iton, *In Search of the Black Fantastic: Politics of Popular Culture in the Post–Civil Rights Era* (New York: Oxford University Press, 2008), 33–34.

82. Iton, 39–40.

83. Pettis Perry, "Strengthen the NAACP: An Open Letter to the Men and Women of the NAACP from a Negro Communist," 1959, Box 3 Folder 9, Pettis Perry Papers MG 354, Schomburg Center for Research in Black Culture, 11.

84. Perry, 19–20.

85. Perry, 13.

86. Perry, 8; Cobb, "Antidote to Revolution: African American Anti-Communism and the Struggle for Civil Rights, 1931–1954," 3.

87. Frazier, "Dallas Convention of NAACP," Memorandum, July 7, 1954, Box 3, Folder 9, Pettis Perry Papers MG 354, Schomburg Center for Research in Black Culture, 4; Cobb, "Antidote to Revolution: African American Anti-Communism and the Struggle for Civil Rights, 1931–1954," 8.

88. Perry, "Strengthen the NAACP: An Open Letter to the Men and Women of the NAACP from a Negro Communist," 5, 3.

89. Steven F. Lawson, ed., *To Secure These Rights: The Report of President Harry S. Truman's Committee on Civil Rights* (Boston: Bedford/St. Martin's, 2004), 85–89.

90. Lawson, 61–11, 164–80.

91. Frazier, "Dallas Convention of NAACP," 2–4. On the NAACP's usage of anticommunism as a tool of racial liberalism, see Carole Anderson, *Eyes Off the Prize: The United Nations and the African American Freedom Struggle, 1944–1955* (Cambridge: Cambridge University Press, 2003), and Anderson, *Bourgeois Radicals: The NAACP and the Struggle for Colonial Liberation, 1941–1960* (Cambridge: Cambridge University Press, 2015).

92. Wiecek, "The Legal Foundations of Domestic Anticommunism," 384.

93. According to the historian Ellen Schrecker, "The federal government was the crucial actor here; its activities transformed the Communist party from an unpopular political group into a perceived threat to the American way of life. But the government's campaign against communism was not monolithic. Different branches adopted different and sometimes competing strategies for handling the communist threat. That competition simply intensified the anticommunist furor as politicians and bureaucrats struggled to gain attention or to ensure that they would not be seen as coddling Communists or worse. Central to the process was a strategically situated network of full-time anti-Communists like J. Edgar Hoover who had dedicated themselves to eliminating communism from all positions of influence in American life. Some of these people were in the government, some outside. Politicians, bureaucrats, journalists, and professional witnesses, they knew each other and collaborated in a surprisingly self-conscious manner. Together they managed to structure much of the campaign against domestic communism and bring it to the forefront of American political life." Ellen Schrecker, "McCarthyism: Political Repression and the Fear of Communism," *Social Research* 71, no. 4 (Winter 2004): 1043–44.

94. Gus Hall-Benjamin J. Davis Defense Committee, "Anti-Communism in the United States," n.p.

95. Griffith, "American Politics and the Origins of McCarthyism," 14.

96. Willmoore Kendall, *The Conservative Affirmation* (Chicago, 1963), 77.

97. Ronald Lora, "A View from the Right: Conservative Intellectuals, the Cold War, and McCarthy," in *The Specter: Original Essays on the Cold War and the Origins of McCarthyism*, ed. Robert Griffith and Athan Theoharis (New York: New Viewpoints, 1974), 64.

98. Wiecek, "The Legal Foundations of Domestic Anticommunism," 378.

99. Griffith, "American Politics and the Origins of McCarthyism," 5.

100. Wiecek, "The Legal Foundations of Domestic Anticommunism," 393.

101. Griffith, "American Politics and the Origins of McCarthyism," 15.

102. Laura McEnaney, "Cold War Mobilization and Domestic Politics: The United States," in *The Cambridge History of the Cold War*, vol. 1, 429.

103. Gid Power, *Not without Honor: The History of American Anticommunism* (New York: Free Press, 1995), 249.

104. Power, 249–50.

105. Power, 250–52.

106. Power, 254.

107. Paul L. Murphy, "Sources and Nature of Intolerance in the 1920s," *Journal of American History* 51, no. 1 (June 1964): 62.

108. Robbie Lieberman, ed., *History in Dispute: The Red Scare after 1945* (Detroit: St. James Press, 2005), 249.

109. Hugh Davis Graham and Ted Robert Gurr, eds., *Violence in America* (New York: Frederick A. Praeger, 1969), 97.

110. Anthony Monteiro, "Race and Empire: W. E. B. Du Bois and the U.S. State," *Black Scholar* 37, no. 2 (Summer 2007): 38.

111. Goldfield, *The Color of Politics*, 30.

112. Michael Goldfield, "The Racial Divide and the Class Struggle in the United States," *Journal of Labor and Society* 11, no. 3 (September 2008): 323.

113. "Anti-American Propaganda Charged to Communist Party," 1930, CPUSA Papers, Box 31, Folder 33.

114. Griffler, *What Price Alliance? Black Radicals Confront White Labor, 1918–1938*, 12.

115. Philp S. Foner, *American Socialism and Black Americans: From the Age of Jackson to World War II* (Westport, CT: Greenwood Press, 1977), 359. Also see Cedric Robinson, *Black Marxism: The Making of the Black Radical Tradition* (London: Zed Books, 1983), 266–77.

116. "There is No Race Problem," *New Solidarity*, September 27, 1919, in *The Black Worker*, vol. 5, *From 1900–1919*, ed. Philip S. Foner and Ronald L. Lewis (Philadelphia: Temple University Press, 2019 [1980]), 530.

117. Quoted in William P. Jones, "Review: 'Nothing Special to Offer the Negro': Revisiting the 'Debsian View' of the Negro Question," *International Labor and Working-Class History* 74 (Fall 2008): 215.

118. Richard B. Moore, "Problems and Struggles of the Negro Workers," *Daily Worker*, June 6, 1929, 6. Emphasis added.

119. Jones, "Review: 'Nothing Special to Offer the Negro': Revisiting the 'Debsian View' of the Negro Question," 222.

120. Keith P. Griffler, "The Black Radical Intellectual and the Black Worker: The Emergence of a Program for Black Labor, 1918–1938" (Ohio State University, 1993) Schomburg Center for Black Culture, New York Public Libraries, 40.

121. Foner, "The IWW and the Black Worker," 59.

122. Cole, *Ben Fletcher*, 42.

123. Cole, 226.

124. *Marcus Garvey Life and Lessons*, ed. Robert A. Hill, 296–99. For a detailed and critical discussion of Marcus Garvey's relationship to communism and anticommunism, see Winston James, "To the East Turn: The Russian Revolution and the Black Radical Imagination in the United States, 1917–1924," *American Historical Review* 126, no. 3 (September 2021): 1001–45.

125. Garvey, "Why the Black Star Line Failed," 140–41.

126. Marcus Garvey, "The Communists and the Negro," in *Marcus Garvey and the Vision of Africa*, ed. John Henrik Clarke (Baltimore: Black Classic Press, 1974), 318–19.

127. Tony Martin, "Some Aspects of the Political Ideas of Marcus Garvey," in *Marcus Garvey and the Vision of Africa*, ed. John Henrik Clarke (Baltimore: Black Classic Press, 1974), 436–37.

128. George Padmore, *Pan-Africanism or Communism* (Garden City, NY: Doubleday and Company, Inc., 1971), 282–84.

129. Martin, "Some Aspects of the Political Ideas of Marcus Garvey," 436–37.

130. Padmore, *Pan-Africanism or Communism*, 287–89.

131. Eric Arnesen, "No 'Graver Danger': Black Anticommunism, the Communist Party, and the Race Question," *Labor: Studies in Working-Class History of the Americas* 3, no. 4 (2006): 15.

132. Arnesen, 26–30.

Chapter Eight

1. "Civil Rights Congress Analysis on Circuit Court of Appeals in the Case of Communist Leaders," Box 146, CPUSA Papers.

2. Patterson, "America and the World Significance of Negro-White Unity: The Deepening Crisis of Racism."

3. Patterson, "America and the World Significance of Negro-White Unity: The Deepening Crisis of Racism."

4. Jerold S. Auerbach, "The La Follette Committee and the CIO," *Wisconsin Magazine of History*, 48, no. 1 (Autumn 1964): 3–20; Auberbach, "The La Follette Committee: Labor and Civil Liberties in the New Deal," *Journal of American History* 51, no. 3 (December 1964): 435–45.

5. Patterson, "We Charge Genocide," speech.

6. Frances Fox Piven and Richard Cloward, *Poor People's Movements* (New York: Pantheon, 1977), 185.

7. Patterson, "We Charge Genocide," speech, 5–6.

8. National Popular Government League, *To the American People* (Washington, DC, 1920), 8.

9. National Popular Government League, 5–7.

10. National Popular Government League, 4–6.

11. National Popular Government League, 3.

12. Justin Goldstein, *American Blacklist: The Attorney General's List of Subversive Organizations* (Lawrence: University Press of Kansas, 2008), 45, 49.

13. Goldstein, xi.

14. Goldstein, xiv, xvi.

15. Goldstein, 25–26.

16. Goldstein, 25, 35.

17. Goldstein, 52, 56.

18. Goldstein, 139.

19. Goldstein, 140.

20. Gus Hall-Benjamin J. Davis Defense Committee, "Anti-Communism in the United States," 5.

21. J. Edgar Hoover, *J. Edgar Hoover on Communism* (New York: Random House, 1969), 78, 79.

22. Hoover, 53–54, 102.

23. Hoover, 103–4.

24. Hoover, 54.

25. Hoover, 102.

26. Hoover, 105.

27. Hoover, 110.

28. Hoover, 114.

29. Hoover, 130.

30. Hoover, 130–31.

31. Hoover, 131–32.

32. Hoover, 76.

33. Hoover, 72.

34. Hoover, 67–68.

35. Hoover, 63–64.

36. Hoover, 80–81.

37. Hoover, 85.

38. Hoover, 86.

39. Hoover, 111.

40. Hoover, 55.

41. Hoover, 116–17.

42. Hoover, 103, 104.

43. Stein, *The World of Marcus Garvey*, 190.

44. Stein, 191.

45. Elkins, "'Unrest among the Negroes': A British Document of 1919," 66.

46. G. E. Chamberlin, US Consul, Georgetown, British Guiana, to the Secretary of State, Washington, DC, May 9, 1919, National Archives, R. G. 28, Unarranged Box no. 53, File no. 398.

47. Elkins, "'Unrest among the Negroes': A British Document of 1919," 66–67.

48. Elkins, 70.

49. Elkins, 70.

50. Elkins, 74.

51. Newton, *FBI Encyclopedia*, 345.

52. Stein, *The World of Marcus Garvey*, 190.

53. E. David Cronon, *Black Moses: The Story of Marcus Garvey and the Universal Negro Improvement Association* (Madison: University of Wisconsin Press, 1969 [1955]), 99. This claim is disputed by Judith Stein, who argues that there was no correlation between the BI's antiradicalism toward Garvey and the Shipping Board's decision to double the bond and delay the sale. Stein, *The World of Marcus Garvey*, 137–39.

54. "Complaint against Marcus Garvey," January 12, 1922, *Marcus Garvey*, vol. 2, 340–41.

55. Stein, *The World of Marcus Garvey*, 191.

56. "First Indictment of Marcus Garvey, Elie Garcia, George Tobias, and Orlando M. Thompson," *Marcus Garvey*, vol. 2, 513–19.

57. Stein, *The World of Marcus Garvey*, 195–96, 200.

58. Stein, 202.

59. Stein, 204.

60. Stein, 205.

61. Stein, 206.

62. Stein, 207.

63. Cronon, *Black Moses*, 118.

64. "Speech by Marcus Garvey," September 13, 1923, vol. 5, 448.

65. Kenneth D. Ackerman, *Young J. Edgar* (Cambridge, MA: Da Capo, 2008), 62.

66. Stein, *The World of Marcus Garvey*, 189.

67. Hill, "'The Foremost Radical Among His Race': Marcus Garvey and the Black Scare, 1918–1921," 226–28.

68. Hill, 229.

69. "Speech by Marcus Garvey," September 13, 1923, vol. 5, 451.

70. Stein, *The World of Marcus Garvey*, 201.

71. Stein, 1919n11.

72. Gus Hall-Benjamin J. Davis Defense Committee, "Anti-Communism in the United States," 5.

73. Wiecek, "The Legal Foundations of Domestic Anticommunism: The Background of *Dennis v. United States*," 377.

74. Laura Weinrib, *The Taming of Free Speech: America's Civil Liberties Compromise* (Cambridge, MA: Harvard University Press, 2016), 4.

75. Weinrib, 4.

76. Weinrib, 7–11.

77. Weinrib, 7–11.

78. Thomas, "*Rouge et Noir* Reread," 2601.

79. Thomas, 2686.

80. Thomas, 2648.

81. Thomas, 2661.

82. Charles M. Martin, *The Angelo Herndon Case and Southern Justice* (Baton Rouge: Louisiana State University Press, 1976), xiii.

83. Herndon, *Let Me Live*, 221.

84. Herndon, 223–25.

85. Herndon, 234–35.

86. Thomas, "*Rouge et Noir* Reread," 2634.

87. Thomas, 2639.

88. Herndon, *Let Me Live*, 237–38. Thomas, "*Rouge et Noir* Reread," 2639.

89. Thomas, "*Rouge et Noir* Reread," 2641.

90. Herndon, *Let Me Live*, 6–7.

91. Thomas, "*Rouge et Noir* Reread," 2688.

92. Martin, "Communists and Blacks: The ILD and The Angelo Herndon Case," 138.

93. Martin, 132.

94. Thomas, "*Rouge et Noir* Reread" 2602.

95. Martin, "Communists and Blacks: The ILD and The Angelo Herndon Case," 139.

96. See Charisse Burden-Stelly and Gerald Horne, *W. E. B. Du Bois: A Life in American History* (Santa Barbara, CA: ABC-CLIO, 2019), 119.

97. Elizabeth Lawson, *20 Years on the Chain Gang?* (New York: International Labor Defense, 1935), 9.

98. Thomas, "*Rouge et Noir* Reread," 2694.

99. Herndon, *Let Me Live*, 286–87.

100. Herndon, 296.

101. Martin, *The Angelo Herndon Case and Southern Justice*, 143.

102. Martin, 143–44.

103. Martin, 144.

104. Martin, 146–47.

105. Martin, "Communists and Blacks: The ILD and The Angelo Herndon Case," 136.

106. Thomas, "*Rouge et Noir* Reread," 2701.

107. Thomas, 2702.

108. Martin, "Communists and Blacks: The ILD and The Angelo Herndon Case," 135.

109. *The Angelo Herndon Case and Southern Justice*, 150.

110. "Federal Jurisdiction. Power of Supreme Court to Determine Constitutional Questions Which Arise because of Unexpected Action of State Appellate Court. Herndon Case," *Columbia Law Review* 35, no. 7 (November 1935): 1137.

111. Osmond K. Frankel, "Constitutional Issues in the Supreme Court, 1934 Term," *University of Pennsylvania Law Review* 84, no. 3–4 (January 1936): 386.

112. "Federal Jurisdiction. Power of Supreme Court to Determine Constitutional Questions Which Arise because of Unexpected Action of State Appellate Court. Herndon Case," 1146.

113. Lawson, *20 Years on the Chain Gang?*, 12.

114. Lawson, 8.

115. Herndon, *Let Me Live*, 316.

116. Martin, *The Angelo Herndon Case and Southern Justice*, 158.

117. Martin, 164.

118. Martin, 168–70.

119. Martin, 176.

120. Thomas, "*Rouge et Noir* Reread," 2600.

121. Martin, *The Angelo Herndon Case and Southern Justice*, 183.

122. Martin, 184.

123. Martin, 187–88, 190.

Chapter Nine

1. Gus Hall-Benjamin J. Davis Defense Committee, "Anti-Communism in the United States," 2.

2. Gus Hall-Benjamin J. Davis Defense Committee, 2–3.

3. Gus Hall-Benjamin J. Davis Defense Committee, 2–3.

4. Gus Hall-Benjamin J. Davis Defense Committee, 3.

5. "Espionage Act of 1917," June 15, 1917, https://iowaculture.gov/sites/default/files/primary-sources/pdfs/history-education-pss-wwi-espionageact-PDF-new.pdf.

6. Ellis, *Race, War, and Surveillance*, 103.

7. Ted Morgan, *Reds: McCarthyism in Twentieth-Century America* (New York: Random House, 2003), 55.

8. Foner, "The IWW and the Black Worker," 63n48.

9. Mark Solomon, "Coerced Loyalty: Racial Equality as Subversion," *Left History* 5, no. 2 (1997): 77–78.

10. Morgan, *Reds*, 56.

11. Wiecek, "The Legal Foundations of Domestic Anticommunism: The Background of *Dennis v. United States*," 387.

12. Ellis, *Race, War, and Surveillance*, xv.

13. Gerald Horne, *Black and Brown: African Americans and the Mexican Revolution, 1910–1920* (New York: NYU Press, 2005), 166.

14. Horne, 173.

15. Horne, 115–16.

16. Horne, 169.

17. Ellis, *Race, War, and Surveillance*, 17.

18. John S. D. Eisenhower, *Intervention! The United States and the Mexican Revolution, 1913–1917* (New York: Norton, 1993), 212.

19. Charles H. Harris III and Louis R. Sadler, "The Plan of San Diego and the Mexican-United States War Crisis of 1916: A Reexamination," *Hispanic American Historical Review* 58, no. 3 (1978): 381, 406.

20. Horne, *Black and Brown*, 166.

21. Ellis, *Race, War, and Surveillance*, 144.

22. Committee of the Judiciary, *Bolshevik Propaganda, Hearings before a Subcommittee of the Committee on the Judiciary* (Washington, DC: Government Printing Office, 1919), 14, 19.

23. Horne, *Black and Brown*, 173–75.

24. Wilfred A. Domingo, "Socialism Imperilled, or the Negro—A Potential Menace to American Radicalism," in *Class Struggle and the Color Line*, ed. Paul M. Heideman (Chicago: Haymarket Books, 2018), 203; Committee of the Judiciary, *Bolshevik Propaganda, Hearings before a Subcommittee of the Committee on the Judiciary*, 15, 82, 155–56.

25. Cohen, "'The Ku Klux Government': Vigilantism, Lynching, and the Repression of the IWW," 43.

26. Kornweibel, *Investigate Everything*, 273.

27. Foner, "The IWW and the Black Worker," 48, 50.

28. Mary Ovington White, "The Status of the Negro in the United States," *New Review*, September 1913, 747–48.

29. James Smethurst, *The African American Roots of Modernism: From Reconstruction to the Harlem Renaissance* (Chapel Hill: University of North Carolina Press, 2011), 135, 136.

30. Domingo, "Socialism Imperilled, or the Negro—A Potential Menace to American Radicalism," 205.

31. Foner, "The IWW and the Black Worker," 51.

32. Foner, 49.

33. William D. Jones, "Solidarity—Black & White," *Messenger*, September 1923, 812.

34. Cole, *Ben Fletcher*, 115.

35. Foner, "The IWW and the Black Worker," 51.

36. "Solving the Race Problem," *Messenger*, July 1921, 215.

37. "The Task of Local 8," *Messenger*, October 1921, 263.

38. Cole, *Ben Fletcher*, 33.

39. Cole, 30.

40. Cole, 25.

41. "Solving the Race Problem," *Messenger*, July 1921, 214.

42. "Shaven IWWs Kiss as Trial Is Postponed," *Chicago Tribune*, April 2, 1918, 7.

43. Cole, *Ben Fletcher*, 27, 29.

44. Kornweibel, *Investigate Everything*, 273.

45. Cole, *Ben Fletcher*, 29.

46. Quoted in William D. Haywood, *Big Bill Haywood's Book: The Autobiography of William D. Haywood* (New York: International Publishers, 1929), 179.

47. Foner, "The IWW and the Black Worker," 58.

48. Gus Hall-Benjamin J. Davis Defense Committee, "Anti-Communism in the United States," 13.

49. American Civil Liberties Union, "Still the Fish Committee Nonsense," May 1932.

50. I. Amter, "They Will Investigate the Communist Party," *Daily Worker*, June 13, 1930.

51. "Red Activities in This Country to Be Probed by Congress," *International Labor News Service*, June 5, 1930(?).

52. "Anti-American Propaganda Charged to Communist Party,"; "Justice Dept. Fears Negroes," *Daily Worker*, June 10, 1930.

53. On antiforeignness, see Charisse Burden-Stelly, "Constructing Deportable Subjectivity: Anti-foreignness, Antiradicalism, and Antiblackness During the McCarthyist Structure of Feeling," 342–58.

54. Charles M. Kelley, "Organized Labor Bars Communism," November 27, 1930, CPUSA Papers, Box 31.

55. James Ford, *The Negro and the Democratic Front* (New York: International Publishers, 1938), 23, 25.

56. Kelley, "Organized Labor Bars Communism."

57. Kelley.

58. Kelley.

59. Kelley.

60. International Labor Defense press release, June 5, 1930.

61. Griffith, "American Politics and the Origins of McCarthyism," 7.

62. Griffith, 7.

63. Doxey Wilkerson, "Mississippi's Ranking Enters Harlem Politics," n.d., Doxey Wilkerson Papers, Box 19, Folder 6, 3.

64. Wilkerson, 1–2.

65. Horne, *Black Liberation / Red Scare*, 160, 164.

66. Committee on Un-American Activities. *The American Negro and the Communist Party* (Washington, DC: Government Printing Office, 1954), v.

67. Committee of One Thousand, Statement on proposed Subversive Activities Control Act of 1948, April 23, 1948, Du Bois Papers, https://credo.library.umass.edu/view/pageturn/mums 312-b117-i481/#page/1/mode/1up.

68. Schrecker, *The Age of McCarthyism*, 66, 69, 70.

69. Schrecker, 63.

70. Newton, *FBI Encyclopedia*, 156.

71. Committee of One Thousand, Statement on proposed Subversive Activities Control Act of 1948, April 23, 1948, Du Bois Papers, https://credo.library.umass.edu/view/pageturn/mums 312-b117-i481/#page/1/mode/1up.

72. Committee on Un-American Activities, US House of Representatives, "100 Things You Should Know about Communism in the U.S.A.," 20.

73. Committee of One Thousand, Statement on proposed Subversive Activities Control Act of 1948, April 23, 1948, Du Bois Papers, https://credo.library.umass.edu/view/pageturn/mums 312-b117-i481/#page/1/mode/1up.

74. Gus Hall-Benjamin J. Davis Defense Committee, "Anti-Communism in the United States," 6.

75. Committee on Un-American Activities, US House of Representatives, *Organized Communism in the United States* 108.

76. Griffith, "American Politics and the Origins of McCarthyism," 8.

77. Griffith, 8.

78. Griffith, 16.

79. Carole Boyce Davies, *Left of Karl Marx: The Political Life of Black Communist Claudia Jones* (Durham, NC: Duke University Press, 2008), 149.

80. Claude Lightfoot, *Chicago Slums to World Politics: Autobiography of Claude Lightfoot* (New York: International Publishers, 1985), 111–12.

81. Claudia Jones, "Autobiographical History," in *Claudia Jones: Beyond Containment*, ed. Carole Boyce Davies (Boulder, CO: Lynne Reiner Publishers, 2011), 14.

82. Jones, *Ben Davis*, 12–13.

83. Lightfoot, *Chicago Slums to World Politics*, 112; Johnson, *I Think of My Mother*, 131.

84. Horne, *Black Liberation / Red Scare*, 210.

85. Pettis Perry, "Your Honor, in Addressing Myself," n.d. [1953], Pettis Perry Papers, Box 4, Folder 5, 17.

86. Lightfoot, *Chicago Slums to World Politics*, 114; Claudia Jones, ". . . [Black] Women Can Think and Speak and Write!," in *Claudia Jones: Beyond Containment*, ed. Carole Boyce Davies (Boulder, CO: Lynne Reiner Publishers, 2011), 8.

87. Hunton, *Alphaeus Hunton*, 84.

88. Jones, *Ben Davis*, 12.

89. Benjamin J. Davis Jr., *Communist Councilman from Harlem: Autobiographical Notes Written in a Federal Penitentiary* (New York: International Publishers, 1991), 182.

90. Civil Rights Congress, *The "Crimes" of Claude Lightfoot and Junius Scales* (New York: Civil Rights Congress, 1955), 4–10.

91. Jones, "[Black] Women Can Think," 7.

92. Hunton, *Alphaeus Hunton*, 79.

93. Davies, "Deportable Subjects," 957–8.

94. American Committee for the Protection of the Foreign Born, *Repeal the Walter Mc-Carran Law*, 1950, Du Bois Papers, http://credo.library.umass.edu/view/full/mums312-b157-i322.

95. Benjamin J. Davis Jr., *Ben Davis on the McCarran Act at the Harvard Law Forum* (New York: Gus Hall-Benjamin J. Davis Defense Committee, n.d.), 12.

96. Lightfoot, *Chicago Slums to World Politics*, 112.

97. James Jackson, "The First Amendment or the Last Liberty," CPUSA Papers, Box 31.

98. Jackson.

99. Bass, *Forty Years: Memoirs from the Pages of a Newspaper*, 189.

100. Johnson, *I Think of My Mother*, 29.

101. Claudia Jones, "I Was Deported Because . . . ," in *Claudia Jones: Beyond Containment*, ed. Carole. Boyce Davies (Boulder, CO: Lynne Reiner Publishers, 2011), 16.

102. Jones, 16.

103. Jones, 17.

104. Johnson, *I Think of My Mother*, 129.

105. Johnson, 13.

106. Gus Hall-Benjamin J. Davis Defense Committee, "Anti-Communism in the United States," 10, 12.

107. Gus Hall-Benjamin J. Davis Defense Committee, "Anti-Communism in the United States," 12.

108. Gus Hall-Benjamin J. Davis Defense Committee, "Anti-Communism in the United States," 7.

Chapter Ten

1. Michael Paul Rogin, *Ronald Reagan The Movie and Other Episodes in Political Demonology* (Berkeley: University of California Press, 1987).

2. William R. Tanner and Robert Griffith, "Legislative Politics and 'McCarthyism': The Internal Security Act of 1950," in *The Specter: Original Essays on the Cold War and the Origins of McCarthyism*, ed. Robert Griffith and Athan Theoharis (New York: New Viewpoints, 1974), 174.

3. Schrecker, *The Age of McCarthyism*, 194.

4. Lightfoot, *Chicago Slums to World Politics*, 112.

5. Committee on Un-American Activities, *Hearings before the Committee on Un-American Activities, June 12 and 13, 1956* (Washington, DC: Government Printing Office, 1956), 4504–9.

6. Michael Joseph Roberto, *The Coming of the American Behemoth: The Origins of Fascism in the United States, 1920–1940* (New York: Monthly Review Press, 2018), 58.

7. Roberto, 34–35.

8. Roberto, 35.

9. Roberto, 53.

10. Roberto, 134.

11. Roberto, 180.

12. Wiecek, "The Legal Foundations of Domestic Anticommunism: The Background of *Dennis v. United States*," 381.

13. Rogin, *Ronald Reagan The Movie and Other Episodes in Political Demonology*, 58, 55.

14. For the link between the Indigenous Red Scare and the discourse of terrorism, see Joanne Barker, *Red Scare: The State's Indigenous Terrorist* (Berkeley: University of California Press, 2021).

15. Rogin, *Ronald Reagan The Movie*, 50–51.

16. Nick Estes, *Our History Is the Future: Standing Rock versus the Dakota Access Pipeline, and the Long Tradition of Indigenous Resistance* (London: Verso, 2019), 107.

17. Estes, 107.

18. Estes, 107.

19. Kyle T. Mayes, *An Afro-Indigenous History of the United States* (Boston: Beacon Press, 2021), 56–57.

20. Barker, *Red Scare*, 10–11.

21. O'Dell, "Foundations of Racism in American Life," 86.

22. Paul Rogin, *Ronald Reagan The Movie*, 50–51.

23. Rogin, xiii–xiv, 51.

24. Rogin, xv, 3.

25. Rogin, 67.

26. Rogin, 70.

27. Rogin, 69.

28. Hill, *RACON*, 36.

29. Hill, 16.

30. Hill, 25; Nancy Weiss, *Farewell to the Party of Lincoln: Black Politics in the Age of FDR* (Princeton, NJ: Princeton University Press, 1983), 36.

31. Hill, 419.

32. Hill, 629.

33. Hill, 410.

34. Hill, 629.

35. Hill, 410.

36. Hill, 629.

37. Hill, 600.

38. Hill, 459.

39. Hill, 674.

40. Hill, 459.

41. Hill, 459, 465.

42. For a representative Black Marxist critique of the Soviet Union and the CPUSA, see C. L. R. James, *State Capitalism and World Revolution* (Chicago: Charles H. Kerr Publishing, 1986). On Trotskyism in the United States, see, e.g., George Breitman et al., *Trotskyism in the United States: Historical Essays and Reconsiderations* (Chicago: Haymarket Books, 2016 [1996]); Paul Le Blanc et al., *US Trotskyism, 1928–1965, Part I: Emergence; Left Opposition in the United States* (Chicago: Haymarket Books, 2017); Le Blanc et al., *US Trotskyism, 1928–1965, Part II: Endurance; The Coming American Revolution* (Chicago: Haymarket Books, 2017); and Le Blanc et al., *US Trotskyism, 1928–1965, Part III: Resurgence; Uneven and Combined Development* (Chicago: Haymarket Books, 2017).

43. Hill, *RACON*, 461, 465.

44. Hill, 467.

45. Hill, 480.

46. Esther V. Cooper, "Negro Youth Organizing for Victory," in *Organize, Fight, Win: Black Communist Women's Political Writing*, ed. Charisse Burden-Stelly and Jodi Dean (London: Verso, 2022), 132–34.

47. Hill, *RACON*, 490.

48. Hill, 612.

49. Hill, 615.

50. Hill, 460.

51. Hill, 466.

52. Hill, 494.

53. Hill, 490–91.

54. Hill, 616.

55. Hill, 487–88.

56. Hill, 495.

57. J. A. Rogers, *Pittsburg Courier*, September 29, 1949.

58. Patterson, *We Charge Genocide*, 3–4.

59. Patterson, "We Charge Genocide," speech.

60. Patterson, *We Charge Genocide*, 3–4.

61. Patterson, "We Charge Genocide" speech.

62. Patterson, *We Charge Genocide*, 5.

63. Patterson, 161.

64. Patterson, 166.

65. Patterson, 163.

66. Patterson, 163–64.

67. Patterson, 164, 165.

68. Patterson, 164, 165.

69. Patterson, 162–63.

70. Patterson, 182.

71. Patterson, 182.

72. Patterson, 183.

73. Lawrence W. Britt, "Fascism Anyone? The 14 Defining Characteristics of Fascism," in *Not Our President: New Directions from the Pushed Out, the Others, and the Clear Majority in Trump's Stolen America*, ed. Haki R. Madhubuti and Lasana D. Kazembe (Chicago: Third World Press Foundation, 2017), 423–25.

74. Jones, ". . . [Black] Women Can Think," 9.

75. Jones, 7.

76. Jones, 8.

77. Jones.

78. Jones, "International Women's Day and the Struggle for Peace," 92–93.

79. Jones, 93.

80. Horne, *Black Liberation / Red Scare*, 12.

81. Doxey Wilkerson, "Race Riots—Hitler's Weapon on the Home Front," radio address, June 27, 1943, Doxey Wilkerson Papers, Box 19, Folder 3.

82. Civil Rights Congress, *We Charge Genocide*, 5–6.

83. Wilkerson, "Race Riots—Hitler's Weapon on the Home Front."

84. Wilkerson.

85. Aric Putman, "Ethiopia Is Now: J. A. Rogers and the Rhetoric of Black Anticolonialism during the Great Depression," *Rhetoric and Public Affairs* 10, no. 3 (Fall 2007): 421.

86. Gus Hall-Benjamin J. Davis Defense Committee, "Anti-Communism in the United States."

87. Johnson, *I Think of My Mother*, 26.

88. Johnson, 129.

89. Pettis Perry, "On a Motion for Acquittal," n.d. [1953], Box 4, Folder 12, Pettis Perry Papers.

90. "We Are Seven," *Jewish Life: A Progressive Monthly*, November 1953, 3.

91. Council on African Affairs, News release from Council on African Affairs, October 13, 1949, Du Bois Papers https://credo.library.umass.edu/view/full/mums312-b124-i122.

92. Doxey Wilkerson, *The Negro People and the Communists* (New York: Workers Library Publishers, 1944), 11.

93. Wilkerson, 14.

94. Wilkerson, 17.

95. Claudia Jones, "Jim Crow in Uniform," in *Claudia Jones: Beyond Containment*, ed. Carole Boyce Davies (Boulder, CO: Lynne Reiner Publishers, 2011), 30.

96. Jones, "International Women's Day and the Struggle for Peace," 90–92.

97. Claudia Jones, "For the Unity of Women in the Cause of Peace," in *Claudia Jones: Beyond Containment*, ed. Carole Boyce Davies (Boulder, CO: Lynne Reiner Publishers, 2011), 104–5.

98. Horne, *Black Liberation / Red Scare*, 247.

99. Patterson, *We Charge Genocide*, 134–35, 167–68.

100. Herbert Aptheker, "American Imperialism and White Chauvinism," *Jewish Life*, July 1950.

101. "Part of discussion on concepts + 'white chauvinism' written by unknown person," n.d., Box 1, Folder 7, Pettis Perry Papers.

102. Schrecker, *The Age of McCarthyism*, 108.

Chapter Eleven

1. Davarian L. Baldwin, "Introduction: New Negroes Forging a New World," in *Escape from New York: The New Negro Renaissance beyond Harlem*, ed. Davarian L. Baldwin and Minkah Makalani (Minneapolis: University of Minnesota Press, 2013), 2.

2. Hill, " 'The Foremost Radical among the Race': Marcus Garvey and the Black Scare, 1918–1921," 215.

3. *Revolutionary Radicalism*, 3435.

4. Alex Carey, *Taking the Risk Out of Democracy: Corporate Propaganda versus Freedom and Liberty* (Champaign: University of Illinois Press, 1997), 21.

5. Carey, 344.

6. State Department of Education, *A Resource Unit: Americanism vs. Communism* (Tallahassee, FL: State Department of Education, 1962), 3.

7. *Revolutionary Radicalism*, 3992.

8. Robert K. Murray, *Red Scare: A Study in National Hysteria, 1919–1920* (Minneapolis: University of Minnesota Press, 1955), 169.

9. Schrecker, *The Age of McCarthyism*, 14.

10. Chamber of Commerce of the United States of America, "Americanization Day, Bulletin No. 8 of the Immigration Committee," July 4, 1917, https://images.socialwelfare.library.vcu.edu /items/show/82.

11. *Revolutionary Radicalism*, 2293.

12. *Revolutionary Radicalism*, 2293.

13. *Revolutionary Radicalism*, 2099.

14. *Revolutionary Radicalism*, 2102.

15. *Revolutionary Radicalism*, 3180.

16. *Revolutionary Radicalism*, 2283.

17. *Revolutionary Radicalism*, 2407.

18. *Revolutionary Radicalism*, 3428.

19. *Revolutionary Radicalism*, 2392.

20. *Revolutionary Radicalism*.

21. *Revolutionary Radicalism*.

22. Roberto, *The Coming of the American Behemoth* 131.

23. Roberto, 115.

24. *Revolutionary Radicalism*, 3489.

25. *Revolutionary Radicalism*, 2283.

26. *Revolutionary Radicalism*, 2103.

27. Murray, *Red Scare: A Study in National Hysteria*, 84–85.

28. *Revolutionary Radicalism*, 2407–8.

29. Schmidt, *Red Scare*, 33.

30. Open Shop Report, *Proceedings of the 28th Annual Meeting of the NAM* (May 1923), 156–59.

31. Robert A. Brady, *Business as a System of Power* (New York: Columbia University Press, 1943), 197–98.

32. Brady, 213, 217.

33. Brady, 219.

34. Brady, 220.

35. Noam Chomsky, *World Orders, Old and New* (New York: Columbia University Press, 1994), 86, 89.

36. Chomsky, 92.

37. *Chomsky*, 348.

38. Nikhil Pal Singh, "Culture/Wars: Recoding Empire in an Age of Democracy," *American Quarterly* 50, no. 3 (September 1998): 490.

39. Carey, *Taking the Risk Out of Democracy*, 18.

40. Carey, 345.

41. Carey, 345.

42. Carey, 352.

43. Barry Shank, "The Continuing Embarrassment of Culture: From the Culture Concept to Cultural Studies," *American Studies* 38, no. 2 (Summer 1997): 96.

44. Schrecker, *The Age of McCarthyism*, 120.

45. Schrecker, 119.

46. Schrecker, 116.

47. Schrecker, 119.

48. Schrecker.

49. Schrecker.

50. Hunton, *Alphaeus Hunton: The Unsung Valiant*, 81.

51. Schrecker, *The Age of McCarthyism*, 38.

52. *Revolutionary Radicalism*, 2279.

53. *Revolutionary Radicalism*, ix.

54. *Revolutionary Radicalism*, 1476.

55. Murray, *Red Scare*, 102.

56. Theodore Kornweibel Jr., *No Crystal Stair: Black Life and the* Messenger, *1917–1923* (Westport, CT: Greenwood Press, 1975), 79.

57. *The Attorney General Report*, 137.

58. Kornweibel, *No Crystal Stair: Black Life and the* Messenger, *1917–1923*, 84.

59. Kornweibel, 85.

60. *Revolutionary Radicalism*, 2291.

61. *Revolutionary Radicalism*, 2285.

62. *Revolutionary Radicalism*, 3977.

63. "Special Bulletin: The Negro Problem in the Army," October 21, 1918.

64. *Revolutionary Radicalism*, 3977.

65. *Revolutionary Radicalism*, 2289.

66. Count Arthur de Gobineau, *The Inequality of Human Race* (London, 1915), 210.

67. *Revolutionary Radicalism*, 1476.

68. Hill, *RACON*, 14.

69. Hill, 631.

70. Hill, 633.

71. Hill, 111.

72. Hill, 81.

73. Hill, 628.

74. Hill, 628.

75. Hill, 113.

76. Hill, 632.

77. Hill, 639–43.

78. Hill, 632.

79. Hill, 627.

80. Hill, 46.

Epilogue

1. The US Department of Justice, "US Citizens and Russian Intelligence Officers Charged with Conspiring to Use US Citizens as Illegal Agents of the Russian Government," Justice News, April 18, 2023, https://www.justice.gov/opa/pr/us-citizens-and-russian-intelligence-officers-charged -conspiring-use-us-citizens-illegal; "FBI Raids Social Justice Organization," *LA Progressive*, August 5, 2022, https://www.laprogressive.com/law-and-the-justice-system/fbi-raids-uhuru-apsp; Patrick E. Eddington, "Indictments and Raids: FBI Moves against Fringe 'Influencers' in Russia Probe," *Cato at Liberty*, August 1, 2022, https://www.cato.org/blog/indictments-raids-fbi -moves-against-fringe-influencers-russia-probe.

2. Eddington, "Indictments and Raids"; People's Dispatch, "FBI Stages COINTELPRO-Like Raid on Black Socialist Group, Alleges Russian Government Connection," *People's World*, August 4, 2022, https://www.peoplesworld.org/article/fbi-stages-cointelpro-like-raid-on-black

-socialist-group-alleges-russian-government-connection/; Black Alliance for Peace, "Black Alliance for Peace Condemns FBI Attack on the African People's Socialist Party," July 30, 2022, https://blackallianceforpeace.com/bapstatements/bapsolidaritywithapsp.

3. Jacqueline Alemany, Josh Dawsey, and Carol D. Leonnig, "Jan. 6 Panel Staffers Angry at Cheney for Focusing So Much of Report on Trump," *Washington Post*, November 23, 2022, https://www.washingtonpost.com/politics/2022/11/23/liz-cheney-jan-6-committee/.

4. Keeanga-Yamahtta Taylor, *From #BlackLivesMatter to Black Liberation* (Chicago: Haymarket Books, 2016 [Kindle Edition]), locations 219–27.

5. Stuart Hall, "The Neo-Liberal Revolution," *Cultural Studies* 25 (2011): 725–26.

6. Hall, 714–15.

7. Clarence Lusane and Randolph B. Persaud, "The New Economy, Globalisation, and the Impact on African-Americans," *Race and Class* 42 (2000): 32.

8. Ruth Wilson Gilmore, *Golden Gulag: Prisons, Surplus, Crisis, and Opposition in Globalizing California*, (Berkeley: University of California Press, 2007); Frances Fox Piven, "The New American Poor Law," *Socialist Register* 48 (2012): 108–24; Loic Wacquant, "Ordering Insecurity: Social Polarization and the Punitive Upsurge," *Radical Philosophy Review* 11 (2008): 9–27; Loic Wacquant, "The Place of the Prison in the New Government of Poverty," in *After the War on Crime: Race, Democracy, and a New Reconstruction*, ed. Mary Louise Frampton et al. (New York: New York University Press, 2008), 23–27; Loic Wacquant, "From Slavery to Mass Incarceration: Rethinking the 'Race Question' in the US," *New Left Review* 13 (2002): 41–60.

9. Barbara Ransby, "The Class Politics of Black Lives Matter," *Dissent* (Fall 2015): 32.

10. Glen Ford, "Democrats Hope to Bury Black Lives Matter under Election Blitz," June 10, 2015, https://blackagendareport.com/democrats_to_bury_black_lives_matter_under_election.

11. Ransby, "The Class Politics of Black Lives Matter," 32.

12. Siddhant Issar, "Listening to Black Lives Matter: Racial Capitalism and the Critique of Neoliberalism," *Contemporary Political Theory* 20, no. 1 (March 2021): 57.

13. Issar, 58.

14. Ransby, "The Class Politics of Black Lives Matter," 32.

15. Alicia Garza, "A Herstory of the #BlackLivesMatter," *Feminist Wire*, October 2017, https://empathyeducates.org/Journeys-to-and-through/a-herstory-of-the-blacklivesmatter-movement-by-alicia-garza/.

16. Taylor, *From #BlackLivesMatter to Black Liberation*, location 136.

17. Ford, "Democrats Hope to Bury Black Lives Matter under Election Blitz."

18. Ford; Garza, "A Herstory of the #BlackLivesMatter." https://empathyeducates.org/Journeys-to-and-through/a-herstory-of-the-blacklivesmatter-movement-by-alicia-garza/.

19. Taylor, *From #BlackLivesMatter to Black Liberation*, location 3179.

20. FBI, *Black Identity Extremists Likely Motivated to Target Police Officers*.

21. FBI, *Black Identity Extremists Likely Motivated to Target Police Officers*.

22. FBI, *Black Identity Extremists Likely Motivated to Target Police Officers*.

23. Goldstein, *Political Repression in Modern America: From 1870–1976*, 429.

24. See, e.g., Charisse Burden-Stelly and Gerald Horne, "Third World International and the Global Color-Line," in *Cambridge History of America and the World*, vol. 4, ed. David Engerman et al., 370–96 (New York: Cambridge University Press, 2022).

25. Goldstein, *Political Repression in Modern America: From 1870–1976*, 432–35, 435.

26. Newton, *FBI Encyclopedia*, 70.

27. Goldstein, *Political Repression in Modern America: From 1870–1976*, 438.

28. Goldstein, 504–9. Also see Micol Siegel, *Violence Work: State Power and the Limits of Police* (Durham, NC: Duke University Press, 2018).

29. Newton, *FBI Encyclopedia*, 68.

30. Dhoruba Bin Wahad, "War Within: Prison Interview," in *Still Black, Still Strong: Survivors of the War against Black Revolutionaries*, ed. Jim Fletcher et al. (South Pasadena, CA: Semiotext(e), 1993), 10.

31. FBI, *Black Identity Extremists Likely Motivated to Target Police Officers*.

32. Bin Wahad, "War Within: Prison Interview," 13, 23.

33. Assata Shakur, "Prisoner in the United States," in *Still Black, Still Strong: Survivors of the War against Black Revolutionaries*, ed. Jim Fletcher et al. (South Pasadena, CA: Semiotext(e), 1993), 205, 208.

34. Black Liberation Army, *Documents of the Black Liberation Army* (Pattern Books, 2021), 110.

35. Tony Perucci, "The Red Mask of Sanity: Paul Robeson, HUAC, and the Sound of Cold War Performance," *Drama Review* 53 (2009): 21.

36. Perucci, 24.

37. Elaine Tyler May, *Homeward Bound: American Families in the Cold War Era* (New York: Basic Books, 2017 [1988]), xxv.

38. FBI, *Black Identity Extremists Likely Motivated to Target Police Officers*.

39. On these phenomena, see, e.g., Layla Brown, "The Pandemic of Racial Capitalism: Another World Is Possible," *From the European South* 7 (2020): 61–74; Elizabeth Hinton, *America on Fire: The Untold History of Police Violence and Rebellion Since the 1960s* (New York: Liveright Publishing, 2021; Keeanga-Yahmatta Taylor, "Voting Trump Out Is Not Enough," *New Yorker*, November 9, 2020, https://www.newyorker.com/news/our-columnists/voting-trump-out-is-not -enough; Gerald Horne, "Racism and a Failed Coup," interview, theanalysis.news, June 30, 2022, https://theanalysis.news/racism-and-a-failed-coup-gerald-horne/; Black Alliance for Peace, "Who Rules Haiti? Black Alliance for Peace Condemns Undermining of Haitian National Sovereignty," September 23, 2021, https://blackallianceforpeace.com/bapstatements/whoruleshaiti; Black Alliance for Peace Solidarity Network Afghanistan Committee, "Timeline Demonstrating U.S. Responsibility for Chaos in Afghanistan," September 7, 2021, https://blackallianceforpeace .com/bapstatements/afghanistantimeline; Black Alliance for Peace, "A Brief Guide on the Situation in Ukraine," n.d., https://blackallianceforpeace.com/resourcesonukraine; Ahiza Garcia-Hodges, "From Essential Status to Strikes, 2021 Was the 'Year of the Worker,'" December 28, 2021, https://www.nbcnews.com/business/economy/essential-status-strikes-2021-was-year-worker -rcna9459; Robin D. G. Kelley, "Where Do We Go from Here? Abolition or Fascism," March 16, 2021, https://mediaspace.wisc.edu/media/Robin+D.+G.+KelleyA++%E2%80%9CWhere+do+We +Go+From+HereFA+Abolition+or+Fascism%22/1_xo32f1af.

40. Mike Gonzalez, "Black Lives Matter Leader Resigns, but This Radical Marxist Agenda Will Continue," *Heritage Foundation*, June 4, 2021, https://www.heritage.org/progressivism/com mentary/black-lives-matter-leader-resigns-radical-marxist-agenda-will-continue.

41. Ryan Teague Backwith, "Read Donald Trump's 'America First' Foreign Policy Speech," *Time*, April 27, 2016, https://time.com/4309786/read-donald-trumps-america-first-foreign-policy -speech/; Tom McTague and Peter Nichols, "How 'America First' became America Alone," *Atlantic*, October 29, 2020, https://www.theatlantic.com/international/archive/2020/10/donald -trump-foreign-policy-america-first/616872/; Caitlyn Oprysko and Anita Kumar, "Trump Pushes Aggressive 'American First' Message to World Leaders," *Politico*, September 24, 2019, https:// www.politico.com/story/2019/09/24/trump-america-first-unga-1509356.

42. Keeanga-Yahmatta Taylor, "'Wokeism' Is Not the Democrats' Problem," *New Yorker*, November 19, 2021, https://www.newyorker.com/news/our-columnists/wokeness-is-not-the-problem.

43. https://www.flgov.com/wp-content/uploads/2021/12/Stop-Woke-Handout-1.pdf; https://www.wptv.com/news/state/gov-ron-desantis-to-host-news-conference-in-wildwood.

44. Andrew Atterburym "DeSantis Pushes Bill That Allows Parents to Sue Schools over Critical Race Theory," December 15, 2021, https://www.politico.com/states/florida/story/2021/12/15/desantis-targets-critical-race-theory-with-bill-that-evokes-texas-abortion-bounties-1400102.

45. Lalee Ibsa, "What to Know about Florida's Anti-riot Law and the Corresponding Legal Challenge," August 7, 2021, https://abcnews.go.com/US/floridas-anti-riot-law-legal-challenge/story?id=79224398; "A Judge Has Blocked the Anti-Riot Law Passed in Florida After George Floyd Protests," *NPR*, September 9, 2021, https://www.npr.org/2021/09/09/1035687247/florida-anti-riot-law-ron-desantis-george-floyd-black-lives-matter-protests.

46. Horne, "Racism and a Failed Coup," interview.

47. Hannah Rabinowitz and Holmes Lybrand, "Oath Keepers Convicted of Charges That Carry a Maximum 20-Year Prison Sentence," *CNN*, November 29, 2022, https://www.cnn.com/politics/live-news/oath-keepers-trial-verdict/h_4113b46c0018f827389e56eaf0675dda.

48. Robert Hart, "Figures Show Stark Difference between Arrests at D.C. Black Lives Matter Protest and Arrests at Capitol Hill," *Forbes*, January 7, 2021.

49. Alanna Durkin Richer, Michael Kunzelman, and Jacques Billeaud, "Records Rebut Claims of Unequal Treatment of Jan. 6 Rioters," *Associated Press*, August 30, 2021, https://apnews.com/article/records-rebut-claims-jan-6-rioters-55adf4d46aff57b91af2fdd3345dace8.

50. Ray Sanchez, "'Self-Defense Is Not Illegal': Kyle Rittenhouse Tells Fox News after Not-Guilty Verdict," *CNN*, November 19, 2021, https://www.cnn.com/2021/11/19/us/kyle-rittenhouse-trial-friday/index.html.

51. Robin Young, "Look for Intent When Comparing the Capitol Mob to Black Lives Matter, Historian Says," January 18, 2021, https://www.wbur.org/hereandnow/2021/01/18/capitol-mob-black-lives-matter.

Index

abolition, 1, 4, 24, 53, 58, 77, 100, 231

Abrams v. United States (1919), 147

accumulation: capitalist racist, 11, 121, 136; primitive, 2, 4, 15, 18, 247, 262n16; war as tool of, 15

Acheson, Dean, 134, 154, 222

Act to Prevent Pernicious Political Activities (Hatch Act) (1939), 148, 167, 199, 205

Afghanistan, 253

Africa, 102, 107, 108, 126, 262n11; Black World and, 62, 101, 103, 109–16, 120; capitalist racism in, 114; "The Emergence of Africa," 118–20

Africa Command (AFRICOM), 244

Africana Critical Theory, 3, 259n9

African Blood Brotherhood (ABB), 18, 59–60, 70, 81, 99, 173, 176

African Communities League (ACL), 59

African Liberation, 110, 116–20

African People's Socialist Party (APSP), 242–45

agitation, Black, 5, 36, 43, 45, 70, 169, 210; capitalist racism and, 44, 55–56; punishment of, 7, 248; True Americanism and danger of, 238–41

Alabama, 1, 17, 28–31, 74–75, 94, 181, 183, 218

Alexander, Sadie T., 154

"alien anarchism," 11, 58, 62, 174

Alien and Sedition Laws (1798), 206

Alien Registration Act (Smith Act) (1940), 37, 43, 148, 165, 179, 199–203, 205, 206, 220

American Committee for the Protection of the Foreign Born (ACPFB), 60, 150

American Communications Association v. Douds (1950), 147

American Defense League, 230

American Defense Society, 157

American Federation of Labor (AFL), 125, 157, 159, 193–95

Americanization, 70, 228–32, 236

"Americanization Work" ("Citizenship Training"), 236

American League for Peace and Democracy, 283n69

American Legion, 157, 195, 230

American Negro Labor Congress (ANLC), 98, 99, 161

American way of life, 4, 72, 88, 214; threats to, 157, 170, 234, 288n93; True Americanism with democracy as, 226–27, 239

Amis, B. D., 93

anti-Black racial oppression, 22, 43–46, 125, 180, 215, 246, 251; anticommunism and, 3, 7–8, 48–49, 95–100, 207–9, 217–25; Countersubversive Political Tradition and, 207–9; CPUSA and, 169; defined, 4; genocide and, 41, 42; labor and, 23; with peace activism punished, 131–36; repression and, 6; True Americanism and, 240; US Capitalist Racist Society and, 42, 71; US global leadership and, 1; white labor and, 40; white supremacist terrorism and, 5

anticommunism, 43, 139, 152, 201, 288n93; anti-Black racial oppression and, 3, 7–8, 48–49, 95–100, 207–9, 217–25; with capitalism, racism, imperialism, and war, 1–2; Countersubversive Political Tradition and, 207–9; defined, 4, 5–6; with fascist character of US, 214–17; labor and, 40–41; legislative branch with state-level, 140; psychoanalysis and, 251; with punishment of peace activism, 131–36; racial liberalism and, 151; Wall Street Imperialism and, 46–47; *We Charge Genocide* petition and, 42–43

anticommunist governance: Countersubversive Political Tradition and, 12, 223, 226, 252; executive branch and, 164, 165–77; judicial branch and, 164, 165, 177–86; legislative branch and,